REA

BIOGRAPHICAL DICTIONARY OF THE MIDDLE EAST

BIOGRAPHICAL DICTIONARY OF THE MIDDLE EAST

YAACOV SHIMONI

Facts On File

New York • Oxford • Sydney

Copyright © 1991 by G.G. The Jerusalem Publishing House Ltd.
39, Tchernechovski Street, P.O. Box 7147, Jerusalem 91071

Facts On File, Inc.	Facts On File Limited	Facts On File Pty Ltd
460 Park Avenue South	Collins Street	Talavera & Khartoum Rds
New York NY 10016	Oxford OX4 1XJ	North Ryde NSW 2113
USA	United Kingdom	Australia

Library of Congress Cataloging-in-Publication Data

Shimoni, Yaacov
    The Biographical dictionary of the Middle East: 1900 to the present.
    p. cm.
    Includes bibliographical references.
    ISBN 0-8160-2458-8
    1. Middle East—History—20th century—Biography. 2. Middle East—
    Biography. 3. Africa, North—History—1882—Biography.
    4. Africa, North—Biography.
    DS62.4.B56 1991   90-32553
    920.5694–dc20   CIP

A British CIP catalogue record for this book is available from the
British Library.

Australian CIP data available on request from Facts On File.

Facts On File books are available at special discounts when purchased
in bulk quantities for businesses, associations, institutions or sales
promotions. Please call our Special Sales Department in New York at
212/683-2244   (dial 800/322-8755 except in NY, AK or HI)   or in Oxford
at 865/728399.

Text design by Margalit Bassan
Jacket design by Techiya Rosenthal
Composition by Yael Kaplan Typesetting Ltd.
Printed in Israel

10 9 8 7 6 5 4 3 2 1

This book is printed on acid-free paper.

EDITOR

YAACOV SHIMONI
Former Ambassador; former visiting professor at the Hebrew University, Jerusalem;
author of several books on the Arab World.

CONTRIBUTORS

YAACOV SHIMONI

PROF. SHMUEL MOREH
Lecturer, Department of Arabic Language and Literature,
Institute of Asian and African Studies,
The Hebrew University, Jerusalem.

DR. YEHIAM WEITZ
Lecturer in Eretz Israel Studies, University of Haifa.

RESEARCHERS

YAACOV HOLTZMAN

HELENE AVRAHAM

ITTAI KAZZAZ

RONEN TRAUBE

PROJECT MANAGER

RACHEL GILON

FOREWORD

The *Biographical Dictionary of the Middle East* provides the reader with approximately 500 biographies of personalities who have played a role in the present and recent past of the Middle East including countries as far west as the Maghrib (Libya, Tunisia, Algeria, Morocco). Kings and rulers, heads of governments, party leaders, religious figures, revolutionaries, and military leaders are portrayed from the point of view of their influence on the political scene of the region. Some leading writers and journalists who influenced the intellectual climate and political opinions have been also included.

This dictionary is by no means an exhaustive Who's Who with full "official" biographies but a ready reference tool for the reader wishing to have quick information on the political figures prominent in events since the beginning of the century.

The Dictionary is arranged in alphabetical order. For Arabic names, the last designation has been taken as the family name and the entry appears accordingly (thus, Nuri Sa'id appears under Sa'id, Nuri). This rule is not applied to kings and princes generally known by their first name (Hussein bin Talal under H; Feisal Ibn 'Abd-ul-'Aziz under F). The Arabic definite article *al-* is disregarded in the alphabetical listing; thus Jamal al-Husseini will be found under H. Names composed of 'Abd-ul- ("Servant of") and one of the epithets of God ('Abd-ul-Fatah, 'Abd-ul-Rahman) are regarded as one name and therefore appear under A (e.g., Gamal 'Abd-ul-Nasser appears under 'Abd-ul-Nasser, Gamal).

Transliteration normally used in the international press has been employed for Arabic terms and names, with some amendment towards a more correct rendition. For example, the guttural aspirate (Arabic *'ayn*, Hebrew *'ayin*) is indicated by an inverted apostrophe ('), except where a name is commonly spelt without it in English (e.g., Iraq). The non-guttural aspirate (Arabic *alif*) is reproduced as an apostrophe (') only where it is needed to separate two vowels (*Ra'uf, Feda'iyin*). To simplify matters, diacritical marks have not been used. A certain freedom has been exercized — within the spirit of the Arabic language — where vowels are concerned, and the generally accepted usage has been followed: Nasser (not Nasir); Hussein, Feisal, but Bahrain, Kuwait. The same goes for the doubling of consonants: Hussein, Hassan (though the *s* is not double in Arabic). A liberal attitude has also been adopted towards "wrong" but accepted transliterations, e.g., Ottoman, 'Oman. Names well known in "wrong" transliteration are also in general left in their usual and accepted form, such as Chamoun (not Sham'un) or, in particular, North African names (Bourguiba — not Abu Raqiba, Boumedienne — not Abu Midyan). There is not therefore full consistency — which is, indeed, unattainable. Repetition of the name of each entry is indicated in the text by its initials. Cross-references to entries on other individuals mentioned are indicated by an asterisk (*) before the name.

All entries on Arab political figures were written by th editor, Yaacov Shimoni, Shmuel Moreh wrote the entries on Arab writers, poets and journalists. Yehiam Weitz, authored the biographies of Israeli personalities. The entries on Iranian and Turkish personalities were researched and drafted by Yaacov Holtzman and Helene Avraham, and rewritten by the editor. The typesetting was done by veronica Bar-Lev, the copy-editing by Edward Levin and the proofreading by Suzy Shabetai. The publishers wish to convey their appreciation and thanks to all of them.

GLOSSARY

Ahdut Ha'avodah — Zionist-Socialist workers' party founded in 1919, considered more radical than its rival, *Hapo'el Hatza'ir*. In 1930 it united with the latter, to form the Labor Party, *Mapai*. In 1944 a radical faction (see *Si'ah B.*) seceded from *Mapai* and reestablished the *Ahdut Ha'avodah* party. That party united in 1948 with *Hashomer Hatza'ir* to form the *Mapam* party, but seceded from *Mapam* in 1954 and again became a separate party. In 1965 *Ahdut Ha'avodah* formed an Alignment with *Mapai*, and in 1969 it reunited with *Mapai* to form the Israel Labor Party.

Alignment — An election and parliamentary union of the Israel Labor Party (*Mapai*) and *Ahdut Ha'avodah* established in 1965. After *Ahdut Ha'avodah* fully merged with *Mapai* in 1969, the reunited Labor Party entered a new Alignment with the *Mapam* party. That Alignment lapsed after the elections of 1984 when *Mapam* decided to contest the next elections separately.

Aliyah — (Literally "ascent") Immigration of Jews to Palestine (*Eretz Israel*). The major waves of pre-State immigration are referred to as the First *Aliyah* (1882); the Second *Aliyah* (1905–14); the Third *Aliyah* (1919–20); the Fourth *Aliyah* (1924–26); the Fifth *Aliyah* (1930s).

Brit(h) Shalom - Small group of Jewish intellectuals in Palestine in the late 1920s and early 1930s advocating a peaceful compromise solution of the Jewish-Arab conflict and favoring a bi-national state in Palestine.

Bilu — Small group of Russian Jews which pioneered the return to Palestine (*Eretz Israel*). Founded after the 1881 pogroms in Russia, it sent its first group of immigrants in 1882.

Eretz Israel — ("Land of Israel"). The traditional Jewish term for Palestine.

Gush Emunim — "Bloc of the Faithful," right-wing organization advocating and conducting settlement activity in the areas occupied by Israel in 1967, considered by them as "Greater Israel."

Haganah — "Defense," Jewish underground self-defense organization in Palestine during the British Mandate. Established in 1920, closely linked with the Labor Movement. It had tens of thousands of members and was the main militay body of the *Yishuv*, transformed in 1948 to the Israel Defense Forces

Hapo'el Hatza'ir — "The Young Worker," Zionist-Socialist party founded by the first pioneers of the Second *Aliyah* in Palestine in 1905.It merged with *Ahdut Ha'avodah* in 1930 into the Labor party, *Mapai*.

Hashomer Hatza'ir — "The Young Watchman," Zionist-Socialist pioneering youth movement founded in Europe in 1916. In Israel it founded the *Kibbutz Artzi* and the *Mapam* party.

Hehalutz — "The Pioneer", organization for the training of Jewish youth in the Diaspora for a pioneering life in *Eretz Israel*. Founded at the end of World War I.

Herut — "Freedom," a political party founded in 1948 by *IZL* and Revisionist Party activists. The main opposition party between 1955 and 1977. The party in power since 1977, in union with the right-wing Liberals first called *Gahal* (1973) and then *Likud*.

Histadrut — Israel Federation of Labor, encompassing trade union, major cooperative and economic enterprises and a sick fund (*Kupat Holim*) providing health services to the majority of Israel's population.

Hovevei Zion — "Lovers of Zion," precursor of the Zionist movement in eastern Europe, founded with the goal of fostering immigration to Palestine; the motivating force behind the first *Aliyah* (1882).

IDF — Israel Defense Forces, the armed forces of Israel.

IZL — (acronym of *Irgun Zevai Leumi* — "National Military Organization"). Underground movement founded in 1937 (splitting from the *Haganah*) and connected with the Revisionist movement. It supported a more militant line than the *Haganah*.

Kibbutz, Kevutzah — Collective settlement, village. During the Third *Aliyah* (after World War I), the term *Kibbutz* came to signify a larger village combining industry and agriculture and open to all, *Kevutzah* usually meant a smaller settlement, closely-knit and composed of graduates of specific youth movements. The distinction has gradually disappeared.

(Ha-)Kibbutz (Ha-)Artzi — A union of *kibbutzim* founded in 1927 by the collective settlements of the *Hashomer Hatza'ir* youth movement. Linked to the *Mapam* party.

(Ha-)Kibbutz (Ha-)Me'uhad — "The United *Kibbutz* Movement," a union of *kibbutzim* founded in 1927, mostly by Third *Aliyah* pioneers, including groups from the *Gedud Ha'avodah* ("Labor Batallion"). Views the *kibbutz* as a large settlement open to all, not just graduates of a specific youth movement. Officially non-party, the *Kibbutz Me'uhad* had close links with the Labor Party (*Mapai*) and specifically to its radical faction (*Si'ah B.*) and formed the nucleus of the *Ahdut Ha'avodah* party seceding from *Mapai* in 1944. The *Kibbutz Me'uhad* split in 1951, supporters of *Mapai* seceding and forming *Ihud Hak(e)vutzot vehakibbutzim*. The two movements were reunited in 1979 into the "United *Kibbutz* Movement" (*Tnu'ah Kibbutzit Me'uhedet, Takam*)

Lehi (acronym of *Lohamei Herut Yisrael*) — "Freedom Fighters for Israel") the Stern Group — a radical underground military formation created in 1940 as a result of the split within *IZL*. The most hard-line among the underground movements.

Lik(k)ud — See *Herut*, above.

Mapai (acronymn of *Mifleget Po'alei Eretz Yisrael* "Palestine/Israel Workers' Party") — Zionist-Socialist party, established in 1930 by the merger of *Ahdut Ha'avodah* and *Hapo'el Hatza'ir*. The dominant party in the *Yishuv* and the State of Israel from the 1930s until 1977. Since 1969 — "Israel Labor Party".

Mapam (acronymn of *Mifleget Po'alim Me'uhedet*, "United Workers' Party") — Radical Zionist-Socialist party. Established in 1948 by *Hashomer Hatza'ir* and *Ahdut Ha'avodah* (the latter seceding in 1954). Represents the left of the Zionist spectrum.

Mizrahi — Religious Zionist movement, founded in 1902 as a religious faction within the World Zionist Organization. In 1956 it merged with the religious workers' movement *Hapo'el Hamizrahi* to found the National religious Party.

Moshav-'Ovdim — Cooperative smallholders' village combining features of both cooperative and private agriculture.

Palmah — An elite group of the *Haganah*. Established in 1941 as the only *Haganah* formation whose members served full-time, working on *Kibbutzim* and doing military service. Its commanders were Yitzhak Sadeh and Yigal Allon.

RAFI (acronym for *Reshimat Po'alei Yisrael*, "Israel Labor List") — Party founded in 1965 as result of a split in *Mapai* led by David Ben Gurion.

Revisionists — Zionist movement advocating political maximalism founded (1925) and led by Vladimir Jabotinsky, the main opposition to Weizmann's leadership and the policies of the World Zionist Organization (*WZO*). In 1935 the Revisionists seceded from the *WZO* and established a separate "New Zionist Organization", NZO, which reunited with the *WZO* in 1946. Forerunner of the *Herut* party.

Si'ah B, "Faction II" — The opposition faction in *Mapai* in the early 1940s. Composed mainly of members of the *Kibbutz Me'uhad* and Tel Aviv activists. It seceded in 1944 and reestablished the *Ahdut Ha'avodah* party.

Va'ad Hatzirim — The Zionist Commission sent to Palestine in 1918 to survey the situation in the land and make plans for the future.

Va'ad Le'umi — "National Council," the executive of the elected National Assembly, *Assefat Hanivharim*, of the Jews of Palestine, the *Yishuv*, from the 1920s until the foundation of the State of Israel in 1948.

Yishuv — The Jewish community in Palestine.

ADDENDUM The delegates to the Madrid Peace Conference: See p.252.

A

'ABBAS HILMI (1874–1945)   Ruler of Egypt (Khedive) 1892–1914, as 'Abbas II, succeeding his father, Tawfiq. 'A.H. was considered to be anti-British and in covert contact with Egyptian nationalists, Islamic revivalists and pro-Turkish elements. His relations with the British administration eased after Lord Cromer was replaced as British Agent and Consul-General (*de facto* Governor) by Lord Gorst in 1907. But friction continued. With the outbreak of World War I and the proclamation of a British protectorate, in 1914, 'A.H. was deposed and went into exile in Turkey. In 1922, his properties were confiscated and he and his family were forever barred from returning to Egypt. He continued cultivating clandestine con-

Ferhat 'Abbas (AP Photo)

tacts and political intrigues, but did not return to play an active role in Egyptian politics. (Excerpts from his memoirs were serialized in the Egyptian daily *al-Misri* in 1950).

'ABBAS, FERHAT(1899–1985)   Algerian nationalist leader. A pharmacist by profession, trained at the University of Algiers, 'A. became active in public affairs in the 1930s and was several times elected to those Algerian administrative and financial assemblies to which an Algerian Muslim was eligible. At first, he opposed Arab Algerian nationalism and advocated full equality for Algerian Muslims and Algeria's integration in France, perhaps with a measure of local autonomy. Disappointed by the failure of the reforms instituted by the French "Popular Front" government after 1936, 'A. gradually shifted to a more autonomist position and in 1938 founded a *Union Populaire Algerienne*; but his influence was limited. After serving with the French army in 1939–40, he was also personally disappointed by the lack of equal opportunity and reward granted to him by Vichy France. After the landing of Allied forces in North Africa, 1942, he presented in Dec. 1942 a message to the French and Allied leaders, proposing a new regime of equality, full freedoms, a vaguely formulated measure of autonomy and Algerian participation in government; these demands were reformulated in Feb. 1943 in a "Manifest," cosigned by a group of Algerian leaders. 'A. was invited in May 1943 to present detailed proposals, but nothing came of these talks. In 1944 he founded an organization, *Amis du Manifeste de Liberation*, which was re-formed in Apr. 1946 as the *Union Democratique du Manifeste Algerien* (UDMA), calling for an autonomous Algeria in federation with France, and seen as a rival and an alternative to *Messali Hajj's more extremist organization. 'A. was now considered anti-French and was several times imprisoned. During those years he despaired of the prospects of federation with France and turned into an advocate of full independence. In 1956, when the armed revolt was in full swing, he escaped to Cairo, where part of the rebel leadership maintained its headquarters, and joined its organization, the FLN. He played no major part in military operations, but when the FLN set up a Provisional Government of the Algerian Revolution in Cairo, in Sept. 1958, he was named Prime Minister. 'A. was, however, unable to accommodate himself fully to the policies and the leadership style of the FLN command, and in Aug. 1961 he was dismissed. He took no active part in the final negotiations for independence. In Sept. 1962 he became President of independent Algeria's first National Assembly. But his opposition to the course the Algerian leadership was taking deepened, and in Aug. 1963 he resigned, bitterly denouncing the totalitarian, "Castroist" trends that had become dominant, the "confiscation of power" by *Ben Bella and his FLN associates (though he could not make that denunciation fully public). He remained in alienated opposition and without a position in power when Ben Bella was overthrown in 1965 by *Boumedienne. In 1976 he was placed under house arrest. This, however, was later relaxed and he was able to publish, in France, several books (*Autopsie d'une guerre*, 1980; *Le Jeune Algérien* — a collection of older essays — 1981; *L'Indépendance confisquée* — his denunciation of Ben Bella's and Boumedienne's regimes — 1984). In 1984 'A. was fully rehabilitated, but now, over 80 years old, he did not resume any political activity. He died in 1985.

'ABBUD, IBRAHIM (1900–83)   Sudanese officer and politician, President of the Sudan 1958–64. His ancestry is described as tribal (in differing versions). Educated at Gordon College and Military College and commissioned in 1918, 'A. served with the Sudan Defense Force established by the British in 1925. During World War II, he served with the Sudanese contingent in the British Army in the Libyan, Ethiopian and Eritrean campaigns. When the Army command was Sudanized, he became, in 1954, Deputy Commander-in-Chief, and with the attainment of independence — Commander-in-Chief, 1956–64. In Nov. 1958 'A. staged a *coup d'état* — reportedly with the encouragement of the outgoing Prime Minister — and became President, Prime Minister and Minister of Defense, while remaining Commander-in-Chief of the armed Forces. His regime was conservative and oppressive and had no clear ideological orientation beyond its aspirations to stability and gradual eco-

nomic improvements. In his foreign policy 'A. was moderately pro-West with a growing neutralist tinge. After having suppressed several attempts to oust him, 'A. was toppled in October 1964 in a *coup d'etat* led by civilian politicians and supported by some army officers. He first ocntinued as a figurehead President, but resigned after three weeks and retired from public life.

'ABD-RABBUH, YASSER (b. 1944)   Palestinian-Arab politician and guerrilla leader. Among the activists of the guerrilla/terror groups formed in the late 1960s, 'A. joined *Hawatma's Leftist Democratic Front for the Liberation of Palestine. Since the 1970s he has been the DFLP's second-in-command and its representative on the Executive Committee of the Palestine Liberation Organization (PLO); within the PLO he has since the 1980s directed the Information/Propaganda Department. In 1989/90 a deep rift developed between him and Hawatma: 'A. supported the PLO's new, *'Arafat-initiated, policies (for a Palestinian-Arab state in the West Bank and Gaza in peaceful coexistence with Israel), while Hawatma opposed it, and since 1990 the DFLP has in fact been split. 'A. was a representative of the PLO in its dialogue with the USA, 1989/90, and frequently appears as a leading PLO spokesman. In his speeches and statements he often reverts, as does 'Arafat, to the PLO's old militant hard line.

ABD-UL-'AZIZ BIN (IBN) 'ABD-UL-RAHMAN of the House of Sa'ud see Ibn Sa'ud.

'ABDUH, MUHAMMAD (1849–1905)   Egyptian Muslim thinker, one of the initiators and main leaders of the renaissance of Islamic thought and its reform and mordernization. After the failure of the *Urabi revolt, 1882, he went into exile and published the *Pan-Islamic journal *al-'Urwa al-Wuthqa* ("Faithful Support") in Paris — together with Jamul-ul-Din al-Afghani (1839–97), the founder of the Pan-Islamic movement, by whom he was strongly influenced. 'A. called for a renewal of Islamic values and their adaptation to modern life; he advocated, for instance, the abolition of polygamy. He maintained that there is no contradiction between the tenets of Islam and those of modern Western civilization, and that the Islamic renaissance he advocated was the answer to Western criticism and an effective defense against the encroachment of Western values. In 1888, 'A. was permitted to return to Egypt, appointed a judge in the Muslim *Shari'a* courts and a member of the board of al-Azhar University and of the Legislative Council. In 1899 he was made Grand Mufti of Egypt. His ideas and writings — intensely debated by supporters and opponents — had a considerable influence on the Islamic movement and Arab nationalism.

'ABD-UL-GHAFFAR (al-Tikriti), HARDAN(1925 –71)   Iraqi officer and politician. As an air force officer, 'A. was, in the early 1960s, in contact with the clandestine *Ba'th* group. He played a leading role in the coup that overthrew the *Qassem regime in Feb. 1963 and became commander of the air force in the *Ba'th* regime that replaced it. When 'Abd-ul-Salam *'Aref took over in Nov. 1963, he was appointed Minister of Defense; but he soon fell out with the President and was dismissed and "exiled" as Ambassador to Sweden — a post which he soon left. After an officer's coup of July 1968 he became Chief of the General Staff and commander of the air force, and after a second coup, the same month, in which the *Ba'th* group took complete control — Deputy Prime Minister and Minister of Defense, and also member of the Revolutionary Command Council; in Apr. 1970 he became Vice-President, giving up the Defense Ministry. He was considered the up-and-coming man, the real power in the government. However, in the complex factional struggle within the ruling *Ba'th* party he ran afoul of rising strongman Saddam *Hussein, who gained the upper hand and had him dismissed in Oct. 1970 (using as a pretext his alleged responsibility for the failure of the Iraqi expeditionary force in Jordan to impose Iraq's will on King *Hussein in his struggle with the PLO). 'A. had to go into exile. In Mar. 1971 he was assassinated in Kuwait — by the agents of the Iraqi regime, as was generally assumed.

'ABD-UL-GHANI, 'ABD-UL-'AZIZ(b. 1937?–1941?) Yemeni politician. As a member of the Sunni-Shafe'i community, 'A. was not closely involved in the incessant struggles of the ruling officers' factions (mostly Zeidi) and between them and the Zeidi tribal leaders and could therefore hold office under various, changing rulers. Trained in the USA as an economist, he served, from 1976/78, in various senior positions — e.g. Minister of Economy and Health, and was Governor of the Central bank from 1971. After Ibrahim *Hamdi's *coup* of 1974 he became a member of Hamdi's Military Command Council and in Jan. 1975 was appointed

Hardan 'Abd-ul-Ghaffar (AP Photo)

Prime Minister. After Hamdi was assassinated, in Oct. 1977, he continued as Premier under A.H. *Ghashmi (serving also on his Presidential Council) and 'Ali 'Abdullah *Saleh, until Oct. 1980, when he became Second Vice-President. From Nov. 1983 until the union of Yemen and South Yemen in May 1990 he again was Prime Minister. In united Yemen, since May 1990, he became a member of the five-man Presidential Council. Considered a "technocrat" and kept in high office mainly to satisfy the Shafe'i community, 'A. did not seem to wield policy-making influence.

'ABD-UL-HADI   Large, prominent Palestinian-Arab clan, centered in Nablus and its rural surroundings. For several generations its sons have provided a long line of administrators for the Ottoman-Turkish Empire, British-mandated Palestine, the Kingdom of Jordan, and local-municipal government, as well as notables active in public and political affairs. In the struggle dividing Palestinian-Arab politics, in the 1920s and 1930s, into two rival camps, the *Husseinis or *Majlisiyyin* (supporters of the Supreme Muslim Council) vs the *Nashashibis or *Mu'aridin* (the Opposition), the 'AuH clan — which is not very closely knit — endeavored to maintain an independent, neutral position. Among its many prominent members: 'Awni *'AuH; **Fakhri 'AuH** — a "black sheep" and outlaw who became one of the top commanders of the guerrilla bands in 1936 and a deputy to Fawzi al-*Qawuqji. In 1938, when the guerrilla activity had turned into internal terrorism, he was one of the commanders of the Opposition's counterterror groups, "the Peace Gangs". He was assassinated in 1943. **Ruhi 'AuH** (1885–1954) served in the Ottoman diplomatic and consular corps, rose to senior positions in the Palestinian administration under the British Mandate, and became a minister in the government of Jordan (Foreign Minister 1949; Justice 1949 and 1952–53).

ABD-UL-HADI, 'AWNI(1889–1970)   Palestinian-Arab, later Joranian, lawyer and politician. Active since his student days in the pre-World War I Arab national movement in the Ottoman Empire, 'A. was a member of the *al-Fatat* nationalist secret society and among the organizers of the Arab nationalist congress of Paris, 1913. He was one of Amir *Feisal's secretaries during his short-lived administration in Damascus, 1919–20, and accompanied him to the Paris Peace Conference. He then served Amir *'Abdullah in Transjordan. 'A. returned to Palestine in 1924, worked as a lawyer and became one of the chief spokesmen of the Palestinian-Arab nationalist movement — for some years as a member of the Arab Executive Committee. He had some — politically unproductive — contacts with Zionist leaders. In 1932 he founded a Palestinian branch of the pan-Arab *Istiqlal* (Independence) party (which never attained much influence); as its head he joined the Arab Higher Committee that directed the Arab rebellion of 1936–39, and served as its secretary, but was arrested and went into exile, 1937–41. In the command of the later stages of the rebellion, from Damascus and Beirut, he played no major role. In Nov. 1945, 'A. joined a new Arab Higher Committee, but in the internal disputes of 1946–47 he opposed the *Husseini leadership, withdrew from the Committee and for some time joined the opposition's rival "Higher Arab Front" (1946). In September 1948 he was appointed Minister for Social Affairs in the abortive "Government of all Palestine" established in Egyptian-occupied Gaza, but resigned soon, and settled in Jordan. He served as Jordan's Minister (later Ambassador) to Egypt, 1951–55, and was a senator, 1955–58. For a short time in 1956 he was Minister of Foreign Affairs and Justice, and in 1958 - one of Jordan's representatives on the Federal Council of the abortive Jordan-Iraq Arab Federation. After 1958 he lived in Cairo and served

for some time as chairman of the Arab League's Judical Affairs Committee. Parts of 'A.'s private papers were published in 1974 in Beirut.

'ABD-UL-HADI, IBRAHIM (1899? 1901?–1981) Egyptian politician. One of the leaders of the Saadist Party. Foreign Minister 1946, Prime Minister 1946/47, Chief of the Royal Cabinet 1947/48, Prime Minister 1948/49. After the officer's coup of 1952, 'A. was accused of having dragged the Egyptian army, against the better judgement of its leaders, into the Palestine war and debacle of 1948, when he headed the King's cabinet. He was charged with high treason, plotting, corruption and terrorism, tried by a revolutionary court and sentenced to death in 1953. The sentence was commuted to imprisonment for life, and in 1954 he was released for reasons of health. His civic and political rights were restored to him in 1960, but he retired from public life.

'ABD-UL HAMID II (1842–1918)   Ottoman-Turkish Sultan from 1876 to 1909. Under pressure from advocates of reforms and liberalization, 'A. in 1876 issued a constitution. But two years later, he abolished it and dissolved the Parliament, claiming that the war against Russia necessitated such action. Thirty years of repressive government followed, during which 'A. exiled many opponents and closely monitored the educational system, banning history and literature courses and emphasizing religious studies. His government did not function well; foreign advisers he appointed to important government posts, including military officers, sometimes issued orders contradictory to those of his ministers. 'A. also created economic chaos by embarking on grandiose plans which contributed to a public debt of 100 million gold lira.

Some reform did take place during Sultan 'A.'s reign. Hassan Fehmi Pasha was permitted to use private funds to establish a Civil Engineering School in Istanbul (1883), which later became a Technical University. Improvements were made in the fields of communications and travel, such as the development of a telegraph and railroad system. 'A. in 1902 had granted Germany the right to construct a Berlin-Baghdad railway system, but British conflicts between Turkey and Great Britain resulted in delays (the project was completed after his reign, in 1914).

Despite strict censorship of the media, underground newspapers and other publications flourished, contributing to the growth of revolutionary activities. Revolutionary groups, calling for liberal policies, won wide support. Finally, groups of "Young Turks" in July 1903 staged a coup. The rebels demanded the reinstatement of the constitution and the reestablishment of the National Assembly. 'A. was compelled to accept the rebels' demands; but in March 1909 he attempted a countercoup — and was deposed and replaced by his brother, Mehmed V. He spent the rest of his life in the Alanti Palace in Salonica.

'A. tried to foster Pan-Islamic ideas and policies, emphasizing his position as Caliph of all Muslims and the loyalty owed to him and the Ottoman Empire by the Arabs, as Muslims. 'A. initiated the construction of the Hijaz Railway to serve the pilgrims to Mecca and strengthen all-Islamic ties.

'ABD-UL-ILAH IBN 'ALI (1912–58)   Regent, 1939–53, and Crown Prince, 1953–58, of Iraq. Born in Hijaz to Sharif *Hussein, both later Kings of Hijaz, 'A. moved to Baghdad with his father in 1925, when Hijaz was conquered by *Ibn Sa'ud. When King *Ghazi of Iraq, his cousin and brother-in-law, died in 1939, he became Regent of Iraq on behalf of the infant King *Feisal II; and when Feisal attained his majority, in 1953, 'A. assumed the title of Crown Prince, retaining considerable influence. He was strongly pro-British throughout his political life. In 1941, during the rule of *Kilani Rashid 'Ali and the officers of the "Golden Square," he was deposed and fled Iraq, returning with the victorious British Army. He, with Nuri *Sa'id, was considered, by anti-British opinion on the right and left as a symbol of reaction and subservience to foreign imperialist domination. 'A. fostered abortive plans for a Greater Syria or a Fertile Crescent Federation and was believed, in the 1950s, to aspire to the throne of Syria. 'A. was killed during the revolution of July 1958, and his body was torn to pieces by the mob.

ABDULLAH IBN 'ABDUL-'AZIZ (b. 1921? 1923?) Sa'udi prince, one of the sons of *Ibn Sa'ud; (his mother came from the *Rashid clan of the Shammar tribes — whose state the Sa'udis overpowered in 1921); Crown Prince and First Deputy Prime Minister since 1982. 'A. belongs to the inner circles of ruling Sa'udi princes and is considered to head a conservative faction (as against the moderate and pro-American advocates of fast development). He served for some time as Governor of Mecca and, from 1962–63, as Deputy Minister of Defense. Since 1962–63 is commander of the National Guard. When Prince Khaled became King and Prime Minister, in 1975, 'A. was appointed Second Deputy Premier, and with Khaled's death and the accession of King *Fahd, June 1982 — Crown Prince and First Deputy Premier. He is therefore supposed to accede to the throne when Fahd dies — but some forsee a potential struggle with Prince Sultan b. 'Abd-ul-Aziz. 'A. is reported to be married to a Syrian woman (said to belong to the 'Alawite sect and to be a relative of President *Asad). In recent years he has advocated — against the pro-Western faction within the dynasty — closer Sa'udi cooperation with the Arab states, including the radical ones (e.g., Syria); he has also become rather more active in Arab politics and has several times tried, without much success, to mediate in the Lebanese crisis, the Syrian-Iraqi dispute, and between Syria and the United States.

'ABDULLAH IBN HUSSEIN (1882–1951)   Amir of Transjordan, 1921–46, King of Jordan, 1948–51. Born in Mecca as second son of Sharif *Hussein ibn 'Ali, scion of the Prophet Muhammad's *Hashemite clan of the Quraishi tribe, 'A. received his education in Istanbul, where he lived from 1891 to 1908 with his father under Ottoman surveillance. He was active in Arab cultural circles and report-

'Abdullah Ibn Hussein (AP Photo)

edly in contact with semi-clandestine Arab nationalist groups in Istanbul. When his father was allowed to return to Mecca, as Amir, after the Revolution of the Young Turks, 'A. went with him. He stayed in Istanbul again, as Deputy for Mecca in the Ottoman Parliament, 1912–14. On his way back to Mecca he met British officials in Cairo to explore the prospects of a British-aided rebellion against Ottoman rule. When his father launched the Arab Revolt in June 1916, 'A. took a leading part in it. From 1917 he also served his father, who had assumed the title King of Hijaz, as political adviser and Foreign Minister. (It was, however, his younger brother *Feisal who was considered the leading figure and who represented Hussein in the peace negotiations.)

In Mar. 1920, at an Arab nationalist congress in Damascus that proclaimed Feisal King of Syria, a group of Iraqi nationalists offered 'A. the crown of Iraq. This corresponded to vague Hashemite concepts of three Arab Kingdoms — Greater Syria; Iraq; and Arabia — ruled by Hussein's sons and federated under King Hussein, but the British, whose zone of influence or domination was to include Iraq, did not seem to favor 'A. as ruler of Iraq. When the French foiled the plans for an Arab kingdom in Syria and compelled Feisal to flee Damascus in July 1920, 'A. assembled troops in Northern Hijaz, planning to march through Transjordan to Damascus to restore Arab-Hashemite rule to Syria. He reached Ma'an in Nov. 1920 and entered 'Amman in Mar. 1921. As the British wished to avoid an armed clash between their Hashemite allies and the French, yet felt obliged towards the Hashemites, the then Colonial Secretary Winston Churchill proposed to 'A. that he settle in Transjordan as Amir of that territory and renounce his plans regarding Syria and the French, as well as his claims to the Iraqi crown.

'A. accepted the British proposal and in Apr. 1921 became Amir of Transjordan. In 1922, the League of Nations endorsed that settlement, within the Palestine Mandate — with the clause referring to the Jewish National Home made, upon Britain's proposal, inapplicable to Transjordan. On these terms Britain recognized Transjordan in May 1923 as an autonomous Amirate. 'A. gradually established an administration — conservative, with some preference given to Beduin tribal chiefs, with the Amir as a powerful, benevolent patriarch — a fully-fledged government, an army (the "Arab Legion," British-officered), a constitution (1928) and first representative institutions (later develop-

ing into a bicameral Parliament). He remained closely linked to the British, dependent on their aid, with a loyalty which he proved during World War II, when he sent his Army to assist in the suppression of Rashid 'Ali *Kilani's rebellion in Iraq (1941). Indeed, many Arab nationalists regarded 'A. as a British puppet, and many foreign countries doubted his independence even after it was formally granted by Britain in May 1946. On that occasion, 'A. assumed the title of King and changed the name of his realm from Transjordan to the Hashemite Kingdom of Jordan; in 1947 he granted a new parliamentary constitution.

Throughout his reign, 'A. continued to cherish the vision of a "Greater Syria." i.e., a union of Syria, Lebanon, Palestine and Transjordan — under his crown — and a Fertile Crescent Federation of that Greater Syria with Iraq, and to cultivate Syrian and Palestinian-Arab politicians that might support his scheme. 'A. publicized these plans mainly after World War II; some elements in Syria, Iraq and Palestine supported them, but most Arab political opinion was hostile. Egypt, Syria and Sa'udi Arabia strongly opposed any "revisionist" plans to change the inter-Arab *status quo*, and even 'A.'s Hashemite cousins and allies in Iraq did not fully back him. The French, who also violently rejected the "Greater Syria" scheme, saw it as a British plot — and so did most Arab opinion. Yet, while some British service branches seem to have supported 'A.'s aspirations to some extent, official British policy never fully backed them.

'A. maintained good relations with the leaders of Jewish Palestine and the Zionist movement over many years. In the early 1930s he favored and invited Jewish settlement in Transjordan — but the British Palestine administration foiled these plans. From 1946 to the final Palestine crisis, 'A.'s contacts with the Zionist leaders intensified and finally led to a secret understanding — unwritten and vaguely general: 'A. — though preferring an autonomous Jewish entity within a Palestinian-Jordanian kingdom under his crown — would not resist or impede the partition of Palestine and the creation of a Jewish State (in accordance with a UN decision then expected), while the Jews, and nascent Israel, would not hinder 'A. from taking over the Arab part of Palestine — in fact, while they would not actually assist him, they encouraged such a takeover; and cooperation, a sort of alliance, would be maintained. Reports or rumors of that agreement inevitably reached the Arab countries, and the resolve to foil it and prevent 'A. from taking over part of Palestine, in league with the Jews, played a major role in the all-Arab decision of May 1948 to invade Palestine (as against a previous decision not to involve the regular armies). In 1947–48, 'A. proved unable to keep his pledge to the full: he told his Zionist contacts (Golda *Meir met him in Nov. 1947, and in a last meeting, later widely reported, in May 1948) that he could not resist the pressure to join the all-Arab camp. The British, too, while generally in sympathy with his ideas, seem to have advised him to take over the Arab part of Palestine in concert with all-Arab moves rather than in a separate agreement with the Jews. He therefore sent his army into Palestine, along with the other Arab forces. Moreover, in a symbolic gesture he was appointed Commander in Chief of all the invading forces; the title, however, was purely nominal. 'A.'s "Arab Legion" took over large parts of Arab Palestine, meeting virtually no resistance. 'A. avoided, however, attacking Israel in the areas allotted to her by the UN plan — a decision coordinated with the British commanders of his forces and conveyed by them to Israel. Fighting did take place in Jerusalem, its vicinity and on the road leading to it — areas not allotted to Israel by the UN plan and not covered by 'A.'s accord with the Zionist leaders. When hostilities ceased, 'A. resumed contacts. In Apr. 1949, while official armistice talks were being held in Rhodes, the most difficult points were settled in secret negotiations directly with the King. These talks continued and led to a draft nonaggression pact, readied for signature early in 1950. 'A., however, again reneged when mounting pressure by Arab states culminated in a threat to expel Jordan from the Arab League.

In return for this renunciation of a pact with Israel, the Arab states acquiesced in the annexation of Arab Palestine by Jordan, which they had previously violently opposed. Late in 1948 'A. had begun to turn the military takeover of the Arab part of Palestine (except for the Gaza Strip, occupied by Egypt) into a full annexation. He had in fact been invited to do so by congresses of Palestinian-Arab notables and local leaders orchestrated by his long-standing supporters, the al-*Nashashibi – led opposition, and unopposed by an extremist leadership that had largely gone abroad and was totally discredited by the defeat of 1948. In 1948 he reaffirmed, with stronger emphasis, the new name of the "Hashemite Kingdom of Jordan" (with former Transjordan as the "East Bank" and Arab Palestine as the "West Bank")

and appointed a large number of Palestinians to senior posts in his administration. This process culminated in a formal act of annexation proclaimed in Apr. 1950. The incorporation of the Palestinian Arabs wrought a basic change in the sociopolitical character and climate of the kingdom: it introduced modern, urban, nationalist politics and a highly active, agitated, traumatized population — many of whom regarded 'A. as a collaborator with the British and the Jews, a traitor to the Arab cause. 'A. was assassinated by a Palestinian in July 1951, while entering al-Aqsa Mosque in Jerusalem for prayer.

'A. published his memoirs in 1945 (abridged English translation: 1950), and a supplementary volume shortly before his death (English: 1954).

'ABDULLAH IBN YAHYA (1916–55)   Yemeni prince and politician. One of Imam-King *Yahya Hamid-ul-Din's sons (titled, like all the Imam's sons, *Seif ul-Islam*, i.e., Sword of Islam), 'A. served, at a time when Yemen had no institutionalized foreign and diplomatic relations, as the Kingdom's chief representative to the outer world at international and inter-Arab conferences. When Yemen was admitted to the UN, in 1947, he also served as her first delegate to that body. From 1949 he was Foreign Minister, sometimes titled Deputy Premier. He was, however, frequently involved in plots — real or rumored — and was said to aspire to the throne. In Apr. 1955, he took part in an attempted coup d'etat against the ruling Imam, his brother *Ahmad; the coup was crushed, and 'A. was captured and executed (together with his brother *Seif ul-Islam* 'Abbas).

'ABD-UL-LATIF (al-Sha‘bi), FEISAL (1935–70) South-Yemeni politician. Linked since the 1950s with the all-Arab "Nationalist Movement" faction (*al-Qawmiyun*), he became one of the main leaders of the extreme "National Liberation Front" (NLF), in the South Yemeni nationalist struggle against British rule in 'Aden. When the "People's Republic of South Yemen" attained independence, in Nov. 1967, 'A. joined her first government as Minister of Economy and Planning. In 1968 he had to relinquish that portfolio, but became Foreign Minister early in 1969. In Apr. 1969 he was named Prime Minister (replacing President Qahtan al-*Sha‘bi), and was also sometimes titled Vice-President. Deeply involved in factional struggles, 'A. was ousted in a coup in July 1969, together with his relative, President Sha‘ni — reportedly because of his Arab-nationalist (as against Marxist) tendencies; he was detained, and later expelled from the NLF. In Apr. 1970 he was killed, "trying to escape".

ABD-UL-MAJID, 'ISMAT (b. 1923) Egyptian diplomat and politican. Born in Alexandria, 'A. studied law at the Universities of Alexandria and Paris and joined the Foreign Service in 1950. He served in various posts in embassies and the Foreign Ministry itself, gradually raising in rank until he reached that of Ambassador in 1970 (Ambassador to France, briefly). From 1970 to 1972 he was Deputy Foreign Minister, and from 1972 to 1983 Chief Representative (Ambassador) to the UN. In July 1984 he was named foreign Minister and Deputy Prime Minister. He held that position, highly respected as the head of Egypt's diplomacy and foreign policy, until May 1991, when he was unanimously elected by the Foreign ministers of all the Arab states as Secretary-General of the Arab League (thus completing the process of Egypt's return, after 11 years, to her position as the leader of the Arab world).

'ABD-UL-NASSER, GAMAL (1918–70) Egyptian officer and statesman, President of Egypt 1956–70. Born in Bani Mor, Asyut district, son of a postal clerk, he graduated from secondary school in Cairo, in 1936, and from the military academy in 1938. He served in Sudan, and from 1941 as instructor at the military academy. After advanced training at the staff college, he commanded a battalion in Egypt's expeditionary forces in the 1948 War. He was besieged with his battalion in the "Faluja Pocket" — a siege lifted only with the armistice agreement of 1949. In 1951 he was promoted to the rank of colonel and appointed lecturer at the military college.

Nasser was a leading member of a clandestine group of "Free Officers" conspiring to remove Egypt's old leadership whom they held responsible for the humiliating defeat of 1948 along with the other ills of Egypt. On July 22, 1952 they mounted a successful coup and took power, forming a Revolutionary Council. General Muhammad *Nagib was appointed to head the Council; according to some, he was a figurehead only, admitted to the plotters' junta at the last stage, while its real leader was Nasser (others dispute that version). In Sept. Nagib took the Premiership. Rivalry soon developed between Nagib and Nasser — a struggle both for power and the shape and character of the

regime to be established. Nagib wished to revert to a parliamentary system and permit the political parties to resume activities, while N. envisaged an army-led populist one-party regime. N. had his way: in Jan. 1953 all political parties were banned and a single organization — the "National Liberation Organization" — established, with N. as its Secretary-General. In May 1953, N. was also appointed Deputy Secretary-General of the Revolutionary Council, and in June, Deputy Premier and Minister of the Interior (while Nagib became President and retained the Premiership).

In Feb. 1954 the struggle between N. and Nagib came to a head. N. became Prime Minister and tried to remove Nagib; but Nagib staged a comeback and deposed N.: demonstrations and counterdemonstrations took place and rival army units moved into position. In Apr. the struggle was resolved: N. became Prime Minister, while Nagib remained President but was stripped of all real power; in Nov. 1954 he was dismissed from that post, too, and put under house arrest. N. now took action against the remnants of the old political parties, seen as nuclei of potential opposition, by conducting a series of purges and trials. Harsh measures were taken against the Muslim Brotherhood in particular. An attempt on N.'s life, in Oct. 1954, was ascribed to them and they were severely suppressed; their leaders were put on show trials and some of them were executed.

From 1952 N. instituted reforms, chiefly an agrarian reform, and some measures of nationalization. From 1955–56, his policies were presented as new doctrine of "Arab Socialism." N. also set about to reshape the political regime. In Jan. 1956, a new constitution was proclaimed, and in a June referendum N., the single candidate, was elected President for a six-year term. With the merger of Egypt and Syria, in Feb. 1958, he was elected President of the United Arab Republic (UAR). After the dissolution of the UAR in Sept. 1961 he insisted on retaining for Egypt the official name of UAR and remained "President of the UAR." N. convened a congress of "popular forces" in 1962, founded a new ruling party — called the "Arab Socialist Union" — and formulated a National Charter as the basic, Arab-socialist, doctrine of the party and the nation. In May 1965, N. was reelected President for six years, again as the single candidate.

In their first years of power, N. and his associates had appeared moderate and pragmatic in their foreign and inter-Arab policy. In 1964 they reached

Gamal 'Abd-ul-Nasser (Bar-David, Tel Aviv)

a final agreement with Britain that had eluded all previous governments for some eight years, and obtained the abolition of the Treaty of 1936, the evacuation of British forces and the termination of any special privileges for Britain. They also conceded, in 1952–53, to Sudan the right of self-determination — which all former rulers had denied. Even in Israel they were, at first, seen as moderates with whom a *modus vivendi* appeared possible — had they not denounced the old regime for its disastrous military intervention in Palestine in 1948, and were they not noticeably reticent on anti-Israel rhetoric?

In the mid-1950s, however, all this seemed to change and N. began adopting increasingly activist, extremist-revolutionary policies. His growing inclination towards the Third World and a neutralist position led him to oppose Western plans for a Middle East defense alliance linked to the West, the Baghdad Pact (indeed, Egypt had opposed such pacts before his time, too). The ensuing confrontation with the West coincided with N.'s first appearance as a leading actor on the international scene — at the Bandung Conference of Asian leaders, 1955, his meetings with Tito and Nehru, and his emergence as one of the architects of a neutralist bloc. It also induced him to conclude an arms deal with Czechoslovakia, 1955 — marking a bud-

ding alliance with the Soviet bloc. In 1956 the USA retaliated by denying her aid to the Aswan High Dam, N.'s pet project (and inducing the World Bank to do likewise). This step led N. to obtain the aid denied by the West from the USSR, and to nationalize the Suez Canal. The confrontation with the West culminated in the Anglo-French invasion, the Suez War; Israel's participation in that invasion was also a turning point in N.'s attitude to peace prospects with Israel (though N. himself repeatedly indicated Israel's retaliatory raid on Gaza, in Feb. 1955, as that turning point). From that crisis of 1956 N. emerged triumphant, as the leader of a small, newly-independent nation that had successfully withstood imperialist aggression, and his international standing was much enhanced. In Dec. 1957, a first Afro-Asian solidarity conference (nongovernmental) was held in Cairo. In 1961, N. co-founded an alliance of leftist-neutralist African countries, the "Casablanca Bloc," and attended a neutralist summit meeting in Belgrade. In 1963, he participated in a summit conference founding the Organization for African Unity — which held its second congress in 1964 in Cairo. Later in 1964, the second conference of nonaligned nations was also held in Cairo, with N. among its leaders. In 1958, N. also paid his first visit to the Soviet Union.

From the mid-1950s, N. took an increasingly activist line also towards the Arab countries. Egypt had always seen herself as the center of the Arab world. In his booklet *The Philosophy of the Revolution* (1954) N. himself had described her position at the center of three circles: Arab, Islamic, and African. But gradually, N.'s policies tended to impose — by fostering "Nasserist" pressure groups in the Arab countries; by Egyptian pressure; by subversion; and if needed, by force — an Egyptian hegemony, in terms of both her interstate power position and her revolutionary Arab-Socialist doctrine. This process led N. to direct military intervention in the Yemen civil war, 1962.

There were ups and downs, tactical shifts, in that activist-interventionist Arab policy. Moreover, statements and policies advocating all-Arab unity based on the inter-Arab *status quo*, cooperation between differing regimes and mutual noninterference (as provided for in the Arab League Charter) existed along with policies aimed at the overthrow of conservative regimes and assertions that such regimes had to go and that only progressive-revolutionary, Arab-Socialist states would cooperate. N. himself and his followers perhaps did not perceive the contradiction. Anyway, after the debacle of the Yemen expedition and the general failure to subvert Arab governments and create regimes in the Nasserist image (as even in countries with Arab-Socialist leanings, such as Algeria, Syria, Iraq and later Libya, national self-interest and particularist tendencies soon prevailed), N. from the early 1960s tuned down his interventionist statements and policies and cooperated with the conservative regimes in renewed efforts at all-Arab cooperation (e.g., regular "summit" meetings from 1964). Yet, harsh statements that no cooperation was possible with "reactionary" regimes also recurred.

In 1966–67, when preparing for war against Israel, N. revived and reinforced his alliance with Syria and, in May 1967, after making war inevitable by proclaiming a blockade of the Straits of Tiran and ordering the UN Emergency Force to withdraw from Sinai, he imposed a close alliance on Jordan, too. The frenzy of the Six Day War, June 1967, orchestrated by carefully built-up mass enthusiasm, brought N. to the pinnacle of his all-Arab leadership; all the Arab countries fervently backed him and many sent troops or equipment to aid Egypt. When the war turned into defeat, N., taking personal responsibility, resigned; but stormy mass demonstrations — seemingly spontaneous, but no doubt carefully staged — "forced" him to retract the resignation. Thus he turned even that day of bitter defeat into a personal victory. N. had indeed become Egypt's sole leader and large masses could not envisage their country without him at the helm.

In the three years left to N. after 1967, his policies were less flamboyant, somewhat subdued — but there was no basic change and the contradiction between his pragmatic position at the center of the inter-Arab *status quo* and his radical revolutionary inclinations, with occasional interventionalist sallies, was never resolved. N. supported, for instance, the PLO's build-up of its state-within-a-state in both Jordan and Lebanon and prevented the governments of the two countries from taking effective measures against it, imposing a precarious coexistence embodied in agreements with the PLO that were formulated under his sponsorship (and never kept by the PLO). When that coexistence broke down in Jordan and King Hussein confronted the PLO in desperate battle, in 1970, N. "mediated," but in fact sided with the PLO and acted to discredit and ostracize King Hussein. N. also led Egypt into an ever-increasing dependence on the Soviet Union (with thousands of Soviet technicians and advisers, civil and military, in Egypt).

N.'s attitude to Israel and to the prospects of an Arab-Israel settlement also remained ambivalent and contradictory. He accepted UN Security Council Resolution 242 of 1967, calling for peaceful coexistence of Israel and the Arab states (interpreting it, as most Arabs did, as providing for Israel's *total* withdrawal from *all* territories occupied in 1967) and did not join the hawkish "Rejection Front" (Syria, Iraq, the PLO, Algeria) that refused in principle to coexist with Israel in any form. Yet he always refused to negotiate with Israel and seldom spoke of the possibility of peace with her. It was N. who formulated the "Three Noes" of the Khartoum summit, 1967 (no peace, no negotiations, no recognition). In numerous speeches he stated that he would not be satisfied with the "removal of the results of the aggression of 1967" (i.e., Israel's withdrawal from the territories occupied), but would continue to struggle for the "removal of the results of the aggression of 1948," i.e., for the destruction of Israel's very existence. He repeatedly said: "What was taken by force, can be regained only by force." And he continued, in his last years, conducting a "war of attrition."

N. died, suddenly, in September 1970. His image has dimmed somewhat since his death. His successors, principally Anwar *Sadat, at first maintained that their policies, though differing from his, were a loyal continuation — or at most a correction, an adaptation — of those bequeathed by him; but gradually they distanced themselves from N. and allowed previously hidden aspects of his rule to be revealed and harsh criticism to be publicly voiced concerning the failure of his economic policies, particularly the state enterprise; the all-pervading corruption; and mainly, the oppressive character of his regime, the police state he created — the suppression of the freedom of speech, organization and the press, the unlawful detention and torture of adversaries. And though "Nasserist" factions still exist in several Arab countries (e.g., Syria, Lebanon), and in Egypt herself, where many remember N.'s rule with nostalgia, "Nasserism" as a doctrine has lost most of its attraction and force.

Final judgement must be left to history. Yet there can be no doubt: N., Egypt's top leader for 18 years, endowed with unusual charisma and wielding an immense, though controversial, influence throughout the Arab world, one of the architects of international nonalignment, was a towering figure among the leaders of modern Egypt and the Arab world and has left a distinctive mark on the history of his country and the Middle East.

'ABD UL-QUDDUS, IHSAN (1918–90)   Egyptian journalist and writer. Born to a Muslim father, Muhammad 'Abd ul-Quddus, who left engineering for the stage, and a Christian mother, Rose al-Yussuf, an eminent Syrian actress who converted to Islam, left the stage for journalism and established the popular political and cultural weekly magazine bearing her name, *Rose al-Yusuf*. 'A. graduated from the Faculty of Law and practiced as a lawyer. In 1945 he became the Editor in Chief of his mother's magazine, a position he kept until 1966, even after the weekly was nationalized in 1960, because of his friendly relations with the Free Officers and *'Abd-ul-Nasser. Later he was editor of the influential weekly *Akhbar al-Yawm* and chairman of its foundation and publishing house (1966–74). In 1974 he became a member of the editorial board of the prestigious daily *al-Ahram* and chaired its board until 1976. 'A. was also a prolific writer of naive didactic-socialist novels, short stories and film scripts in support of the Egyptian revolution and its leader 'Abd ul-Nasser, and of women's liberation. Many of his novels were filmed for cinema and TV.

'ABD UL-RAZIQ, 'ALI (1888–195? 6?)   Egyptian Muslim religious scholar, and writer. Born to a wealthy family in Abu Girg in the Minya province, 'A. studied in his village *kuttab* (Qur'an school) and at al-Azhar Mosque and Academy in Cairo, where he received his *'Alim* degree after twelve years of studies. He was a disciple of the Islamic reformer Muhammad *'Abduh. He attended some university classes on Arabic literature given by the Italian Orientalist Nallino and on Muslim philosophy given by Santillana, and for a year, in 1912, studied English in England. In 1915 he was appointed a religious judge in Alexandria, then in Mansura and later in Jiza in Cairo. There he lectured at al-Azhar on Arabic rhetorics. He published several articles defending women's rights and liberation and called for abolishing the veil. Unlike most Muslim scholars, 'A. advocated and accepted the abolition of the Ottoman Sultanate (1922) and the Caliphate (1924) and the separation of state and religion. In 1925 he published his book *al-Islam wa-Usul al-Hukm* (Islam and the Principles of Government), which was considered as departing from the tenets of Islam and which caused a storm

among Muslim religious circles (some even seeing it as an Egyptian plot to transfer the caliphate to Egypt's King *Fu'ad).

A court of al-Azhar scholars unanimously found 'A. guilty of unorthodoxy, declared him incapable of holding any religious office and dismissed him from his positions. This verdict caused a crisis in the Egyptian government, when the Minister of Justice, 'Abd ul-'Aziz Fahmi Pasha, resigned in protest, charging that it was a political, not religious, decision. Several books were published to rebuff 'A.'s thesis and prove al-Azhar right.

In 1937 the committee of scholars of al-Azhar rehabilitated 'A., and in 1945 he was appointed a member of the Senate. Later he lectured at the Faculty of Law of King Fu'ad University and from 1947 to 1949 he was Minister of *Awqaf* (religious endowments), considered to be a representative of the Liberal-Constitutional Party.

'ABD-UL-RAZZAQ, 'AREF (b. 1924) Iraqi officer and politician. In Feb. 1963 he became commander of the air force. As a Nasserist, he opposed the *Qassem regime, and later the *Ba'th*, but had some affinity to the ideologically fluctuating semi-Nasserist regime of the *Aref brothers. He served them, in 1963/64, as Minister of Agriculture. In Sept. 1965, after Nasserist pressure and a reported semi-*coup*, he became Prime Minister, but was dismissed after two weeks and went into exile to Egypt. In 1966 'A. was involved in an abortive Nasserist *coup* and detained. He was, however, released in 1967 without having stood trial. He remained a Nasserist, was sometimes consulted when the faction in power wished to form a broader united front, and was again involved in a *coup* attempt in Oct. 1968 and detained for some time. With the consolidation of the *Ba'th* regime, from 1968 on, 'A. ceased his political activities.

ABU ---, (Arabic: Father of ---).   Calling a man Father of his first-born son as an honorific added to his name is a widespread custom in Arab society. In most cases, the honorific is known only to close acquaintances; in some, it becomes public knowledge — particularly in underground organizations, where the honorific may serve as a *nom de guerre* (Abu 'Amar — Yasser *'Arafat; Abu Lutf — Faruq Qaddumi). In many instances, the *nom de guerre* is used rather than the real name (Abu Iyad — Salah *Khalaf; Abu Jihad — Khalil al-*Wazir; Abu Nidal — Sabri al-*Banna; and many other PLO activists). There are also many family names with "Abu ---" — such as Abu-(a)l-Huda, *Abu-(a)l-Fath, or in the North-African form (usually in the French transcription) *Bourguiba, Bouteflika, Boucetta; these stay in the family, in contrast to the honorifics and *noms de guerre* which are tied to the person bearing them.

ABU GHAZALA, 'ABD-UL-HALIM (b. 1930) Egyptian officer and government leader. Graduated 1949 from military college and joined the artillery; four years of advanced training in the Soviet Union; author of several artillery manuals. In Oct. 1973, A.-Gh. became commander of the artillery. Later he headed army intelligence and subsequently was military attache in Washington. In May 1980 he was appointed Chief of Staff, but relinquished that post in Mar. 1981 when he became Minister of Defense. In Apr. 1982, he was promoted to the rank of Field Marshal, and from Aug. 1982 he served, in addition to being Defense Minister, as Deputy Prime Minister. Some considered him as Egypt's "strong man" behind President Husni *Mubarak. In Apr. 1989 he was dismissed (because he had grown too strong, rivaling the President?).

ABU IYAD see Khalaf, Salah.

ABU JIHAD see Wazir, Khalil.

ABU-(A)L-FATH   Egyptian family of several brothers prominent as journalists, writers and publishers. Mahmud (1892–1958), Hussein and Ahmad (b. 1917) AF founded, owned and co-edited with Muhammad al-Tabi'i and Karim Tabit the daily *al-Misri* (1936) which became a chief organ of the *Wafd* party; they supported — and their writings influenced — the liberal-progressive wing of the party. In 1946, Ahmad AF became Editor-in-Chief, and in 1950 a Wafdist member of Parliament. In 1952, the AF brothers inititally suported the Free Officers' revolution; indeed, Ahmad was considered close to Abd-ul-*Nasser. But they soon turned against the anti liberal, authoritarian-populist tendencies of the new regime. In 1954, Mahmud and Ahmad went into exile; their paper was closed by the government and their property confiscated. In one of the regime's purge trials, 1954, Mahmud was sentenced, *in absentia*, to prison for 15 years, while Hussein's identical sentence was suspended. Mahmud and Ahmad became spokesmen for the anti-Nasserist opposition in exile (where Mahmud died); they formed a "Free Egypt Committee" and

Ahmad wrote a bitterly anti-Nasser book (*L'affaire Nasser*, 1962). In 1963, Hussein's prison sentence was reconfirmed, *in absentia*, and extended to Ahmad. However, in 1974, *Sadat, Nasser's successor, quashed the sentence. and Ahmad returned to Egypt. He began writing again, occasionally, for Egyptian papers. His own paper, however, was neither restored to him nor permitted to reappear.

ABU NIDAL see Banna, Sabri.

ADONIS (b. 1930)   Pseudonym of 'Ali Ahmad Sa'id Asbar, Syrian 'Alawi poet and writer, born in the village of Kassabin near Latakia. The name Adonis was given to him by Antoun *Sa'adeh, the leader of the Syrian Social-Nationalist Party of which A. was an active member. In 1954 A. graduated from Damascus University in Philosophy.

Because his political activities in the right-wing, mainly Christian S.S.N. Party were considered subversive, A. was sentenced to a long term of imprisonment. In 1956 he escaped to Lebanon. In Beirut he continued his studies and got his Ph.D. from St. Joseph University with a thesis on "The Eternal and Ephemeral in Arab Culture"; he also was interested in Islamic mysticism (Sufism).

In Beirut, A. expanded his literary and journalistic activity. He was coeditor, with Yusuf al-Khal (1917–1987), of the *avant-garde* poetry and criticism magazine *Shi'r* (1956–63, 1967–69), and worked on the editorial staff of the literary magazine *al-Adab* (1962–63) and the Beirut daily *Lisan al-Hal*. Later he established his own journal, *Mawaqif* (Attitudes) (1968–80?). For some years A. was a leading proponent of "Phoenicianism," basing Lebanon's civilization and nationalism on its ancient Phoenician roots (rather than its Arab identity).

After publishing two anthologies in the conventional form of the Arabic *qasida* (ode), he became devoted to the new technique of the French *poeme en prose* (*qasidat al-nathr*). He replaced the images of both Arab romantic and realistic poetry with a complex technique of unusual images to convey an intuitive existentialist, mystical vision of revolutionary change, portraying himself, in his book *Introduction to Arabic Poetry* (Beirut, 1971), as the herald of post-modernist Arabic poetry. His rebellious poetry speaks of political suppression and submissiveness; he decries the industrial smoke in the town and the emptiness and degradation of city life, and his references to Syria and Damascus are hostile. Yet the poverty, enslavement and misery of his village is reflected in the image of a boy "brought up to pray and be a shoeblack... a slave to hunger, tears and home." A.'s poetry is distinguished by historical images and symbols reflecting the tragic past and present of his country, the invasions by foreign races such as the Mongols, the destruction and stagnation it underwent and its enslaved present. The legendary Phoenix, burning to death and reborn from the ashes, is, besides Christ and Tammuz, his symbol of the revival of the Arab civilization from its last stage of decay; he identifies the Phoenix with Tammuz who with his return to life will bring rain and harvest, lifting the three ancient curses of his nation: idleness, poverty and illiteracy.

After the civil war in Lebanon, A. left for France where he teaches and writes.

'AFLAQ, MICHEL (1910–89) Syrian political thinker, founder of the *Ba'th* party. Born in Damascus, a Greek-Orthodox Christian, 'A. studied in Paris and was close to the Communist Party. In the late 1930s he developed his own brand of revolutionary-socialist Arab nationalism, stressing the aim of immediate all-Arab unity. In the 1940s he organized, together with Salah-ul-Din *Bitar, a group of like-minded students and young intellectuals as the "Arab Renaissance (*al-Ba'th*) Party." The party first appeared on the political scene in the Syrian elections of 1947: 'A. stood as a candidate, but failed. In 1949 he served briefly as Minister of Education (in Hashem al-*Atassi's government, following the Sami *Hinnawi coup), but was again defeated when he stood for Parliament. He remained Secretary-General of the *Ba'th* party when it merged, in 1953, with Akram *Hourani's "Arab Socialist Party" and in 1959 authoritatively summarized the party's doctrine in his book *In the Ways of the Ba'th*. In the factional struggles that split the party after it came to power through the coup of Mar. 1963, 'A. (with Bitar) sided with the "civilian wing" considered more moderate, i.e., with the faction that lost out in Syria — in the 1966 coup of the "military wing" — and won in Iraq. In 1966, 'A. left Syria. He continued leading the "National (i.e., all-Arab) Command" of the *Ba'th* seated in Beirut and Baghdad — to which the Syrian party no longer paid allegiance. In 1967, 'A. emigrated to Brazil, abandoning all political activity; but late in 1968 he went to Baghdad to resume his position of leadership. In 1970 he left Baghdad in protest against Iraq's failure to send troops against Jordan in support of the Palestinian guer-

rillas; but in 1974 a reconciliation was effected and he returned to Iraq. While highly respected as an ideologist and party intellectual, 'A. did not retain much effective influence on party and state policies (determined by political and military interests, as judged by a junta of officer-politicians, rather than by ideology or doctrine).

AHMAD BIN YAHYA (HAMID-UL-DIN) (1895–1962) Ruler of Yemen and Iman of her Shi'i-Zeidi community, 1948–62. The eldest son of Imam *Yaha, he was groomed for the succession and entrusted with various state missions (as a prince, he bore, like all the Imam's sons, the title *Seif-ul-Islam*, "Sword of Islam"). In his campaigns against rebellious tribes in the 1920s and 1930s, he acquired a reputation of cruelty. When his father was assassinated, in Feb. 1948, A. was chosen by the ruling Zeidi notables — the *Sada* — to succeed him as Imam. He continued strengthening the central royal power — building a modern army, subduing recalcitrant tribes and reducing the influence and power of the *Sada*. In Aug. 1955 he had to suppress, with the help of his eldest son Muhammad al-*Badr, a coup attempt launched by rebellious officers and the *Sada* as well as two of his brothers, *Seif-ul-Islam* 'Abdullah and *Seif-ul-Islam* 'Abbas (who were both executed). A. continued slowly to establish regular foreign relations, with both superpowers eager to respond. In his later years, A. was plagued by illness and delegated much of his power to his son al-Badr and his brother *Seif-ul-Islam* Hassan. His death, in September 1962, triggered the revolution that toppled Yemen's monarchy.

AHMAD, JALAL (1923–69) Iranian Islamic revolutionary intellectual whose thought inspired many of the Shah's rivals. Though his family was a clerical one, he chose a Western-style education. At the age of 20, he showed an affinity for the Communist Party but later joined socialist-nationalist movements. In the early 1960s, he returned to Islam by fulfilling the pilgrimage to Mecca (*Hajj*).

During the 1960s, A. was noted for his writings on social and political issues. He criticized both the West and the Iranian political system, calling for a return to traditional Islam as a way to solve the country's social problems. He accused the wealthy nations of the West of supressing the poorer nations or weakening them to ensure their dependence on the West. He claimed that the rapid Westernization of Iran would deepen its dependence on the West; that Western universities trained Iranian intellectuals in nonproductive occupations, perpetuating the need for foreign advisers; and that the purchase of industrial equipment from the West led to a reliance on foreign parts and experts. He coined the term *"urbazdag"* (Westoxication) to define the Iranian reality: a society blinded by the West and being pushed toward the loss of national identity.

A. was a member of a group of thinkers who had a major influence on the ideology of the *Khomeini revolution in its early stages, serving as a bridge between the political and the religious resistance to the Shah.

AL-AHMAR, 'ABDULLAH HUSSEIN   Yemeni tribal leader and politician. Chief of all the Zeidi Hashed tribal confederation, Yemen's strongest tribal group. He succeeded his father, Sheikh Hussein ibn Nasser al-Ahmar, who was reportedly executed in 1958/59 as a rebel, together with his eldest son, by the Imam *Ahmad ('Abdullah himself was detained). Since the Hashed tribal leaders had resisted the Imam and his royal regime whenever they infringed upon the tribes' traditional privileges and semi-autonomy since the coup of 1962, A. supported the Republican rebels in the civil war, at the head of a contigent of Hashed tribal warriors. He also served, on behalf of the Republic, as Governor of the Hajja district (controlled by his tribes). His support was not, however, unreserved: he envisaged a Republic conservative in character and respecting tribal autonomy, in which the tribal leaders would play a principal role. He called for an Advisory Council of tribal and religious elders and selected conservative elements to manage or supervise the affairs of the Republic, and convened, between 1963 and 1967, several tribal conferences to voice these requests. In alliance with conservatives among the Republicans (such as al-*Iryani, al-Zubeiri, al-*Nu'man), he opposed the radical, "leftist" officers who emerged as the Republic's leaders. He also wanted Egypt's intervention to end and her expeditionary forces to be withdrawn. He was supported and aided by Sa'udi Arabia. A.'s relations with the Republic and its chief leaders fluctuated — sometimes to the point of actual armed clashes.

A. particularly opposed the Republic's leader, 'Abdullah *Sallal, when Sallal returned from Egyptian exile and resumed control; in 1965/66, he tried to arrest A. — who escaped to his tribal stronghold and organized armed resistance to Sallal and his forces. A. returned to San'a, with his warriors, after the withdrawal of Egyptian forces in 1967 and was instrumental in the removal of Sallal in Nov. 1967. He wielded much influence behind the scenes of the post-Sallal conservative-moderate regime. He also brought most of the northwestern tribes over to the Republican camp and was instrumental, with Sa'udi help, in the reconciliation with the Royalists that ended the civil war, abolished the Imamate-Kingdom and firmly established the Republic. When under the Constitution of 1970 an Advisory Council was set up — as he had demanded since 1963 — A. became its chairman. After Ibrahim *Hamdi's coup of 1974, the abolition of the Advisory Council and Hamdi's attempts to impose a centralized administration, A. and his tribes again became restive and a tribal semi-rebellion ensued in 1977. A. was not appointed to the new Constituent Assembly Hamdi set up in early 1978. After Hamdi was toppled (and killed) in 1978, A.'s relations with his successors — Ahmad Hussein al-*Ghashmi in his short-lived Presidency, and 'Ali 'Abdullah *Saleh — improved: he was also made a member of the Constituent Assembly and, in 1979, of a reestablished Consultative Council. He did not, however, regain the predominant position he had enjoyed in the heyday of the conservative Republic, 1968–74. His opposition to Yemen's union with South Yemen, and to the regime's reconciliation with the leftist-radical underground, as well as to its tendency to enhance relations with the Soviet bloc, created renewed tension between him and Saleh and his regime and caused a decline in his influence.

AL-'AINI-MUHSIN (b. 1932/33)   Yemeni politician. Studied at Sorbonne and Cairo Universities, graduating in law and economics (1959). 'A. joined Yemen's civil service and served *inter alia* as Crown Prince al-*Badr's private secretary. However, close to leftist-revolutionary ideas of the *Ba'th*, he joined the "Free Yemen" underground and in 1959 exiled himself to 'Aden. There he was active in the 'Aden Trade Unions' Congress (which advocated a union of Yemen and South Yemen and claimed to represent Yemen, too) and took part in missions and conferences abroad. In Jan. 1961 he was expelled from 'Aden by its British goverment. After the Yemen coup of 1962 he joined the Republic, and after a few weeks as Foreign Minister was appointed Ambassador to the UN, and from 1963 concurrently to the USA. In 1965 he was Foreign Minister in A.M. *Nu'man's short-lived government. Despite his leftist inclinations he thus joined the conservative-rightist faction headed by the tribal leaders and their allies al-*Iryani, al-*'Amri, Nu'man, and then as an opponent of al-*Sallal's ruling faction he was exiled to Egypt, where he was kept in semi-detention. 'A. returned to Yemen after the ouster of Sallal, in 1967, and became Prime Minister. However, he never kept office for long — apparently because of his intellectual-ideological vacillation and his factional instability. His first Premiership lasted for one month only, after which he became briefly Ambassador to the UN, then special representative of Premier 'Amri, and, in 1968, Ambassador to the USSR. In 1970 he was again Prime Minister, serving also as Foreign Minister. In 1971 he lost office for a few months, going to France as Ambassador, then resumed it — until Dec. 1972 when he became ambassador to Britain. After Ibrahim *Hamdi's coup, 1974, he was made Prime Minister again, but was dismissed in Jan. 1975 and sent again to France as Ambassador. He stayed in semi-exile and was kept under surveillance in Egypt. Later he was allowed to go to other Arab capitals. While in exile, he was suspected of plotting — with Libya, according to some reports — and of masterminding the assassination (in London) of conserative, pro-Sa'udi ex-Premier 'Abdullah el-*Hajri, in 1977.

AIT-AHMAD, HUSSEIN (b. 1919)   Algerian nationalist, guerrilla leader and politician. Closely linked with the Berber-dominated Kabylia region, A. was one of the nine "historic leaders" of the Algerian nationalists who in 1954 founded the "National Liberation Front" (FLN) and began a bloody eight-year rebellion against France. He fought as a rebel leader — in his Kabylia mountains and with the rebel high command abroad, in Egypt and Tunisia — until captured by the French in Oct. 1956 (with four other leaders, in a commercial airliner the French forced to land). He was imprisoned in France until the 1962 agreement on Algeria's independence. In nascent independent Algeria he strongly opposed the ruling faction of *Ben-Bella and his associates. Ben-Bella, who ruthlessly suppressed all opposing factions, dared not take similar action against A. He made A. a member of the FLN Politbureau, but A. soon resigned, in 1962, and went underground. He was elected in 1963 to the National Assembly, on the FLN list, and returned from exile, but soon went underground again and started militant guerrilla action against Ben-Bella's regime. He was captured in Oct. 1964 and sentenced to death, but was

pardoned by Ben-Bella. In Apr. 1966 he escaped. In exile in France A. tried to organize various shifting opposition groups plotting against the Algerian regime — sometimes even in cooperation with Ben-Bella (himself now in exile), but mostly in rivalry with him; his main organizations in the 1970s and 1980s were the Party of Socialist Revolution and the Front of Socialist Forces (FFS). After the liberalization of Algeria's regime in the late 1980s, under *Ben-Jedid, A.'s FFS was legalized in Nov. 1989, and A. returned to Algeria from his 23-year exile. He tried to build the FFS into a main democratic opposition party, strongly anti-FLN and again based mainly on Kabylia and Berber elements (but not overtly speaking for the Berbers — in contrast to the rival, openly Berber, RCD). A. and the FFS oppose the growing Islamic-fundamentalist agitation of the FIS group (in accord with the regime and the FLN on this issue). They boycotted the June 1990 local and municipal elections, the first free multiparty elections in Algeria, and their strength has not yet been tested.

'ALA, HUSSEIN (1883? 1885–1964)   Iranian diplomat and politician, Prime Minister 1951, 1955–57. Born in Tehran, his father was a Prime Minister and ambassador and a leader of the Constitutional Revolution, 1906. 'A. studied at Westminister School (later the University of London). He joined the diplomatic service on the eve of World War I and served as a junior minister during the war. After the war he was a member of the Iranian delegation to the Paris Peace Conference (not admitted to full participation because of Iran's neutrality during the war). In the early 1920s 'A. served as ambassador to Spain and later to the USA During his stay in the USA, he was elected to the *Majlis* (Parliament), where he opposed the deposition of *Ahmad Shah, the last of the Qajar dynasty, and the enthronement of *Reza Khan (Pahlavi) as Shah, 1925. He was therefore out of favor with Reza Shah and was not given any position, but in the late 1920s he was named ambassador to France. In 1932, he became Comptroller of the National Bank. When Britain presented her oil dispute with Iran to the League of Nations in 1932/33, 'A. served as Iran's representative to that organization, and in 1933–34 became ambassador to Britain. He served as Minister of Commerce (1935), Chief of Government Monopolies (1936), again Governor of the National Bank (1941), and Minister of the Court, 1942–45. From 1945/46 to 1950 he was again ambassador to the U.S.A. When the USSR's refusal to withdraw from Iran's territory was debated at the UN in 1945/46, he headed the Iranian delegation to the Security Council. He was briefly Foreign Minister in 1950 and again in 1951, and was instrumental in the acceptance of U.S. military and economic aid and the bestowal of oil concessions to American companies.

Following the assassination of 'Ali *Razmara, 'A. was appointed Prime Minister, in Mar. 1951, but had to resign after a month in the context of the Anglo-Iranian oil crisis, as he was considered not sufficiently hard-line, and again became Minister of the Court. He was forced out of that position by Prime Minister *Mossaddeq, but regained it after Mossaddeq's fall in 1953. He again was Prime Minister from 1955 to 1957 and Minister of the Court from 1957 to 1963.

ALAM, ASSADULLAH (1915-?) Iranian politician. His father, Shawkat ul-Mulk, was a prominent khan in Baluchistan. Born in Birijand, A. graduated from the College of Agronomy in Karaj and continued his studies at Oxford University. He entered the Ministry of Agriculture in 1942 and was a supervisor in the Ministry of the Interior. After a brief stay in Great Britain, he became governor of Baluchistan in 1948. From Jan. 1950, he was Minister of the Interior, and from Nov. 1950, Minister of Labor. In Muhammad *Mossaddeq's government, 1951, he served as Comptroller of the Treasury, but he fell out with Mossaddeq and was fired and exiled to Birijand. After Mossaddeq's fall in 1953, he returned to his previous office.

In 1955 A. became Minister of Interior in Hussein *'Ala's cabinet, until 1957. He also was the Secretary-General of the *Mardom* (People's) Party, but resigned after the elections of 1960. He was elected to the *Majlis* (Parliament) in 1961, but relinquished his seat. He was Prime Minister, 1962–64.

A. also served as general secretary of the Pahlavi Foundation (1961), Chancellor of Pahlavi University, and editor of *Iran-i-Ma*.

AL-'ALAMI, MUSSA (1897–1984) Palestinian Arab politician. Son of a prominent Jerusalem family (his father, Feidi al- 'A., 1865–1924, was Mayor of Jerusalem, 1906–09, and represented the Jerusalem District in the Ottoman Parliament, 1914–18), 'A. studied law at the American University of Beirut. He joined the Legal Department of the Palestine Government, attaining the senior position of Government Advocate. He took some

part in the Arab nationalist movement, but was not very active. He was related to the al-*Husseini family and considered close to the al-Husseini political camp, but was never fully identified with any faction. In the mid-1930s — before and during the rebellion of 1936–39 — he met Jewish leaders for talks on the possibility of an Arab-Jewish agreement, but the talks were abortive. In 1937 he was dismissed from government service because of his alleged involvement with the leadership of the Arab rebellion, and went in exile to Syria and Iraq; he returned to Palestine in 1941. In the absence of a Palestinian-Arab representative body, he was appointed by the conveners of the Arab League to represent the Arabs of Palestine at the Preparatory Conference of Alexandria, Oct. 1944, and at the foundation of the Arab League, Mar. 1945. In 1945, he was also appointed to a new (or reconstituted) Arab Higher Committee, as a neutral notable not identified with any faction, but soon withdrew from the Committee and the factional struggle around it, to devote himself to two special independent projects: he founded Palestinian-Arab Information (or propaganda) offices in London, Washington, Beirut and Jerusalem, selecting mostly younger intellectuals — without paying attention to their factional or clan affiliation; and he initiated a "Constructive Scheme" to develop the Palestinian-Arab village and its lands so as to prevent the sale of Arab lands to Jews (as against an Arab "National Fund" (*sanduq al-Ummah*), established by a rival faction, that planned to attain the same goal by the purchase of such lands). Both his enterprises were approved and supported by the Arab League. Both collapsed in the Arab-Jewish war of 1948.

After the war, 'A. devoted himself to a training farm for Palestinian-Arab youth, particularly orphans, near Jericho, supported by funds from abroad — a remnant of his "Constructive Scheme." Reports of his involvement in political activities in Jordan — e.g., as a co-founder of a branch of the *al-Ba'th* party or a faction sponsored by Iraq — were never substantiated. After 1967 he lived in London and 'Amman, paying visits to Jerusalem and Jericho. In 1971 he returned to Jerusalem, but took no part in public life. He died in 'Amman in 1984.

'ALAVI, BOZORG (b. 1905) Iranian writer. Born in Tehran, 'A. studied German language and literature in Germany. 'A. served as an instructor at the Technical School and a teacher of German at the Industrial College in Tehran. In 1936, he was accused and arrested with 53 others for planning to establish a Communist party. Following the conquest of Iran by the Allied forces in 1941, he was released from jail. 'A. joined the pro-Soviet *Tudeh* Party and was associate editor of the party's newspaper *Mardom* (The People).

When the *Tudeh* Party was outlawed in the late 1940s, he migrated to East Germany and has resided there since. He served as a professor of Iranian language and literature at Humboldt University. Among his books: *Her Eyes* (1952); *The Suitcase* (1955); *Letters* (1961); *The Salaris* (1978); *Mirza* (1978); and *Demon! Demon!* (1978). He has also written a scholarly book about the Persian and German languages and literature, as well as translations.

'ALI IBN HUSSEIN (1880–1935)   King of Hijaz, 1924–25. The eldest son of *Hussein ibn 'Ali, the *Hashemite Sharif of Mecca and later King of Hijaz, 'A. led, together with his brothers *Feisal and *'Abdullah, the Hijazi Arab Revolt (the "Revolt in the Desert") against the Turks, 1916, but played no major role in operations. The Hashemites' vague plans for an Arab Federation to be established after the defeat of the Turks envisaged 'A. as ruler of Hijaz (with his brothers ruling Syria and Iraq, and their father as overall king or Caliph). Therefore 'A. remained with his father in Mecca while Feisal and 'Abdullah left for the countries of the Fertile Crescent to claim them. 'A. seems to have had little influence on his father's policies. When the Hashemite Hijazis' conflict with *Ibn Sa'ud, the Wahhabi ruler of Najd, culminated in 1924 in armed clashes and the defeat of the Hijazis, King Hussein, to save the throne for his dynasty, abdicated in favor of 'A. and went into exile. 'A., however, could not save the kingdom and Mecca was conquered by the Sa'udis late in 1924. 'A. renounced the throne late in 1925 and left Hijaz, thus ending Hashemite rule in Hijaz (which became part of Sa'udi Arabia). 'A. spent the rest of his days in Baghdad, at the court of his brother King Feisal I. His daughter 'Aliya (d. 1950) married Feisal's son King *Ghazi (King *Feisal II thus was his grandson), and his son *'Abd-ul-Ilah was Regent of Iraq from Ghazi's death in 1939 until Feisal II reached the age of 18 in 1953.

'ALI, AHMAD ISMA'IL (1913? 1919?–74) Egyptian officer and politician. Graduated from Military College c. 1938, staff school 1950, advanced training in Russia (1957) and the Nasser Academy (1965). Appointed in 1967 to command the infantry, Chief of Operations 1968, Chief of Staff 1969. He was dismissed the same year following an Israeli raid on the Red Sea area. Considered close to *Sadat, 'A. was restored to army service in 1971 and appointed Chief of Intelligence. In Oct. 1972 he became Minister of Defense, in 1974 also Deputy Premier. He died in Dec. 1974.

ALI, KAMAL (-UL-DIN) HASSAN (b. 1920) Egyptian officer and politician. Graduated from staff school, 1946. Battalion commander in the Palestine war of 1948. Led the Egyptian expeditionary force in the Yemen civil war of 1962–67. Commanded an armored brigade in the October War, 1973 (and was seriously wounded). 1975 - Assistant to Defense Minister *Gamassy, 1976–77 — Chief of Intelligence and Security. In Oct. 1978, 'A. replaced Gamassy as Minister of Defense and Commander-in-Chief. In this capacity he took part in the peace negotiations with Israel. From May 1980 he served as Foreign Minister and Deputy Prime Minister, and in July 1984 became Prime Minister. He resigned in Sept. 1985, because of ill health. He then wrote a book on the peace negotiations.

'ALI, RASHID see *Kilani, Rashid 'Ali.

'ALI, SALEM RUBAI' (1934/35–78)   South Yemeni politician, President of South Yemen 1969–78. A schoolteacher and law student, 'A. was active in the 'Aden nationalist movement against British rule — first as a youth leader, and from 1963 within the main and extreme nationalist faction, the NLF — in its leftist-Marxist wing linked with the "Arab Nationalist Movement" (*Harakat al-Qawmiyyin*). When South Yemen became independent in 1967, under the NLF, 'A. was suspected of factional plotting and went into exile. In June 1969 he took part in a successful coup against President Qahtan al-*Sha'bi and his faction, and became chairman of a new Presidential Council (which he continued purging and reshaping in 1970 and 1971). From 1970, he was also a member of the NLF Central Committee and Executive. 'A. was considered pro-Chinese (as against a pro-Soviet faction headed by 'Abd-ul-Fattah *Isma'il), and during his rule South Yemen remained leftist-extremist in her international and inter-Arab policies. But he gradually mitigated his views and became more pragmatic and moderate, later described as "rightist"; and the rivalry between him and Isma'il grew more pronounced. In June 1978 'A. became involved in a strange drama that has never been clarified: a special envoy he sent to A.H. al-*Ghashmi, the President of (North) Yemen, assassinated al-Ghashmi with explosives he carried in his diplomatic briefcase (and was himself killed). According to one version, 'A. had tried to enlist al-Ghashmi's help in a coup he was planning, but his plot had been discovered and his envoy caught and replaced. At the same time, a brief struggle took place in 'Aden: according to one version — an attempt on 'A.'s part to oust his rival 'Abd-ul-Fattah Isma'il and his faction, with the help of the army; in another version — a coup by Isma'il, aided by the NLF's People's Militia, to oust 'A. 'A. was defeated and executed.

ALLON (original name: Faikovitch), **YIGAL** (1918–80) Israeli military and political leader. Born in Kfar Tavor in the lower Galilee to a family of farmers, he studied at Kadduri agricultural school, and was one of the founding members of Kibbutz Ginossar on the shores of the Sea of Galilee. In 1941 he was one of the founders of the *Palmah* and in 1945 became its chief commander. He was one of the prominent commanders during the 1948 War of Independence commanding the Yiftah Battalion, and afterwards, at age 30, he was appointed commander of the Southern Front. In retrospect he reached his zenith during this period — at no later time did he manage to attain the glory which he then achieved.

Towards the end of 1949, when members of the *Mapam* Party were removed from the army's higher echelons, A. too lost his command. After studying at Cambridge he entered politics for the *Ahdut Ha'avodah* party. In 1955 he was elected to the Knesset and in 1961 served as Minister of Labor in *Ben Gurion's government. After *Mapai* (the Labor Party) and A.'s *Ahdut Ha'avodah* founded the "Alignment" (1965), he became Prime Minister Levi *Eshkol's chief defense advisor, but in 1967, Moshe *Dayan, his longtime rival, received the defense portfolio, to A.'s bitter and lasting disappointment.

In 1968 he was appointed Deputy Prime Minister and Minister of Absorption and in 1969 — Minister of Education and Culture. Following the Yom Kippur War in 1973 he became Foreign Minister and Deputy to Prime Minister Yitzhak *Rabin — formerly his subordinate in the *Palmah*. After the victory of the Right in 1977 he vied with Shimon *Peres for the leadership of the Labor Party. In the middle of this contest he suddenly died. His death, deeply mourned, was considered the end of an era and a symbol of the failure of an entire generation which saw A. as one of its beloved sons.

Yigal Allon was considered to symbolize the missed political opportunities connected with the generation born in Palestine. He never shook off the sense of awe in which he held the founding generation — Ben Gurion, *Tabenkin and afterwards Golda *Meir whom he served as deputy. When he reached political maturity he cleared the stage for Yitzhak Rabin. The major political idea with which he was identified — the "Allon Plan," dealing with the territories occupied by Israel since 1967 — was unrealistic from its outset.

ALONI (original name: Adler) **SHULAMIT** (b. 1929) Israeli politician. Born in Tel Aviv, A. graduated from a teachers' college and the Hebrew University Law School. She produced radio programs dealing with law, justice and civil rights. In 1959 she joined *Mapai* and in 1965 was elected to the Sixth Knesset. In 1969, due to her worsening relationship with Golda *Meir, she was not placed on the list for the Seventh Knesset. When in 1973 she was again not allotted a place on the Labor Party's list for the Eighth Knesset, she resigned from the party and founded an independent party — the Citizen's Rights Movement (CRM).

That list won three seats in the Knesset. In June 1974 she joined the government formed by Yitzhak *Rabin as Minister without Portfolio. In Nov. 1974, after the National Religious Party joined the government, A. left it, against the wishes of the majority of her party's Council. In the 1977 elections the CRM won only one seat in the Knesset, and until 1984 A. was the CRM's sole representative. She was considered one of the Knesset's most vocal members and one of the leaders of the opposition, the main spokesperson on civil rights and a fierce opponent of religious coercion. From 1984 onward the electoral strength of her party has been on the rise. A. is one of the outspoken leaders of the dovish-liberal camp.

ALTERMAN, NATAN (1910–70) Israeli poet and playwright, considered one of the great modern Hebrew poets. Born in Warsaw, A. immigrated to Palestine in 1925 and studied in Gymnasia Herzliah high school in Tel Aviv. He then studied agriculture in Nancy, France. Upon his return, in 1932, he began to publish poems in the periodical *Turim* ("Columns"). From 1934 to 1943 he wrote for

Ha'aretz. In 1938 he published his first book of poems *Kokhavim Bahutz* ("Stars Outside"), and in 1941 *Simhat Aniyim* ("Joy of the Poor"). While his first book was distinctly lyrical, many researchers regard the second as expressing the fear of a possible conquest of Palestine by foreign powers.

In 1943 A. joined the editorial board of *Davar* and for 22 years published in that paper a weekly column, *Ha-Tur Hashevi'i* ("The Seventh Column"), which gave poetic expression to major issues arising in the Jewish *Yishuv* in Palestine and afterwards in the State of Israel. A. was a member of *Mapai* and maintained close relations with its leaders, particularly David *Ben Gurion. He supported the party in various public debates, e.g., the "*Kasztner Trial." Yet he maintained an independent position on various issues, such as the attitude towards the Arab minority and the question of accepting reparations from Germany (which he opposed).

In the early sixties he was one of Ben Gurion's most vocal supporters in the "*Lavon Affair." He also seceded from *Mapai* along with Ben Gurion to form *Rafi* in 1965. After the Six Day War he was one of the founders and leaders of the "Movement for the Whole *Eretz Yisrael*" (Greater Israel) — parting company on this matter with Ben Gurion, who strongly opposed the annexation of territory.

'AMER, 'ABD-UL-HAKIM (1919–67)   Egyptian officer and politician. Graduated from the Military Academy in 1938 and served in the War of 1948.

'Abd-ul-Hakim 'Amer (Bar-David, Tel Aviv)

One of the founders of the "Free Officers" group that planned and mounted the coup of July 1952; member of the Revolutionary Council it established. Promoted to General, and appointed Commander in Chief of the Armed Forces in June 1953; from 1954 also Minister of War. With the union of Egypt and Syria in 1958, 'A., promoted to the rank of Field-Marshal, became Vice-President and War Minister of the UAR. When opposition to the regime increased in Syria, he was sent there in 1960 as special commissioner to enforce the will of the central government. After the dissolution of the UAR in 1961, he continued serving as Minister of War in Egypt, becoming also a member of the Presidential Council in 1962. In 1964 he was appointed First Vice-President and Deputy Commander in Chief of the Armed Forces. In June 1967 he was considered responsible for the Egyptian debacle in the Six Day War and resigned, or was dismissed. In Aug. 1967 he was accused of plotting a military coup and was arrested; he committed suicide in prison in Sept. 1967.

'A., who came from a wealthy peasant family and himself acquired quite a fortune and extensive landed property (he was also involved in some questionable deals), was considered "right-wing" within the officers' junta, conservative in his political leanings, and upper-class in his life-style. He had reservations regarding the populist-socialist regime *Nasser introduced, as well as Egypt's growing alliance with the USSR, and strove to enhance the leading role and special status of the armed forces and their top commanders. On this account he clashed several times with Nasser; yet his divergent tendencies never crystallized to become a rival doctrine and he always deferred to Nasser. Until the final crisis of June 1967 he enjoyed a close personal friendship with Nasser and was considered nearest to Nasser of all the Free Officers' group.

AMIN, 'ALI (1914–76) and **AMIN, MUSTAFA** (b. 1914)   Prominent Egyptian journalists and publishers, twin brothers of an upper-class family (their father, Amin Yusuf, was Ambassador to the USA, 1935–38). The brothers A. edited various papers. Mustafa was chief editor of the weeklies *Akher Sa'a* 1938–41 and *al-Ithris,* 1941–44. They rose to prominence when they founded, in 1944, the popular weekly *Akhbar al-Yawm,* which they owned and edited. Though jealously maintaining its independence, the paper was close to the Royal Court and anti-*Wafd.* Both brothers were Members of Parliament in the 1940s. In 1946 they enlarged their growing press empire by purchasing *Akher Sa'a* too, and in 1952 they founded *Al-Akbar*, which became Egypt's largest daily with a circulation of over 700,000. They also published, in 1956–57, an Arabic edition of *Reader's Digest* (*al-Mukhtar*). In 1960 their papers were nationalized, with the rest of the Egyptian press. In 1962 the brothers A. were reappointed as editors and board chairmen of the papers they no longer owned, but be ng nonconformist and insisting on a freedom of the press which was no longer granted (they boasted of having been harassed and frequently arrested under all previous governments, too), they soon fell out with the *Nasser regime and lost their positions. 'Ali went into exile in 1965; Mustafa was accused of espionage for the USA, put on trial and sentenced in 1966 to life imprisonment. He managed to smuggle out of prison some of the articles he continued writing and to publish them in the Beirut press under a pseudonym.

In 1974 President *Sadat pardoned and released Mustafa, and permitted 'Ali to return to Egypt, and both were reinstated in managerial and editorial positions in the papers they had owned and founded. For some time they were considered close to Sadat, but being unable to conform even to the milder rules of the Sadat regime, they were again dismissed in 1976. 'Ali died in 1976; Mustafa continues writing as a highly respected freelance columnist with no editorial responsibilities. Mustafa also wrote two books on his prison years — one of the first to describe publicly the dark side of Nasser's police state.

AMINI, ALI (b. 1905?)   Senior Iranian politician and former Prime Minister. He was born into an affluent landowning family of partly royal descent. His maternal grandfather, Muzzaffar ul-Din Shah of the Qajar dynasty, ruled Iran from 1896 to 1907. His father was the son of Amin al-Dowla, the Grand Wazir of Nasser ul-Din Shah who ruled from 1848 to 1896.

After graduating from Paris University, A. served in the Ministries of Law, Finance, and Customs, becoming Director-General of the Ministry of Economics (1939). He joined Qavam-al-Saltanch's first cabinet, 1942, as Deputy Prime Minister. After economic research in India he returned to Iran in 1946. The following year he was elected to the *Majlis* (Iranian Parliament). He was Minister of National Economy in the cabinet of 'Ali *Mansur in 1950, resigned, but was again appointed Minis-

ter of Economy by Muhammad *Mossaddeq in 1952. A. became Finance Minister under Fazlullah *Zahedi in 1953 and in that capacity signed the Petroleum Agreement with the International Oil Consortium in 1954. He was Minister of Justice in Hussein *'Ala's cabinet, 1955, and became ambassador to the U.S. (1956–58). He was Prime Minister from 1961 to 1962.

In 1968, A. was accused of plotting against the government to reestablish himself as Prime Minister. Following the Islamic Revolution of 1979, he supported the establishment of a broad-based coalition among all opposition forces, but failed in his attempt. Early in 1982 he tried to form a "Front of the Salvation of Iran" and called on all those who opposed Ayatullah *Khomeini to unite to free Iran of its "illegal and bloodthirsty regime," but failed.

AMMASH, SALEH MANDI (b. 1924)   Iraqi officer and politician. From the 1950s one of the leading officers connected with the underground *Ba'th* party, 'A. was imprisoned several times under the *Qassem regime, 1958–63. He was one of the leaders of the coup of Feb. 1963 which overthrew Qassem, and became Defense Minister in the new *Ba'th*-dominated government. When that government was deposed by President *'Aref, in Nov. 1963, he went into exile, but returned in 1966. After the first al-*Bakr coup of July 1968 'A. became a member of the revolutionary Command Council and Minister of the Interior, and after Bakr's second coup, later the same month, Deputy Prime Minister as well. In 1970 he was appointed Vice-President and gave up the Interior Ministry. In the factional struggles inside the *Ba'th* and the government, 'A. headed a faction opposing Hardan *'Abd-ul-Ghaffar (al-Tikriti), then considered the strong man. After the latter was assassinated, in Mar. 1971, 'A. was seen for some time as the next leader, but lost out to Saddam *Hussein (al-Tikriti). In Sept. 1971 he was deposed and sent abroad, into semi-exile, as Ambassador — first to Moscow, in 1974 to Paris, and in 1975 (a further demotion) to Finland. He was rumored to be involved in further coup attempts, and reportedly refused to return to Iraq from his ambassadorial post; but in recent years he has disappea ed from the public stage.

AL-'AMRI, HASSAN (b. 1916)   Yemeni officer and politician. Received his military education in Iraq, graduating in 1939. 'A. took part in the coup of Sept. 1962, was a member of the Revolutionary

Council and became one of the leaders of the Republican government, as Minister of Transport, 1962, and Communications, 1963. Later in 1963 he became Vice-President and in 1964 briefly Prime Minister. However, he opposed and rivalled the then top leader of Republican Yemen, 'Abdullah al-*Sallal. 'A.'s faction, while staunchly anti-Royalist, was considered somewhat more conservative, fostering strong ties to the great tribal federations, and rather more reserved towards the Egyptians, who then controlled Yemen through their military aid and expeditionary force. When the Egyptians wished to extricate themselves from the Yemen war, in 1965, they made 'A. Prime Minister, removing Sallal into semi-detention in Egypt. In 1966, when Sallal returned, 'A. lost the Premiership and was taken, in his turn, to Egypt, where he was kept in semi-detention. In Oct. 1967, following Sallal's fall, A. returned and was appointed a member of the Presidency Council (to 1971), Prime Minister (to 1969) and Commander in Chief. He led the Republican forces that saved the capital San'a from being taken by the Royalists (Dec. 1967–Feb. 1968). In 1971 he again became Prime Minister, but was ousted after a week or two both as Premier and as a member of the Presidential Council — officially because he was involved in an unsavory incident and accused of murder. The real reason for his overthrow was, reportedly, that he had fallen foul of his powerful tribal allies and was trying to abolish the consultative-representative institutions that served as a stronghold of the tribal leaders and a brake on the government. After three years of exile, 'A. returned to Yemen in Jan. 1975; he has not regained a position of influence or power.

AMUZEGAR, JAMSHID (b. 1923)   Iranian engineer and politician. The son of former Senator Habib A., A. completed his engineering studies at Tehran University and in the United States (Ph.D., Washington University and Cornell). He was a lecturer in hydraulics and civil engineering at Cornell and served as an underground water expert for the United Nations. While in the U.S., he published books on sanitary engineering and hydraulics, and articles on economics and oil.

After returning to Iran, he directed the Engineering Department of the administration of the U.S. ("Point-Four"). In 1957 he became Minister of Agriculture, and in that capacity initiated a land reform bill. From 1965 to 1976 he was Minister of Finance (including for some time matters of the oil

industry), and in 1975–76 Minister of the Interior. In 1976 he became Secretary-General of the *Rastakhiz* (Renaissance) Party, which the Shah was at that time trying to build up as a single party.

In Aug. 1977 the Shah appointed A. Prime Minister, with plans for liberal reforms that would gain popular support. However, the steps he took antagonized the middle class and turned it against the Shah, and in Aug. 1978, A. was dismissed.

ANTONIUS, GEORGE (1892–1942)   Palestinian-Arab writer. A Greek-Orthodox Christian born in Lebanon and educated in Egypt, A. came to Palestine in 1921 and served until 1930 in the British Mandatory Government's Department of Education. In 1930 he entered the employment of the New York Institute of Current World Affairs headed by C.R. Crane. A. was an eloquent spokesman, orally and in his writings, of the Arab case on Palestine and Arab nationalism in general, and fostered close contacts with British governmental and political circles. He appeared before the Peel Commission (1936/37) and participated, as an adviser to the Arab delegations, in the London Round Table Conference of 1939. In 1938 he published his book *The Arab Awakening* which, though obviously pleading a cause, has become a classic on the Arab nationalist movement. A., though apprehensive of Muslim extremism and sympathetic to the idea of a Greater Syria of which Palestine would be a part, was close to the Mufti Hajj Amin al-*Husseini and his faction. He met Zionist leaders several times to explore the possibility of a Jewish-Arab compromise, but nothing came of these meetings.

'AQIL, SA'ID (b. 1912)   Lebanese poet. A symbolist and nationalist and a leading representative of the "Phoenician" trend. Born in Zahla, he started his literary life as a lyrical romantic poet under strong French influence. He was the first Arab symbolist poet to influence many young poets in the Arab world. Later he advocated the use of the colloquial Lebanese Arabic in poetry, and of Latin characters. He applied these ideas in a unique anthology, *Yara*. 'A.'s Lebanese-"Phoenician" nationalism induced him to advocate Lebanon-Israel cooperation and friendship.

AL-'AQQAD, 'ABBAS MAHMUD (1889–1964) Egyptian journalist, poet and writer. Born in Aswan, 'A. finished primary school only and completed his education as an autodidact. In 1907–1909 he joined the editorial staff of the National Party's pan-Islamic *al-Dustur* newspaper, contributing literary and cultural articles. From 1910 he wrote for various magazines, mainly *al-Bayan* (1911) and '*Ukaz*. In 1914 he became an editor at the pan-Islamic *al-Mu'ayyad*, as well as at *al-Ahali* and *al-Ahram*. In 1921 he became the editor of the Wafdist *al-Balagh*.

In 1925 'A. was elected for the *Wafd* Party to the Senate, and in 1929 to the House of Representatives; his struggle in Parliament for constitutional liberties led to nine months' imprisonment (1930) after the suspension of the constitution by Prime Minister Isma'il *Sidqi. Later he fell out with the leaders of the *Wafd* and was expelled in 1935; in 1937 he joined Ahmad *Maher's new Saadist Party, represented it in Parliament for several years and edited its newspaper *al-Asas*.

During World War II he took an anti-Fascist line and supported the Allies in articles and books (*Hitler fi 'l-Mizan* [Hitler in the Scales], 1940 and; *al-Naziyya wa-l-Adyan* [Nazism and the Religions], 1940.

His political activity came to an end after the Egyptian revolution of 1952; but he backed its reforms and became Chairman of the Poetry Committee of the Supreme Council for Arts, Literature and Social Sciences. In 1959 'A was awarded the State Prize for Literature.

'ARAFAT, YASSER (b. 1929) Palestinian-Arab politician and guerrilla leader. A distant relative of the prominent *Husseini family, 'A. was educated in Egypt and graduated from Cairo University as an engineer. In the 1950s he was chairman of the Palestinian Students' Union centered in Gaza and was active as a political organizer while working in Kuwait as an engineer, 1957–60 (reportedly after briefly serving in the Egyptian army in 1957). In the late 1950s 'A. was a co-founder of the *al-Fatah* guerrilla group forming in the Palestinian-Arab diaspora in Arab countries and among students in Europe; he emerged in the 1960s as its chief leader. When in mid-1968 the Palestine Liberation Organization (PLO) became a roof organization of various guerrilla groups, *al-Fatah* gained control of the organization, and in Feb. 1969 'A. became Chairman of the PLO's Executive Committee and its main leader and Commander in Chief. In this capacity he was recognized by the Arab states as the top leader of the Palestine Arabs, particularly since the 1974 all-Arab summit of Rabat recognized the PLO as the sole legitimate representative

Yasser 'Arafat (Israel Sun Ltd.)

of the Palestinians. He attends all-Arab summit conferences, maintains permanent contact with Arab heads of state; Third World, nonaligned, and Islamic states and organizations similarly recognize his status, and treat him as the authorized spokesman and leader of the Palestine Arabs; in Nov. 1974 and Dec. 1988 he was invited to address the UN General Assembly. He constantly travels between Arab capitals and frequently visits other world centers.

As head of *al-Fatah* and from 1969 of the PLO, 'A. led the planning and execution of continuous sabotage and terror operations in Israel (which began, according to *al-Fatah* chronology, in Jan. 1965), abroad, and against international aviation. From the mid-1970s 'A. and his mainstream faction disaproved of hijacking and terrorist operations against foreign aircraft; but as Chairman of the PLO he remained responsible for such operations continued by the PLO's more extremist factions, as well as for frequent assassinations of dissenters and factional rivals within the PLO. 'A. was the chief architect of a large PLO organization and transformed it, with huge funds put at his disposal by the Arab states, mainly the rich oil countries, from a feeble association of small guerrilla bands into a wealthy, multibranched establishment conducting military, economic-financial, social, medical and educational operations. In the late 1960s he built a veritable state-within-a-state in Jordan and Lebanon — without their consent and against their interest — and brought about a critical confrontation with these countries (Jordan: "Black September," 1970).

In the course of Israel's Lebanon War, from June 1982, the PLO establishment was expelled from South Lebanon and evacuated from West Beirut (late Aug. 1982) and 'A., while stepping up his constant travels, established his headquarters in Tunis. He maintained a command base in Syrian-occupied East Lebanon (the Biqa) and North Lebanon (Tripoli), but Syrian-instigated anti-'A. factions within the PLO and al-Fatah rebelled in 1983 and with Syrian army support expelled 'A.'s forces from the Biqa; 'A. personally was expelled from Syria in June 1983. As 'A. rallied his forces in Tripoli and the Palestinian camps around it, fighting soon spread to that area; 'A. was defeated by the Syrian-supported rebels, and in Dec. 1983 the remnants of his forces were evacuated from Tripoli (to Yemen, South Yemen, Algeria, Tunisia) and 'A. returned to his political and administrative headquarters in Tunis; military/terrorist commands and operative departments were dispersed in various Arab countries. 'A. himself kept up his constant travels to Arab and world capitals, carefully cultivating his image as the tough, fatigues-clad guerrilla leader.

'A. has always been considered, within the PLO, a man of the center, the mainstream. He was not a moderate; he saw "military" action, i.e., sabotage and terrorism, as the main method of struggle, and he was instrumental in the formulation of the PLO Charter of 1968 — an extremist document totally denying Israel's right to exist, negating any link between the Jews and Palestine and refusing any kind of compromise or coexistence. But against various rival PLO factions, particularly the leftist ones of *Habash and *Hawatma with their Marxist-Maoist doctrines, and those linked to extremist-rejectionist Arab states, 'A. insisted that the unity of the Palestinian movement must be maintained at all costs and that all internal social-ideological struggles concerning political orientations should be postponed. Such a position is considered by leftists as right-wing; indeed, 'A.'s own inclination was patently conservative, with a measure of Islamist tendencies.

Since the 1970s, 'A. has been considered by many observers as moderate. He opposed terrorism against foreign countries and international aviation, as practiced by the extremist factions. He initiated, in 1974, a resolution by the PLO National Council stating that the PLO would establish a "national authority" in any part of Palestine vacated by Israel; and though that resolution did not renounce the claim to all Palestine or pledge peaceful coexistence of the proposed Palestinian "national authority" with Israel — nor did 'A. himself commit himself to such a coexistence — some observers interpreted it as implying that 'A. and the PLO might content themselves with a Palestinian state in part of Palestine, in coexistence with Israel. 'A., in some of his many and often conflicting statements, also began to emphasize political solutions, implying that he would prefer diplomatic efforts to military-terrorist operations. He spoke of joining international efforts to negotiate a settlement, he hinted that Security Council Resolution 242, considered by most countries as the key to any settlement, might be acceptable if amended to recognize the national rights and aspirations of the Palestine Arabs, i.e., an independent state. 'A. did not object to all-Arab plans, e.g. the "*Fahd Plan" or the Fez Summit Resolution of 1982 advocating a settlement based on the recognition of the Palestinians' right to independent statehood and acquiescence in the peaceful existence of "all states in the region," i.e., by implication: of Israel, too. 'A. advocated and held meetings with Israelis — primarily those of the dovish Zionist left or the anti-Zionist Communists; such contacts were based, explicitly, on the acceptance of the Jews of Israel as inhabitants of the country (contrary to the PLO Charter) and, implicitly, on the assumption that some settlement between Israel and the Palestine Arabs is feasible (again contrary to the PLO Charter). Yet 'A. frequently invalidated or counterbalanced moderate statements by renewed expressions of extremism.

Since 1982, 'A. negotiated with King *Hussein of Jordan, mainly on two issues: a confederation between a future Palestinian-Arab state and Jordan: and joint Palestinian-Jordanian action towards a general peace settlement, possibly a joint negotiating delegation. They reached an agreement in Feb. 1985; but rejected by the traditional PLO factions, it was abrogated by the PLO in Apr. 1987. However, after a period of friction and dissent, 'A. resumed cooperation with King Hussein, keeping open the possibility of joint representation in

Arab-Israel peace negotiations and adhering to the concept of a future Jordanian-Palestinian confederation.

'A., who in 1978–79 had fully supported the all-Arab steps against Egypt, also resumed, since 1982–83, close relations with President *Mubarak's Egypt — to a point that there was talk of a "moderate bloc" formed by Egypt, Jordan and 'A.'s wing of the PLO. Yet 'A. was unable to unequivocally accept Mubarak's proposals, and in Apr. 1987 he had to accept the radicals' demand to suspend relations with Egypt. They were resumed after some time, but remained cold and reserved on Egypt's part, especially after *Mubarak and 'A. followed diametrically opposed policies in the Iraqi/Gulf War crisis of 1990/91.

'A.'s status and position were questionable since 1982. He lost his main base of operation in South Lebanon and was reduced, except for some marginal, indecisive terrorist ventures, to a feeble traveling diplomacy. His "moderate" policies and his *rapprochement* with Jordan and Egypt deepened the rift with Syria — a rift that had originated with 'A.'s refusal to submit to Syrian guidance and Syria's refusal to accord the PLO full freedom of action — and the extremist, Syria-guided factions of the PLO. The *al-Fatah* rebellion of 1983 deprived 'A. of his last power base in the Biqa and the Tripoli area and caused a deep, perhaps irreversible, split within the PLO. It was fully supported by some of the extremist factions, while the two leftist ones of Habash and Hawatma half-sympathized with it and tried to mediate. The rebels and their supporters demanded 'A.'s dismissal, and boycotted all meetings and sessions of the 'A.-loyal PLO. In Nov. 1984 'A. succeeded in convening, in 'Amman, a session of the National Council that was attended only by 'A.-loyalists; it endorsed 'A.'s policies and his leadership. Since 1985–86 he has also reestablished, despite protracted clashes with the Shi'i *Amal* militia, a strong presence of his PLO wing in the Palestinian-Arab camps in South Lebanon, and less so in Beirut (in the south, 'A.'s faction suppressed rival groups, particularly that of *Abu Nidal, in bloody clashes; in Beirut, pro-Syrian anti-'A. groups had the upper hand in the Palestinian camps). In Apr. 1987, 'A. achieved reconciliation with some of the radical factions within the PLO. To achieve this, he had to accept some of the policy changes they demanded (mainly concerning PLO relations with Jordan and Egypt). Syria and the factions guided by her were not reconciled with 'A.

In Nov. 1988, at the 19th Palestine National Congress in Algiers, 'A. proclaimed a "State of (Arab) Palestine"; no government-in-exile or administration was set up, the "State" had no territorial basis and was symbolic-declaratory only with no factual existence — but 'A. was solemnly acclaimed "Head of State" and has since been so treated by Arab and other pro-PLO countries. At the same Nov. 1988 Congress, 'A. spelled out radically new policies — virtually those he had been hinting at since 1974: he accepted Security Council Resolutions 242 and 338; the Palestine State to which he aspired would be set up in the West Bank, Gaza and East Jerusalem - the "occupied territories," and would no longer aim to seize the whole of Palestine but live in peaceful coexistence with Israel. He had his new policy endorsed by the PLO's National Congress (Habash and his PFLP voted against some clauses, but accepted the majority decision; Hawatma and his DFLP took a similar position; the pro-Syrian extremist factions boycotted the Congress). Yet, while admitting in informal comments that the PLO Charter of 1968, emphatically contrary to the new policy and precluding it, was not "obsolete," 'A. did not revoke or amend it; and while he renounced "terrorism," he insisted on the PLO's right to conduct "military" operations against Israel (but then, he had never accepted the definition of PLO raids as terrorism).

'A. reiterated and further explained his new policies in Dec. 1988 to a group of American-Jewish public figures who came to Stockholm to meet him, to the UN General Assembly (specially convening in Geneva, as the USA would not permit 'A. to come to New York), and to a Geneva press conference. The USA now agreed to hold a dialogue with his PLO, conducted through her Ambassador in Tunis. But the talks made little progress; 'A. found it difficult to translate his new principles into actual political steps and compromises. When he could not bring himself unequivocally to denounce a terrorist raid foiled by Israel and to discipline or expel its leader (a member of the PLO executive), the USA in June 1990 suspended the dialogue. Moreover, 'A. hedged and equivocated in his frequent general policy statements — partly, no doubt, in order to appease his Arab denunciators and critics in the extremist factions within and without the PLO — to a degree that raised doubts as to the validity and trustworthiness of his policy professions. (Many Israelis, e.g., suspected that the West Bank/Gaza Palestine State was conceived by 'A. and the PLO as a stage towards a future assault on Israel). This mistrust, and the resulting decline in 'A.'s standing beyond his PLO and the Palestinians, culminated when in Aug. 1990 and the months following 'A. took a stridently pro-Iraqi line in the Gulf crisis caused by Iraq's invasion of Kuwait and violently denounced the USA and her allies — thus antagonizing not only the West, the USSR and most of the world, but the majority of the Arab countries, including Egypt, Syria, Sa'udi Arabia and the principalities of the Persian Gulf (on whose aid and finance he had always depended).

After the defeat of Iraq (Feb. 1991), 'A. began rebuilding his position and prestige — but they were badly shaken. He continued issuing self-confident statements, but as he was no longer welcome in many Arab capitals, he cut down sharply on his travels, previously incessant, and remained mainly holed up in Tunis. Even in the ranks of his supporters inside al-Fatah and the PLO — weakened by the assassination of his closest associates Abu Jihad (in Apr. 1988, reportedly by Israeli commandos) and Abu Iyad (in Jan. 1991, by Palestinian rivals, reportedly the Abu Nidal group) — the possibility of his replacement was sometimes mooted. Yet, 'A. still was the "Head of State" of the "State of Palestine" and the Chairman of the PLO ("the sole and legitimate representative of the [Arab] people of Palestine"), and Palestinian Arabs, the Arab states and most world leaders and public opinion still seemed to regard him as the chief and most representative Palestinian-Arab leader.

ARAN (original name: Aharonovitch), **ZALMAN** (1899–1970) Israeli political leader. Born in Russia. During the 1920's he was active in the Zionist movement in Russia. In 1926 he immigrated to Palestine and immediately afterwards joined the political leadership of *Ahdut Ha'avodah* and the *Histadrut*. He was a member of the Secretariat of the Tel Aviv Worker's Council and during the early 1930s, its Secretary. During the 1930s and 1940s he held central positions in the *Histadrut*. He was its Treasurer, a member of its Executive Secretariat, and chairman of the Department of Information. He founded the School for *Histadrut* Activists and was its first director. After the founding of the State he was elected Secretary of *Mapai*. He was a Member of the Knesset from the First Knesset in 1949 until 1969. In the First Knesset (1949–1951) he served as Chairman of the Committee on Foreign Affairs and Defense. In 1954 he joined the government as Minister without Portfolio.

In 1955, after the elections to the Third Knesset, he was appointed Minister of Education and Culture. He held this position for many years (1955–1960 and 1963–1969). These years were considered to be the pinnacle of his political career. As opposed to other Ministers of Education, he did not see this as a stepping-stone to other positions, but dedicated all his efforts to this task and initiated several reforms, such as reforming the structure of the schools, introducing the junior high school and system and educational integration.

Aran was one of the most prominent figures in his party. Together with Golda *Meir and Pinchas *Sapir, he was a member of a "troika" which for years was the central force within the party. He was a colorful figure: an intellectual, a poet and a man with a rich rhetorical capability. In 1969 he resigned from public life and passed away several months later.

ARAS, TEVFIK RÜSTÜ (1883–1972) Turkish politician. Born in Canakkale, A. studied medicine in Beirut and Paris. He served in the army medical service and as Inspector of Public Health in Salonica. In 1908 he participated in the Young Turks Revolution and became Inspector-General of Public Health of the Ottoman Empire. He was close to Kemal *Ataturk.

During World War I, A. served as a medical officer. After participating in Turkey's war of independence (1918–23), he joined the First National Assembly. He served as Minister of Public Health in the early 1920s and chaired the Turkish Committee for the Exchange of Population between Turkey and Greece, 1923. He was Foreign Minister (1925–38), a respected figure at the Council and Assembly of the League of Nations and at times their President. From 1939 to 1942 he was Ambassador to Great Britain.

In the 1940s he retired from public and political activities, but in 1950 Turkey appointed him, a respected elder statesman, as her representative on the Palestine Conciliation Commission for several years.

'AREF, 'ABD-UL-RAHMAN (b. 1916) Iraqi officer and politician. President of Iraq, 1966–68. 'A. was a member of the "Free Officers" group that toppled the monarchy in July 1958. A brother of 'Abd-ul-Salam *'Aref, he became involved in the struggle between his brother and *Qassem, the head of the ruling junta, 1958/59, and his military career was jeopardized when his brother was ousted. But when his brother became President, after the Feb. 1963 coup, 'A. was rapidly promoted, serving as acting Chief of Staff, 1963–66. When 'Abd-ul-Salam 'Aref was killed in an air crash, in Apr. 1966, the Revolutionary Command Council chose 'A. an inoffensive compromise candidate, as President. As President — and for some months in 1967 concurrently Prime Minister — he followed his late brother's policies: a strongly nationalist, independent, moderately pro-Egyptian, foreign policy, and an authoritarian regime of conservative state socialism at home. But he seemed to be lacking his brother's shrewd leadership qualities. 'A. was ousted in July 1968 by a coup headed by Ahmad Hassan al-*Bakr and 'Abd-ul-Rahman al-Na'if, and went into exile (in England).

'AREF, 'ABD-UL-SALAM (1920–66)   Iraqi officer and politician. President of Iraq, 1963–66. Son of a Sunni middle-class Baghdad family, 'A. was trained as a professional officer. He served with the Iraqi expeditionary force in the Arab-Israel war of 1948. He was a leading member of the "Free Officers" group that overthrew the monarchy in July 1958 and commanded the task force that took over Baghdad. *Qassem, the leader of the junta, appointed him Deputy Commander in Chief, Deputy Prime Minister and Minister of the Interior — i.e., in practice, the number two member of the new regime. However, as 'A. was strongly Nasserist, advocating union with Egypt (the UAR), and obviously aspired to the top leadership, he soon fell out with Qassem. In Sept. 1958 he was dismissed, and in Nov. he was arrested and put on trial; in Feb. 1959 he was sentenced to death by a "Peoples Court" for plotting against the regime and planning to assassinate Qassem, but the latter did not confirm the sentence, and in 1961 'A. was set free. He was one of the organizers of the coup of Feb. 1963 (together with officers of the *Ba'th* group) that overthrew Qassem, and became President. As long as the *Ba'th* officers were in control, his powers were nominal only; but in Nov. 1963 he ousted the *Ba'th* group in a bloodless semi-coup, and henceforth he exercised real power.

As President, 'A. at first endeavored to model his regime on a Nasserist pattern and sought a close association with *Nasser's Egypt. In May 1964 he agreed with Nasser to establish a political union with Egypt, with a Joint Presidential Council and close military and economic coordination. In July he decreed far-reaching nationalization measures, on the Egyptian model, and established an "Arab

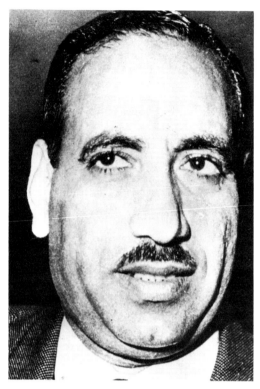

'Abd-ul-Salam 'Aref (Israel Sun Ltd.)

Socialist Union" as a single party. However, the union with Egypt scheduled to be fully consummated within two years did not materialize, as 'A. insisted, in effect, on Iraq's complete independence. Iraq's transformation on the Egyptian pattern was also halfhearted and incomplete and 'A. soon ceased advancing it; few of the nationalization decrees were put into practice, and the ASU did not come into being. 'A. followed no clear ideological line; his policy was based on nationalism and a pragmatic, rather conservative state socialism. Though most of his colleagues and supporters were army officers, he entrusted the Premiership to a civilian ('Abd-ul-Rahman al-*Bazzaz, Sept. 1965). 'A. and Bazzaz were keen on solving two issues troubling Iraq — but failed on both: an agreement with the Kurdish rebels was reached in June 1966, but was not implemented; and an agreement with the Iraq Petroleum Co. was signed in 1965, but was not ratified by Iraq because of leftist and nationalist pressure. 'A. was killed in Apr. 1966 in an air crash (and succeeded by his brother 'Abd-ul-Rahman *'Aref, who was overthrown in July 1968).

ARENS, MOSHE (b. 1925)   Israeli politician. Born in Kovno, Lithuania, immigrated to the USA in 1939. From 1944 to 1946 he served in the American army and later studied aeronautical engineering at M.I.T. He was active in Betar, the Revisionist youth movement, and served as its leader in the USA. In 1948 he immigrated to Israel and settled in Mevo-Betar, a *moshav* near Jerusalem.

After he left the *moshav*, he worked in his field — aeronautical engineering. He was a Professor at the Technion, Haifa and during the 1960s was assistant director of Israel Aircraft Industries. In 1974 he was elected to the Eighth Knesset for the *Likud* Party. After his party won the elections of 1977, he was appointed chairman of the Knesset Committee for Foreign Affairs and Defense and held that position until 1982. He opposed Menahem *Begin's Camp David Agreements (1978) and the peace treaty with Egypt (1979), abstaining in the Knesset vote. He therefore refused to accept the position of Defense Minister offered to him in 1980, after Ezer *Weizman's resignation.

In 1982 he was appointed Ambassador to the United States. In 1983, he replaced Ariel *Sharon as Defense Minister. During his term as Defense Minister the army maintained its presence in Lebanon and paid a bloody price for this involvement.

In the National Unity Government established in 1984 he became Minister without Portfolio. In 1987, he resigned from the government in protest against the cancellation of the "Lavie" aircraft project but returned to it in April 1988. In December 1988 he became Foreign Minister and in 1990, after the National Unity Government was dissolved, Defense Minister. A., a hard-liner, is considered to be close to Prime Minister *Shamir and a potential candidate to replace him as Prime Minister.

ARIDOR (original name: Liebermann), **YORAM** (b. 1933)   Israeli politician. Born in Tel Aviv to a family active in the Revisionist Party. A. studied law and economics at the Hebrew University. During the 1960s he was active in the *Herut* youth movement. In 1969 he was elected to the Seventh Knesset. A. was a member of Knesset continuously until 1988. A. was also active in the *Histadrut* as joint chairman of the *Tchelet Lavan* faction (*Herut* in the *Histadrut*; his co-chairman was David *Levy).

In 1977, after the *Likud*'s election victory, he became Deputy Minister in the Prime Minister's Office. In this capacity he dealt for several months with a number of government ministries to which

ministers had not yet been appointed. In 1978 he was the *Likud*'s candidate for Treasurer of the Jewish Agency; its Executive Board did not elect him. In Jan. 1981 he joined the government as Minister of Communications and soon after was also appointed Finance Minister. His economic policy was called the "correct economics" and consisted primarily of lowering taxes and prices as a means of reducing inflation; it was seen as one of the main reasons behind the *Likud*'s victory in the elections for the Tenth Knesset in the summer of 1981. He continued these policies after the elections, but they brought Israel's economy to the brink of ruin and anarchy. In October 1983 the banks stocks collapsed, causing $1 billion losses. A., though personally considered highly intelligent and capable, was forced to resign, leaving behind him an economy with a virtually uncontrollable inflation (over 500%) and almost without foreign currency reserves. A. did not recover politically and did not even present his candidacy on the *Herut* list for the 1988 elections. In 1990, Foreign Minister David Levy rescued him from the political wilderness and appointed him Ambassador to the United Nations.

ARLOSOROFF, HAIM (1899–1933)   Labor-Zionist political leader. Born in the Ukraine, A. moved to Germany with his family as a child and received his education there. He studied at the University of Berlin where he was awarded a doctorate in economics. In 1918 he joined *Hapoel Hatzair* and became editor of its newspaper, *Die Arbeit*. In 1923 he was elected to the Zionist Executive, as its youngest member. In 1924 he immigrated to Palestine, joined *Hapoel Hatzair* and, despite his youth, became one of its leaders, displaying brilliant writing and analytical ability. In 1926 he was elected secretary of the party.

On the eve of the union between *Hapoel Hatzair* and *Ahdut Ha'avodah* he expressed his doubts about this step, but with the establishment of *Mapai* in 1930 he became one of its prominent central leaders. In 1931 he was elected to the Jewish Agency Executive and was placed in charge of its Political Department. Thus, at the age of 32, he was the "foreign minister" of the State in the making. A. was a moderate, and as head of the Political Department ably maintained contacts with the British Mandatory Government in Jerusalem and the British Government in London and made great attempts to find a *modus vivendi* between Jews and Arabs in Palestine.

In 1933, after Hitler's rise to power in Germany, he negotiated an agreement with the German government to enable Jews to leave Germany with most of their property. The right-wing Zionist Revisionists opposed that agreement and *Brit Habiryonim*, their extremist faction in Palestine, attacked A. with unprecedented harshness. In June 1933 A. was murdered on the seashore of Tel Aviv. His murder brought the *Yishuv* to the verge of civil war. The Labor Movement blamed the Revisionists for the murder, while the Revisionists claimed that the assassin was an Arab and that the Labor Party was raising a "blood libel" against them. Two suspects from *Brit Habiryonim* were tried by a British Mandate court, but were acquitted for lack of evidence. Labor circles, however, maintained that they were guilty, and the issue continued agitating public opinion — both before and after the establishment of the State of Israel. In 1982 the *Begin government appointed a new Commission of Inquiry; but in its report, June 1985, it was unable to reach a clear, definite conclusion as to the identity of the murderer(s).

His death was deeply mourned, and the shocked *Yishuv* felt that a leader blessed with unique qualifications had been cruelly cut down.

ARSALAN (often spelled **ARSLAN**; also called **YAZBAKI**) Clan of Lebanese Druze notables, whose chiefs bear the hereditary title of Amir; until the late 19th century — the semifeudal lords of the southwestern regions of Mount Lebanon, centered in the al-Gharb area east of Beirut. Since the 17th and 18th centuries, the A. clan headed one of the rival factions competing for the overall leadership of Lebanon's Druze community — mainly against the *Junbalat clan. The A.-Junbalat rivalry became pronounced in the late 19th century, after the elimination of the semi-Druze Shihab dynasty, with whom the A.'s had been allied. During the French Mandate, the A.'s were usually opponents of the Mandatory regime; some of them took an active part in the Pan-Arab nationalist movement and opposed Lebanon's separate status. Thus — 'Adel A. (1882–1954), a right-wing Syrian politician briefly Deputy Premier and Foreign Minister in 1949, after the Zaim coup, and Syrian Minister to Turkey 1949–1951 (dismissed, because he publicly advocated, in contradiction to his government's policy, Syria's accession to a Middle East Defense Pact proposed by the Western Powers). Since 1943, the A.'s in Lebanon have supported the unwritten "National Pact" and the Maronite-led establishment based mainly on a Maronite-Sunni coalition. Their leader was **Majid A.** (1943–83), from 1937 many times a minister, usually Defense Minister. As the Junbalats increasingly became the chief spokesmen of Druze demands and opposition, the A.'s influence declined, particularly during and since the civil war from 1975 onward (in which they tried to avoid becoming involved and, in contrast to the Junbalats, maintained no real organized militia). Since the death of their chief **Majid A.**, in 1983, and the succession of his son, **Feisal A.**, this decline has been aggravated by the lack of strong leadership and an organized military force.

ARSALAN, SHAKIB (1869–1946) Syrian Pan-Arab writer, poet, historian and politician, of Lebanese-Druze origin. A district governor in the Ottoman Empire, A. remained loyal to the Sultan and joined the Arab nationalists only after World War I. In the 1920s A., mostly in exile, was active in the "Syrian-Palestinian Congress," which strove to keep Pan-Arab endeavors alive, and was a leading member of its permanent delegation in Geneva. He edited the Pan-Arab weekly *La Nation Arabe* and cultivated contacts with world statesmen (including unsuccessful talks with Zionist leaders). A. later exhibited near-Fascist tendencies and maintained strong ties with Italy and Nazi Germany. He also converted to Islam and drew nearer to Pan-Islamic views. Many of his numerous writings concern Islamic topics, including a detailed biography of the modern Islamic thinker Muhammad Rashid *Rida. A. returned to Syria in 1937, but took no active part in Syrian political affairs. During World War II he returned to Switzerland, where he resumed his contacts with the Axis powers and called on the Arabs to collaborate with the Axis.

AL-ASAD, HAFEZ (b. 1929?) Syrian officer and statesman, President of Syria since 1971. Born in Qardaha near Lataqia, of 'Alawi origin ('Alawis — a dissident sect on the fringe of Islam), A. became a professional officer in the air force. In the 1950s he joined the clandestine officers' cells linked to the *Ba'th* party. He took a leading part in the coup of Mar. 1963 that brought the *Ba'th* officers to power, and became Commander of the Air Force (promoted to the rank of *Fariq*, Lieutenant-General, in 1968). From 1965 A. was a member of the *Ba'th* High Command — both the "national," i.e., all-Arab, and the "regional" (Syrian) one. In the incessant factional struggles that rocked the Syrian

Ba'th and caused frequent changes in party, army and government leadership, A. sided with the "military" faction of the extreme, doctrinaire "left" which opposed the **'Aflaq-*Bitar-al-*Hafez* faction then in control. He was one of the leaders of the military wing's coup of Feb. 1966 and became a leading figure in the regime it established, serving as acting Defense Minister. However, A. soon fell out with Salah *Jadid, the top leader of the new junta, and his associates, and formed a "nationalist" faction. He opposed Jadid's doctrinaire leftism, rejected rigid ideological definitions and preferred a pragmatic approach to political and economic issues. He opposed total identification with the Soviet Union, chafed at Syria's growing isolation within the Arab world and aimed at closer all-Arab cooperation and a stronger emphasis on the fight against Israel. In Feb. 1969, in a bloodless semi-coup, A. gained control of the government and party command, but accepted — reportedly on Egyptian and Russian advice — a compromise providing for a coal tion and leaving some of his adversaries in positions of power (e.g. Nur-ul-Din al-*Atassi as President and Prime Minister). When, however, the power struggle resumed, A. seized full control in another semi-coup in Nov. 1970 — and this time he kept power, purging and dismissing his opponents and detaining their leaders (for over ten years, as it turned out). He assumed the Premiership, retaining the Defense Ministry, and became Secretary-General of the *Ba'th*. In Feb. 1971 he nominated a "People's Council," and that Council appointed him President, after the *Ba'th* command had nominated him. In Mar. 1971 a plebiscite endorsed that election, with A. as the only candidate and 99.2% of the votes in his favor. He was reelected in Feb. 1978, and for a third seven-year term in Feb. 1985. (Since Syria's President must be a Muslim, A.'s election implied a recognition of the 'Alawis as Muslims — which many Muslim-Sunni fundamentalists secretly opposed).

Since 1971 A. has given Syria a regime of remarkable stability, with the reins firmly in his own hands. He continued an economic policy of nationalization and a pragmatic state socialism. He established firm constitutional patterns: a Constitution was adopted in 1973, and elections for a People's Council were held, from 1973, every four years — with a *Ba'th*-led "National Progressive Front" (including the Communist Party) as the only permitted party list, but with *Ba'th*-approved independent candidates admitted. In fact, the *Ba'th*

Hafez al-Asad (IPS, Tel Aviv)

apparatus was in firm control, with A. himself as its undisputed chief, and behind the facade of semidemocratic and populist instititutions the regime was harshly authoritarian, underpinned by a powerful all-pervasive secret police.

Opposition, apart from exiled politicians, came mainly from orthodox and fundamentalist Muslim-Sunni groups, such as the outlawed Muslim Brotherhood, and it was aggravated by the fact that A., the Head of State, and many of his close associates belonged to the heretic 'Alawite sect. A. ruthlessly suppressed the Brotherhood and broke its resistance. Other political and factional struggles were conducted semiclandestinely within the ruling army and party junta. These intrigues turned into a bitter fight for the succession, as A.'s health deteriorated, since 1983.

In his foreign and inter-Arab policies. A. at first effected a measure of *rapprochement* with the all-Arab main line, taking Syria out of her isolation. He reinforced relations with Egypt, joining in 1971 a "Federation of Arab Republics" with her and Libya, and entering a close partnership with Egypt towards and during the October 1973 war against Israel. He also obtained all-Arab endorsement for his military intervention in Lebanon in 1976. But then he adopted increasingly hard-line, extremist policies, leading Syria back into the isolation from which he had sought to extricate her. Differences with Egypt had emerged even during the October War; they deepened when Syria joined the "Rejectionist" camp and became its mainstay, and turned into complete estrangement after *Sadat's moves towards peace with Israel, from 1977, when Syria headed the extremist camp clamoring for Egypt's boycott and expulsion. Tension and mutual hostility between Syria and Iraq mounted under A., to the point that Syria supported Iran against Iraq in the Gulf War, 1980–88 — contrary to the all-Arab line. When A. joined Egypt and Sa'udi Arabia, after Iraq's invasion of Kuwait in Aug. 1990, in a USA-led coalition against that invasion and even sent troops to aid Sa'udia's defense, he was motivated, at least in part, by that Syrian-Iraqi hostility. A. turned Syria's Arab-endorsed intervention in Lebanon into a permanent occupation of northern and eastern Lebanon, and though he took care not to be dragged into the Lebanese quagmire, he became the arbiter of Lebanese internal affairs, through client factions' "militias," and acquired near-total domination of Lebanon (without being able to fully control the situation, end the civil war and implement his plans).

Towards Israel A. took a very hard line — though he strictly adhered to disengagement agreements reached and also prevented terrorist attacks from Syrian soil (while encouraging such raids from Lebanese territory). He strove to attain "strategic parity" with Israel, opposed American peace plans, totally rejected Egypt's peace with Israel, and vehemently objected to the Jordanian King's efforts to work out a formula for peace negotiations. His relations with Jordan, aggravated by those efforts and by King *Hussein's alliance with the PLO under *'Arafat, were anyhow far from friendly — though there were ups and downs, and periods of *rapprochement* in 1975–76 and again from late 1985. A.'s bitter dispute with 'Arafat, originating in the latter's refusal to accept his guidance and subject the PLO to Syrian dictates, was exacerbated by 'Arafat's moderate line and accommodation with Jordan. A. cultivated PLO factions subservient to Syria, instigated and supported an armed revolt within the PLO's main faction, *al-Fatah*, in 1983, and waged a war against the PLO forces loyal to 'Arafat, expelling them from Syria and Syrian-occupied eastern and northern Lebanon. Despite his opposition to his predecessors' close alliance with the USSR, A. further cemented that alliance and made Syria even more dependent on the Soviet Union.

In contrast to the erratic flamboyance of Libya's *Qadhdhafi, his close ally, A. conducts both his authoritarian rule of Syria and his extremist foreign policies with cool calculation and suave tactics. Whether A.'s policies of leftist-authoritarian extremism were ultimately successful, only history will judge; in their execution, in any case, A. proved himself a master-politician.

AL-ASAD, RIF'AT (b. 1936)   Syrian officer and politician, of 'Alawaite origin, President Hafez al-*Asad's brother. Since 1984 Vice-President of Syria. A. came into prominence in the 1970s as commander of the "Defense Detachments," a semi-autonomous formation, variously estimated at 15–30,000 men, entrusted chiefly with the enforcement of internal security and endowed with special privileges (its own armor, intelligence, prisons — and much higher pay for its troopers). A. and his brigades were hated by many as brutal oppressors; a massacre of Muslim-Sunni opponents detained in Palmyra prison camp (1980) and the killing of many thousands in Hama (1982) were ascribed to them. There was also tense hostility between A. and several senior officers, commanders of other formations, from the Chief of Staff down. A. was reputed to be thoroughly corrupt; he owned real estate and considerable properties abroad, was fond of luxuries and high living, and was said to control widespread smuggling operations. Politically, A. was thought to be a dissident, favoring free enterprise and an alliance with the USA rather than the Soviet bloc.

A., long rumored to plot towards succeeding his brother as Head of State, made an open bid for it when his brother's health seriously deteriorated in late 1983. Early in 1984 his pictures and posters appeared all over Damascus and troops loyal to him took key positions and deployed tanks. However, his foes commanding other army formations took countermeasures. An armed confrontation between rival army units ensued, and several clashes were reported. To prevent internecine warfare, President Asad imposed a new division of powers (never clearly proclaimed) and appointed his brother as one of three Vice-Presidents — according to most reports *second* Vice-President. This did not solve the issue of the succession (now less immediate, as the President had recovered), and further clashes occurred. In late May 1984 A. was sent, together with two of his chief rivals, on a mission to Moscow — and did not return, remaining, with a large retinue, in Switzerland and France. It was never clarified whether A. was ordered to absent himself from Syria or whether his exile was self-imposed. In Nov. 1984 he was told to return and assumed his duties as Vice-President in charge of security. He was no longer in direct command of his Defense Detachments (which were much reduced in power and status and lost some of their privileges); but while he seemed to have lost part of his power base, his claim to the succession persisted. He still resides most of the time in France and Switzerland.

AL-'ASKARI, JA'FAR (1885–1936)   Iraqi officer and politician. A graduate of the military academy of Istanbul, 'A. became a professional officer in the Ottoman army. During World War I he was sent to Cyrenaica in 1915 to organize Sanussi units for guerrilla operations against the Italians, and against the British in Egypt. Taken prisoner, he was recruited from the prison camp in Egypt for Sharif *Hussein's army of the Arab Revolt, 1916, and became one of its leaders. In 1918 'A. was appointed military governor of 'Amman and in 1919–20, during Amir *Feisal's reign in Syria, governor of Aleppo. After Feisal's expulsion from Syria 'A. settled in Iraq. In 1921 he became Minister of Defense and was one of the architects of the Iraqi army. He was Prime Minister in 1923–24 and again in 1925–27, Iraqi Minister to Great Britain 1928–30, and again Minister of Defense 1935–36. 'A. was strongly identified with the *Hashemite dynasty and its conservative pro-British governments. He was assassinated in Oct. 1936 by a group of officers in the course of the first Iraqi military coup d'etat (the Bakr *Sidqi coup). — Ja'far 'A.'s brother **Tahsin 'A.** (1892–1947) was also active in Iraq's Army and politics and a minister in several governments in the 1940s.

AL-ASNAJ, 'ABDULLAH (1933–81)   South Yemeni and Yemeni politican. Employed in 1951–62 by 'Aden Airways, A. was active in the 'Aden Trade Unions Congress and became its Secretary-General. In 1962 he formed and led a political wing of the TUC, the People's Socialist Party, which joined the nationalist anti-British agitation and demanded the union of South Yemen with Yemen. In the mid-1960s he went into exile. In Jan. 1966 he was one of the founders of the "Front for the Liberation of Occupied South Yemen" (FLOSY) and became its Secretary-General. After the take-over of South Yemen by the rival "National Liberation Front" (NLF), 1967, he remained in exile and settled in Yemen. He joined the Yemen Government in 1971 as Foreign Minister, Minister of Economy 1971–74, and again Foreign Minister 1975–79. When he was dismissed — reportedly to please South Yemen — he continued serving as the President's adviser on foreign affairs, but lost that post in 1980. He was rumored to be linked to Sa'udi intrigues or attempted coups and to Iraqi, British and American intelligence. In Mar. 1981 he was arrested, his immunity as a member of the Constituent People's Assembly was lifted, and he was put on trial. The outcome of the trial was not announced, but according to unconfirmed reports he was executed.

AL-'ASSALI, SABRI (b. 1903)   Syrian politician and lawyer. Active in the nationalist movement since the 1920s, including the revolt of 1925–27 (the "Druze Revolt"), 'A. in 1930 joined the "National Bloc," the mainstream of Syrian nationalism, but later in the 1930s was also active in other, more extremist groups (e.g., the "League of National Action"). He was several times elected to the National Assembly. When the National Bloc disintegrated in 1947, he was one of the founders of the "National Party" that tried to replace it, and became its Secretary-General and main leader. From 1945 on he served as minister in several governments. After the coup that ousted Adib *Shishakli in Feb. 1954, 'A. became Prime Minister. Between 1954 and 1958 he headed four governments, while the real power was in the hands of shifting groups of army officers. With the Syrian-Egyptian Union (Mar. 1958), 'A. was appointed one of the four Vice-Presidents of the UAR; but when it was revealed in an Iraqi trial that he had been involved in 1954 in talks aiming at a possible Syrian-Iraqi union (and he could not accommodate himself to Egyptian domination and the new Nasserist regime), he resigned after a few months. Since 1958 'A. has not been active in political life. After the Ba'th officers' coup of 1963 he was disqualified, along with other "old regime" politicians, from public office and political activity, and also detained for about a year.

AL-ATASSI   Syrian landowning clan of notables which provided many leaders of modern Syria. It was centered in Homs and wielded considerable influence in all of northern Syria. When Syria had a parliamentary regime and political parties were operating, leaders of the A. clan were often in opposition to the mainstream of nationalist movement and the Damascus government. In the 1940s they were among the founders and leaders of the "People's Party."

The following were prominent members of the family: **Adnan A.** (b.1905), the son of Hashem *A. — in the 1950s among the leaders of the "People's Party" and Minister in several governments. Accused, in 1956-57, of playing a leading role in an "Iraqi-British-American plot," tried and sentenced to death in Feb. 1957 (commuted to prison for life), pardoned by *Nasser in Sept. 1960 and released into forced residence in Cairo, he did not return to play an active part in Syrian politics. **Feidi A.**, also a leader of the "People's Party" in the 1950s and a minister in several governments. He was accused in 1956-57 of involvement in the Iraqi plot mentioned, tried (*in absentia*, as he had fled) and acquitted. He was not further active in Syrian politics.

AL-ATASSI, HASHEM (1874?-1960) Syrian politician, three times President of Syria. Educated in Istanbul, A. served as a district governor in the Ottoman administration. In 1920 he chaired the nationalist Syrian-Arab Congress and was for a short time Prime Minister of the government Amir

Hashem al-Atassi (AP Photo)

*Feisal tried to set up in Damascus. Under the French Mandate he was one of the leaders of the "National Bloc" which fought for Syrian independence. He headed the delegation which signed the Franco-Syrian Treaty of 1936 providing for Syria's independence with certain privileges for France — a treaty that was not ratified by France and remained abortive. He was President of Syria, 1936-39. In the 1940s A. drifted away from the mainstream Damascus faction of the National Bloc. He took no active part in the final struggle for complete independence, 1945-46, and the Syrian governments that ensued. In 1949, after *Hinnawi's coup, he became Prime Minister, and in Dec. 1949, following *Shishakli's coup, President; but Shishakli was the real, behind-the-scenes ruler. and the President's powers were limited, almost nominal. When the politicians failed in their struggle with the dictator, A. resigned in 1951 and began working for the overthrow of Shishakli. Following Shishakli's fall, A. returned to the Presidency in 1954; but as real power was again in the hands of shifting officers' cliques, he was frustrated, resigned in Sept. 1955, and retired from politics.

AL-ATASSI, NUR-UL-DIN (b. 1929?) Syrian politician. President of Syria 1966-70. A physician (Damascus University, 1955), A. was close to the *Ba'th* group. After the *Ba'th* officer's coup of 1963 he became Minister of Interior, 1963-64, Deputy Prime Minister, 1964-65, and a member of the Revolutionary Council and the Presidential Council, 1964. In the struggle between rival *Ba'th* factions he was close to the extremist leftist "military" group, and after that faction came to power in the coup of Feb. 1966, he was made President and Secretary-General of both the "national" (i.e., all-Arab) and "regional" (Syrian) command of the *Ba'th* party (the wing ruling Syria). From 1968 to 1970 A. also served as Prime Minister. In the struggle between the factions of Hafez al-*Asad and Salah *Jadid, he sided with the latter, but tried to mediate. After Asad's semi-coup of 1969, A. retained his posts, as part of a compromise settlement; but when Asad took full control in Nov. 1970, A. was dismissed from his three posts as President, Prime Minister and Secretary-General, and imprisoned. There were conflicting reports concerning his release. He was reportedly offered a release late in 1980, but was returned to jail or house arrest when he refused to cooperate. Apparently he was released later, but was not allowed to return to political activities.

ATATÜRK, KEMAL MUSTAFA (1881–1938)

Founder and first President of the Turkish Republic. Born in Salonica, M.K.A. graduated from the Military Academy in Istanbul in 1905, and served in Syria, Macedonia and Tripolitania. After a brief spell as military attache in Sofia, he distinguished himself in World War I in the Dardanelles and on the Caucasian and Palestinian fronts. Initially, he had supported the Young Turks and taken part in their conspiracies, but after the 1908 revolution he gradually became disenchanted with their policies. After the Armistice of Mudros, 1918, he was recalled from Syria to Istanbul and subsequently appointed Inspector of the Ninth Army in Erzurum. In May 1919 M.K.A. began to organize nationalist resistance to Allied plans for the dismemberment of the Turkish heartland of Anatolia and to Greek attempts to take over Western Anatolia. He convened two nationalist congresses in Erzurum and Sivas, 1919, and the Grand National Assembly in Ankara, 1920. M.K.A. led the nationalists, in their victorious struggle against the Allies, the Greeks and the Ottoman Sultan's government in the War of Independence, the deposition of the Sultan and the proclamation of the Turkish Republic, 1923, and the abolition of the Caliphate, 1924 (the title *Ghazi*, "The Victor," was bestowed upon him in recognition of this). He was elected the first President of the Republic and served in this office until his death in 1938. During this period A. — the surname he chose in 1935 — imposed on the Republic an ambitious program of transformation into a modern, Westernized, secular state. Religious schools and religious courts were abolished and religious orders suppressed; civil and criminal law codes based on European models replaced the Muslim *Shari'a*; polygamy was outlawed, civil marriage instituted; traditional clothing was banned (e.g., the oriental fez was replaced by European hats); the Arabic alphabet was replaced with the Latin one.

Though A. proclaimed democracy as the final goal, only his Republican People's Party was permitted to operate (for a short time, in 1930, he allowed an opposition party, but after unrest and religious riots, this opposition was again banned; a multiparty system was introduced only after A.'s death). A. became a model for the leaders of many developing countries. His concepts and ideas ("Kemalism") became the official doctrine of the state, and though their inviolability has become blunted, they still play a very important part in Turkish politics. A. is still revered by his countrymen.

Kemal Mustafa Ataturk (Bar-David, Tel Aviv)

AVIGUR (original name: Meirov), **SHAUL** (1899–1978) A leader of the Israel Labor Movement and one of the creators and mentors of the *Haganah* and Israel's defense and security system. Born in Russia, A. immigrated to Palestine in 1912 and was in one of the first graduating classes of the Gymnasia Herzliah high school, Tel Aviv. During the First World War he was inducted into the Turkish army. He was a member of the *Ahdut Ha'Avodah* party since its establishment (1919) and from 1920 until his death was a member of *Kvutzat* Kinneret.

From 1922 A. was a member of the *Haganah* command, dealing mostly with intelligence and the procurement of arms. He also headed the organization for "illegal" immigration (*Mossad Le 'Aliyah Beth*) from its establishment in 1939. He was loyally linked to the leadership of the Labor Party (*Mapai*).

On the eve of the establishment of the State of Israel and during the War of Independence A. was active in procuring weapons in Europe and the USA. He was a deputy to Minister of Defense David *Ben Gurion and one of the founders of Israel's military industries. For many years he remained responsible for the immigration of Jews from Eastern Europe and contacts with the Jews of the Soviet Union. He was one of the editors of a multi-volume *History of the Haganah*. In 1973 he was awarded the Israel Prize.

'AWN, MICHEL (b. 1935)   Lebanese, Maronite-Christian, officer and politician. After completing the Military Academy, 'A. became a professional officer; he was sent for complementary and staff training in France (1958/59 and 1966) and the USA (1978–80). In 1984 he was promoted to the rank of Brigadier-General and appointed Commander in Chief of the Lebanese armed forces (Lebanon was then in the throes of a continuing civil war, since 1975, and the army, split in practice into communal formations, was lying low and trying to avoid involvment in that war). When in Sept. 1988 President Amin *Jumayyil's term ended and Parliament was unable to meet, overcome factional strife and elect a new President, Jumayyil appointed 'A. to take over the government as Prime Minister and acting President. It was the outgoing President's constitutional right to appoint a temporary successor in the absence of a new elected President; but the Prime Minister had to be, by strictly kept tradition, a Sunni Muslim. At any rate, 'A.'s appointment flew in the face of political-factional realities; acting Prime Minister Salim al-*Huss disputed it, claiming that he and his government were the only legal authority, and even dismissed 'A. from his army command. 'A. controlled only Beirut and parts of the region surrounding it; even there he soon clashed with the Christian "Lebanese Forces" (his potential allies) and suppressed them in bloody fighting in Feb. 1989 and again in Jan. 1990. From Mar. 1989 he was involved in battles with Druze militias southeast of Beirut, backed by Syrian troops, which imposed a tight blockade on his area; he declared an all-out "war of liberation" against Syria, to defend Lebanon's independence — but could do little more than maintain control of Beirut. When in Oct. 1989 Parliament met (in Ta'if, Sa'udi Arabia) and elected a new President — R. *Mu'awwad, and after his assassination the same month, Elias *Harawi — 'A. refused to accept that election, manipulated by Syria, and maintained that his was the legal government. In Oct. 1990 the various militias arrayed against him attacked Beirut and quickly overcame 'A.'s troops (whose resistance was not joined even by his erstwhile allies, the "Lebanese Forces"). 'A. ordered his troops to reintegrate into the Lebanese army and submit to its discipline, while he himself sought asylum in the

Michel 'Awn (AP Photo)

French Embassy. There he stayed, the Lebanese government refusing to fly him to Paris until he first repay large amounts of money which it claimed he had unlawfully appropriated. Permission was granted finally and A. was flown to France in late Aug. 1991.

AYBAR, MEHMET (Muhammad) ALI (b. 1910) Turkish politician, one of the former leaders of the Turkish left. A. graduated from Istanbul Law School and received his Ph.D. in international law in France. Upon his return to Turkey he joined the faculty of Istanbul University.

A. was active since the 1940s in attempts to organize leftist groups and resist the increasing influence of the U.S. in Turkey, and was sometimes close to Communist factions advocating an independent "Eurocommunism." Because of his political views, he was dismissed from his position at the University and detained several times. He practiced Law in Istanbul and tried to publish various magazines, all of which were banned by the government.

In 1962, he joined the Turkish Labor Party (TLP) founded the year before and became its chairman. He was elected to Parliament in 1965 and 1969. In 1967 he was a member of the international "Russell

Tribunal" which condemned U.S. operations in Vietnam. A. lost his chairmanship of the TLP in 1968 because of his outspoken criticism of the Soviet Union's involvement in Czechoslovakia. In 1970, he resigned from the TLP with a group of associates and founded a "Socialist Workers' Party," and in 1975 he regrouped his faction as the "Socialist Party," or "Socialist Revolutionary Party," which was licensed but failed to win a seat in the elections of 1977. After the military coup of Sept. 1980, A. retired from political life.

AL-AYYUBI, JAWDAT 'ALI (1885–1969)   Iraqi politician. Born in Mosul, A. graduated from the Military College of Istanbul and served as an officer in the Ottoman Army. He deserted in 1916 and joined the forces of Sharif *Hussein's "Arab Revolt." During Amir *Feisal's rule in Syria, 1919–20, he was Governor of Aleppo. He returned to Iraq in 1921 and served as governor of several provinces. A. was Minister of the Interior 1923–24, of Finance 1930–33, Chief of the Royal Court and Private Secretary to King Feisal 1933, Prime Minister 1934–35, Speaker of Parliament 1935, Minister to Great Britain 1933–37 and to France 1937–39, Foreign Minister 1939–40. During Rashid 'Ali *Kilani's pro-German regime, 1941, A. left the country, to return after the restoration of the pro-British regime. He then served as Minister to the USA 1944–48, Senator and Foreign Minister 1948–49, Prime Minister 1949–50, Deputy Premier 1953–54, Prime Minister 1957. After General *Qassem's coup of 1958 he settled in Lebanon. Although A. was among the leaders of the right-wing *al-Ikha'* party which opposed the Anglo-Iraqi Treaty of 1930, he belonged to the group of conservative pro-British politicians loyal to the *Hashemite dynasty. Though he served in high posts and was considered dependable, he never figured among the first-rank top leaders of that group.

AL-AYYUBI, MAHMUD (b. 1932)   Syrian politician, reportedly of Kurdish origin. As one of the second-rank leaders of the *Ba'th* group, A. was Minister of Education 1969–71 and concurrently Deputy Premier 1970–71. In Apr. 1971 President *Asad appointed him Vice-President. From Dec. 1972 to Aug. 1976 he was Prime Minister, a position that carries in President Asad's regime rather less decision-making weight than in most countries.

AL-AZHARI, ISMA'IL (1900? 1902?–69)   Sudanese politician. Educated at Gordon College, Khartoum, and the American University of Beirut, A. served in the Sudan Department of Education, 1921–46. In 1938 he organized the "Graduates' General Congress," the association of graduates of Gordon College and intermediate schools, most of them civil servants, that formed the nucleus of Sudan's nationalist movement. A. himself was its secretary. In 1943 he organized Sudan's first political party, the *Ashiqqa'* (Brothers). He and his group favored union with Egypt, collaborating with the *Khatmiyya* order. In 1952, various "Unionist" factions merged in the "National Unionist Party" (NUP) and A. became its President. The NUP won the 1953 elections, during the transition period towards self-rule, and in Jan. 1954 A. became Sudan's first Prime Minister. Although in principle favoring union with Egypt, he and his government led Sudan to independence in Dec. 1955–Jan. 1956. He continued as independent Sudan's Prime Minister, heading a coalition, but in July 1956 lost his majority and became leader of the opposition until the fall of the parliamentary regime in 1958. In 1961–62 he was detained by General *'Abbud's military regime. A. played a part in the 1964 coup which restored civilian political government. In 1965 he was elected a member, and later permanent chairman, of the Presidential

Isma'il al-Azhari (Bar-David, Tel Aviv)

Council, i.e. Head of State, a post he held until *Numeiri's coup of May 1969. The new regime kept him under house arrest until his death in Aug. 1969.

AZIZ, TAREQ (b. 1936)   Iraqi politician. Born in Mosul, a Christian of the Nestorian-"Assyrian" community, 'A. received his MA from the University of Baghdad. He began working as a journalist from 1958 at al-Jumhuriyya; being close to the al-Ba'th group, he edited the al-Jamahir paper, considered the party's mouthpiece, after the Ba'th coup of 1963. From 1969, after the Ba'th firmly established itself in power, he edited its main organ, al-Thawra. In the 1970s, reportedly from 1972, 'A. was co-opted to the Revolutionary Command Council ruling Iraq — apparently, since he had not been a major political leader, in order to have a representative of the Christian communities on the Council — as well as to the Ba'th Party High Command (from 1974 to the "national," i.e. Iraqi-run all-Arab one, and from 1977 to the "regional," Iraqi one). From 1974 to 1977 'A. was Minister of Information, and in 1979, after Saddam *Hussein took full power, he became Deputy Prime Minister. From Jan. 1983 to Mar. 1991 he was Foreign Minister, and since Mar. 1991 he is again Deputy Prime Minister. 'A. was not a decision-making political leader but loyally represented the foreign policies of his master Saddam Hussein to the outer world. During the Gulf crisis and war of 1990/91 he was much in the limelight as Iraq's chief negotiator.

AL-'AZM, KHALED (1900–65)   Syrian politician. Scion of a wealthy family of Damascus notables which dominated the city in the 18th century and continued to provide administrators and notables. 'A. was an independent, not belonging to the mainstream "National Bloc" that led Syria to independence and governed her in the first years after independence; sometimes he formed short-lived parliamentary factions of his own. He was a minister in many governments and several times Prime Minister — in 1941–42 under the French Vichy regime; 1948–49 (until removed by the coup of Husni *Za'im); 1949–50; and 1951 under *Shishakli. In 1955–57 he served as Minister of Defense, Finance and Deputy Prime Minister. Although himself a wealthy landowner and industrialist, he vigorously fostered close ties between Syria and the Soviet Union and was therefore considered by some as a "leftist." 'A. was not among the advocates of Syrian-Egyptian union, and when the two countries merged into the United Arab Republic in 1958, he ceased political activity. After Syria's secession in 1961 and the reestablishment of her independence, he became once more Prime Minister, in 1962–63. He was overthrown by the Ba'th officers' coup of Mar. 1963 and went into exile in Lebanon, where he died. A volume of 'A.'s memoirs was published posthumously in 1973.

AL-AZMA, YUSSUF   Syrian politician, scion of a family of Damascus notables. In 1920, 'A. was Minister of War in Amir *Feisal's short-lived administration. When the French Army advanced on Damascus from Lebanon, he organized and commanded an Arab force of soldiers and volunteers to resist the French. His troops were defeated at the Maisalun Pass, and 'A. was killed in the battle. After his death he became a national hero and a symbol of the resistance to French rule. "Maisalun Day," 26 July, is a day of national mourning in Syria.

Other membes of the 'A. clan were also active in the nationalist movement and held various government positions in Syria. Thus Nabih 'A. was active in Pan-Arab nationalist organizations, but did not find a prominent place in independent Syria's establishment. 'Adel 'A. (died 1952), also active in the nationalist struggle, became a governor and, in 1948–49, a Minister. Bashir 'A. was briefly Prime Minister in 1962.

'AZOURI, NAJIB (d. 1916)   Arab nationalist journalist and writer. A Lebanese of Greek-Catholic faith, 'A. served in the Ottoman administration of the Jerusalem district, but left at the beginning of the century for France, and later Egypt. In 1904 he founded — in Paris, and apparently with French support a Ligue de la Patrie arabe which published pamphlets calling for Arab independence and unity — one of the first to clearly voice that demand. In 1907–8 he published a monthly, Indépendance arabe. His doctrine of Arab independence — in the Arabian Peninsula and the "Fertile Crescent" which would secede from the Ottoman Empire (Egypt and North Africa were outside the scope of his scheme, as he considered them not fully Arab) — was expounded in his book Le Reveil de la Nation Arabe (Paris, 1905); it included a proposal to establish an Arab-Muslim Caliphate in Mecca, to be entrusted to the *Hashemite Sharifs. 'A.'s publications were addressed mainly to the Western world; they had little influence on the

Arab nationalist societies then forming, and 'A. did not become a leader of the movement.

'AZZAM, 'ABD-UL-RAHMAN (1893?–1976)

Egyptian diplomat and politician. Studied medicine in London, but did not become a practicing physician. From his youth an active Arab nationalist, 'A. for some time joined Libyan guerrillas resisting the Italian conquerors, after 1911–12. He was a member of Parliament, 1924–36. At first he was an adherent of the *Wafd*, but since the 1930s he joined the anti-Wafdist camp and was, among its various factions, particularly close to 'Ali *Maher. From 1936 to 1945 'A. joined Egypt's diplomatic service — first as Minister to Iraq, Iran and Sa'udia, and from 1940 as Minister to Turkey; in 1939 he briefly was counselor to the Arab delegations to the London Conference on Palestine. His diplomatic service was interrupted for a year, when he joined 'Ali Maher's government, 1939–40, as Minister of *Waqf* (religious endowments), and later of Social Affairs.

From the early 1930s 'A. actively advocated an "Arab orientation" of Egypt's policy, promoted her involvement in pan-Arab affairs, and himself took part in several all-Arab congresses and in continuous efforts at all-Arab organization. He combined a fervent Pan-Arabism with pronounced Islamic tendencies. When, in 1945, the League of Arab States was established, 'A. became its Secretary-General and chief architect. He served as Secretary-General until 1952. As he was *persona non grata* with the Nasserist regime, he was not politically active since 1952 and even absented himself from Egypt. He returned in 1972, but did not resume political activities. His memoirs were serialized in Arabic, in Egyptian and Lebanese weeklies in 1950 and 1972.

B

AL-BADR, MUHAMMAD (b. 1926) Yemeni prince, Imam of Yemen (i.e. head of the *Zeidi community and ruler of the state), 1962–70. Eldest son of Imam *Ahmad b. Yahya, Prince al-B. served his father in various capacities, both consultative and executive. His status and influence increased after he succeeded, in 1955, in rallying the northern Bakil and Hashed tribal federations to save his father from defeat by a serious rebellion. In 1956 and 1958 he visited Russia and China as his father's representative (and got the reputation of being somewhat Leftist and of pushing Yemen towards growing links with the Soviet Bloc). In Imam Ahmad's absence, e.g. in 1959, al-B. acted as Imam, and in 1961 his father formally appointed him Crown Prince. On the death of Imam Ahmad, in Sept. 1962, al-B. became Imam. A week later he was overthrown by an officers' coup and reported killed. But early in Oct. he reappeared in the northern mountains and soon rallied various tribes to lead them into war against the Republic proclaimed in San'a. In the civil war that ensued, he retained or recovered control of parts of Yemen -changing with the shifting fortunes of war. He was generally supported by the northern Zeidi tribes, and by Sa'udi Arabia (while Egypt sent an expeditionary force to support the Republic). But his control of his own Royalist camp was precarious, and other princes, mainly his uncle Prince Hassan b. Yahya, frequently had to support (or, virtually, to dispute) his flagging leadership. A sick man, Imam al-B. had to go for a cure in Sa'udia and was out of Yemen during the critical period of Nov. 1966 to Sept. 1968. Late in 1966 his power was formally reduced, in his absence, by the formation of an "Imamate Council" under Prince Muhammad b. Hussein. early in 1969, however, al-B. resumed power. The Royalist-Republican reconciliation that ended the civil war in 1970 by-passed him, as it was based on the general acceptance of a republican regime, the abolition of the Imam-King and the permanent exclusion of the royal Hamid-

ul-Din family. Al-b. has not formally abdicated, not has he renounced his claims and titles; but he acquiesced in the abolition of the royal regime and the Imamate and went into exile in London. No serious efforts to restore the royal imamate has been reported.

BADRAN, MUDAR (b. 1934) Jordanian officer and politician. After completing law studies at Damascus University (1956), B. joined Jordan's armed forces and in 1965 became one of their legal consultants. In 1968 he was appointed Director of Intelligence (Security), with the rank of Lieutenant-General. In 1970 he became Chief Chamberlain, and later Secretary-General, of the Royal Court and in 1972 Security Adviser to the King. Concurrently, he was deputy head of the Office for the Occupied Areas (i.e., the Palestinian "West Bank"), with the rank of Minister. In 1973–74 he served as Minister of Education, and late in 1974 he became Chief of the Royal Court. B. was Prime Minister from July 1976 to Dec. 1979, also holding the Defense and Foreign Affairs portfolios; from Aug. 1980 to Jan. 1984, serving as his own Defense Minister; and since Dec. 1989, again keeping the Defense Ministry. As to his views and political line, reports were contradictory, but it would appear that B. was an administrator (with a strong security and intelligence background) rather than a decision-making political leader.

BAGHDADI, 'ABD-UL-LATIF (b. 1917) Egyptian officer and politician. Vice-President of the UAR 1958–61 and of Egypt 1962–64. A graduate of the military academy and a professional officer, B., then a Lt. Colonel, was a leading member of the "Free Officers" who staged the coup of July 1952 and the Revolutionary Council they established; when the officers banned all political parties and set up their own single "Liberation Organization" in Jan. 1953 he became its Inspector-General. He also chaired several purge trials of old-regime politicians. In June 1953 he joined General *Nagib's government as Minister of Defense; when *Nasser took over, in 1954, B. was switched to the less prestigious Municipal Affairs portfolio, to which he added in 1956 the Planning Ministry. Within the junta, he was considered conservative and right-wing. In Aug. 1957 he left the Cabinet, to become President of the National Assembly. When Egypt and Syria merged to form the UAR, in Feb. 1958, B. was appointed one of the new state's Vice-Presidents, in charge of economic affairs; he was concurrently Minister of Planning of the UAR and Minister of Finance of the Egyptian "regional" government. After the secession of Syria in 1961, B. continued as Finance and Planning Minister in the reconstituted Egyptian government, with the rank of Deputy Premier. In Sept. 1962 he became Vice-President (one of five), and concurrently resumed his Presidency of the National Assembly. In 1964 he was dropped as Vice-President and resigned his National Assembly post. He has not been politically active since, though as a former Vice-President and one of the original Free Officers he is respected and sometimes volunteers advice and opinions. B. was, like other'old Nasser associates, critical of *Sadat's new line, especially regarding Sadat's peace treaty with Israel which he publicly denounced (jointly with three other former Vice-Presidents). While he seems to have accepted Egypt's growing links with the USA, he criticized the 1971 Treaty of Friendship with the USSR (a confidential memorandum he presented to Sadat in 1972 was leaked to the press and led to his detention for a short time).

BAIDANI, 'ABD-UL-RAHMAN Yemeni politician, of the Sunni-Shafe'i community, of partly Egyptian descent. Involved in subversive activities against the royal regime, B. spent several years in exile. After the revolution of Sept. 1962, he was named as a leader of the Shafe'i community, a member of the Revolutionary Council, Deputy Premier and Foreign Minister. However, in the factional struggles among the new rulers he was ousted in 1963 and kept in semi-detention in Egypt until 1966.

When 'Abdullah al-*Sallal returned to power, in 1966, B. was appointed ambassador to Lebanon, where he acted as a major, but controversial, spokesman for the republican regime. He was dismissed late in 1968, and has not returned to a position of influence in Yemeni politics, living in exile in Egypt.

BAKDASH, KHALED (b. 1912) Syrian politician, Communist Party leader. Born in Damascus, of Kurdish origin, B. studied law at the University of Damascus. Active in the underground Communist Party since the 1930s, its Secretary-General since 1932 or 1936, he was imprisoned during the French Mandate and went as an exile to the USSR, where he studied at the Communist International College. He returned to Syria in the 1940s. Though the Communist Party was illegal, B. stood for Parliament several times as an independent, and failed; in 1954 he was elected and served in Parliament until 1957–58. When Syria was led into union with Egypt, in 1958, the Party, always ridden by factional disputes, was divided. B. himself seems to have opposed the merger, though not very vigorously. As the UAR regime began suppressing the Communist Party along with other organizations outside the single party permitted, B. again went into exile. He tried to return in 1961, after Syria's secession from the UAR, but was barred by the ruling officers. B. always loyally followed the line laid down by Moscow. He reportedly resisted, in the mid-1960s, a Soviet directive to cooperate with the Ba'th Party, but eventually accepted that "United Front" line. He returned to Syria in the fall of 1966; but while Communists served as government ministers since 1966, B. remained somewhat in the background. He was also involved in factional intra-Party disputes and splits. B. was replaced as Secretary-General in 1968, but remained a senior Party leader. He resumed his post as Secretary-General in 1974. Despite Ba'th-Communist cooperation in a "National Progressive Front" formally set up in 1972, B. did not seem to have much policymaking influence on the regime. Yet, he has remained the most senior Communist leader in the Arab world.

BAKHTIAR, SHAHPUR (1914–91) Iranian politician. Graduated (Ph.D.) in international law and political science from Paris University. In 1940, while in France, B. was recruited to the French army for 18 months; his participation in the war against the Nazis had a great influence on his personality.

B. returned to Iran in 1946 and until 1948 worked for the Ministry of Labor. He was associated with the leftist Iran Party: in 1951/52 he joined *Mossaddeq's National Front Government for that party, as Deputy Minister of Labor. After the fall of Mossaddeq in 1953 he was forced to retire from public service and practiced law, continuing his

Shahpur Bakhtiar (IPS, Tel Aviv)

activities in opposition groups. He constantly criticized the Shah, comparing his rule to the Nazi regime and his secret police (*Savak*) to the Gestapo. His subsequent arrests only increased his hostility toward the regime.

When the Shah's power was shaken by a growing Islamic rebellion and US advisers counseled him to appoint a government not associated with his autocratic and corrupt regime, B., seen as a pro-Western social democrat, was in Jan. 1979 appointed Prime Minister. Though he had struggled against the Shah for years, he did not call for his deposition, but for a British-type constitutional monarchy.

As a modernist, secularist and liberal, opposed to the influence of the Islamic clergy, he declined an alliance between his National Front and the Islamic opposition headed by *Khomeini. B. abolished the *Savak* and declared that Iran would no longer be the policeman of the Persian Gulf. But neither the Islamic fundamentalists nor the left accepted him, seeing him as a representative of the old regime. He was expelled from the National Front, and when the Islamic Revolution won in Feb. 1979 and Khomeini returned to Iran, he was dismissed — after only 38 days in power. He was arrested, but after a time was permitted to leave Iran. He settled in Paris and founded the National Resistance Move-ment. He advocated cooperation among all opposition groups, but in fact refused to cooperate

with some of them. He attacked *Bani-Sadr, *Raja'i of the *Mujahidin Khalq*, and the left. The only one he cooperated with was the Shah's son.

B.'s struggle against the Shah had made him popular, but he was swept away by the Islamic Revolution. His reported meetings with Iraq's Saddam *Hussein in order to brief him on the weaknesses of the Iranian regime on the eve of the Iraq-Iran War, and his eagerness to initiate a counterrevolution, also turned public opinion against him. In his Paris exile he had little influence. In July 1980 he escaped an assassination attempt. (Iran for years demanded the release of his attacker, imprisoned in France.) B. was assassinated in Paris in Aug. 1991.

AL-BAKR, AHMAD HASSAN (1912? 1914?–82) Iraqi officer and politician, President of Iraq 1968–79. B. belonged to the group of "Free Officers" who plotted and carried out the revolution of July 1958; but, favoring a more active Pan-Arab policy and an Iraqi-Egyptian union, he soon fell out with *Qassem, the new ruler, and was removed from the army. He took a leading part in the *Ba'th*-led coup that toppled Qassem in Feb. 1963 and became Prime Minister. When his *Ba'th* Government was dismissed by President 'Abd-ul-Salam *'Aref, in Nov. 1963, B. continued serving in the new regime for a few weeks as Deputy Premier, but

Ahmad Hassan al-Bakr (Bar-David, Tel Aviv)

resigned in Jan. 1964. While probably not belonging to the inner core of the original *Ba'th* officers' group, he was in close contact with them. In July 1968 he led a group of *Ba'th* members and other officers in a coup that toppled 'Abd-ul-Rahman *'Aref, and became President. Less than two weeks later he ousted his non-*Ba'th* partners, Col. 'Abd-ul-Razzaq Na'if (Nayef), then Prime Minister, and his group. In the *Ba'th* regime that ensued he assumed, in addition to the Presidency, the Premiership and the supreme command of the armed forces, and also became chairman of the Revolutionary Command Council. B. and his associates consolidated the *Ba'th* rule by cruel purges, first of non-*Ba'th* opposition groups, then of intra-*Ba'th* factional rivals, and by an all-pervasive secret service. He kept the Iraqi *Ba'th* firmly in the hands of the "right," anti-Damascus, wing and took an extremist line in inter-Arab affairs, making Iraq a mainstay of the "Rejectionist" camp, while seeking, inside Iraq, an accommodation with the Kurd rebels (an agreement he reached with them in Mar. 1970 later broke down) and the Communists (with one of whose factions he concluded, in 1973, a "National Front" pact — but whom he suppressed again in 1978–79). In the Iraqi *Ba'th*'s internal factional struggles B. was considered close to the "rightist" group, but he tried to position himself above the factions, mediating between them and keeping them together, leaving the purges and the infighting to his chief lieutenants. Among those, Saddam *Hussein (al-Tikriti) emerged dominant, since the early 1970s, eliminating his rivals one by one. In fact, due to deteriorating health, B. had been losing control since the mid-1970s and turning into a figurehead, while Saddam Hussein became the real ruler. In July 1979, what had been a fact was openly formalized: B. resigned all his posts — officially for reasons of health, in reality probably ousted by Saddam Hussein, who took over all power. B. spent his last three years in retirement, shunted aside and nearly forgotten.

BANI-SADR, ABU'L-HASSAN (b.1933) Iranian politician, first President of Iran after the Islamic Revolution of 1979. As a student of theology, economics, and sociology at Tehran University B.S. associated with anti-Shah groups, such as *Mossaddeq's National Front. After Mossadeq's defeat in 1953, he joined underground movements. He was arrested by the *Savak* secret police and in 1964 was exiled from Iran. He settled in Paris and studied at the Sorbonne, earning his Ph.D. in econom-

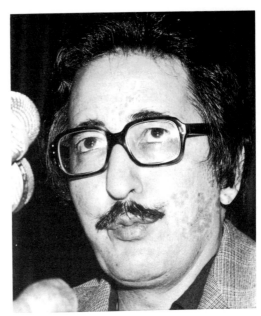

Abu'l-Hassan Bani-Sadr (AP Photo)

ics and sociology, and was active in the Union of Iranian Students.

After meeting Ayatullah *Khomeini in Najaf, Iraq, in 1977, B.-S. became one of Khomeini's close advisers when the Ayatullah moved to Paris in 1978. He was part of a group of intellectuals (most of them anticlerical) who bridged the distance between the political opposition and the rebellious anti-Shah clergy. After the Islamic Revolution, 1979, he published a daily newspaper, *Inqilab*, but at first declined any official post in the government. Yet, in Nov. 1979 he was appointed Minister of Foreign Affairs and Minister of Economics and Finance.

B.-S. was elected President of Iran in Jan. 1980. Khomeini also appointed him Chairman of the Supreme Defense Council. However, B.-S. failed to build up a basis of support in the *Majlis* (Parliament). He was attacked by the radical faction of the ruling, clergy-dominated Islamic Republic Party, headed by its Secretary-General, Ayatuallah Beheshti, *inter alia*. for his anti-Soviet stand after the Soviet intervention in Afghanistan, his stance in the Iran-Iraq conflict, and especially his position on the American hostage crisis and his attempts to restrain the militant students.

In June 1980, Khomeini dismissed him as head of the Defense Council. A committee of inquiry found him guilty of violating the constitution and of disobeying the Imam's orders. He escaped from Iran to France, and the *Majlis* declared him unfit for the Presidency, transferring his former posts to his adversaries.

In their Paris exile in 1981, he and Mas'ud *Rajavi of the *Mujahidin Khalq* founded a National Resistance Council. However, their alliance broke up when B.-S. objected to Rajavi's contacts with Iraq. B.-S. continued to consider himself Iran's legal President, claiming that he enjoyed the support of the army.

B.-S. is considered an important theoretician of the revolution. In three books and about fifty articles he advocated a combination of socialism and the principles of equality which characterized the beginning of Islam. He saw Islamic thinking as the framework of his beliefs. He supported the existence of a religious-clerical leadership, but rejected its actual leaders. He was suspicious of the USA and the USSR, denounced Iran's economic dependence on the West, and called for the stabilization of Iran's economy and the foundation of a classless society. In his book *My Turn to Speak* (1991) he tells the inside story of his political career and the circumstances in which it grew.

AL-BANNA, HASSAN (1906–49)   Founder and leader of the Muslim Brotherhood in Egypt. Born in Isma'iliyya to a pious Muslim family, B. graduated from the Cairo Teachers' College and became a teacher of Islam in Isma'iliyya and Cairo schools. He regarded himself as a follower of the Islamic thinker and reformer Rashid *Rida. In 1929 he founded, in Isma'iliyya, the Muslim Brotherhood — initially an association for religious teaching that turned into a conservative-fundamentalist organization aspiring to the purification of Islam, the return to its pristine doctrine, imposition of Islamic Law, and the transformation of Egypt into an Islamic state. B. was the mentor and sole leader, the "Supreme Guide" (*al-Murshid al-'Aam*) of the Brethren. His simple, forceful doctrine attracted considerable support — chiefly among the lower classes and uneducated folk, but also among some younger intellectuals, mainly students — and his frugal ways and charisma earned him much sympathy, but his organization's increasing radicalization, its subversive fanaticism and advocacy of political assassination caused the government to suppress it and drive it underground. After Prime Minister *Nuqrashi was murdered, in Dec. 1948, by the Brotherhood, B. himself was assassinated in revenge, in Feb 1949. He was replaced as "Supreme

Guide" by Sheikh Hassan Isma'il al-Hudeibi — but neither al-Hudeibi nor those who followed him were able to fill his place as a leader. While B. did not write a systematic exposition of his doctrine, collections of his speeches and articles have been printed several times, as well as a book of memoirs.

AL-BANNA, SABRI ("ABU NIDAL") (b. 1934? 1937?)   Palestinian-Arab terrorist leader. Born in Jaffa, Abu N. left emerging Israel in 1948 and grew up in Gaza. Since the 1960s he has headed a terrorist group considered the most extreme and most brutal among the Palestinian-Arab factions and guerrilla/terror gangs. Officially called "*Al-Fatah* Revolutionary Command," Abu N.'s band appeared under various names (Black September, Black June, Black March) and in shifting links with other groups, and was kept secret even from the PLO, with confusing disinformation deliberately spread concerning its location, operations and identity. A long list of the most brutal terrorist attacks, hijackings and assassinations — including the murder of rival Palestinian leaders — is ascribed to Abu N. and his group. As he refused to submit to the decisions and discipline of the PLO leadership, he and his group were reportedly expelled from the PLO in 1972 or 1974, and he was sentenced to death by the PLO. Abu N. and his group were reportedly hosted and supported by Iraq (until the late 1970s), and then by Syria, until 1985, and Libya, and since 1990 again by Iraq. Their attempts to gain control of Palestinian camps in South Lebanon were defeated by *'Arafat's mainstream *Fatah* in bloody battles in 1990. There have been reports of internal rifts and power struggles inside Abu N.'s group, but information is contradictory and confusing.

BARAZANI (or **BARZANI**)   Kurdish tribe and clan in Iraq, leaders of Kurdish rebellions. Originally a branch of the Muslim-Sunni Naqshabandi Dervish order, the B.'s assumed the characteristics of a tribe in the 19th century. Their center is the village of Barzan, c. 50 mi. north of Erbil. The B. sheikhs, always involved in feuds with rival Kurdish clans and in constant competition for predominance among the tribes, were traditional, semifeudal, tribal-type leaders maintaining a *de facto* semi-autonomy in their mountain valleys, closely linked to related tribes across the border in Iran. Whenever a government - Ottoman, British (for Iraq), or Iraqi - tried to impose tighter control, they resisted. They were thus usually, in a state of semi-rebellion that often erupted into fully-fledged revolt. This near-constant rebellion gradually established links to Kurdiah nationalist groups in the towns or in exile and grew into a revolutionary nationalist upheaval. The B. tribal sheikhs thus turned into national, though never uncontested revolutionary leaders.

Since 1915 the head of the tribe was Sheikh **Ahmad B.** (died 1969) - a religious eccentric often considered mentally disturbed. In the 1920s, he was not the top leader of the Kurds (that place was taken by Sheikh Mahmud, a non-B.). During the 1930s and early 1940s he was identified with the leaders of the Kurdish rebellions, but later he again faded out of the political and military struggle.

The leader of the Kurds in their national struggle since the late 1930s was Sheikh Ahmad's younger brother, **Mulla Mustafa B.** (1901/2/4?-79). Involved in the rebellion, he was jailed with his brother Sheikh Ahmad in the early 1930s and spent the years following in and out of prison, and in exile (mainly in Iran). He returned in 1943 and assumed the leadership of a new rebellion. In 1945–46 he again crossed into Iran, and in 1946 he commanded the army of the short-lived Kurdish Republic of Mahabad. After its collapse he escaped with a band of followers to the USSR (though he was no Communist; the Soviet Union had supported the Mahabad republic). He stayed in Russia until permitted to return to Iraq after *Qassem's coup of 1958. He and his men supported Qassem against both Nasserist and Communist attempts to take over, but he himself was not permitted to leave Baghdad. When Kurdish hopes were disappointed by the Qassem regime and a new rebellion began fermenting, B. escaped to the Kurdish mountains in 1960/61 and assumed the leadership of the re-erupting rebellion. The military fortunes of that rebellion were changing, but Iraq's armed forces were unable to liquidate it. B. had obtained significant aid from the Shah of Iran and was able to use Iranian territory as a supply base and staging area. He also got aid, training etc. from Israel.

While B.'s leadership remained essentially traditional and tribal, he maintained a firm alliance with political nationalist groups and formally headed the modernist-socialist "Kurdish Democratic Party" that led the national struggle since the 1950s. Yet his leadership was beset by both tribal and political-factional rivalries and defections, and his rivals (such as Jalal *Talabani) frequently collaborated with the Iraqi authorities. Throughout the rebellion B. conducted, on and off, negotia-

Mulla Mustafa Barazani (Popper Agency, London)

tions with Iraq, offering to end the rebellion for far-reaching autonomy for the Kurds. An agreement conceding a large part of B.'s demands was reached in June 1966; but as it was not implemented, the rebellion re-erupted in 1968. A new agreement, even more far-reaching, was signed with the *Ba'th regime in Mar. 1970. Again, the Kurds held that it was not honestly implemented, and in Mar. 1974 B.'s fighters, the *Pesh Merga*, resumed battle. But in Mar. 1975, Iraq reached an agreement with Iran after which the Shah stopped his aid to the Kurdish rebels, and closed his territory to the rebels and their supplies. The rebellion collapsed and on 20 Mar. 1975 B. announced its end in defeat. B. himself was among more than 100,000 refugees who escaped to Iran. He later went to the USA, where he died in 1979, a refugee and a broken man.

One of B.'s sons, **'Ubaid-ullah**, was reported to be collaborating with the Baghdad Government. Two others, **Idris** and mainly **Mas'ud**, since the late 1970s to rebuild the Kurdish Democratic Party and resume armed resistance; collaborating, against the Iraqi regime with *Khomeini's Iran (while a rival Iranian wing of the Party, rebelling against Khomeini, collaborates with Iraq). Idris died in

Jan. 1987, and Mas'ud B. became the main leader of the Kurdish rebels (still competing, and frequently cooperating with Talabani). A new rebellion since Mar. 1991, after Saddam *Hussein's defeat in the Gulf War, was encouraged but not affectively aided by the USA; it was partly successfull and reestablished Kurdish control of a wide area in northern and north-eastern Iraq. Since June 1991 B. and Talabani have been negotiating with the Iraqi government for the reestablishment of an autonomic Kurdish region; so far, no agreement has been reached.

AL-BARAZI, HUSNI (1893?-1975) Syrian politician. Scion of a prominent landowning family of Kurdish origin centered in Hama, B. was a right-wing conservative, considered close to Western interests and to King *'Abdullah of Jordan, and never belonged to the mainstream of Syrian nationalism. In World War II, after the conquest of Syria by the British and the Free French (1941), he served in 1942 as Prime Minister. Later he continued to wield some influence behind the scenes, but never returned to power or an official position of prominence. B. was one of the very few Arab politicians to oppose the mainstream Arab hostility to Jewish endeavors in Palestine, to agree to the establishment of a Jewish state and to envisage Arab cooperation with it. In 1946, he confidentially advised the Anglo-American Committee studying a possible settlement of the Palestine conflict that the partition of the country into a Jewish state and an Arab state was the only feasible solution. In the mid-1950s he was frequently accused of plotting with the West, Turkey, Iraq or Jordan, and went into exile. In 1959 he was sentenced, *in absentia*, to imprisonment for life, for "provoking foreign aggression." He did not return to Syria and died in exile in Turkey.

AL-BARAZI, MUHSIN (d. 1949) Syrian politician. Son of a prominent landowning family of Kurdish origin, centered in Hama. A conservative of pro-Western leanings. B. played no prominent part in the mainstream of Syrian nationalism. He served as a minister in several cabinets in 1941-42 (after the conquest of Syria by the British and the Free French), and again in 1947-48 (Interior, and subsequently Foreign Minister). He was President al-*Quwwatli's personal assistant and speechwriter in 1948-49), and the same year briefly served as Minister to Egypt. When Husni *Za'im, after his coup of Mar. 1949, was elected President, in June

1949, B. became his Prime Minister. He was arrested, together with Za'im, during Col. Sami *Hinnawi's coup in Aug. 1949, sentenced to death by a summary military court, and executed. (A relative later killed Hinnawi in revenge.)

BASHIR, 'OMAR HASSAN (b. 1935) Sudanese officer and politician, since July 1989 ruler of Sudan. During his long years of service in the Sudanese army, rising to the rank of Major-General, B. was not involved in political affairs and did not become prominent. However, as Sudan's civilian, elected government (established in 1985/86, after the fall of *Numeiri) deteriorated in continuous crisis, he staged a coup on June 30, 1989, with a group of fellow officers. He dismissed the government, dissolved Parliament, suspended the constitution and banned political parties; he also detained several leaders of the regime he deposed. In July B. formed his own government. He has ruled Sudan since 1989 as *de facto* Head of State and Prime Minister. B. has not emerged as an inspiring leader and has not seriously tackled any of Sudan's major problems — such as her economic crisis, leading to repeated famines, the continuous civil war with the rebellious African tribes in the South, or the imposition of the punishment code of Islamic Law (the *Shari'a*). As to the future regime of Sudan, including a settlement of the southern rebellion, he has convened several consultative conferences, where a federal system of government was mooted as a solution; but nothing was done about this and no serious talks were held with the rebels.

Several attempts to topple B. have been vaguely reported; but his rule has so far not been seriously challenged. Most observers consider B. and his junta to be closely linked to Islamic-fundamentalist circles and think that these Islamic leaders in fact rule the country behind the scenes.

BAYAR, CELAL (1882? 1884?-1986) Turkish politician; third President of the Republic of Turkey 1950-60 and first President with no military background since the Young Turks' Revolution of 1908. Born in Umurbey, Gemelik, B. attended the French Lyceum in Bursa. He worked for a short time as a bank clerk, but soon entered politics. In 1908, he was executive secretary of the Izmir branch of the Committee of Union and Progress — the political organization of the Young Turks. In 1919, he joined the Kemal *Ataturk-led war of independence against the Greeks (1919-1922), as one of the leaders of the resistance in the Aegean area. He was elected to the "Grand National Assembly" (Parliament) in 1920, and was appointed Minister of the National Economy in 1921. He was acting Minister of Foreign Affairs (1922), a member of the Turkish delegation to the Lausanne Peace Conference in 1923 and under the Lausanne Treaty was appointed Minister for the Exchange of Population and Land Settlement. In 1924 he became Minister of Reconstruction and the same year withdrew from the government, founding a government-backed bank (Is Bank) and managing it from 1924 to 1932. Then he rejoined the government as Minister of the National Economy (1932–37) and for a short time was acting Prime Minister. From 1937 to 1939 he was Prime Minister. Throughout the 1920s and 1930s he was largely responsible for Kemalist Turkey's economic policies. In Jan. 1939 he stepped down as Prime Minister.

In 1945, after his differences with President Ismet *Inonu escalated — e.g., over land reform laws, and mainly over increasing efforts to break the monopoly of the ruling Republican People's Party (RPP) and introduce a multi-party system — B. left the RPP and with *Menderes, *Korltan and *Koprulu founded the Democratic Party (Jan. 1946). Six months later, he and 63 other representatives of the new party were elected to Parliament. In May 1950, the Democratic Party won the elections (408 seats, against 69 RPP) and in May 1950 B. was elected President. During his ten-year presidency Turkey strengthened her relationship with NATO, mainly in reaction to the USSR's claims to Turkish territories.

B.'s presidency ended with the military coup of May 27, 1960. With the other top leaders of the Democratic Party regime of 1950–60 he was tried by a special tribunal (the Yassiada Trials) and sentenced to death; but his death sentence was commuted to prison for life (Sept. 1961). In prison, his health deteriorated and he was hospitalized. Under an amnesty of 1964, B. was released and in 1974 his full political rights were restored. As a former President he was entitled to a position as Senator for life, but he refused it. He did not resume an active role in politics, but was regarded as an elder right-wing statesman. He published six volumes of memoirs. In his last years, as a centenarian, his health and general state deteriorated.

BAZARGAN, MEHDI (b. 1905) Iranian politician; first Prime Minister, 1979, in Ayatullah *Khomeini's Islamic regime. Born in Tabriz to a well-known family of merchants, B. graduated in thermodynamic engineering from Paris University. He began his political career in the 1940s as a Deputy Minister in *Mossaddeq's radical government (1951–53), and its chairman of the Committee for Oil Nationalization. During the 1950s he was also General Manager of the Tehran Water Board and Dean of the Tehran University Technical College.

After Mossaddeq's fall in 1953, B. was active in anti-Shah groups, such as the revived National Front in the early 1960s, and in 1961 founded his own Iran Liberation (or Freedom) Movement. He was also among the founders of the Human Rights Association in 1977. B. was arrested several times.

In the course of the Islamic Revolution, Khomeini in Jan. 1979 appointed him Prime Minister, as head of a transitional government composed mainly of members of the National Front and B.'s Liberation Movement. B. was also appointed to the Central Committee of the ruling Islamic Republic Party and was in charge of labor affairs in the Council of the Islamic Revolution. His appointment was an expression of Khomeini's appreciation of his personal integrity, Islamic fervor and his struggle against the Shah, rather than a mandate for his faction, and the real power remained in the hands of Khomeini, the Council of the Islamic Revolution, the Revolutionary Guards, and the clergy. B. tried to resign in Mar. and Aug. 1979 in protest against the closing of newspapers, the banning of party activities and mass executions; but Khomeini refused to accept his resignation. On Nov. 5, 1979, however, a day after the seizure of the American hostages, his resignation was finally accepted.

B. was allowed to continue expressing moderate opposition to the new regime — the only politician to be so allowed. In 1980 he was elected to the *Majlis* (Parliament), where he continued to criticize the government (calling, e.g., for an end to the Iran-Iraq war). He was however, restricted, frequently harassed, and not permitted to maintain an active organization or publish a newspaper. In 1984 he refused (or was forbidden) to run again for the *Majlis*, and in 1985 the regime prevented him from presenting his candidacy for the Presidency. In 1986 he tried to set up an "Association for the Nation's Sovereignty and Freedom," but it was not permitted to function.

B. remains the only Iranian politician permitted, though harassed and restricted, to express some cautious opposition to the Islamic regime.

AL-BAZZAZ, 'ABD-UL-RAHMAN(1913–73) Iraqi politician and jurist, a Sunni Muslim, born in Baghdad. A fervent nationalist. B. was detained in 1941, after the defeat of the Rashid 'Ali *Kilani regime, for his anti-British and pro-German attitude. From 1955 he was Dean of the Baghdad Law College. In 1957, he was arrested for "Nasserist" anti-regime activities. After the July 1958 revolution of General *Qassem, B. was among those pushing the new regime towards Nasserist policies, and in 1959 was arrested for his suspected involvement in a Nasserist plot. After Qassem's fall in 1963, he became Ambassador to Cairo (briefly) and London, and in 1964–65 served as Secretary-General of OPEC (the Organization of Petroleum Exporting Countries). In Sept. 1965 B. was appointed Deputy Premier and Foreign Minister, and two weeks later became Prime Minister, retaining the Foreign Ministry. He tried to restore civilian-political rule and thus soon fell out with the army officers really in control. B. was the chief architect of an agreement of June 1966 with the Kurdish rebels that made far-reaching concessions to the Kurds and granted them partial autonomy. The agreement was never implemented, as it proved unacceptable to most of the nationalist military establishment, and the controversy around it contributed to B.'s fall, in Aug. 1966. After the *Ba'th* coup of July 1968, B. was arrested for plotting with the Western powers. He was released in 1970 and went into exile to England, where he died in July 1973.

BEGIN, MENAHEM (b. 1913) Israeli statesman. Born in Brisk (Brest-Litovsk), Poland. Graduated from the University of Warsaw Law School. From 1929 active in *Betar*, the Revisionist youth movement, he was appointed in 1948 Commander of *Betar* in Poland. He took a more radical line than Jabotinsky and in 1938 publicly challenged him.

At the outbreak of the Second World War he escaped to Vilna and did not return to occupied Poland — a grave decision that remained traumatic for him. In 1940 he was arrested by the KGB and sent to a detention camp. In 1941, after Germany invaded the Soviet Union, he was released and inducted into Gen. Anders' Polish army. He reached Palestine as a soldier in 1942. After his demobilization he was named Commander of the underground IZL in 1943. As head of the IZL he proclaimed a revolt against the British in Palestine in Jan. 1944 and in Oct. 1945 and was one of the

initiators of the "Movement for Hebrew Resistance" — the roof organization of all the underground movements. In the summer of 1946, after the IZL bombed the British Mandatory government offices in King David Hotel, the *Haganah* ceased cooperation with the IZL and the roof "Movement."

After the establishment of the State of Israel, B. established a new political party, the *"Herut* Movement founded by the IZL," and was its undisputed leader for decades. In 1949 he was elected to the First Knesset and was a member of Knesset until 1984. In 1952, during the dispute over the acceptance of reparations from Germany, which B. opposed, he organized a demonstration that tried to break up by force a Knesset debate — an action that led many to question his loyalty to the democratic system.

From 1955 onward B., heading the largest party in opposition, was the leader of the opposition in the Knesset. As such he was a parliamentarian and a legalist in many matters, such as his liberal position on the emergency laws. On the other hand, he led his party as the sole leader and whoever tried to challenge him (Eri Jabotinsky, Hillel Kook, Shmuel Tamir, Ezer *Weizman and others) was cast out. He was also involved in several incidents (such as the motorcycle demonstration of 1959, on the eve of the elections to the Fourth Knesset which had dictatorial undertones) which did not conform to accepted democratic ethics. During all those years *B. and his party were boycotted by* *Ben-Gurion, who ruled them out as a partner in any coalition and refused to call B. by his name (instead referring to him as "the man who sits next to Knesset member Bader").

In 1965 the *Herut* Movement joined the Liberal Party to form the *Gahal* bloc, thus beginning a process of legitimization of the party. In May 1967, on the eve of the Six Day War, B. joined the *Eshkol government. He was a member of that government until July 1970, when it agreed to accept UN Resolution 242 which calls for Israel's withdrawal from territories occupied in 1967. In 1973 the *Likud* was formed and Begin led a political bloc which included all the right-wing parties.

After the *Likud* election victory, B. formed the government in June 1977 and served as Prime Minister until October 1983. Among his several achievements during his Premiership were the Camp David Agreement with Egypt, 1978, for which he was awarded the Nobel Peace Prize, and the Peace Treaty of 1979. He also strictly protected

Menahem Begin and Anwar Sadat (GPO)

democratic values and the freedom of the press. However, he also had several great failures. One was economic; at the end of his term inflation reached 400% a year and was uncontrollable. Another failure was the war in Lebanon which involved Israel in a bloody, controversial war with hardly any achievements. In Sept. 1983 B. resigned (without publicly explaining his reasons), retired from public life and became a recluse.

B., both as leader of the opposition and as Prime Minister, was a controversial figure. However, even his opponents see him as a great statesman and one of the outstanding Prime Ministers which the State of Israel has had.

AL-BEID, 'ALI SALEM (b. 1938)   South Yemeni politician, since May 1990 Vice-President of Yemen. Of tribal, Haddamauti background, B. was active in the South Yemeni nationalist struggle and gradually rose in the ranks of its leading party, the NLF (renamed in 1978 "Yemen Socialist Party"). In the factional struggles within that party, ruling South Yemen since it attained independence in 1967, he was close to the hard-liner 'Abd-ul-Fattah *Isma'il.

B. joined the government in 1973 as Minister of Planning, in 1976 as Minister of Location/Municipal Affairs, and in 1980 as Deputy Prime Minister. In the 1980s he increasingly opposed President 'Ali Nasser *Muhammad, and in the bloody confrontation of Jan. 1986 between Isma'il and 'Ali Nasser

Muhammad he took the side of Isma'il. He was reported killed or executed, but survived. In Feb. 1986, with Isma'il dead and 'Ali Nasser Muhammad ousted and exiled, B. became Secretary-General of the ruling Yemen Socialist Party and (with a weak President and Prime Minister) the *de facto* ruler of South Yemen. He gradually moderated his hard-line policy, promised a measure of liberalization and vigorously pushed ahead with the implementation of long-standing plans for the merger of South Yemen and (North) Yemen. When the union of the two countries was achieved, in May 1990, he became Vice-President of the new united Yemen.

BEN-AHARON (original name: Nissenbaum), **YITZHAK** (b. 1906)   Israeli politician. A prominent member of the Labor Party and leader of the *Kibbutz Hameuhad*. Born in Bukovina, Rumania, where he was a leader of *Hashomer Hatzair*. He immigrated to Palestine in 1928, and in 1933 cofounded Kibbutz Givat Hayim. During the 1930s he was Secretary of *Mapai*, together with Pinhas Lavon, and Secretary of the Tel Aviv Workers Council. In this capacity he assisted in forming a coalition of the *Kibbutz Hameuhad* and the opposition to the leadership of *Mapai*, thus creating a faction which was eventually to split the party.

During the Second World War, in defiance of the position taken by the leaders of the *Kibbutz Hameuhad*, he joined the British army and in 1941 was taken prisoner in Greece. After the war he joined the *Ahdut Ha'avodah* faction, which cofounded the *Mapam* Party in 1948 (seceding from it in 1954). In 1949, B.-A. was elected to the First Knesset, and except for short intervals he served as a member of the Knesset until 1977. From 1959 to 1962 he was Minister of Transport and from 1969 to 1973 Secretary General of the *Histadrut*.

B.-A.'s influence went far beyond the formal positions he held. He has been one of the major ideologues of the Labor Movement. His article, "The Strength to Change Before Disaster," published in *Davar* in 1962, was one of the catalysts for the establishment of the Alignment between *Mapai* and *Ahdut Ha'avodah* in 1965. More often than not, his opinions were opposed to those of his party's leaders. While serving as Secretary-General of the *Histadrut* he came out strongly against the political positions of Prime Minister Golda *Meir, and against the socioeconomic policies of Minister of Finance Pinhas *Sapir. These attacks created a deep rift between him and his party's leaders, causing him to resign from his post. The dovish position he took since 1967 brought him into conflict with his faction and Yitzhak *Tabenkin, head of the *Kibbutz Hameuhad*, whom he considered to be his leader and mentor.

Since leaving the political scene he has often expressed his opinions in books and articles. He is considered to be one of the informal leaders of the doves in the Labor Party and those who consider it to be a socialist and not a center party.

BEN-'ALI, ZEIN-UL-'ABEDIN (b. 1936)   Tunisian officer and politician, President of Tunisia since Nov. 1987. B.-'A., trained at the French military academy, with additional training in the USA, mainly in the field of intelligence, served mostly in Tunisia's intelligence and security apparatus. He was director of military intelligence 1958–74, military attache in Morocco 1974–77, head of the secret services 1977–80, with the rank of Secretary of State. In 1980 he was removed and sent abroad, as Ambassador to Poland, but in 1984 he returned to his post. When government deteriorated, with aging and declining President *Bourgiba trying to maintain his *de facto* one-man rule against much discontent, B.-'A. was made Minister of Public Security in late 1985 and Minister of the Interior in Apr. 1986, beginning in fact to control the government. He was also named, in June 1986, Secretary-General of the ruling *Dustour Socialist Party* (formerly *Neo-Destour*). In Oct. 1987 he took over as Prime Minister, keeping also the Ministry of Interior (and Security). After one month, in Nov. 1987, he staged a coup, deposed Bourguiba and proclaimed himself President. In Apr. 1989 he was elected President, as the single candidate, with over 99% of the popular vote. As President, B.-'A. tightened the government and initiated several reforms; he permitted multiparty competition for Parliament, but saw to it that the ruling party (the former *Neo-Destour*, which he renamed *Rassemblement Constitutionnel-Democratique*) continued to win all the seats in the elections of Apr. 1989. His chief opponent — and Tunisia's main problem — was the growing Islamic-fundamentalist movement; he did not permit it to establish a legal organization and tried to suppress it by various means.

BEN-BARKA, MEHDI (1920–65)   Moroccan nationalist leader and politician. One of the younger leaders of the *Istiqlal* party, B.-B. served as chairman of the Consultative Assembly, 1956–59, that preceded the establishment of elected representative and legislative bodies. Within the *Istiqlal* he headed a leftist faction opposed to the traditional leadership, and in 1959 he seceded with his faction and founded the *Union Nationale des Forces Populaires*. Accused of involvement in subversion and plots, he soon went into exile in France. In 1963–64 he was tried *in absentia* and sentenced to death, though the King later pardoned him. In Oct. 1965 B.-B. disappeared in France and it was generally assumed that he had been abducted and murdered by the Moroccan secret services (though his body was never found). The "B.-B. Affair" caused a grave crisis in French-Moroccan relations for several years. In Jan. 1966 the French issued an arrest warrant against Muhammad Oufkir, the Moroccan Minister of the Interior and Head of the Secret Services. A trial was held in France from Sept. 1966; of the accused, Oufkir was absent, but one of the heads of the secret service, Ahmad Dlimi, gave himself up. Sentence was pronounced in June 1967: Oufkir was condemned to imprisonment for life, and Dlimi was acquitted. The French-Moroccan crisis over the "B.-B. Affair" was patched up in 1969.

BEN-BELLA, AHMAD (or sometimes **Muhammad**) (b. 1916? 1918?)   Algerian politician and leader of the nationalist revolt. President of Algeria 1963–65. B.-B. emerged as a nationalist leader after World War II. After serving in the French Army during the war, he joined the MTLD party led by *Messali Hajj, which advocated full independence for Algeria. He soon began advocating armed struggle and set up, with a group of like-minded associates (Belkacem Krim, Muhammad Khidr, Hussein *Ait-Ahmad), an underground *"Organisation Speciale"* for that purpose, thus breaking with Messali and the MTLD. In 1950 he was arrested and sentenced to seven years' imprisonment. He escaped in Mar. 1952 to Cairo and established there the headquarters of the groups preparing an armed revolt. In 1953 his *Organisation Speciale* turned into a *Conseil Revolutionnaire pour l'Unite et l'Action*, out of which grew the *Front de Liberation Nationale* (FLN) in 1954. When the FLN began an armed revolt in Nov. 1954 B.-B. was its most prominent leader. In Oct. 1956, when B.-B. was flying from Morocco to Tunis, the French secret services arranged for the pilot to land at Algiers and arrested B.-B. and four other rebel leaders, including Khidr and Ait-Ahmad. While B.-B. was in prison in France and could no longer lead the rebellion, his colleagues kept his place in their leadership bodies and managed to consult him; he was named, for instance, Deputy Premier in the FLN's Provisional Governments of 1958 and 1961.

B.-B. was released in Mar. 1962, with the French-Algerian agreement and cease-fire. He immediately assumed a vigorous leadership and took bold positions in the factional splits that developed. He advocated leftist-neutralist, anti-Western policies on Nasserist lines and a one-party state socialism, with the party dominant; in the rift between the guerrillas inside Algeria and the rebel army under *Boumedienne entering Algeria from Tunisia he backed the latter. In June 1962 he convened the FLN leadership in Tripoli, Libya, and imposed his line. He ignored the two rival governments struggling for control — the one set up provisionally by the French-Algerian agreement, and Yussuf Ben-Khedda's FLN government - and imposed his own politbureau's control (with the FLN government acquiescing). In Sept. 1962 the provisional arrangements were ended and B.-B. formed the government of independent Algeria. He continued imposing his strict, hard-line rule and began suppressing all oppositional trends within and without the FLN. In Apr. 1963 he became Secretary-General of the FLN in addition to holding the Premiership. In Sept. 1963 B.-B. was elected President in a referendum, as the only candidate, nominated by the FLN; he kept the Premiership, too, but from 1964 ceased using the title Prime Minister and treated his government as a presidential one. He made Algeria an ally of the Soviet bloc (he received the Lenin Peace Prize in 1964) and a mainstay of the leftist-neutralist camp, aspiring to a position of leadership in that camp.

B.-B.'s harsh policies and his suppression of opposition leaders with a proud FLN fighting record caused much unrest and dissatisfaction. In June 1965 he was overthrown by his associate and protege Boumedienne, and imprisoned. His confinement was eased from 1979, after Boumedienne's death, and in Oct. 1980 he was released. He refused, however, to associate himself with the regime in power and soon went into voluntary exile in France, where he co-founded various opposition groups in exile — adopting an increasingly Islamic and pro-Libyan line (these groups, factionally split, did not have much impact on political realities in Algeria). In 1982 he co-founded an "International Islamic Commission for Human Rights." After the liberalization of Algeria's regime by President *Ben-Jedid B.-B. returned to Algeria in Sept.

Ahmad Ben-Bella (IPS, Tel Aviv)

1990. Taking an extreme militant line, he has since endeavored — apparently with very limited success — to rebuild a party of his own and a position of influence.

BEN-GURION (original name: Green), **DAVID** (1886–1973)   Israeli statesman, one of the founding fathers of the State of Israel, prominent leader of the Labor Movement. Born in Plonsk, Poland (then Russia). From 1904 he studied in Warsaw, where he he was active in the Zionist Socialist party *Poalei Zion*. In 1906 he immigrated to Palestine and worked as a farmer — first in Petah Tikvah and later in Sejera in Lower Galilee, continuing his activities in *Poalei Zion*; in 1910 he co-founded its organ *Ha'ahdut*.

In 1911 he travelled to Constantinople to study law. With the outbreak of the First World War he returned to Palestine, but was expelled by the authorities and travelled to the United States. There he worked to foster contacts between the workers in Palestine and the local Jewish Labor movement. He co-initiated volunteering for a "Jewish Legion," and was one of the first to volunteer himself.

At the end of the war he returned to Palestine

David Ben-Gurion (GPO)

where he was one of the founders of the *Ahdut Ha'avodah* Party and the *Histadrut* of which he was general secretary 1920–1935. He was one of the architects of the merger of the factions of the Labor movement as the Labor Party, *Mapai* (1930), and one of the new party's top leaders. From the early 1930s onward he successfully strove to turn the Labor Party into the dominant factor in the Zionist movement and he stood at the forefront of the struggle at the end of which *Mapai* appeared as the ruling party in the Zionist movement. From 1935 to 1948 he headed the Jewish Agency Executive and led the political struggle for the establishment of the State of Israel.

In 1937 he supported the partition plan proposed by the Peel Commission, against the opposition of his *Mapai* leadership associates Berl *Katznelson and Yitzhak *Tabenkin. He led the struggle against the British White Paper of 1939, but decided on full cooperation with the British in the Second World War, while intensifying the Zionist movement's struggle to achieve Jewish sovereignty in Palestine; in 1942 he was the chief initiator of the "Biltmore Plan" proclaiming the creation of a Jewish Commonwealth State in Palestine as the aim of Zionism. At the end of the war he supported an active struggle against the British, up to and including action

by the underground *Haganah*, but was prepared for political compromises in order to achieve his goal; he rejected, and fought, the more extremist methods of the Revisionist party and *IZL* and their separate action in defiance of the national leadership. In 1947 he supported the United Nations partition plan endorsing the establishment of the State of Israel.

In May 1948 B.G. became the first Prime Minister and Defense Minister of independent Israel. He led Israel in the critical War of Independence. At the same time he struggled to establish the authority of the new State and prevent the emergence of separate or dissident centers of power. Thus he ordered artillery fire on the *Altalena*, a ship trying to land arms for the *IZL*, and disbanded the headquarters of the *Palmah*, dismissing several senior *Haganah-Palmah* commanders. B.G. was also responsible for the decision to bring hundreds of thousands of Jews to Israel — despite the war and the difficult security and economic situation of the new State. Another major decision he took was to begin negotiations with West Germany over reparation payments — a decision which almost plunged the country into a civil war. He instituted a unified national school system, disbanding separate education streams. On foreign, defense and security matters he took forceful positions. During the first years of the State B.G. was its leader, though he was sharply attacked by the opposition, both right and left.

In Dec. 1953 B.G. resigned from all his positions, transferring the Premiership to Moshe *Sharett, and settled in Sdeh Boker, a small *kibbutz* in the Negev. For a year he held no official positions, but he remained a center of power in his retreat at Sdeh Boker. When in Feb. 1955 P. *Lavon resigned as Minister of Defense, because of the "Lavon Affair," B.G. returned as Defense Minister and at the end of that year became Prime Minister once again. In Oct. 1956, against what Israel perceived as escalating Egyptian aggression, he decided on military action and the Sinai Campaign, in coordination with British and French operations.

B.G.'s decline began after the "Lavon Affair" was reopened in 1958–60, and he resigned in 1961 in protest against a government endorsement of a committee decision to clear Lavon. In Feb. 1961 Lavon was forced to resin from his post as Secretary-General of the *Histadrut*, to facilitate B.G.'s return as Prime Minister and Defense Minister — but the latter's standing was weakened and his dominance diminished. In 1963 he resigned and began a struggle against his successor, Levi *Esh-kol. This vendetta greatly harmed B.G.'s public image and brought about a split in *Mapai*, and B.G. created a new party — *Rafi*. In the elections to the Sixth Knesset, 1965, the new party won only ten mandates and B.G. found himself on the opposition benches. In 1968 Rafi returned to the Labor Party, and B.G. founded a new party — *La'am* ("To the People"); it won only four mandates in the elections of 1969, and in 1970 B.G. retired from political activity. After the Six Day War he took a dovish position, saw the continued occupation of the West Bank and Gaza as a danger to Israel and opposed their annexation.

After his death in 1973 and with the passing of time admiration for B.G., the architect of the State of Israel, its defense and its democratic society in the first fifteen years of statehood, has deepened, and even his political opponents admit his great leadership. Several biographies have been written about him, the most important by Shabtai Tevet. B.G. himself has left, in addition to many articles and several books, detailed diaries by now largely published, and voluminous documentation.

Chadli Ben-Jedid (IPS, Tel Aviv)

BEN-JEDID, CHADLI (al-Shadhili) (b. 1929) Algerian officer and politician, President of Algeria since 1979. Born in eastern Algeria into a peasant family, B.-J. received no higher education. According to French reports never confirmed by Algerian sources, he served in the French Army in the early 1950s. He joined the FLN forces of the armed revolt in 1955 and rapidly rose in rank, soon named Colonel. In 1961 he was appointed to the General Staff of *Boumedienne's rebel army in Tunis, and from 1962 was a member of the Revolutionary Council. In the factional struggles of 1962–63 he supported Boumedienne (and therefore *Ben-Bella), and was named commander of the Constantine region. From 1963–64 he commanded the Oran region for fifteen years and, while supporting Boumedienne, ruled it with a strong hand as his personal fief. He took no part in ideological debates or factional struggles.

When after the death of Boumedienne in Dec. 1978 the struggle for the succession seemed to be deadlocked, B.-J. emerged as the Army's candidate and a generally acceptable compromise. Nominated by the FLN as the single candidate for the Presidency, he was elected in Feb. 1979 in a referendum. As President, he kept the Defense Ministry to himself until mid-1990. He appointed a Prime Minister — the first separation of the Premiership from the Presidency since 1962–63. He was also elected Secretary-General of the FLN. He was reelected President, as the only candidate, in 1984 and in Dec. 1988. B.-J. purged the FLN, the government and the army of elements he considered extremist or undesirable. While he made no major changes in Algeria's policies of state socialism and radicalism, he fostered the influence of technocrats, de-emphasized ideological-doctrinal elements and relaxed Algeria's regime, ending the monopoly of the FLN and gradually legalizing, from 1988–89 and under a new constitution of Feb. 1989, rival political parties. He also toned down Algeria's radical foreign policies, e.g., gradually dissociated her from the inter-Arab "Rejection Front." In recent years B.-J. faced increasing difficulties, as the economic situation deteriorated (serious unrest was suppressed in Oct. 1988 with bloody violence), the old, dogmatic and antireform FLN cadres became restive, and the new multiparty system allowed opposition forces to grow — e.g., adherents of Berber nationalism and, particularly, Islamic fundamentalists.

BEN-ZVI (original name: Shimshilevitch), **YITZHAK** (1884–1963) Israeli politician, President of Israel 1952–63. One of the fathers of the Labor

Movement. Born in Poltava, Ukraine. From his youth he was a Zionist activist; in 1906 he and Ber Borochov founded *Poalei Zion*, the first Zionist-socialist political party. In 1907 he immigrated to Palestine and became one of the main leaders of the Labor Movement. He was one of the founders of the "Bar-Giora" and *Hashomer* self-defense associations, and a co-founder and editor of *Ha'achdut*, the organ of *Poalei Zion* in Palestine. From 1912 he studied law in Istanbul; there he sought contacts with the "Young Turk" leaders, as he advocated the realization of Zionist efforts within the framework of the Ottoman Empire.

At the outbreak of the First World War he returned to Palestine. But in 1915 he was exiled by the Turkish authorities, together with David *Ben-Gurion and went to the USA. There he organized a *Hehalutz* movement, in cooperation with the Labor Zionist movement. He was one of the founders of the Jewish battalions in the British army, the "Jewish Legion."

After the British conquest of Palestine he returned to that country and in 1919–20 was one of the founders of *Achdut Ha'avodah* and the *Histadrut*, and of the Labor Party, *Mapai*, in 1930. He was active within the framework of *Knesset Yisrael*, the Representative Assembly of the *Yishuv*, and its National Council the *Va'ad Le'umi*; and in 1931, after *Mapai* won in the elections for the Assembly, he was elected chairman (retitled President in 1945) of the *Va'ad Le'umi*. During those years he fulfilled an important task but lost some of his central position, since the focal point of the *Yishuv's* strength and activity had shifted to the Jewish Agency Executive.

With the establishment of the State of Israel B.-Z. was one of the signers of the Declaration of Independence and was elected to the First and Second Knesset. In 1950 he headed the *Mapai* list for the Jerusalem municipality, but was not elected Mayor. In 1952, after the death of Chaim *Weizmann, he was chosen as *Mapai* candidate for President (winning over Yosef *Shprinzak, by a tight margin), and was duly elected by the Knesset in the fourth round of voting, against M. Nurock, the candidate of the right wing.

He was reelected President in 1957 and 1962 and held this post until his death. He was well beloved for his modesty and his simple way of life, and during his term the President's home was open to all members of the public. B.-Z. was deeply interested in history and ethnography, especially that of "lost," mostly Oriental, Jewish tribes and com-

munities. Among several books he wrote is one on such communities (1936) and one on the population of Palestine under Ottoman rule (1955).

BERRI, NABIH (b. 1930? 1937?)   Lebanese lawyer and politician, political leader of the Muslim-Shi'i community. Born in Freetown (Sierra Leone), where his father had migrated, B. was returned to the town of his family's origin, Tibnin in South Lebanon, and brought up there. He later studied law at the Lebanese University of Beirut. He was, in his student days, active in the *Ba'th* Party and frequently visited Damascus. For some time he was president of the students' union. Later he studied for some time at the Sorbonne in Paris, lived with his father in Sierra Leone, and then went to the USA. There he married a Lebanese-American, but later divorced her; his divorced wife and some of their seven children remained in the USA (he remarried in 1982).

B. returned to Lebanon in 1975 and joined the Shi'i leader Sheikh Mussa al-*Sadr and his recently formed paramilitary organization, al-Amal. During the civil war that erupted in 1975, the Shi'is of Lebanon — until then a backward community that had not been given a fair share in the distribution of political power — began asserting their strength and organizing to claim the power due to them. B. gradually became one of their main younger leaders. He soon became a member of al-*Amal's* Political Committee, then its Secretary-General (1978) and its Chairman (1980); and though his direct control of the organization and its militia remained in doubt, he emerged as the chief Shi'i leader.

In the civil war itself, from 1975, the Shi'is did not actively join either of the rival camps and restricted their militias, *al-Amal* and local guards, to the protection of their villages and quarters. There were tension and frequent clashes between them and the Palestinian PLO guerrillas dominating South Lebanon. In the early 1980s however, and particularly after the Israeli occupation of South Lebanon in 1982 and with the increasing Shi'i resistance to that occupation, B. allied himself to the "leftist," antigovernment camp led by the Druze chief Walid *Junbalat. He did not formally join the several "National Front" coalitions set up by Junbalat in 1983 and 1984, but he joined their efforts to force on the Christian-led government a pro-Syrian and anti-Israel policy and far-reaching changes in Lebanon's political structure; officially he and his Druze allies demanded the abolition of the communal structure, but in fact they aimed at — and

Nabih Berri (AP Photo)

achieved — the enhancement of the Shi'i and Druze share in that structure and the creation of Shi'i-ruled and Druze-ruled districts (parallel to the Christian-ruled "canton" of Mount Lebanon). When a "Government of National Unity" was set up in Apr. 1984, under Syrian pressure, B. joined it as Minister of Justice. He refused, however, to take his seat until he was given the additional post of a Minister of State for South Lebanon, aiming at total control of that region. Even after that he did not fully participate in the work of the Government, boycotting most of its sessions — together with Junbalat — and sabotaging its efforts to impose unified control. He resided for much of the time in Damascus.

In 1984–85, his Shi'i militias conducted military operations against both the Army and Government (of which he was a member) and against local Sunni militias (*al-Murabitun*) and took control of West Beirut and its southern suburbs and, after the withdrawal of Israeli troops, of the southern coastal plain and most of South Lebanon. These operations were conducted in cooperation with Junbalat's Druze forces, and in July 1985 he cemented

that alliance in a "National United Front." From May-June 1985 B.'s forces attacked the Palestinian guerrilla camps of Beirut and South Lebanon and liquidated PLO control of those in Beirut.

B. became internationally known through his part in the June 1985 hijack of an American airliner by Shi'i extremists. Acting partly as mediator, partly as negotiator for the hijackers, partially taking over from the extremist hijackers, he, together with Syria eventually took credit for the release of the hostages. In Dec. 1985 he and Junbalat agreed with a leader of the Christian "Lebanese Forces" on a plan for a new political structure for Lebanon, in line with Syria's conceptions and demands; but the agreement was rejected by the Christian leadership and remained abortive. B. supported — reluctantly and halfheartedly — the Syrian-sponsored "Ta'if Accord" of Fall 1989 on a new regime for Lebanon (opposed by Christian hardliners), the operations of Fall 1990 by the Army and militias supporting it against General 'Awn and his Christian forces, and the takeover of Greater Beirut by the Army. He did not join the government formed by Salim *Huss after the Ta'if Accord; he was named Minister of State in 'Omari Karameh's government of Dec. 1990, but apparently did not in fact take up that post.

B. and his *al-Amal* have been under constant pressure from more extremist Shi'i groups (*Hizbullah, al-Amal al-Islami, al-Jihad al-Islami*) and inspired and directed by Iran's *Khomeini and his partisans — groups which clamor for control of the Shi'i community and its *al-Amal* militias, for much more extreme political aims (the transformation of Lebanon into an Islamic state, and total war against Israel). Clashes between *al-Amal* and *Hizbullah* escalated from 1988 into a veritable war for control of South Lebanon and the Shi'i southern suburbs of Beirut; this war was defused by Syrian and Iranian intervention.

B. is considered by many as essentially a moderate with limited aims: the enhancement of the Shi'i share of power, and full Shi'i control of South Lebanon and the Biqa'. Towards Israel, too, he may content himself with the achievement of a full Israeli withdrawal from Lebanon and oppose attacks on Israel herself, though he refuses to establish fully-fledged contacts with Israel and reach an agreement with her. He opposes any return of an armed PLO presence to South Lebanon and Beirut. But under the pressure of the extremist Shi'i groups, he frequently adopts more extremist positions so as to maintain his leadership.

BITAR, SALAH-UL-DIN (1912–80) Syrian politician. Born in Damascus to a prominent family, B. studied physics at the Universities of Damascus and Paris and worked as a teacher. In 1940, together with Michel *'Aflaq, he founded among Syrian and Arab students and intellectuals in Paris a leftist-nationalist Pan-Arab group, *al-Ba'th al-'Arabi* (Arab Renaissance), and became editor of its organ, *al-Ba'th*. When the *Ba'th* group became a political party of growing importance, in the late 1940s and the 1950s, B. was one of its chief leaders. In 1954, after the overthrow of *Shishakli, B. was elected to Parliament. In 1956–57 he was Foreign Minister and worked, with his *Ba'th* associates, for the union of Syria and Egypt. When that union was established, in 1958, B. became Minister of State for Arab Affairs, and later Minister of National Guidance, in the government of the UAR. He resigned in 1959, when Abd-ul-*Nasser began curbing the influence of the *Ba'th* leaders and drove them into opposition. In 1961, after Syria's secession from the UAR, B. lost his seat in the elections. After the *Ba'th* officers' coup of 1963, B. became Prime Minister and Foreign Minister. As the *Ba'th* government increasingly turned into an officers' regime, with the civilian politicians and ideologues

losing whatever influence they had, B. had to step down late in 1964 for General Amin al-*Hafez; he also lost his position in the *Ba'th* party high command. With the decline of Hafez, B. briefly became Prime Minister again in Jan. 1966, but was overthrown in the Feb. 1966 coup in which the *Ba'th* leftist "military" faction seized power. He was arrested, but escaped to Lebanon. He was expelled, together with 'Aflaq, from the *Ba'th* party — i.e., from the faction now ruling Syria. In his Lebanese exile, B. was not active in the rival wing of the *Ba'th* controlled by 'Aflaq and linked with the Iraqi *Ba'th*, and later he moved to Paris and dissociated himself from both wings of the *Ba'th*. In 1969 he was sentenced to death *in absentia* by the Syrian court, but in 1971 he was pardoned. In the late 1970s he briefly returned to Syria, but finding cooperation with the al-*Asad regime impossible, he soon left again for Paris, where he became the rallying point for various dissident groups in exile. B. was assassinated in Paris in July 1980 — according to anti-Syrian *Ba'th* spokesmen, by the Syrian secret service.

BIZRI, 'AFIF (b. 1914) Syrian officer and politician. Born in Sidon, Lebanon, to a family report-

Salah-ul-Din Bitar and President Nasser (Bar-David, Tel Aviv)

edly of Kurdish origin. In 1938 B. joined the local armed forces recruited by the French Mandate authorities and from 1945–46 rose in the ranks of the Syrian army. In the early 1940s, while studying in Paris, he became a leftist; while it is not certain whether he formally joined the Syrian Communist Party, he was close to it. He also maintained contacts to the Ba'th group and its officers' cells. In 1955 B. attained the rank of colonel and in 1957 he headed a military court trying prominent politicians for alleged plots with Iraq and the Western powers. The same year he was appointed Chief of Staff and promoted to general. He was considered, in 1957–58, the most influential officer-politician in Syria and was co-instrumental in bringing about her union with Egypt as the UAR. However, he soon fell out with Abd-ul-*Nasser and the Egyptian-dominated regime of the UAR, was dismissed and went into exile. He returned to Syria after her secession from the UAR in 1961, but after the 1963 takeover by the Ba'th he was dismissed from the army in 1965 by General Amin al-*Hafez. After the fall of the latter in the 1966 coup of the extreme "military" faction of the Ba'th, B. tried to regain a position of influence, but did not succeed.

BOUMEDIENNE, HOUARI (Hawari; original name: Muhammad Boukharouba) (1925?–78) Algerian officer and politician. Born in the 'Annaba (Bone) region of eastern Algeria, the son of a farm laborer, B. was later said to have studied Arabic literature at Tunis and Cairo's Al-Azar Universities. He stayed on in Cairo, working as a teacher. It was there that he met *Ben-Bella and other leaders of the incipient Algerian revolt; in 1954 he joined their FLN and soon became one of the revolt's commanders. In 1955 he landed in Western Algeria with a group of rebels and soon headed the rebel formations in the Oran region. He later returned to FLN headquarters, (now in Tunis), became a member of the Revolutionary Council set up in 1956, and in Mar. 1960 was appointed Chief of Staff of the rebel army. After the French-Algerian Agreement of 1962 he led that army into Algeria. When tensions between the guerrillas inside Algeria and the "regular" rebel army entering from Tunisia led to armed clashes, B. firmly insisted on the primacy of the regulars. He also became involved in factional struggles, vigorously backing Ben-Bella. In July 1962 he was dismissed by the FLN Prime Minister Ben-Khedda, but, firmly backed by Ben-Bella, he ignored this order, marched into Algiers and imposed the rule of his army and

Ben-Bella's faction. When Ben-Bella set up the first government of independent Algeria in Sept. 1962, B. became his Defense Minister, and from Sept. 1963 also Deputy Prime Minister (and some thought that he held the real power). But tension developed between the two men; Ben-Bella did not trust B. and saw him as a rival, and B. loathed Ben-Bella's factionalism and his treatment of former comrades-in-arms, his allures of grandeur and his aspirations to all-Arab and African leadership.

In June 1965 B. overthrew Ben-Bella in a coup and imprisoned him. He set up a new Revolutionary Council with himself as chairman. He was now Head of State and Prime Minister — without formally assuming these titles — and remained Minister of Defense. For nearly eleven years he ruled Algeria without seeking a formal institutionalization or popular endorsement of his titles and positions. Only in 1976 did he convene an FLN leadership conference and had it draw up a new "National Charter," which was endorsed by a plebiscite; a "National Conference" under that Charter enacted a new constitution, and under that constitution B. was elected President, as the only candidate, in a referendum in Dec. 1976.

In his over thirteen years as Head of State, B. made no major changes in Algeria's policies. He put less emphasis on ideology and doctrine and stressed the internal regime and economic rather than foreign and international policy, but his regime remained strict, allowing no deviation from the line he laid down and keeping power within the circle of his associates. He not only purged the establishment within Algeria, but during his rule — i.e., probably under his orders — prominent opposition leaders in exile were eliminated by assassination, including Muhammad Khidr and the revolution's most prominent leader after (or with) Ben-Bella, Belkacem Krim. His state socialism remained leftist-radical and his alliance with the Soviet bloc, international leftist neutralism and the inter-Arab "Rejection Front" was firm. While B. had little charisma, his leadership was unquestioned until his death in Dec. 1978.

BOURGUIBA, AL-HABIB (b. 1903) The most prominent leader of Tunisian nationalism, who led Tunisia to independence. President of Tunisia, 1957–87. Born in Monastir, B. studied law in France and began practicing as a lawyer. He was active in the nationalist movement represented by the *Dustur* (Constitution Party). In 1934 he was among a group of younger activists who seceeded

Habib Bourguiba (Popper Agency, London)

from the party, dissatisfied with its traditional leadership and lack of vigor, and founded the *Neo-Dustur* Party which soon became the chief spokesman of Tunisian nationalism. B. was imprisoned in 1934–36 and again from 1938. He was released in 1942 by the German occupiers of France (and from Nov. 1942 also of Tunisia). His official biographers are silent concerning his relations with the Germans after his release; he seems to have collaborated with them to some degree, but this has not been fully clarified. In 1945 he escaped renewed French surveillance and harassment and went to Cairo, where the nationalists of the three Maghrib countries established their headquarters. In 1950 he went to France to negotiate, but when these talks failed he was again arrested. For the final negotiations on Tunisia's independence, 1954–55, he was released but kept under surveillance. During those years B. had to face more extremist elements within his movement — both the guerrillas fighting an armed struggle, and a faction of the *Neo-Dustur* led by his rival Saleh Ben-Yussuf — but he won out.

After Tunisia attained partial independence in 1955 and full independence in Mar. 1956, B. was elected President of the Constituent Assembly in Apr. 1956, and the same month he formed the first government of independent Tunisia, keeping the Defense and Foreign Ministry portfolios himself. With the abolition of the monarchy in July 1957 he was proclaimed President of Tunisia (though the Constitution was completed and adopted only in 1959). He was reelected President, as the only candidate, in 1959, 1964, 1969 and 1974 and in Mar. 1975 was proclaimed President for life. As President he also kept the Premiership until Nov. 1969.

For three decades B. was the supreme leader of Tunisia, determining the character and policies of the state, its regime and its administration. He endeavored to give Tunisia a modernist and moderate, liberal, pro-Western shape. He abolished polygamy, restricted the rule of Islamic law and made the secular institutions of the state supreme. He intervened personally several times to prevent pogroms or mob excesses against Tunisia's Jews. Despite several sharp conflicts with France, he kept Tunisia close to France and the USA, with the French language and French cultural influence nearly dominant. While supporting all Arab cooperation, he had little sympathy for Pan-Arab rhetoric or for the radical leftist-"progressive" regimes and doctrines prevalent in several Arab countries, such as Egypt or Algeria. He frequently clashed with Egypt's *Abd-ul-Nasser. In the spring of 1958, on the eve of Tunisia's admission to the Arab League, he accused Egypt, and Nasser personally, of assisting in plots to subvert Tunisia and assassinate him (the reference was to Saleh Ben-Yussuf, his leading rival, who had found asylum in Egypt since 1956); in Oct.-Nov. 1958 he repeated these accusations in public speeches, severed relations with Egypt and ordered Tunisia's representative to walk out of the first Arab League meeting Tunisia attended, denouncing the League as Egypt's tool. In 1961 he resumed relations with Egypt and returned to the League, but relations remained cool.

B. did not conform to all-Arab positions on Israel. Although he had no sympathy for Israel, he held that the Arab states did not have the military power to solve the conflict by war but should negotiate with Israel and peacefully coexist with her if she accepted their conditions. As to these conditions and demands, B. hardly differed from other Arab leaders; but the prospect of peaceful coexistence he held out in public was in the 1950s and 1960s unusual and unacceptable to the Arab states.

His dissent reached a peak in the spring of 1965 during a tour of the ME when he expounded his ideas to journalists, students and political circles in Egypt, Jordan and Lebanon and formulated them into a plan. There was a storm of protest, the Arab states denounced him and recalled their ambassadors, he was called a traitor and was informed that Tunisia's participation in Arab League sessions was undesirable. B. dissented also on other issues. In 1965 he refused to sever relations with West Germany, as most Arab states did, and in the early 1960s Tunisia was the only Arab country to accept Mauritania's independence. B. absented himself from the all-Arab summit of Casablanca, 1965. In 1966 B. again severed relations with Egypt. In the crisis of 1967 and the Six Day War B. returned to the fold and declared his solidarity with Nasser. But after the war relations reverted to the old pattern: B. was sharply critical of Nasser's Egypt, boycotted Arab League meetings and severed relations with Syria in 1968. After Nasser's death in 1970 relations with Egypt improved. B. also mended relations with Algeria. Those with Libya, on the other hand, sharply deteriorated; in Jan. 1974, B., ailing and very old and with his faculties declining, was persuaded by Libya's al-*Qadhdhafi to proclaim the merger of Tunisia and Libya, and when Tunisia cancelled the merger soon after, tension was aggravated.

The liberal image B. was trying to impart to Tunisia, and to himself, was not borne out by his internal regime. He installed and maintained a *de facto* one-party system, and though in later years rival parties were permitted, B.'s *Neo-Dustur* (since 1964: "Socialist *Dustur*") remained in full control and the only party represented in Parliament. Within the party and the government, B. ruled with an iron fist, ousting and purging any not wholly conforming to his wishes. He also resented any of his aides and associates growing too strong or independent; thus he dismissed Prime Ministers Ladgham (1970), Mouira (1980, after nearly ten years of Premiership) and Mazali (1969, after over six years). Even within his own household his rule was harsh and tainted by plots and intrigues; in 1986 he divorced his wife (whom he had married in 1962 after divorcing his first, French-born, wife) amid rumors of a widespread intrigue, and he broke with his son, al-Habib B. Jr., who had served him in senior posts for many years. As his rule became oppressive and his senility obvious, his succession was for years Tunisia's major problem. He was deposed in Nov. 1987 in a coup headed by Zein-al-'Abedin Ben-Ali who became President. B. was permitted to retire and has since been living in isolation and under strict surveillance.

BURG, JOSEPH (b. 1909)   Israeli politician. A leader of the National Religious Party (NRP). Born in Dresden, Germany, B. studied philosophy at the University of Leipzig. A leader of the *Brit Halutzim Dati'yim* (Union of Religious Pioneers) in Germany. In 1939 he immigrated to Palestine. During the 1940s he worked as a teacher and was one of the leaders of the *Hapo'el Hamizrahi party*.

In 1949 he was elected to the First Knesset, holding his seat there until 1988. In the First Knesset he acted as Deputy Speaker. From 1951 he served in the government for close to 35 years: he was Minister of Health, 1951–52; Post 1952–1958; Welfare 1950–1970; Interior 1970–1984; Police (within the framework of the Ministry of the Interior) 1977–84; Religious Affairs 1981–1986. After his retirement he was appointed World President of the *Mizrahi* and Chairman of the International Council of Yad Vashem. From 1970, after the death of M.H. *Shapira, he became the leader of his party, the NRP.

Burg is known as an intellectual, fluent in many languages, a witty and fascinating orator. However, his influence upon the political scene was minor. Despite his personal political moderation he assisted in the radicalization of his party. Though he was the head of the *Lamifneh* faction, a faction with socialist tendencies, during his time the "historical pact" between the religious Zionists and *Mapai* came to an end and his party became a partner of the *Likud*. During the last few years of his leadership of the NRP, that party lost a great deal of its power. In the 1984 elections it won only four seats in the Knesset, as opposed to the twelve seats which it held after the elections of 1977.

BUTRUS-GHALI   Prominent Egyptian Coptic family. The best-known of its sons was **Butrus B.-Gh.**, Foreign Minister at the end of the 19th century, and in that capacity cosignatory, with Lord Cromer, of the 1899 Anglo-Egyptian Convention which established the condominium over Sudan. Later he was Justice Minister; in that capacity he was responsible for the trial, in 1906, of the Egyptians involved in the Dinshawi Incident, which aroused much resentment and nationalist agitation — and bitter hatred of B.-Gh. personally and anti-Copt incitement in general. In 1908 B.Gh. became Prime Minister — Egypt's first and only

Mirrit Butrus-Ghali (IPS, Tel Aviv)

Coptic-Christian Premier. As Prime Minister he advocated a 40-year extension of the Suez Canal concession — which again caused violent nationalist agitation and was rejected by the National Assembly. B.-Gh. was assassinated in 1910.

Wassef B.-Gh. (1877–1958), the former's son, was Foreign Minister in several governments of the *Wafd* Party — in 1924–25, 1928, 1930 and 1936–37.

Mirrit B.-Gh. (b. 1922), also a grandson of the first-listed, a jurist and political scientist educated in Cairo and Paris, since 1949 teaching at Cairo University, and the author of several studies of international problems. In 1977 he was appointed by President al-*Sadat as Minister of State for Foreign Affairs. He played an important part in the Egypt-Israel peace negotiations, and while he drove a hard bargain and adamantly stuck to positions laid down by Egypt's leaders (and some of his statements were resented in Israel), he strongly advocated peace. He wields considerable influence and is a chief operative of Egypt's foreign policy, though formally he has not attained the position of Foreign Minister (apparently because he is a Copt, a non-Muslim).

C

CAGLAYANGIL, IHSAN SABRI (b. 1908) Turkish politician. After earning a law degree from the University of Istanbul, C. joined the Ministry of the Interior where he served as governor of Antalya (1943–53), Canakkale (1953–4), Sivas (1954), and Bursa (1954–60). Following the military coup in 1960, he was tried in the military court in Yassiada, as he was seen to be identified with the deposed regime of the Democratic Party, but was released. He reentered the political arena for the Justice Party founded to replace the Democratic Party. In 1961 he was appointed to the Senate. He was Minister of Labor (Feb.-Oct. 1965), Foreign Minister in Demizel's governments (1965–1971, 1975–77 and 1977–78). C. was for some time also President of the Senate. Following the military coup of Sept. 1980, he was detained for some time.

CEBESOY, ALI FUAD (1882–1968) Turkish general and politician. Born in Istanbul, into a prominent family (his grandfather, Marshal Mehmet Ali Pasha, represented Turkey at the Berlin Congress, 1878, and his father, Ismail Fazil Pasha, was the first Minister of Public Works in the Turkish Republic), C. attended St. Joseph's Lyceum in Istanbul, Istanbul War College (where he was a classmate of Ataturk), and the Academy of War in Istanbul.

From 1908, C. served in various military posts — Military Attache in Rome in 1908, commander of a division and chief of staff of an army corps in the Balkan Wars in 1911–12 (wounded three times). In 1914, he commanded the first World War I attack on the Suez Canal, and also saw action on the Russian front; he commanded the defense of Jerusalem in 1917.

After the war, as the Commander of the Central Anatolian Army Corps, he forced the Sultan's government in Istanbul to submit to the resolutions of the National Congress (1919). After the revolution, he became Vice-President of the National Assembly. He left politics in 1926 after a dispute

with Ataturk, returning in 1933 as a representative of Konya in the National Assembly. He was assistant to the chairman of the Turkish Parliament, Minister of Public Works 1939–42 and of Communications and Transport 1943–46. In 1947–48 he was elected Speaker/President of Parliament. In the later 1940s he broke with the ruling Republican People's Party and became a leading figure of the opposition. From 1950 to 1954 he represented Eskisehir in Parliament as an independent elected on the list of the Democratic Party (in power since 1950). He was also Ambassador in Moscow.

C.'s writings include *The Political and Military State of the Ottoman Empire during the First World War* (1937); *Memoirs of the National Struggle Movement* (1953); *Memoirs of Moscow* (1955); and *My Political Memoirs* (1957).

CEMAL (JAMAL) PASHA (1872–1922) Turkish officer and politician, one of the chief leaders of the "Young Turks." C. graduated from the Cadet School and the War Academy in 1861 and served in Macedonia and Thrace. As a young officer he joined underground groups preparing a rebellion (organized in 1908 and the "Committee of Union and Progress") and their Revolution of 1908, as became a member of the military government. He later served as governor of Adana and Baghdad provinces, head of the security forces, and Minister of Public Works.

In 1913 he staged a coup, together with *Enver Pasha and *Talat Pasha, that reinstated a government of the "Young Turks," became Military Governor of Istanbul, Minister of Naval Affairs, and together with Enver and Talaat in fact ruled Turkey during the First World War. In 1914, he commanded the Palestine front and the unsuccessful offensive against Egypt. As governor of Syria, he prevented and suppressed stirrings of Arab nationa-lism and oppressed the Armenian minority. His rule in Syria bore elements of a personal dictatorship. Following Turkey's defeat in World

Cemal (Jamal) Pasha (Popper Agency, London)

War I, he escaped to Germany, to Afghanistan, and later to Tiflis, where he was assassinated in 1922 by an Armenian nationalist. His *Memoirs of a Turkish Statesman* were published in 1922 in Munich and London.

CHAMOUN, CAMILLE (**Sham'un, Kamil**) (1900–87) Lebanese politician. President of Lebanon 1952–58. One of the top leaders of the Maronite-Christian community. Born in Deir al-Qamar in southern Mount Lebanon (the Shuf) — a region that remained his home and power base until 1983, when in the civil war it was taken over by Druze militias. C. graduated from the French Law College of Beirut (1925). He was a member of most Parliaments since 1934. He became a Minister in 1938 (Finance) and again in 1943 (Interior). In that year he played an important role in the talks leading to the unwritten intercommunal "National Covenant." In 1944 he was appointed Minister to Great Britain and in 1946 headed Lebanon's delegation to the UN, as Ambassador. Chamoun belonged to Bishara al-*Khouri's "Constitutional

Bloc" that stressed Lebanon's Arab character and advocated her integration in all-Arab alignments and the termination of special ties to France. He was considered anti-French (and pro-British). In 1947–48 he served again as a Cabinet Minister. However, when President Khouri arranged, in May 1948, to have the Constitution amended so that he could be elected to a second term (as he duly was, in 1949) C. resigned and joined the opposition. As resistance to Khouri increased during his second term and he was accused of corruption and malpractices, C. staged a semi-coup in the summer of 1952 that forced Khouri to resign. In Sept. 1952 C. was elected President, with 74 of Parliament's 77 votes.

As President, C. followed a policy of close relations with the West and cautious neutrality towards the other countries. His pro-Western attitudes brought him into growing conflict with the swelling tide of leftist-Nasserist tendencies inside and outside Lebanon. These forces also resented his authoritarian inclinations and accused him of rigging the elections of 1957. When Syria and Egypt merged in 1958, C. stoutly opposed leftist and Muslim trends pushing Lebanon to join the Syrian-Egyptian camp. Clashes, that developed in May 1958 into a civil war, were also fanned by rumors that C. intended, like his predecessor, to seek a constitutional amendment to secure his reelection for a second term. C. was the main force behind Lebanon's complaint to the UN Security Council against the Syrian-Egyptian intervention and her request for the help of the U.S. armed forces leading in mid-July to the dispatch of U.S. Marines. A compromise agreement that ended the civil war in Sept. 1958 included C.'s renunciation of any plan to run for a second presidential term, and with the end of his term, the same month, he stepped down. He now founded a political party of his own, the "National Liberal Party," and remained an elder statesman and a powerful influence; but he returned to a governmental position only for a year as Minister during the civil war of 1975–76 and as Finance Minister in the "National Unity" Government since 1984 — two governments that did not really function.

In the years since 1958 C. became a spokesman for the Christian camp resisting Lebanon's active integration in Pan-Arab alignments and wishing to preserve her pluralistic character under Christian-Maronite leadership and her communal structure protecting that pluralism. In the 1960s C. and his National-Liberal Party established a "Triple

Alliance" with the camp's other factions — Pierre *Jumayyil's "Phalanges" and Raymond Edde's "National Bloc," but their cooperation was never complete and the three factions frequently followed divergent policies. During the civil war from 1975 onward C. headed a rather loose "Lebanese Front" of various Christian-Maronite-dominated factions that resisted a Muslim-leftist takeover; but his chairmanship was little more than nominal and the real decisions were taken by the leaders of the factions and their "militias." C. and his party set up armed militias of their own — the "Tigers," active mainly in the area of his power base southeast of Beirut. In 1980, however, the Phalanges' hardening claim to complete domination and exclusive leadership of all Christian forces led to escalating clashes between them and C.'s Tigers, and finally the Tigers were completely eliminated as a fighting force (their remnants were incorporated in the Phalanges-led "Lebanese Forces"). Thus C. did not play an active role in the post-1982 regime headed by the Jumayyil brothers. When the Phalanges' and Bashir *Jumayyil's cooperation with Israel was at its height, in 1982, C. seems to have been somewhat more reserved (in the past he had never openly advocated cooperation with Israel — though he had later delegated his son Danny, groomed as his political heir, to maintain contact). Yet, when President Amin *Jumayyil reneged on his brother's policies and annulled the May 1983 agreement with Israel, C. opposed that step and recommended continuing Lebanon-Israel cooperation. However, he agreed to join, in Apr. 1984, the "Government of National Unity" Jumayyil was compelled to form — a government headed and dominated by C.'s leading adversaries; but he

Camille Chamoun (IPS, Tel Aviv)

seemed to regard this as a token contribution to national reconciliation and was not very active in the affairs of the Government or his Ministry. C. published his memoirs in 1949 and, in a revised edition, in 1963, as well as a book on the Lebanese crisis, in 1978.

C.'s son **Danny Chamoun** (1934–90), took over the leadership of his father's camp when C. died in 1987. He was murdered in Oct. 1990, with his wife and two small sons, during the takeover of Beirut by the army and the pro-Syrian militias.

D

AL-DAJANI Prominent Palestinian-Arab family, Jerusalem. The large clan is divided into several branches, some of which bear additional names, such as Wafa' D., al-Dawudi D. Many sons of the D. clan have been prominent as administrators, professionals, political activists. Among them: **'Aref D.,** a leader of the national movement in the early 1920s, President of the Muslim-Christian Association and of several congresses and committees. **Hassan Sidqi D.,** one of the main leaders of the al-*Nashashibi-led opposition, was assassinated in 1938; his assassination signified the escalating terror employed by the dominating al-*Husseini faction against the opposition that induced the latter to organize armed counterterror squads. In the 1940s and 1950s his son **'Omar Sidqi al-D.** was a confidant and political agent of King *Abdullah of Jordan (though he was never appointed to high office). **Sa'id Wafa' D.** (b. 1915) was a district officer in the Mandate government, served in the Jordanian administration, and from 1965 was a Cabinet Minister several times. **Kamal D.** and **'Ali D.** also were Jordanian government ministers in the 1960s, as were **Nijm-ul-Din D.** in the 1970s, after serving as Ambassador, and **Raja'i D.** in the 1980s. **Ahmad Sidqi D.** is a senior PLO functionary, a member of the PLO Executive Committee 1977–85, a director of the PLO research center and co-founder of its organ *Shu'un Filastiniyya*. Another prominent D. family, from Jaffa, is not related to the Jerusalem D.'s.

DARWISH, MAHMUD (b. 1941) Palestinian-Arab poet and writer, the most prominent of the Israeli Arab poets of nationalist resistance and since 1987 a member of the Executive of the Palestine Liberation Organization (PLO). Born in the village of Barwa near Acre, during Israel's War of Independence in 1948 his family fled to Lebanon, but a year later they infiltrated back to Israel and lived in the village of Deir al-Asad in the Galilee. D. went to high school in nearby Kafr Yasif. He then worked at a printing press in Acre and published several poems in Israeli Arabic journals.

He became a journalist and joined the editorial board of the Communist biweekly *al-Ittihad* and the monthly cultural and literary magazine *al-Jadid*; later on he joined the Communist Party. In his anthologies *Olive Leaves* (1964), *Lover from Palestine* (1964) and *Birds without Wings* (1961) he depicted in lyrical poems the dispersion and suffering of the Palestinian refugees in their camps. After a year in Moscow, 1970, in 1971 D. left for Cairo, where he announced his decision to leave Israel and stay in Arab countries; this was received with disappointment by his Communist collegues in Israel but applauded in the Arab world. In Cairo he contributed to the daily newspaper *al-Ahram*.

In 1972 D. went to Beirut and became an editor of *Shu'un Falastiniyya (Palestinian Affairs)*, the monthly magazine of the Palestine Liberation Organization (PLO), and in 1975 Director of the PLO Research Center. Since 1982 he has edited *al-Karmel*, the organ of the Palestinian Writers and Journalists Association (published in Cyprus) and was also elected the Chairman of the Association.

Many of his poems were translated into several languages (e.g., *The Music of Human Flesh*, London-Washington 1980, selected and translated by Denys Johnson-Davies).

During Israel's Lebanon War D. was with *'Arafat during the siege of Beirut and the expulsion of the PLO in August 1982 (he went to Cyprus). He wrote several poems and books about this traumatic experience. D. was awarded the Lotus Prize by the Union of Afro-Asian Writers, 1969, the Shield of the Palestinian Revolution 1981, the Ibn Sina Prize bestowed by the USSR, 1982, and the Lenin Prize, 1983.

DAWALIBI, MA'RUF (b. 1907) Syrian politician. Born in Aleppo, a Sunni Muslim, D. studied law in Aleppo, Damascus and Paris and from 1935 to 1939 practiced law in Aleppo.

During World War II, D. stayed in Paris and headed a pro-Axis association of Syrian students which enjoyed the patronage of the Mufti of Jerusalem, Hajj Amin al-*Husseini, then in Berlin. These contacts introduced him to inter-Arab and Islamic activism. After the war he reopened his law practice and from 1947 also taught at the law faculty. He belonged to the Aleppo-centered "People's Party" and was elected to Parliament on its list. After *Shishakli's first coup, Dec. 1949, he served as Minister for Economic Affairs, and in 1951 as President of Parliament. In Nov. 1951, during the crisis between Shishakli and the politicians, he was Prime Minister for a single day (removed by Shishakli's second coup). Following Shishakli's fall, 1954, D. was Defense Minister for a few months. He put a strong Islamic emphasis on his political posture. In the 1950s he opposed the growing influence of radical officers' cliques, particularly the *Ba'th* group, and opposed the union with Egypt. The period of that union, the United Arab Republic, 1958–61, he spent in self-imposed exile in Lebanon. After the dissolution of the UAR, D. was Prime Minister, 1961–62, until removed by the officers coup of Mar. 1962. Since 1962 he has lived in exile — most of the time in Sa'udi Arabia, where he has served the king as a legal adviser,

Moshe Dayan (GPO, Jerusalem)

special envoy and chairman of Islamic congresses and committees. Since 1974 he has been President of the "World Muslim Congress" headquartered in Karachi, Pakistan.

DAYAN, MOSHE (1915–81)   Israeli military and political leader. Born in the Degania *kvutzah* (communal settlement); his father Shmuel D., who came to Palestine with the Second *Aliyah*, was a prominent *Mapai* activist. When D. was six the family moved to the first *moshav* (smallholders' cooperative) — Nahalal — cofounding it. As a youth, D. was active in the *Haganah*. He was arrested by the British in 1939, charged with the possession of illegal firearms and sentenced to ten years' imprisonment. In 1941 he was released to lead an auxiliary force of the *Haganah* cooperating with the British army in the conquest of Lebanon, then under Vichy rule. He was severely wounded in Lebanon and lost his left eye. The eye patch he wore from then on became well-known worldwide.

During the War of Independence D. commanded a battalion which took Ramle and Lod. Later he was put in charge of the Jerusalem area. From then on his progress up the military ladder was swift — he was *Mapai's* counterbalance to the generals of the War of Independence, most of whom were *Mapam Ahdut Ha'avodah* men. In 1950 he served as Commander of the Southern Region; in 1952, as Commander of the Northern Command; later, as Chief of Army Operations; and from 1953 to 1958, as Chief of Staff. During the four years he headed the army he turned it into a well-trained fighting force and was considered an outstanding Chief of Staff. His military leadership reached its zenith during the Sinai Campaign of late 1956.

After his release from the army Dayan turned to politics within the framework of *Mapai*. He was elected to the Fourth Knesset and from 1959 to 1964 served as Minister of Agriculture. At the same time he was a member of the "Young Generation" — a group to which *Ben Gurion wanted to hand the reins of leadership, over the heads of the veterans. In 1964 he resigned from the government due to a difference of opinion with Prime Minister Levi *Eshkol. Several months later, after much hesitation, he formed a new political party — *Rafi*. This earned him the reputation of a fence sitter, unwilling to be fully loyal to a party or a leader.

On the eve of the Six Day War, 1967, D. was co-opted into the government as Defense Minister — as a result of public pressure and political manipulations. Thus he came back from the "political wasteland" which he had inhabited for several years. He served as Defense Minister until 1974. These years were the pinnacle of his public activity. His popularity rose to new heights. He used this popularity and repeated threats to leave his party (the Labor Party, with which his *Rafi* group had reunited in 1968, and the Alignment) and form an independent political group, to force his position upon his party's leaders. For example, during the summer of 1973 he forced them to accept the "Galili Document" whose gist was the rapid development of the occupied territories, including the construction of a deep-water port in Yamit.

The Yom Kippur War in 1973 shattered his political image — he was identified with its "failure" and many questions were raised regarding the way he functioned during the war. Following the war he was forced to leave his position as Defense Minister.

In 1977, after the political victory of the right-wing *Likud*, he crossed the lines and became Foreign Minister in Begin's government. In this capacity he was one of the architects of the peace treaty with Egypt. But in 1979 he resigned from the government and in 1981 he formed his own party. That party won only two mandates in the elections — a failure that may be seen as a symbol of his decline from a political and military oracle into a sick and lonely old man. Soon after the elections he died.

D. was one of the *sabra* generation (men born in Israel) reaching the highest political and military rank. He was a man of contradictions. He was innovative in his concepts and his way of thinking and flouted convention and rules. He was a brave military leader, but as a politician did not fight for his convictions (for example, his proposal in 1971 that Israel withdraw from the Suez Canal and allow it to reopen), and more than once shirked taking responsibility for his actions. He had much to do with building up the fighting spirit of the army — but also with destroying norms in Israeli society.

DEMIREL, SÜLEYMAN(b. 1924)   Turkish politician, Prime Minister 1965–71, 1975–77, 1977–78 and 1979–80. Born in a village in the province of Isparta, D. studied civil engineering in Istanbul and the USA. He entered the Civil Service and became Director of the State Water Board. After the military coup of 1960 he joined the Justice Party, newly formed to replace the ousted and banned Democratic Party, and in 1964 succeeded

Suleyman Demirel (Bar-David, Tel Aviv)

Gen. *Gumuspala as leader of the party. In 1965 D. joined Suat *Urguplu's coalition cabinet as Deputy Premier, and after his party won the elections later the same year, he became Prime Minister. During his Premiership of over five years, D. took care not to antagonize the army, restrained the right wing of his party and followed a middle-of-the-road policy in both external and internal affairs, strongly maintaining democratic order. However, social reforms were slow in coming and political pressures on the government degenerated into continuous disorders. In March 1971 D. was forced to resign after an ultimatum presented by the chiefs of the armed forces. During the years of shifting coalition governments that followed, D. headed three governments in 1975–77, 1977–78 and 1979–80. But as unrest escalated and terrorism spread, the armed forces again intervened in Sept. 1980 and ousted D. and his government. D. was exiled into forced residence for some time, and when released, was banned from any political activity and public appearances. He was reported to be behind a new Great Turkey Party in 1983, but the party was banned and D. was again exiled for three months. The ban on D. and other pre-1980 politicians had been lifted in Sept. 1980 by a referendum, and D. took over the chairmanship of a new right-wing True Path Party that had been forming since 1983. The party won only 59 seats in the elections of 1987, leaving *Ozal's Motherland Party as the main representative of the right and the party forming the government, and D. has since been vocal in the opposition to Ozal's regime.

D's party emerged as the largest group in the Oct. 1991 elections, and D. was expected to form a coalition goverment.

DENKTAS (DENKTASH), RA'UF (b. 1924) Turkish-Cypriot lawyer and politician, President of the "Turkish Republic of North Cyprus" since 1975. Born in Paphos, educated at Lincoln's Inn, London. In legal practice in Cyprus 1947–49; Crown Counsellor and Acting Solicitor-General 1949–58; Chairman, Federation of Turkish Cypriot Associations 1959–60; elected President of the Turkish Communal Chamber 1960. As a result of the inter-communal disturbances of December 1963, D. was denied permission to return to Cyprus after a journey to London, and lived in Turkey 1964–68 (an attempt to return clandestinely to Cyprus in 1967 failed and he was deported). Permitted to return in April 1968, he became Vice-President of the Turkish-Cypriot "Transitional Administration."

He formed a hard-line faction among the Turkish Cypriots which became from 1970 dominant in their representative bodies. When the Turkish Cypriots seceded in 1974 and formed their own separate state, aided by invading Turkish troops (and recognized only by Turkey), D. became the new State's President. He was reelected in 1976, 1981, 1985 and 1990.

DINUR (original name: Dinaburg), **BEN-ZION** (1884–1973)   Israeli historian, educator and politician. Born in the Ukraine, D. studied at the Universities of St. Petersburg and Bern. From 1921 he was director of the Beit Hakerem Teachers' College. He also taught at the Department of Jewish History of the Hebrew University in Jerusalem, stressing the longing for Zion and the Zionist dream as the center of the history of the Jewish people. D. was also active in public affairs, e.g., in *Mapai*; during the Holocaust he was one of the heads of the "*Al Domi*" group which criticized the *Yishuv's* leadership's lack of action in face of the destruction of European Jewry.

After the establishment of the State of Israel, D. was elected on the *Mapai* list to the First Knesset. From 1951 to 1955 he was Minister of Education and Culture. During his term of office, the law of compulsory public schooling was passed and the political trends in the educational system were abolished. Another law passed during his term established Yad Vashem as a national memorial authority to commemorate the Holocaust; D. himself was its first chairman 1953–59.

D. wrote many books and published source books and documentation on the history of the Jewish people. He was awarded the Israel Prize twice: first for his work as a historian and the second time as an educator.

DIZENGOFF, MEIR (1860–1936)   One of the founders of Tel Aviv and its first mayor, a leader of the moderate right wing in the Yishuv. Born in a village in Bessarabia (then part of Russia), he volunteered for the Russian Army in 1882 and drew close to revolutionary circles. In 1885 he was arrested and jailed for eight months. After his release he founded a group of *Hovevei Zion* (Lovers of Zion) and afterwards went to Paris to study chemical engineering. In 1892, after completing his studies, he was sent by Baron Rothschild to set up a wine bottle factory in Tantura, south of Haifa (one of the first attempts to found a factory in Palestine).

After the factory failed he returned to Russia where he was elected to the central committee of *Hovevei Zion*. He was a delegate to the Fifth and Sixth Zionist Congresses (1901, 1903). In 1904 he founded the Geula company for purchasing land in Palestine and returned to Palestine. In 1909 he was one of the founders of the Ahuzat Bayit quarter near Jaffa which became the city of Tel Aviv. D. was elected to lead the neighborhood council.

During the First World War he was active in alleviating the plight of those arrested and expelled by the Ottoman authorities, e.g., the Jews of Jaffa and Tel Aviv expelled in 1917. From the end of the war as Mayor of Tel Aviv, he devoted all his energies to developing the "First Hebrew City," which during the 1920s and 1930s grew to a city of 150,000 and became the center of the Jewish *Yishuv* in Palestine.

Dizengoff was also active in the general politics of the *Yishuv*. In 1926–27 he was a member of the Executive of the Zionist Organization. He was the most prominent leader of the moderate right wing, but did not succeed in organizing it in a general political framework.

E

EBAN, ABBA (b. 1915)   Israeli diplomat and political leader. Born in South Africa and raised in Britain. During the Second World War he served with British intelligence in Cairo and Jerusalem. After the war he joined the Political Department of the Jewish Agency and served as liason to UNSCOP and a member of the delegation to the special assembly of the United Nations discussing Palestine.

In 1949, following Israel's admission to the United Nations, he was appointed head of the delegation to the UN and a year later in 1950 he became ambassador to the USA. Until 1959 he served concurrently in both these posts — the most important positions in Israeli diplomacy. E., a brilliant orator and gifted diplomat, excelled in presenting and defending Israeli policy — even when he disagreed with it. A prime example of this was his speech at the UN defending the "Kinneret operation" in December 1955, while simultaneously, he wrote to *Ben-Gurion expressing his reservations concerning that operation. (Ben-Gurion answered that he, too, had had reservations about the operation, but after hearing E.'s speech at the UN, he had become convinced of its necessity.)

Upon his return to Israel in 1959 E. joined *Mapai* and entered political life. He was elected to the Fourth Knesset and was a Minister without Portfolio. After the resignation of Zalman *Aran, during the summer of 1960, he became Minister of Education and Culture, a position in which he served for three years. In July 1963, he became Levi *Eshkol's Deputy Prime Minister. From 1966 to 1974 he was Foreign Minister in Levi Eshkol's and Golda *Meir's governments. After the Six Day War he was one of the architects of UN Resolution 242.

As Foreign Minister in Golda Meir's government his position was problematic. His views were considerably more moderate than those of the Prime Minister, and he had to publicly represent policies with which he did not always agree. Also, Yitzhak *Rabin, as ambassador to Washington, maintained direct contact with the Prime Minister behind his

Abba Eban (Israel Sun Ltd.)

back. When the Rabin government was formed in 1974, E. was not included. Between 1984 and 1988 he served as Chairman of the Knesset Committee for Foreign Affairs and Defense. In 1988 E. was not included in the Alignment list of candidates to the Knesset — an omission which angered many in Israel and abroad.

E. is a man of many talents — he is fluent in many languages and even after being out of the government for many years, his name is known throughout the world. However, his influence on the formation of Israeli politics, including its foreign policy, has been limited, and in recent years, negligible.

ECEVIT, BÜLENT (b. 1925)   Turkish politician.

Born in Istanbul to an upper-class family, E. graduated from the prestigious Robert College High School (1944) and studied at the Istanbul University Faculty of Letters. He joined the government press agency in Ankara. From 1946 to 1950 he was an assistant in the London Turkish Embassy Press Office and studied in London University. In 1950 he returned to Turkey and joined the editorial staff of *Ulus*, the daily paper of the Republican Peoples's Party, (RPP — since 1950 no longer in power). In the mid-1950s he studied at Howard University in Washington, on a Rockefeller Foundation scholarship. In 1957 E. was elected to Parliament, for the RPP. Thanks to his close relationship with Party leader Ismet *Inonu and his association with a group of reformist intellectuals headed by Turhan *Feyzioglu, he gained increasing influence in the party. After the 1960 coup, he was appointed by his party to the nominated assembly that drafted the constitution of 1961. That year he was reelected to the Turkish Parliament and in Nov. 1961 joined Inonu's government as Minister of Labor, until 1965. He continuously strengthened his position in the RPP leadership and apparatus and was the party's General Secretary, 1966–71, pushing it further to the left. In March 1971 he resigned in protest against the party's collaboration with the military intervention or semi-coup. He thus broke with Inonu. In May 1972, backed by a majority at an emergency congress of the party, he forced Inonu to retire and was elected in his place as chairman of the RPP.

When the RPP emerged from the elections of 1973 as the strongest party, though without a majority, E. founded a coalition government. He was Prime Minister Jan.-Nov. 1974, June-July 1977, and Jan. 1978-Nov. 1979. He failed to halt the anarchy, terrorism and inflation that plagued Turkey. In Nov. 1979 he was forced to resign after 11 of his ministers had already done so.

When the army headed by Kenan *Evren intervened in Sept. 1980, the RPP was banned and E. was arrested; he was released after a month, but was exiled and barred from making any public political statements (and was rearrested several times for violating that ban).

When political parties were repermitted in 1983, time was too short for E.'s group to organize for the elections of Nov. 1983 (the RPP did not revive, and E. himself was barred from political activity). In 1985 a Democratic-Socialist Left Party was founded, with E.'s wife in the chair, and some members of Parliament joined it. The ban on E. was lifted in Sept. 1987 only and he assumed the charimanship of his Democratic Left Party. However, the party won only 8.5% of the vote and not a single seat in the elections of 1987, and E. resigned in 1988. He was reelected party chairman in Jan. 1989, but Erdal *Inonu's Socialist-Democratic Party (SODEPOP) had become the main organization of the moderate left, and E.'s group was nearly eclipsed.

EDDE, EMILE (1886–1949)   Lebanese politi-

cian, President of Lebanon 1936–41. A Maronite Christian, French-educated lawyer, E. was one of the advocates of the creation of "Greater Lebanon" in 1920. Later he realized that the addition of a large Muslim population, jeopardizing the Christians' primacy in Lebanon, was a grave mistake, and contemplated a reduction in Lebanon's territory to restore that primacy (though such a view was hardly aired in public in his lifetime).

E. served in the administration of the French Mandate and was Prime Minister in 1929–30. In the 1930s he emerged as the leader of the camp that took a pro-French attitude, wanted Lebanon to remain a pluralistic, multi-community state, protected by France, with the Christian Maronites as the predominant community, and opposed the notion that she was part of the Arab world and should cultivate close ties with it and be integrated in pan-Arab formations. E. was also willing to reach an agreement with the Jews in Palestine; he had several meetings with *Weizmann and other Zionist leaders and agreed, in general terms, that Maronite-led Lebanon and Jewish Palestine should cooperate — though he concluded no formal agreement.

In 1934, E. organized his camp in the "National Bloc" party, and in 1936 he was elected President, defeating Bishara al-*Khouri. He continued as Head of State even when the French suspended the Constitution, in Sept. 1939, and resigned only in 1941. With the restoration of a parliamentary regime in 1943, his supporters sought to have him reelected as President, but eventually his candidacy was not put to the vote (8 pro-E. members of Parliament absented themselves from the session that elected his rival Khouri). In the crisis of Nov. 1943, E. agreed to be appointed Head of State by the French. However, when British and American pressure compelled France to retreat and to reinstate the President, government and Parliament, E. was deposed, thoroughly discredited; in Mar. 1944 he was expelled from Parliament and his political career ended.

E.'s sons Raymond and Pierre continued to lead his "National Bloc" — but their views were not as clear-cut as their father's, their factional-tactical positions vacillated, and the party declined. **Raymond Edde** (b. 1913) has been a member of Parliament since 1953 (except for a defeat in the elections of 1964 — repaired in a 1965 by-election) and led the small parliamentary group of his party (usually 3–6 seats) in a loose "Triple Alliance" with *Chamoun's "National Liberals" and *Jumayyil's Phalanges; but factional rivalries between him and both Chamoun and Jumayyil prevented the formation of a strong, stable bloc of Christian parties. In 1958–59 Raymond E. was one of the four ministers of the compromise government set up after the civil war of 1958. He served again as a minister in 1968–69, but usually he was in opposition. He was mentioned as a candidate for the presidency in 1976 and again in 1982, but no formal candidacy was put to the vote. For some years Raymond E. strongly opposed the use of Lebanese territory as an operational base by the Palestinian guerrillas and the "Cairo Agreement" of 1969 that was intended to regulate that use, and suggested an international peace force. He also opposed Syrian ambitions and policies in Lebanon, but he was prepared to compromise on the preservation of Lebanon's communal regime and Christian predominance. In the civil war since 1975 he did not actively support the Christian-conservative camp, and his National Bloc did not establish a militia. In recent years he mostly lives in France and is no longer politically active.

Pierre Edde (b. 1921) was a member of Parliament several times from 1951, and briefly served as Finance Minister four times, but usually has been active mainly in the economic and financial arena.

EHRLICH, SIMHA (1915–83)   Israeli industrialist and politician. Born in Poland, E. immigrated to Palestine in 1938. During the 1950s he was active in the Tel Aviv branch of the General Zionist Party. In 1955 he was elected to the Tel Aviv Municipal Council and during the 1960s was deputy to Mayor Mordechai Namir.

E. was first elected to the Knesset in 1969 and, after the death of Yosef *Sapir and Dr. Elimelech Rimalt's retirement, he became the head of the Liberal Party. In 1977, after the *Likud's* victory, he became Finance Minister. In that capacity he initiated an "economic upheaval," a liberalization,

abolishing the limitations placed on foreign currency. This step had dire consequences for Israel's economy leading to a large increase of imports and rapid inflation reaching 25% in 1977 and 100% in 1979. E. was forced to resign, but was appointed Deputy Prime Minister. After the 1981 elections he became Minister of Agriculture.

E. was the first of the Liberal Party leaders who fully accepted Menahem *Begin's leadership, and though his own political position was more moderate than Begin's, he did not oppose him.

ENVER, PASHA (1881–1922)   Turkish military and political leader. Born in Istanbul, E. graduated from the Military Academy and, as a professional officer, played an active part in the events in Macedonia leading to the 1908 revolution of the "Young Turks." He served as military attache in Berlin and returned to fight against the Italians in the Tripolitanian War, 1911. In January 1913 E. led a coup which brought down the Liberal Party then in power in Istanbul; together with *Talat Pasha and *Jemal Pasha he then formed a "triumvirate" that ruled Turkey until 1918. Having become a military hero by recapturing Edirne (Adrianople) from the Bulgarians in the second *Balkan War, 1913, E. was promoted to the rank of General and appointed Minister of War. With strong *Pan-Turkish and pro-German inclinations, he was instrumental in bringing about Turkey's entry into World War I as an ally of Germany. During the war he led the Ottoman Third Army in a disastrous campaign on the Russian front. After the Armistice he was tried and sentenced to death; he fled to Berlin and then to Russia and Turkestan, where he intrigued against the new Kemalist Turkey and took part in a Muslim nationalist insurrection in the course of which he was killed.

EQBAL, MANUCHEHR (1908? 1909?–77)   Iranian politician, Prime Minister 1957–1960. E. was born in Mashhad to a prominent family. One of his brothers, Khosrow, was a deputy to the counsel of the Anglo-Iranian Oil Company in London, while another, Ali, was elected to the *Majlis* (Parliament) several times. E. studied medicine in Montpellier and Paris, specializing in infectious and tropical diseases.

After returning to Iran, he completed his army service as a doctor at the Government and Military Hospital and Director of the Health Department in Mashhad. From 1939 he was assistant professor in medicine at Tehran University. He served as

Minister of Health (1940–41, 1942–44 and 1945), Education (1944–45), the Interior (1949), and Communications (1950), and as Governor of Azerbaijan and Chancellor of Tabriz University. From 1954 to 1957 he was Dean of Tehran University.

In 1953 E. was named a member of the Senate and in 1956 served as a Minister of the Imperial Court. He was Prime Minister from 1957 to 1960 (he resigned after the general elections of 1960 were cancelled because of irregularities). The following year he was elected to the *Majlis*. He headed the Iranian delegation to UNESCO. In 1963, E. was appointed Chairman of the Board and General Director of the National Iranian Oil Company.

ERIM, NIHAT(1912–80)   Turkish educator and politician. Born in Kandura, he studied at the Universities of Istanbul (1936) and Paris (1938). He taught international law and political science at Ankara University from 1939. In 1943 he was appointed editor of *Ulus*, the newpaper of the Republican People's Party (RPP), and also served as a law consultant in the Foreign Office. In 1945 he was elected to Parliament for the RPP. He served as Minister of Public Works (1948) and Deputy Prime Minister (1949–50). From 1950 to 1954 he was again editor of *Ulus*. In 1959 he headed the Turkish delegation to negotiations on Cyprus. E. became Prime Minister from Mar. 1971 to Apr. 1972 as an independent, after his ties with the RPP had loosened and he had finally left the party. E., considered a moderate reformist, was assassinated in 1980 — apparently by leftist extremists. He published books and articles and was a member of the *Academie Diplomatique Internationale*.

ESHKOL(original name: Shkolnik), **LEVI**(1895–1969) Israeli statesman. Born in the Ukraine, E. immigrated to Palestine in 1914. He worked as an agricultural laborer and joined *Hapo'el Hatza'ir*. In 1918 he volunteered for the Jewish Battalion of the British Army, in opposition to his party's position. In 1920 he was one of the founders of Kvutza (now Kibbutz) Degania B where he remained a member until his death.

In the 1920s he was among the co-founders of the *Histadrut's* economic institutions, such as *Nir*, the Agricultural Center and the *Histadrut's* housing company. In the 1930s he was an emissary in Germany, mainly for financial arrangements and transfers, and from 1937 to 1946 he directed the *Histadrut's* Water Company which later became

Levi Eshkol (GPO, Jerusalem)

Mekorot. In the late 1930s and 1940s he was a member of the national headquarters of the *Haganah* and in the 1940s secretary of the Tel Aviv Workers Council. During the War of Independence he was *Ben Gurion's deputy in the Defense Ministry, responsible for the economic and financial aspects of the war. In 1948 he was elected to the Jewish Agency Executive and was made Head of its Settlement Department. In this position, which he held until 1963, he was the main architect of large-scale rural settlement, responsible for the establishment of hundreds of agricultural settlements, mainly of the cooperative *moshav* type, by the new immigrants streaming into Israel. For some years he was also the Treasurer of the Jewish Agency.

From the early 1950s E. was part of the *Mapai* leadership. In 1951 he was elected to the Knesset and held a seat until his death. In 1951–52 he was Minister of Agriculture and Development. In 1952 he replaced Eliezer *Kaplan as Finance Minister. In this position, which he held until 1963, shared the responsiblily for the rapid economic development of those years. He strengthened his position as Ben Gurion's right hand man and as a *Mapai* leader. In the crisis over the "Lavon Affair" he brought about *Lavon's forced resignation and put together the new Ben-Gurion government after the 1961 elections. But the aftermath of the "Lavon Affair" caused a deepening rift between Ben-Gurion and the *Mapai* leaders, and principally E.

After Ben-Gurion's resignation in 1963 E. was the natural candidate to replace him as Prime Minister and Defense Minister. During his first years in this position he carried out several reforms, including a liberalization of the economic regime. He abolished limitations placed on the Arabs of Israel. He turned the Broadcasting Authority from a department in the Prime Minister's Office into an independent authority. As Defense Minister he strengthened the army and developed security and arms-purchasing agreements with the United States. He passed a government decision to bring Ze'ev *Jabotinsky's remains to Israel for reburial, thus easing the relationship between the government and the opposition. However, Ben-Gurion continued his attempts to undermine E.'s position and authority, resigned from *Mapai*, during the summer of 1965, and entered the elections of that year with a separate party. But E. and *Mapai* won the elections and E. again headed the government.

In May 1967, on the eve of the Six Day War, the growing crisis and political pressure forced E. to widen his government into a national coalition. He had to resign as Defense Minister in favor of Moshe *Dayan of Ben-Gurion's *Rafi* party. For the first time, *Gahal* entered the National Unity Government, with Menahem *Begin serving as Minister without Portfolio. He was also seen by many as an overcautious hesitater. He was deeply wounded by these developments. Yet he continued heading the government until his death.

After his death esteem of E. greatly deepened and he was seen as a moderate, shrewd statesman with great achievements in the fields of economy, political leadership, and national defense.

EVREN, KENAN (b.1918) Turkish officer and politician; President, 1982–89. Born in Alasehir in western Turkey, E. studied at the War College and the Army Staff College (1938–39). During his long military career he served as Artillery Commander (1947–57), Chief of Operations and Training Officer

of the Turkish Brigade in Korea (1958–59), Chief of Army Staff Schools and Chief of Operations (1959–61), Deputy Chief of the General Staff (1975–76), Aegean Army Commander (1976–77), Land Forces Commander (1977–78) and Chief of the General Staff (1978–83).

While Chief of Staff, E. led the military coup of Sept. 12, 1980, intended to end the terrorism that had plagued Turkey for over two years and killed 5,000. The government was dismissed, Parliament dissolved, the constitution suspended and martial law imposed. Approximately 30,000 people suspected of terrorism were arrested and a score were hanged. Harsh emergency measures included restrictions on the press, trade unions and public meetings.

The ruling military junta named E. Head of State; a military man, Admiral Bulent Ulusu, formed a government.

In Nov. 1982, after two years of military rule, which drastical reduced terrorism, decreased the rate of inflation from over 120% to 40%, and streamlined the bureaucracy, E. held a referendum which endorsed a new constitution and elected him President for a seven-year term. (He was the only candidate and received more than 90% of the vote.) The new constitution gave the President wider powers; it also barred many former leaders, such as ex-Prime Ministers *Ecevit and *Demirel from taking part in political life until 1992 (a ban eased in 1986 and lifted after a referendum in Sept. 1987), and restricted the rights of political parties and trade unions and the freedom of the press. In Nov. 1983 E. held general elections, in which only three parties were allowed to run; E. favored a "National Democratic Party" headed by the retired general Turgut *Sunalp. The elections were won by the "Motherland Party" headed by Turgut *Ozal. In Dec. 1983 Ozal formed a government, and thus civilian-political government was restored. E. turned from a military ruler into a constitutional, civilian President who cooperated with the government; he exerted a moderating, stabilizing influence and was, until his retirement at the end of his term, in Nov. 1989, a highly respected and widely admired President.

F

FAHD IBN 'ABD-UL-'AZIZ (b. 1921? 1922?) King of Sa'udi Arabia since June 1982. A son of *Ibn Sa'ud (his mother came from the Sudairi tribal clan of Najd). Prince F. served as Minister of Education, 1953–60, during the reign of his half brother *Sa'ud. In Oct. 1962, when his half brother *Feisal ascended the throne, F. became Minister of the Interior, and from 1968 also Second Deputy Prime Minister. When Feisal was assassinated, in Mar. 1975, and another half brother, Khaled, became King, F. was promoted to be Crown Prince and First Deputy Prime Minister; he retained the Home Ministry for half a year. Upon Khaled's death, in June 1982, F. became King and Prime Minister.

F. is considered relatively liberal, an advocate of development and modernization, moderate in his foreign policies, and an ally of the USA. His name is linked to a plan for a Middle East peace settlement based on the total withdrawal of Israel from all the territories occupied in 1967, including the removal of settlements established, and the establishment of a Palestinian-Arab state, following which "all states of the region" would "be able to live in peace" (or their "right to live in peace would be recognized"; versions differ) — implying Arab acceptance of, or acquiescence in, the existence of Israel. This "F. Plan" was launched in Aug. 1981 by a press interview granted by F., then Crown Prince. It was one of the causes for the breakup of the 12th All-Arab Summit at Fez, Nov. 1981, but was eventually adopted — with several significant changes — at the Summit's resumed second session, Sept. 1982. Now usually called the "Fez Plan," it has since been regarded as the Arab master plan for a Middle East settlement. When Iraq invaded Kuwait, in Aug. 1990, threatening Sa'udia, King F. called in U.S. and Arab (Egyptian, Syrian) troops to defend Sa'udi Arabia and restore Kuwait's independence, and joined the military operations against Iraq which were begun in Jan. 1991.

FAHMY, ISMA'IL (b. 1922)   Egyptian diplomat and politician. The son of a wealthy landowning family, F. graduated in political science from Cairo University. He joined the foreign service in 1945/46. From the late 1950s he dealt particularly with international and UN matters, for several years as a member of Egypt's delegation to the UN (elected in 1967 chairman of the General Assembly's Political Committee). F. was Ambassador to Austria, 1968–71. In 1971 he became Under-Secretary of State, but was dismissed in 1972 after publicly criticizing Soviet policy and Egypt's efforts to rebuild closer relations with the USSR. He was soon reinstated, after President *Sadat expelled the Soviet military advisers, and appointed Ambassador to West Germany. He did not take up that post, as in 1973 he joined the cabinet as Minster of Tourism. He soon took a leading role in talks with the USA (Kissinger) and became Foreign Minister later the same year. In that position he was Egypt's leading negotiator with the U.S. and Israel, 1973–77. In Nov. 1977 he strongly opposed President Sadat's dramatic journey to Jerusalem and his policy of seeking a peace agreement with Israel, and resigned — the only senior member of Sadat's team to do so at that time (his successor did likewise a year later). Later reports of a comeback did not materialize. F.'s candidacy for a seat in the People's Assembly (1979) was disqualified. He joined the opposition "Socialist Labour Party" (reported 1980) or the *Wafd* (1984). F. wrote a book on his diplomatic experience and his views, *Negotiating for Peace in the Middle East*, 1983.

FAROUQ (1920–65)   King of Egypt, 1936–52. The son of *Fu'ad, Sultan and later King of Egypt, F. was educated in England and Egypt. On the death of his father in May 1936, he succeeded to the throne; as he was a minor, a Regency Council ruled for him until July 1937. F. continued, even intensified, the struggle between the royal court and the *Wafd* party and encouraged the rise of anti-*Wafd*

King Farouq and his daughter Fawzia

parties, such as the existing Liberal-Constitutional Party and the newly created Saadist Party. and reportedly also extra-parliamentary rightwing groups. He was considered anti-British; during World War II he was reported to share the pro-Italian and pro-German sentiments that permeated the administration, the officers' corps and public opinion and led to several cases of desertion and treason. The British had to put pressure on him before he would honor Egypt's obligations under the treaty of 1936 and render the wartime assistance it stipulated; it was also only under pressure that he dismissed subversive government and army officers. In Feb. 1942, the British forced F. to dismiss the government and appoint the *Wafd* leader Mustafa Nahhas Prime Minister (F. removed him in Oct. 1944 — as soon as the British, the danger of an Axis victory having passed, ceased actively intervening in Egyptian internal affairs). The decision of May 1948 to have the Egyptian armed forces march into Palestine — in disregard of previous decisions not to involve the regular forces, and against army advice — was imposed on the government and the army, so their leaders later claimed, by F. personally. The defeat of 1948 and ensuing revelations of corruption in the palace, the

bureaucracy and the army undermined F.'s position, as did his luxurious life and his reputation as a playboy. In the crisis of 1951, when a *Wafd* government abrogated the Anglo-Egyptian Treaty, F. was proclaimed "King of Egypt *and Sudan*." In July 1952, F. was deposed in the officers' coup led by Gen. *Nagib and Col. *Nasser. He was allowed to go to Italy with his family. F. had three daughters and (after divorcing his wife, Queen Farida, in 1949) a son from a second marriage, Ahmad Fu'ad (b. 1952). The latter was proclaimed King in 1952 (with a Regency Council ruling for him) — until the abolition of the monarchy in 1953. F., known throughout his life as a voluptuary, a gambler, jet-setter and frequenter of the night-club circuit, continued his high living in his Rome exile. He died in Rome in July 1965.

FAWZI, MAHMUD (1900–81)   Egyptian diplomat and politician. Prime Minister 1970–72, Vice President 1972–74. The son of a Cairo middle-class family, F. graduated in law at Cairo University, with further studies in history, political science, etc., at Liverpool, Columbia (New York), and a Ph.D. from Rome (1929). He joined the foreign service in 1926 and held various consular posts in the U.S. and Japan; from 1941 to 1944 he was Consul-General in Jerusalem. From 1946, F. was Egypt's representative at the UN, and in 1952 served briefly as Ambassador to Britain. In Dec. 1952, the Free Officers' regime made him Foreign Minister — a post he held until 1964, including

Mahmud Fawzi (Bar-David, Tel Aviv)

King Feisal Ibn 'Abd-ul-'Aziz and Queen Elizabeth (Bar-David, Tel Aviv)

three years as Foreign Minister of the Egyptian-Syrian UAR (1958–61). He was thus one of the few leading public servants of the monarchy retained and promoted by the new regime. He remained nominally responsible for foreign affairs 1964–67, as Deputy Prime Minister (with Mahmud *Riad as Foreign Minister really in charge), and from 1967 to *Nasser's death in 1970 was relieved of government duties to serve as the President's special adviser on foreign affairs. In 1968, Nasser also had him co-opted to the Executive of the Arab Socialist Union, Egypt's single party, though F. had never been active in internal or party politics, and entrusted him with the reorganization of the party. *Sadat, Nasser's successor as President, appointed F., in Oct. 1970, Prime Minister; in Jan. 1972 he relinquished that post to become Vice-President and, again, special adviser to the President on foreign affairs. He retired in Sept. 1974. F. was respected as a refined diplomat and a man of wide culture and considered a liberal with pro-Western tendencies; he served the radical-revolutionary

officers' regime as a respectable spokesman to the external world — but he went along with whatever policy was laid down by the decision-making leadership, being essentially a diplomat-"technician" with no political influence.

FEISAL IBN 'ABD-UL-'AZIZ (1904? 1905?–75) King of Sa'udi Arabia 1964–75. The second son of 'Abd-ul-'Aziz *Ibn Sa'ud (after the death of two elder half brothers). In 1927 his father appointed him governor, later with the title Viceroy, of the Hijaz, which had recently been conquered from the Hashemite King *Hussein and his son *'Ali, and entrusted him with its integration into the Sa'udi kingdom. In 1928 F. was also made chairman of the Council of *Ulama* (Islamic savants), acting as an advisory state council. Prince F. frequently represented Sa'udia in foreign affairs and negotiations and, with Ibn Sa'ud maintaining no formal Council of Ministers in the Western pattern, was considered a kind of foreign minister. In 1953, after the death of Ibn Sa'ud, F.'s elder half brother, F.

was designated Crown Prince, Deputy Prime Minister (the King himself taking the Premiership) and Foreign Minister. A half-concealed fight for power between Sa'ud and F. flared up in 1958, when Sa'udia experienced a severe economic crisis and a deterioration of relations with Egypt (with *Nasser and Sa'ud accusing each other of assassination plots). Sa'ud was forced to grant F. full powers in fiscal, internal and foreign affairs and to make him Prime Minister in 1962. F. instituted financial and administrative reforms, took economy measures and attempted to eliminate waste and corruption. He managed to retrieve the economic situation and pay all state debts by 1962. The struggle with King Sa'ud continued intermittently, with F. the virtual ruler. In 1964, Sa'ud demanded the restoration of his power, but F. refused and a new crisis ensued. On 2 Nov. 1964, the Council of *Ulama'* deposed Sa'ud (who went into exile) and proclaimed F. King.

During his reign, F. promoted and accelerated the development and modernization of Sa'udi Arabia, made possible by the continuous growth of oil production, but made few changes in the ultra-conservative system of government. He followed a more active, inter-Arab policy and became a much-respected all-Arab leader. He endeavored to mend relations with Egypt (which had again deteriorated as the two countries were involved, since 1962, on opposing sides in the Yemen civil war), but frequently refused to go along with Nasser's policies, and emerged as the leader of a bloc of conservative moderately pro-Western Arab states. He also cultivated relations with the Islamic states and was instrumental in the formation of a permanent consultative group of these states from 1969-70. F. was assassinated in Mar. 1975 by a nephew, Feisal Ibn Musa'id, who was executed for the murder.

Of F.'s eight sons, several fill senior positions. Prince Sa'ud Ibn F. (b. 1941) has served since 1975 as Foreign Minister, Turki (b. 1945) is Director of Foreign Intelligence.

FEISAL I, IBN HUSSEIN(1885-1933)   King of Iraq, 1921-33. Born in Ta'if, Hijaz, as the third son of Sharif (later King) *Hussein of the Hashemite dynasty, F. grew up in Istanbul, where his father lived in exile. He returned to Hijaz with his father in 1908, when Hussein was appointed Amir of Mecca. On the eve of World War I he established contact with Arab nationalists in Damascus. When his father launched the "Arab Revolt" in Hijaz,

1916, F. took command of the "Northern Army" which harassed Turkish forces in guerrilla operations and from 1917 advanced northwards into Transjordan as part of General Allenby's British and Allied forces. F. and his contingent were allowed to enter Damascus on Oct. 1, 1918, and assume control of inner Syria in the name of Arab nationalism and under the supervision of the Allies' provisional military administration. F. set up an Arab government and administration, composed of and supported by Arab nationalist leaders (some with administrative experience in Ottoman-Turkish service). But France regarded Syria, under the wartime secret Sykes-Picot Agreement, as being in her zone of influence, and made it clear that she would not accept Syrian-Arab independence free of French control. In the meantime, F. presented his dynasty's claim to an independent Arab kingdom (or federation of kingdoms), and Arab nationalist claims in general, at the Paris Peace Conference (where he also signed, after earlier meetings since June 1918, an agreement on future Arab-Jewish cooperation with the Zionist leader *Weizmann). In Mar. 1920 an Arab-Syrian national congress proclaimed F. King of Syria (meaning a "Greater Syria," including Lebanon,

King Feisal I

Palestine, and Transjordan, though no borders were specified). At the same time, the San Remo Conference of the Allied powers confirmed French control of Syria by conferring upon her a Mandate to administer that country. Maybe an accommodation could have been found between French control and a semiindependent Arab kingdom under F. (such as the British arranged in Iraq and Transjordan); but French forces soon clashed with hastily assembled troops and volunteers of F.'s regime, and after a battle at Meisalun, in July 1920, F. gave up the fight and left Syria. As the British felt committed to the Hashemite dynasty, Colonial Secretary Churchill, on the advice of T. E. *Lawrence and the British "Arab Office" in Cairo, secured for F. the Kingdom of Iraq. A "plebiscite" of notables was arranged in July 1921, and in Aug. 1921 F. was proclaimed King of Iraq.

During his reign, F. proved himself an astute politician. He avoided alienating the nationalists, most of whom were anti-British and regarded the King as a foreign implantation; yet he remained on good terms with the British and was their loyal ally. He also continued, not very vigorously, to advocate a settlement with the Jews of Palestine within the framework of a general Middle East confederation or alliance. He promulgated an Iraqi Constitution in 1925, laid the foundations for an independent administration, at first under British tutelage, and led Iraq, through the Anglo-Iraqi Treaty of 1930, to formal complete independence and admission to the League of Nations in 1932 — the first Arab country to attain that status. In 1933 he tried to restrain mounting violence against the Assyrian minority — an attempt that cost him much of his popularity and persuaded observers that he was losing his grip. F. died in Sept. 1933 and was succeeded by his only son, *Ghazi.

FEISAL II, IBN GHAZI (1935–58) King of Iraq 1939–58. The only son of King *Ghazi and grandson of *Feisal I (and, through his mother, of ex-King *'Ali of Hijaz, the brother of Feisal I), F. became King on his father's death in 1939, when he was not yet four years old. His uncle *'Abd-ul-Ilah (his father's cousin and his mother's brother) became Regent. During the crisis under the Rashid 'Ali *Kilani regime in 1941 — when the Regent and other leaders of the conservative, pro-British regime fled — F. and his mother were in the power of the rebellious nationalist government, but remained unharmed. After the war, F. was educated along English lines, partly in England (Harrow). On

Feisal Ibn Ghazi (AP Photo)

coming of age, in 1953, F. assumed his royal-constitutional duties. In Feb. 1958 he became head of the short-lived "Arab Federation" of Jordan and Iraq. F. was not a forceful personality and had no appreciable influence on his country's policies. He was murdered during the revolution of July 1958; his murder was probably planned with the intention of depriving adherents of the old order of a possible rallying point.

FEYZIOGLU, TURHAN (b.1922) Turkish politician; chairman of the Reliance Party and former Deputy Prime Minister. Born in Kayseri, he graduated in law at Istanbul University (1945) and earned his LL.D. degree in Paris and London. He was appointed to a chair at the School of Political Science in Ankara, but was forced to resign due to his criticism of Prime Minister Adnan *Menderes.

F. was elected to Parliament in Oct. 1957 for the Republican People's Party (RPP). After the May 1960 coup he was appointed Dean of the Middle East Technical University. In 1961 he served briefly as Minister of Education, later as Minister of State, and in 1962-63 as Deputy Prime Minister under Ismet *Inonu.

At the 1966 convention of the RPP he was defeated in his bid to become General Secretary by the leftist Bulent *Ecevit, and in 1967 he seceded from the RPP, and together with over 40 other right-wingers founded the Reliance Party, which won 15 seats in the elections of 1969 and merged in the 1970s with several other small right-wing groups. In the late 1970s he rejoined the RPP, but did not regain a leading position.

F. was a member of the Turkish Parliamentary delegation to the European Council. Following the military coup of 1980, F. left the political arena. For a brief period he was an adviser to the Turkish Republic of Northern Cyprus.

FORUHAR, DARIUS (b.1928) Iranian politician. Leader of the Iran National Party. Born in Tehran, F. studied law in Isfahan and Tehran. While practicing law, he was one of the founders of the Pan-Iran Party and later of the Iran National Party; both of these groups joined the "National Front" Coalition supporting *Mussaddeq against the Shah, 1951-53. After Mussaddeq's fall in 1953, F. continued backing the National Front, now half-underground as an opposition group. He was arrested several times and spent a total of 15 years in jail. After *Khomeini's Islamic revolution of 1979, while the "National Front" was still half-permitted to function, he served for some months as Minister of Labor in *Bazargan's goverment. F. was one of the many candidates for the presidency in 1980, but not a prominent one, and failed to attract a significant share of the vote. Under the Islamic regime, he could no longer be politically active.

FRANJIYEH, SULEIMAN (b. 1910) Lebanese politician. President of Lebanon 1970-76. Members of the Christian-Maronite F. clan, centered in Zagharta, northern Mount Lebanon, are the chief leaders of the Maronites in the north and largely in control of their region. They are in near-constant rivalry with the Maronite chiefs of central Mount Lebanon (al-*Khouri, *Edde, *Chamoun, *Jumayyil) over a leading role in general Lebanese-Christian politics. The main political exponent of the F.'s was S.F.'s elder brother **Hamid F.** (1907? 1909?-81), from the late 1930s a member of Parliament and many times Minister, frequently Foreign Minister, and in 1952 a candidate for the Presid-

ency (he withdrew in favor of Camille Chamoun) — while S.F. acted as the organizer and strong-arm man of the clan and its armed guards. After Hamid F. suffered a stroke in 1957, S.F. became the main leader of the clan and entered politics. In the civil war of 1958 he aligned himself and his militia on the Nasserist side and against President Chamoun; but his political position was complex and shifting, and after 1958 he was considered pro-American or at least neutral. From 1960 he was a member of Parliament and served several times as a Minister (1960-61, 1968-70). In Aug. 1970 he was elected President, against Elias *Sarkis, the candidate of the strongest Parliamentary group, the "Shiha-bists"; the vote was 50-49 — the smallest majority ever.

S.F. did not become a strong President. He had publicly denounced the armed presence of the Palestinian guerrilla formations, and their operations from Lebanese territory, as a danger to Lebanon — both externally, for exposing the country to Israeli counteroperations, and internally, for endangering the cohesion of Lebanon's communal structure. But as President he took no action to avoid that danger; and when the dreaded crisis erupted, in Apr. 1975, and turned into a civil war, he was weak and indecisive. He did not order the army into action to defend the regime and public order, fearing (rightly, as it turned out later) that the army would split and break up if it became involved in the civil war; nor did he throw his support to the conservative, Christian-led camp, to whose leaders (Chamoun, Jumayyil) he remained deeply antagonistic, despite their crucial vote for his election. He stayed neutral and even evinced some sympathy for the leftist-revolutionary, mainly Muslim, camp. From late 1975 F. became very close to Syria, recognizing her as the only power capable of imposing both an end to the civil war and basic reforms as a more permanent solution. In Jan.-Feb. 1976 he evolved, together with Syrian President *Asad and his associates, a plan for reforms in Lebanon's political-communal structure. The plan was based on the replacement of the Christian majority in Parliament, which no longer corresponded to demographic realities, by a 50:50 division of representation between Christians and non-Christians (Sunni, Shi'i and Druze), but retained the constitutional principle of predetermined communal main power positions as informally agreed in the "National Pact" of 1943 (with a Maronite President, a Muslim-Sunni Prime Minister and a Muslim-Shi'i President of Parliament).

Suleiman Franjiyeh (AP Photo)

The plan has remained Syria's and F.'s basic formula for Lebanese reforms. When, in early 1976, the Asad-F. plan was rejected by the leftist-Muslim-Palestinian camp, F. encouraged, or even invited, Syrian armed intervention.

F.'s presidential term was slated to end in Sept. 1976. For some time, he resisted demands, reinforced by formal Parliamentary votes, to reaffirm that he would step down, maintaining that in the conditions of civil war no election could be properly held and implying that his term should be extended (as Parliament had extended its own term). But eventually he bowed to pressure, his Syrian allies failing to support his bid for extension. In May 1976, a new Syrian-backed President, Elias *Sarkis, was elected, and in Sept. F. stepped down.

Out of office, F. maintained his position as the chief of the Maronites of the Zagharta region and North Lebanon, and built up his militia, the *Marada*. The tension between him and the main Maronite leadership flared up in the late 1970s, when the Phalanges, the main military formation of that leadership, and the "Lebanese Forces" they had established, claimed exclusive control of all Christian militias, and F. refused to integrate his force. During the clashes that ensued, F.'s son Antoine (Tony) — a budding politician, member of Parliament since 1970, a Minister 1973–75, and his father's political heir — was killed, with his wife and small daughter, by the Phalangists; F. held the Jumayyil clan personally responsible, and the old antagonism was aggravated by a bitter blood feud. When Bashir *Jumayyil was murdered in Sept. 1982, F. openly expressed joy. He had, anyway, bitterly opposed Jumayyil's policy of cooperation with Israel — before, during and after the Israeli invasion of June 1982 — and his election to the Presidency.

In July 1983, F. joined the Druze chief *Junbalat and the Muslim-Sunni leader *Karameh in a "National Salvation Front" founded to oppose President Amin *Jumayyil and his government and to step up resistance to the Israeli occupation. At the conference of national reconciliation of Oct.-Nov. 1983 (Geneva), and Mar. 1984 (Lausanne), F. was aligned with the Sunni, Shi'i and Druze leaders against President Jumayyil and the conservatives. However, his allies went beyond the "Asad-F. Plan" and demanded the gradual total abolition of the communal representation system, and a far-reaching limitation of the powers of the Maronite President for an immediate transition period; F. could not go along with that and parted company with his allies or at least dissociated himself to a large extent. F. remained close to Syria, but did not take part in the 1985 efforts of the Druze and Shi'i leaders to work out a reform plan. He rebuilt contacts with Maronite leaders — including even Chamoun (but not President Jumayyil, whose resignation or dismissal he continued demanding), and also the new leader of the "Lebanese Forces," Elie Hobeika, who was no longer loyal to and dominated by the Jumayyil faction. In Sept. 1985 he resubmitted a plan for reforms, which was in fact the old "Asad-F. Plan" of 1976; it was vaguely implied that it was now backed also by other Christian leaders. In the clashes between rival Christian militias that broke out in Jan. 1986, after Hobeika reached an agreement with the Druze and Shi'i militias that was repudiated by Jumayyil and the Phalanges, F.'s militia joined Hobeika and the Druze and Shi'i forces in their unsuccessful assault on Jumayyil and the Phalanges. In late 1989 F. backed the "Ta'if Agreement" devising a Syrian-guided reformed regime (along the lines of F.'s plan). He and his militia supported the fall 1990 military moves against General *'Awn and the takeover of Greater Beirut by the Army and the pro-Syrian militias. In recent years, F. seemed to indicate that he aspired to a new term as President, though he staked no formal claim.

FU'AD (full name: Ahmad Fu'ad) (1868–1936) Sultan of Egypt 1917–22, King of Egypt 1922–36. The youngest son of the Khedive Isma'il (ruled 1863–79). In 1917 the British arranged for F. to succeed his brother Hussein Kamel as Sultan of Egypt — a title they had introduced in 1914, when they made Egypt a protectorate and deposed Khedive *'Abbas Hilmi. In 1922, following Britain's unilateral declaration of Egypt's independence, F. was proclaimed King (he relinquished his claim to the title "King of Egypt *and Sudan*" only under intense British pressure). During his rule, Egypt's government and nationalists continued to struggle for complete independence and a treaty with Britain recognizing and assuring it — a struggle in which the King did not play an overt part. While, officially, Egypt rejected the unilateral British declaration of her independence and the reservations limiting it, the foundations of independent Egypt's constitution (promulgated in Apr. 1923) and government were in fact based on that declaration. The King and his Court desired a strictly conservative system of government with limited power for Parliament and its political parties, and throughout his reign F. struggled with the nationalist, radical *Wafd* party over this issue and strove to exclude the *Wafd* from power, preferring prime ministers from conservative circles close to him. During the last year of his life, in Dec. 1935, F. reinstated the liberal-parliamentary constitution that had been suspended in 1930, thus opening the way for the *Wafd*'s return to power, and nominated an all-party delegation for negotiations with Britain that led to the Anglo-Egyptian Treaty of 1936; he did not live to see its completion. He died in Apr. 1936 and was succeeded by his only son, *Farouq. When the University of Cairo was modernized and turned into a Western-type institution, 1925, it was named "King F. University"; his name was removed in 1953, after the "Free Officers" revolution and the abolition of the monarchy.

G

GADDAFI see *Qadhdhafi.

GALILI (original name: Brechenko), **YISRAEL** (1911–86) Israeli political leader. Born in the Ukraine, immigrated to Palestine with his family in 1914. A leader of the *Noar Ha'Oved* (Working Youth) Movement and, from 1930, one of the founders of Kibbutz Na'an where he was a member until his death.

From an early age he was active in matters of defense and in 1941 he became the *Histadrut* representative in the *Haganah* Central Command. He was one of the leaders of *Mapai*'s leftist opposition faction (*"Si'ah Bet"* and from 1944, after *Mapai* split, of the *Ahdut Ha'avodah* party. In the summer of 1947 he was named chairman of the *Haganah* Central Command, but in the summer of 1948, at the height of the War of Liberation, *Ben Gurion forced him to resign his command — a step which caused a severe crisis.

After the War of Liberation, when his *Ahdut Ha'avodah* party co-founded the *Mapam* party, he became one of its leaders and represented it in the First Knesset. After *Mapam* split in 1954, he became General Secretary and leader of *Ahdut Ha'avodah*. He was one of the initiators of the alignment between his party and *Mapai* in 1965.

G. first joined the government in 1966, as Minister without Portfolio, and held that position until 1977. Though he had no defined ministerial responsibilities, he wielded a great deal of influence in the government. He acted as chief adviser to Prime Ministers Levi *Eshkol and Golda *Meir and was responsible for many government decisions. He took hawkish political positions; in 1969, for instance, during a press debate with historian Jacob Talmon, he held that the Palestinian-Arabs were not a "nation." His hawkish views, his closeness to Prime Minister Meir and the "Galili Document" caused him to be held responsible for the political position which made the Yom Kippur War and its political setback inevitable. Despite this, he was co-opted into Yitzhak *Rabin's government; but his influence was no longer as it had been in the past.

GAMASY, (MUHAMMAD) 'ABD-UL-GHANI (b. 1921)   Egyptian officer and politician. Graduated from the Military Academy in 1939, Staff and Command School 1950, courses in the USA and USSR, the Nassar Academy 1966; Major-General 1965. Military posts included command of an armor battalion, later a brigade, staff officer at the General Staff, chief of operations of the land forces 1966, in the war of 1967 Chief of Staff of the Second Army, after the war Deputy Chief of Intelligence, 1972, Chief of Operations (in which capacity he prepared plans for the October War of 1973) and Deputy Chief of the General Staff. In the war of 1973 G. was credited with the initial successes and put in charge of the Suez front. He had sharp differences with Chief of Staff Sa'd-ul-Din Shazli (Shadhili), and when the latter was dismissed by President *Sadat, G. replaced him as Chief of Staff (this was announced in Dec. 1973, but had actually happened in Oct.) and was promoted to Lt.-General. He conducted the 1973–75 negotiations with Israel that led to the Disengagement and Interim Agreements of 1974 and 1975. In Dec. 1974 G. was appointed Minister of War (renamed in 1978 Minister of Defense) and Deputy Prime Minister. He fully backed Sadat in his peace initiative of Nov. 1977 and took a leading part in the negotiations that led to the Egypt-Israel Camp David Agreements of Sept. 1978 and peace treaty of Mar. 1979. He was considered by some as the strong man behind Sadat. He resigned in Oct. 1978 in circumstances never fully clarified (because he had become too strong a potential rival?) and became President Sadat's special adviser on military affairs. He was relieved of that post, too, in 1981 after suffering a stroke.

GEMAYEL see *Jumayyil.

AL-GHASHMI, AHMAD HUSSEIN (1938? 1939–78) Yemeni officer and politician, President of Yemen 1978. Gh., himself of a leading clan of the Zeidi Hashed tribal federation, served as liaison between the post-1962 republican regime and the powerful tribes, but he was frequently in conflict with Sheikh 'Abdullah al-*Ahmar, the Hashed federation's chief leader. After Ibrahim *Hamdi's coup of June 1974, Lt.-Col. Gh. was appointed Chief of Staff, Deputy Commander in Chief and member of the Military Command Council. When Hamdi was assassinated, in Oct. 1977 (according to some reports in Gh.'s house, or at least with his collaboration), he became Commander in Chief and chairman of a three-man Military Command Council. He had to maneuver between the powerful Zeidi tribal leaders on one side and urban leftist pressures, largely Shafe'i, on the other, but he was seen as a conservative, close to the tribes and to Sa'udi Arabia. In Feb. 1978 he reestablished an appointed "People's Constituent Assembly" that had been abolished by Hamdi, thereby responding to tribal demands; but the chief leaders were not among those appointed. Tribal fighting, in Mar. 1978, was seen by some as a rebellion, and in Apr. an officers' coup led by his associate on the Command Council, Paratroop Commander 'Abdullah 'Abd-ul-'Alem, had to be put down. In Apr. 1978, the Assembly decided to replace the Military Council by a Presidential Council and elected Gh. President. Gh. was assassinated in June 1978 by an envoy from South Yemen carrying a booby-trapped briefcase that killed Gh. and its bearer — a bizarre episode apparently connected with South Yemeni factional infighting but never fully clarified.

GHAZI IBN FEISAL (1912–39) King of Iraq 1933–39. Born in Hijaz, the only son of Amir (later King) *Feisal, the third son of Sharif (later King) *Hussein, Gh. became heir apparent to the Iraqi throne when his father was installed as King of Iraq in 1921. He was educated in Iraq, with a brief, unhappy spell in England (Harrow). He succeeded to the throne in 1933, upon his father's death. He married his cousin 'Aliya, daughter of *'Ali ibn Hussein. Gh. was popular in Iraq for his Arab nationalism and his hate of the British, but carried little political weight; he had no influence on the officer cliques, the real rulers of Iraq after 1936. Gh. was killed in Apr. 1939 in a road accident.

GLUBB (PASHA), SIR JOHN BAGOT (1897–1986) British officer and writer, commander of the Jor-danian Army 1939–56. G. served in Iraq 1920–30. In 1930 he went to Transjordan, where he raised Bedouin units within the Arab Legion, the Transjordanian Army. He became the Legion's second-in-command and from 1939 its commander (from 1948 — Chief of the General Staff), attaining the Jordanian rank of *Fariq* — Lieutenant-General. Although he served Jordan under contract (not seconded from the British Army), the nationalists in Jordan and other Arab countries regarded him as a symbol of British imperialist domination. They blamed him for the limitation of Jordan's military role in the Palestine war of 1948, her non-adherence to Arab overall strategic-military plans, and specifically the Arab Legion's failure to capture West Jerusalem, the loss of Ramle and Lydda, and Jordan's withdrawal from Umm Rashrash to become Eilat) near 'Aqaba. As the tide of nationalism rose in Jordan and King *Hussein felt compelled to ally himself with Egypt and Syria, the King abruptly dismissed G. in Mar. 1956. G. retired to Britain. He wrote many books and continued expressing strongly pro-Arab views, especially on the Arab-Israel conflict.

GÖKALP, ZIYA (1875?-1924) Turkish poet and writer. The theorist of Turkish nationalism. Born

Ghazi Ibn Feisal (AP Photo)

in Diyarbekir (Eastern Anatolia), G. made contact with the Young Turks at an early stage, and after the revolution of 1908 he was elected to the council of the "Committee of Union and Progress" in Salonika. There, and later in Istanbul where he became Professor of Sociology at the University, G. wrote his main nationalist essays and became the spiritual leader of the Young Turks. After the Proclamation of the Republic, 1923, he was elected to the National Assembly. Prior to the dissolution of the Ottoman Empire, G. favored the preservation of the supranational state, but called for the revival and promotion of Turkish national culture, the acceptance of European scientific and technical knowledge, and the relegation of Islam to an ethical and personal religion. For some time an advocate of Pan-Turkism, later his thoughts grew closer to those of *Ataturk. His social and cultural ideas paved the way for many reforms during the Republican period.

His only book, *The History of Turkish Civilization*, was written a short time before he died with only one volume completed.

GOLOMB, ELIYAHU (1893–1945)

One of the leaders of the *Yishuv* in Palestine during the Mandate period. Born in Russia, he immigrated to Palestine in 1909 and graduated in the first class of the Gymnasia Herzlia in Tel Aviv, the first Hebrew high school. He then went to work as a farmer and a watchman in Degania and Kinneret, the first *kibbutzim* then founded.

During the First World War G. opposed service with the Turkish-Ottoman army; he was one of the initiators of the Jewish Battalions within the British army and was one of the first to volunteer. For some time he was the secretary of *Ahdut Ha'avodah* and remained a member of the leading bodies of that party and later, from 1930, the Labor Party (*Mapai*).

During the Mandate period, most of his activity revolved around the *Haganah*, created in 1920. He did not at first hold a formal position in the *Haganah*, but guided and inspired it and was its ethical and political source of authority, in fact its commander and the informal "Minister of Defense" of the State in the making. He built up the defense organization and made it subordinate to the civil-political leadership of the *Yishuv*. He was one of the initiators of "illegal" immigration and of the dispatch of Palestinian-Jewish parachutists to Europe during the Second World War. He was also one of the founders of the *Palmah*.

GREENBERG, URI ZVI (1896–1981)

One of the great Hebrew poets of the 20th century. The chief poetic voice of the Revisionist nationalist right wing. Born in Eastern Galicia, G. studied in Lvov. In 1912 he began to publish poems in Hebrew and Yiddish and in 1915 his first book of poems appeared, in Yiddish. From 1915 to 1918 he served in the Austrian army; in 1918 he deserted and returned to Galicia, and in 1921 went to Warsaw. In 1923 he immigrated to Palestine and worked as a pioneer in the Jezreel Valley and in Petah Tikvah. At that time he was a member of the Labor Movement and the *Ahdut Ha'avodah* party and published poems and articles in their organs *Kuntres* and *Hapoel Hatzair*. He was one of the regular contributors to the *Histadrut* daily *Davar* from its foundation. That same year he published his first book of poems in Palestine. After his immigration to Palestine he wrote only in Hebrew, identifying with the revival of the Hebrew language and the pioneering enterprise in Palestine. Only in the 1950's did he again write poetry in Yiddish.

After the 1929 Arab riots G. left the Labor movement and joined the Revisionists, and together with Abba Ahimeir and Yehoshua Heshel Yevin he led their radical wing which disputed *Jabotinsky on various issues, such as the position towards Britain and the attitude to democracy. From 1931 to 1935 he edited the Revisionists' Yiddish newspaper in Warsaw, *Di Velt*, and from 1938 to 1939 their paper *Der Moment*. His book of poems *The Book of Prosecution and Faith* (*Sefer Hakitrug Veha'emunah*), 1937, deeply impressed *Betar*, the Revisionist youth and the *IZL*. Thus G. became the poet of the radical right and a bitter poetic adversary of the Labor movement.

In 1939, with the outbreak of war, he returned to Palestine. During the war years he wrote nothing about the events occurring in Europe. His poetry on the Holocaust — a central topic in his writings — was written after the war and collected in 1951 in *The Book of the River Streets* (*Sefer Rechovot Hanahar*). After the establishment of the State of Israel he joined the *Herut* movement and was a member of the First Knesset on its list. In 1967, after the Six Day War, he was one of the founders of the "Movement for the Whole *Eretz-Yisrael*" (Greater Israel).

G.'s poems were controversial and much debated — particularly due to his hatred for the Labor movement and its accessories, including the *kibbutz* movement. But since the 1950s he has been acclaimed as one of the greatest Hebrew poets of the modern era. He was awarded many prizes, including the Israel Prize (1957) and the Bialik Prize (three times — in 1947, 1954, 1977). He refused to publish new editions of his books during his lifetime and only after his death were his collected works published.

GRUENBAUM, YITZHAK (1879–1970)   Israeli, Zionist politician. Born in Warsaw, from his youth he was active in the Zionist movement. In 1906 he was a delegate to the "Helsingfors Conference" where he was a proponent of *"Gegenwartsarbeit"* ("work at present"), i.e., for Zionist efforts to strengthen the position and rights of Jews in the Diaspora. After the First World War he was elected to the Polish *Sejm*, and during the 1920s he headed the "minority bloc" in the *Sejm* and led the struggle to obtain for the Jews the status and rights of a national minority. He was a leader of the Zionist movement in Poland, and of Polish Jewry in general, and a prominent figure in the Jewish world. In the Zionist movement he headed an *"Al Hamishmar"* faction opposing *Weizmann's pro-British position and his plan to establish an enlarged Jewish Agency. On this issue he cooperated with *Jabotinsky and the Revisionist movement.

At the Zionist Congress of 1933 he was elected to the Jewish Agency Executive and, following this, immigrated to Palestine. From 1933 to 1935 he headed the *Aliyah* (Immigration) Department of the Jewish Agency and afterwards its Labor Department. After his immigration to Palestine his position as one of the foremost leaders of the Zionist movement gradually weakened, as he was cut off from the Jews of Poland whom he had led and did not develop an alternative group of followers.

During the Second World War he was chairman of the United Rescue Committee and his activities in this capacity were the subject of great criticism. After the war he traveled to Europe to look for his son Eliezer who had been a *Kapo* in Auschwitz. He found his son in France. With the establishment of the State of Israel he joined the Provisional Government as the first Minister of the Interior. He was one of the signers of the Declaration of Independence. In 1949 he headed his own list to the First Knesset but was not elected — a tragedy for a man who had been the leader of millions and who could now not obtain the 5,000 votes needed to win a seat.

G. remained a member of the Jewish Agency Executive for a short time and afterwards settled in Kibbutz Gan Shmuel where his son Benyamin lived. His final years were devoted to writing, particularly for the *Mapam* daily *Al Hamishmar*.

G. was considered a leader who courageously stood up for his principles, endowed with charisma and a gift for both written and oral expression. Though admired by his followers, he did not attain a position of top leadership after the State of Israel was established.

GÜMÜŞPALA, RAGIP (1897–1964)   Turkish officer and politician. Born in Edirne, graduated from military college, and served in World War I and in the war against Greece and for independence, 1920–22. In 1948 he was promoted to the rank of general. After the military coup of May 1960, in which he commanded the Third Army in the Eastern Provinces, he became Chief of Staff, but resigned the same year. In Feb. 1961 G. was among the founders of the Justice Party (the heir to the Democratic Party toppled by the 1960 coup) and was named its chairman. G. opposed the continuation of the military rule that followed the 1960 coup and pressed for the reinstallation of democratic parliamentary government, achieved with the elections of Oct. 1961. G. became a member of Parliament, but did not regain a leading position.

GUNALTAY SEMSETTIN (1882? 1883?–1961) Turkish politician and historian, Prime Minister 1949–50. A graduate of Istanbul Teachers' College (1905) and Lausanne University, G. taught Turkish history and comparative religion at Istanbul and Ankara Universities. He was a member of the Ottoman-Turkish Parliament from 1915. After World War I he joined *Ataturk's nationalist revolution and held a seat in Parliament from 1923 until 1954. He also was a member of the Istanbul city council and deputy mayor. As Prime Minister (1948–50) he instituted some economic and electoral reform. His greatest accomplishment was organizing the first truly free elections. When in the late 1940s the monopoly of the Republican People's Party was ended and other parties were admitted, he was chosen in Jan. 1949 as a RPP man considered independent and moderate, to head the government holding the multiparty elections of May 1950 (won by the opposition Democratic Party).

G. co-founded the Turkish Historical Society (1931) and was its President from 1941 until his death. He wrote on history and religion in the Middle East.

GÜRSEL, CEMAL (1895–1966)   Turkish army officer and politician, fourth President of the Turkish Republic, 1961–66. Born in Erzurum, G. graduated from the military college in Erzincan. As an officer in World War I, he was a prisoner of war in Egypt for two years.

After the war he joined the national movement of Mustafa Kemal (*Ataturk) and commanded a unit in the War of Independence. After slowly rising in rank, in 1958 he was appointed Commander of Land Forces.

He opposed the decision of the *Menderes government (which he saw as reactionary and repressive) to use the army to suppress the opposition and expressed his reservations in a letter to the Minister of Defense (which was ignored). On May 27, 1960, he headed a group of 38 military officers in a coup which overthrew the government, and headed the ruling National Unity Committee and was Prime Minister and *de facto* President. In Nov. 1960, he ejected 14 radical officers headed by Colonel *Turkesh, claiming that this group was antidemocratic, nearly causing a second revolution. Shortly after, he suffered a heart attack from which he never fully recovered.

After a new constitution was adopted and a new Parliament elected in 1961, G. was elected President. In early 1966, due to his failing health, G. was

Cemal Gursel (Bar-David, Tel Aviv)

replaced as President by Cevdet *Sunay; he died the same year.

H

HABASH, GEORGE (b. 1924? 1925? 1926?) Palestinian-Arab guerrilla leader and politician. Born in Lod (Lydda), a Greek-Orthodox Christian, H. graduated in medicine from the American University of Beirut. After the Arab-Israel war of 1948 he settled for some years in 'Amman. In the 1950s, he was one of the founders, and the ideological mentor, of the Arab Nationalist Movement (AMN; *Harakat al-Qawmiyyin al-'Arab*) — an extreme nationalist, pan-Arab group, largely underground, with its leaders never publicly identified, that opposed the established Arab governments and increasingly adopted Marxist-Maoist doctrines. In 1969 H. was a co-founder of the Pop-

ular Front for the Liberation of Palestine (PFLP), an extremist guerrilla/terrorist formation strongly influenced by and connected with the ANM. The PFLP, of which H. has remained the leader, advocates all-out guerrilla war against Israel and opposes a political solution involving compromise.

H. is a bitter rival of the mainstream of Palestinian-Arab politics and guerrilla/terrorism led by *'Arafat and cooperates only partly in their joint roof organization, the PLO (he boycotted the PLO Executive and Central Council from 1974–75 to 1981, and again from 1984), and does not submit to its discipline. In 1970 his organization staged several brutal hijackings of foreign civilian airliners,

George Habash (with female Guerilla) (Bar-David, Tel Aviv)

holding the passengers hostage, and continued such operations even after the PLO, in the mid-1970s, decided to discontinue them. H. was also thought to have triggered the bloody clashes that erupted in 1970 between PLO guerrillas in Jordan and the Jordanian government. Relations between H. and the governments of the Arab states, including those hosting him and his group, have always been difficult. For some years, *Nasser of Egypt sponsored and protected him, hoping to cultivate his group as a "Nasserist" faction; but the alliance soon fell apart. The same held true, in the late 1960s, for the *Ba'th* government of Syria; despite ideological elements common to the *Ba'th* and the ANM and PFLP, doctrinal-factional disputes, and H.'s refusal to submit to the guidance and discipline of any government, made a full alliance impossible. H. was even detained for some time by Syria, in the late 1960s.

Since the 1970s, H. has been residing mostly in Syria and is close to her rulers, and his PFLP is headquartered there; but relations remain reserved, and the alliance partial. H. did not fully join the Syrian-instigated intra-PLO rebellion against 'Arafat and his faction, in 1983. Though he continues rejecting 'Arafat's leadership, he is, in contrast to the Syrian-guided rebels, prepared to negotiate and maintains, together with *Hawatma and his Popular Democratic Front for the Liberation of Palestine (PDFLP), a middle position between the rebels and 'Arafat's faction. H. co-founded, with the PDFLP and some other groups, an anti-'Arafat "Democratic Alliance" within the PLO (May 1984). In Mar. 1985 he joined with the pro-Syrian "National Alliance" in forming a new "Palestine National Salvation Front" (this time without his ally Hawatma). In an Apr. 1987 reconciliation he rejoined the PLO National Council and Executive, but remained a focus of opposition (thus he opposed the Palestine National Council's decision of Nov. 1988 to accept a Palestinian-Arab state in *part* of Palestine and in peaceful coexistence with Israel — but announced that he would abide by the decision of the majority). Despite H.'s intense, high-pressure activity his PFLP has remained a small group and his influence is limited.

HABIBI, EMIL (b. 1921) Palestinian-Arab writer, journalist, and politician in Israel. Formerly one of the leaders of the Israel Communist Party. Born in Haifa to a Christian family and educated in Haifa and Acre high schools, H. worked in various jobs and was an announcer at the Palestinian Broadcasting Service, 1940–42. He joined the Communist Party in 1940. Conforming to that party's line, he supported the partition of Palestine and the creation of the State of Israel in 1947/48 and stayed in Israel when many of his associates left as refugees. Between 1951 and 1973 he was four times a member of the Knesset for the Israeli Communist Party and served on the party's leadership bodies. H. published many cultural, literary and political articles in the Arab Communist periodicals in Israel such as *al-Ghad, al-Ittihad, al-Jadid* and *al-Tariq* and served on their editorial boards. From 1985 to 1989 he was Chief Editor of *al-Ittihad*, the main Communist organ. In 1989 he dissented from his party's line and resigned (or was removed from) his party offices.

In 1969 H. published his first short story collection, *The Sextet of the Six Day War*, dealing with the exciting reunion of the Arabs of Israel with the Palestinian Arabs after the Six Day War. Later on he published the novels *The Optimist-Pessimist* (1974), *Luka' bin Luka'* (1980), *Ikhtiyya* (1986) and *Saraya Bint al-Ghol*, 1991. Some of his novels were translated into Hebrew, English and French.

HADDAD, SA'D (1937–84) Lebanese officer. Born in Marj 'Ayoun, South Lebanon, a Greek-Catholic Christian, H. joined the army as a professional officer. In 1976 he was appointed commander of the forces in South Lebanon, with the rank of Major. He strongly opposed the guerrilla/terrorist operations of the Palestinian-Arab PLO from Lebanese soil and its *de facto* control of South Lebanon, and semisecretly cooperated, from about 1976–77, with the Israeli army. In 1978 he assisted it in its occupation of South Lebanon, which lasted three months and was intended to eliminate the PLO bases. When the Israeli forces withdrew, he established, with their aid, a "South Lebanese Army" (SLA), to continue preventing the use and domination of the area by the PLO. The SLA, equipped and trained largely by Israel, numbered 1,500–2,000, mostly Christians (his efforts to recruit also Shi'is, who constitute the majority of South Lebanon's population, had but little success), and controlled a 15–30 km. wide strip of territory along the border. As his operations, and his collaboration with Israel, did not have the approval of the Lebanese high command (virtually nonoperative because of the Lebanese civil war) and government (wielding little actual control, with the various regions ruled by rival militias), H.

was dismissed from the army. He appealed, since he regarded himself as a loyal Lebanese patriot; the matter was never fully clarified, but he and those among his men who were Lebanese army soldiers seem to have continued drawing army pay. In 1979 H. proclaimed a "Free Lebanon" entity in the area under his control; but he apparently regarded that as a symbolic declaration only, for he did not actually establish such an entity, and maintained partial links with the Beirut government or its Christian components. In June 1982, H. and his force collaborated with the invading Israeli forces and took part in the military administration Israel set up in the occupied area. H. died in Jan. 1984 and the command of the SLA was taken over by General Antoine Lahad, a retired Maronite-Christian officer of the Lebanese Army.

AL-HAFEZ, AMIN (b. 1920? 1921?)   Syrian officer and politician. President of Syria 1963–66. Aleppo-born, H. was an NCO in the French-Syrian "Special Forces" and in 1947 graduated from the Syrian Army's military academy. A veteran member of the *Ba'th* Party group of officers, H., after the *Ba'th* took power in the coup of Mar. 1963, was recalled from his post as military attache in Argentina to become Deputy Prime Minister and Minister of the Interior in the *Bitar cabinet. He soon emerged as the most prominent leader of the new regime. In July 1963 he became Chairman of the Revolutionary Council, i.e., *de facto* head of state, a post he retained when in May 1964 that body was reshaped as a Presidential Council. Concurrently he was, for some months in 1963, Defense Minister, Commander in Chief and Chief of Staff, and twice — Nov. 1963 to May 1964 and Oct. 1964 to Sept. 1965 — Prime Minister. In the factional struggles within the ruling *Ba'th* group H., though trying to stay above the factions and keep the regime united, gradually became identified with the "civilian" faction of *'Aflaq and Bitar, which was considered more moderate and "rightist." In Aug. 1965, he ousted Salah *Jadid, the head of the extremist "military faction," from his post as Chief of Staff.

In Feb. 1966 H. was overthrown by a coup of Jadid's military faction, wounded and imprisoned. He was released in June 1967 and went into exile in Lebanon. There he took part in efforts to organize the ousted wing of the *Ba'th*. In 1968 his faction joined a "National Progressive Front" of several groups opposed to the Syrian regime. As his *Ba'th* wing retained control of Iraq, he moved, with 'Aflaq and others, to that country. In 1968 he was

Amin al-Hafez (AP Photo)

accused, in Syria, of involvement in 1966 and 1967 coup attempts and plots by Salim *Hatum and tried *in absentia*; however, the verdict in that trial, in Jan. 1969, indicated that H. and some others would be tried separately. In Aug. 1971, he was sentenced to death, with four other leaders of the pro-Iraqi *Ba'th*, all *in absentia* (commuted in Nov. to life imprisonment). H. has remained in Iraq, as a member of the leadership of the pro-Iraqi *Ba'th* wing and its "national," all-Arab command. His formal post is not quite clear — in 1970, e.g., it was reported that he had been relieved of his official position to ease the way for a reconciliation between the rival *Ba'th* wings. But he remains involved in anti-Syrian activities on behalf of the Iraqi regime and the "National Alliance for the Liberation of Syria," a loose coalition of anti-*Asad factions.

HAITHAM, MUHAMMAD 'ALI (b. 1940?) South Yemeni politician, Prime Minister and member of the Presidential Council 1969–71. A school teacher, H. was active in the nationalist movement of 'Aden and South Yemen, and a member of the Central Committee of its leading organization, the NLF. When South Yemen became independent, in 1967, H. was named Minister of the Interior.

In 1969 Qahtan al-*Sha'bi, the Head of State, dismissed him in the course of a factional and personal struggle. The same year, however, Sha'bi was overthrown in a coup in which H. seems to have had a hand, and H. became Prime Minister and a member of the five-man Presidential Council (from 1970 — its deputy chairman) and of the FLN Executive Committee. In 1971 he also took over the Foreign Ministry. In the factional struggles that ensued, H. was considered right-wing, too close to tribal interests and linked to Sa'udi Arabia. He also ran afoul of 'Abd-ul-Fattah *Isma'il, then the strong man of the regime. In Aug. 1971 he was ousted and went into exile. He has since been living in Egypt. In 1975 and 1976, unsuccessful attempts were made to assassinate him. In his exile, he organized and headed political groups trying to operate against South Yemen's Marxist regime.

AL-HAJRI, 'ABDULLAH (1911? 1916?–77) Yemeni jurist (Islamic *Qadi*) and politician, Prime Minister 1972–74. After the Sept. 1962 revolution, H. was arrested as a Royalist. After a long period of detention he joined the Republicans, but within the Republican regime he maintained a conservative, right-wing line and was always suspected of Royalist tendencies. In 1972 he became a member of the Presidential Council headed by *Qadi* 'Abd-ul-Rahman *Iryani, and later the same year he was appointed Prime Minister, but between him and Iryani there was constant antagonism and rivalry. As Prime Minister, H. suppressed leftist unrest and detained many leftist activists, while admitting many former Royalists to government service. He was closely linked to Sa'udi Arabia, stonewalled plans for Yemen's union with leftist South Yemen, and was reported to be in secret contact with the former *Imam*, al-*Badr. In Feb. 1974 he was dismissed by Iryani and went into exile. He returned the same year, after Ibrahim *Hamdi's coup and Iryani's fall, and became Deputy Chief Justice. H. was assassinated — with his wife and a Yemeni diplomat — in Apr. 1977, in London (where he was again rumored to be engaging in plots with the Royalists). The identity of his murderers was never established, but it was assumed that they were leftist-radical or South Yemeni agents.

AL-HAKIM, TAWFIQ (1898? 1902–1987) Egyptian playwright and novelist. Born in Alexandria to an Egyptian father and a Turkish mother, H. was the first Arab dramatist to study Greek and European, especially French, drama and to infuse new blood into Arabic literature. H. became interested in theater and started writing plays while studying law at the University of Cairo (from 1921). From 1925 to 1927 he studied law in Paris, deepening his interest in Greek and European literature and drama.

Failing to get a doctorate in Paris, H. returned to Cairo and served in the office of the Public Prosecutor at the mixed court of Alexandria, and in 1929 he was promoted to Deputy Prosecutor and served in various towns. He described his experience in this office in his novel *Diaries of a Prosecutor in the Countryside*, 1937, translated into many languages, (English: *Maze of Justice*, 1947).

He became director of the Research Department of the Ministry of Education in 1934 and of the Information Service of the Ministry of Social Affairs in 1939.

From 1951 H. served as Director of the National Library in Cairo. After the Free Officers' revolution of 1952 he also worked in journalism. Abd-ul *Nasser considered him the spiritual father of his Egyptian Revolution, and in 1956 he was appointed, together with Taha *Hussein, a member of the Superior Arts Council headed by the young officer and writer Yussuf al-Siba'i. In 1959 he represented Egypt with UNESCO in Paris. In 1960 H. received the State Prize for Literature.

H., who had reflected on Egypt's social and national aspirations in 1933, in his novel *'Awdat al-Ruh (The Return of the Soul)*, felt disappointed with Nasser's political record and after Nasser's death denounced Nasser's despotism and his defeats in Yemen and the Six Day War in a booklet, *The Return of Consciousness*, 1975.

After the Yom Kippur War of 1973 he was, together with Nagib Mahfuz, the first Arab writer who advocated peace with Israel, which would enable Egypt and the Arab world to restore their economic and cultural life.

H. endeavored to adapt Greek tragedies to suit Arab-Muslim culture and to express his own philosophy, especially in his dramas *King Oedipus* (1949) and *Pygmalion* (1942), as well as in plays derived from the Qur'an and the Arabian Nights, such as *Suleiman al-Hakim* (1943), *Ahl al-Kahf* (1933) and *Shehrezad* (1934).

HAMDI, IBRAHIM (1939? 1943?–77) Yemeni officer and politician, President of Yemen 1974–77. H., son of a *Qadi* (Islamic judge) and trained as a *Qadi*, joined the army after the revolution of Sept. 1962, though the new Republican regime had at first detained him as a suspected Royalist. He held several command posts and served as confidential secretary to Gen. Hassan al-*'Amri, who was in the later 1960s several times Chief of Staff and Prime Minister. In Sept. 1971, Prime Minister al-*'Aini made him Deputy Premier and Minister of the Interior, and late in 1972 he became Deputy Chief of Staff with the rank of Lt.-Colonel. In June 1974, H. staged a bloodless coup, dissolved the Presidential Council and the Consultative Council, and formed a new Military Command Council with himself as chairman, i.e., head of State. He was at that time considered a "rightist" and closely linked with Sa'udi Arabia. However, in the complexities of Yemeni politics this label did not prove to be wholly fitting. H. did endeavor to foster relations with Sa'udia and managed to obtain increased aid from her, but he also took a "leftist" line in efforts to mend relations with South Yemen; and he clashed with Sa'udia's main allies in Yemen, the tribal federations of the North, and particularly the Hashed tribes who rose in rebellion — and was supported in that policy by the 1976-founded leftist and semiunderground "National Democratic Front." In effect, H. was trying to establish himself as a strong leader able to keep both the tribes and the leftists in check. H. was assassinated in Oct. 1977 — together with his brother, Lt.-Col. 'Abdullah Hamdi, the commander of an elite brigade. The identity of the murderers was never established; it was assumed that they came either from the right wing and the tribes or, more probably, from a group of officers plotting for power.

HAMMER, ZVULUN (b. 1936)   Israeli politician, a leader of the Zionist-religious movement. Born in Haifa, did his army service in the *Nahal* and then studied at Bar-Ilan University. He began his political activity at an early age in the framework of the "young generation" of the National Religious Party (NRP), which he headed for many years.

In 1969 he was elected to the Seventh Knesset and has since held a Knesset seat. His political position was considerably more hawkish than that held by the older NRP leadership and he contributed greatly to the party's political radicalization. He was a staunch supporter of settling the West Bank and a leading supporter of *Gush Emunim*. He also opposed the disengagement agreements concluded with Egypt in 1975.

In 1973 he was appointed Deputy Minister of Education and Culture and from 1975 to 1976 was Minister of Welfare in the *Rabin government. On the eve of the elections to the Ninth Knesset, 1977, he led the group which deposed Yitzhak Rafael

from the NRP leadership. This enabled him to dissolve the "historic pact" between the NRP and the Labor Party and to conclude an alliance with the *Likud*. After the *Likud's* election victory of 1977 he was appointed Minister of Education and Culture, a position which he held until 1984. He was considered a serious Minister of Education who saw in this position an end in itself — not a stepping-stone to another position. During his years as Minister of Education his political position became more moderate, and during the War in Lebanon he was one of the chief opponents of Minister of Defense Ariel *Sharon. H. was considered as sharing the responsibility for the NRP's loss of votes in 1984 and 1988, and after Yosef *Burg's retirement, he was not chosen to head the NRP list to the Knesset in his place, but was forced to settle for second place.

In 1984 he was not appointed to the government, but returned in 1986 as Minister of Religious Affairs. In 1990, after the National Unity Government was dissolved, he was again appointed Minister of Education and Culture.

HARAWI, ELIAS (b. 1930)   Lebanese politican, President of Lebanon since Nov. 1989. A Maronite Christian, born in a village of the Zahla region in East Lebanon to a landowning family, H. did not pursue the law studies he had started, but took a first degree in business administration and devoted himself to the management of his lands and to agricultural interests.

He was elected to Parliament in 1972 (the last Lebanese Parliament elected). From 1980 to 1982 he served as Minister of Public Works. When in Nov. 1989 Rene *Mu'awwad, the President just elected, was killed, H., though not a major leader, was found acceptable to Syria and the Syrian-guided rump Parliament meeting outside Lebanon (in Ta'if, Sa'udia) to set up a new regime against Michel *'Awn's government in East Beirut, and was elected President of Lebanon. As President, H. has not given his country inspiring, rallying leadership; but he has succeeded in gradually extending, with the support of Syrian troops, the area his regime controls — including, for the first time in many years, large parts of South Lebanon (1991) — and in arranging for the dissolution of the various rival militias and their integration into the army and government establishment. H. fully "coordinates" his policies with Syria and accepts her "guidance," formalized in a Lebanese-Syrian Treaty of May 1991.

HAR'EL (original name: Halperin), **ISSER** (b. 1911)   One of the heads of Israeli intelligence. Born in Russia. Immigrated to Palestine in 1931. A member of Kibbutz Shefayim. During the 1940s he was active in the *Haganah* and was one of the heads of the *Shai*, its intelligence service. During the War of Independence he commanded the *Shai* in the Tel Aviv area. In 1952 he was appointed head of the Israel Intelligence Agency (*Mossad*) and for many years he was the central figure in Israeli intelligence. In addition to his being the head of the *Mossad*, he was also responsible for all the security services. Under his supervision, the *Mossad* succeeded in 1960 in capturing Adolf Eichmann and bringing him to Israel. In 1963 H. resigned his position due to serious differences with Prime Minister *Ben Gurion over the means of dealing with the German scientists then working in Egypt. His resignation hastened that of Ben Gurion, which occurred several months later.

After his resignation, H. served as Prime Minister Levi *Eshkol's intelligence adviser and was a member of the Seventh Knesset (1969–1973) for the *La'am* party, headed by Ben Gurion. In 1976 he was one of the founders of the Democratic Movement headed by Yigal *Yadin. Over the years he wrote several books about his years of service in the security forces.

H. wielded a great deal of influence over the political system during his years as head of the *Mossad*. He was very close to the inner circle of *Mapai* in general and to Prime Minister Ben Gurion in particular.

HASHEM, IBRAHIM (1884? 1888?–1958)   Jordanian politician, born in Nablus, Palestine. Prime Minister of Jordan 1931–38, 1945–47, 1955–56, and during the crises of Apr. 1975 when he aided King *Hussein to keep control. As Deputy Prime Minister of the short-lived 1958 Jordan-Iraq "Arab Federation" he was assassinated in July 1958 in Baghdad during the Iraqi coup.

HASHEMITES, HASHEMIS, HOUSE OF HASHEM   Banu Hashem are the family, or clan, of the Qureish tribe to which the Prophet Muhammad belonged. In the 20th century, the H. has come to refer specifically to the family of the Sharifs of Mecca, from which came the Kings of Hijaz, Iraq, briefly Syria, and Jordan. They are descendants of the Prophet Muhammad through his daughter Fatima and his son-in-law 'Ali, and their son al-Hassan. They thus carry, like all descendants of that line, the title Sharif, and one of them usually bore the honorific Sharif of Mecca.

The Sharif *Hussein Ibn 'Ali (1852–1932) was appointed Amir of Mecca in 1908. In 1916, after obtaining promises of British support through an exchange of letters with Sir Henry McMahon, the British High Commissioner in Egypt, he staged an "Arab Revolt" against the Ottoman Empire and proclaimed himself King of Hijaz. In 1924 he took steps to declare himself Caliph, but this was not accepted by the Islamic world. The same year he was defeated by *Ibn Sa'ud and abdicated in order to save his throne for his dynasty (he died in exile). His son *'Ali (1879–1935) succeeded to the throne of Hijaz, but after less than a year he was driven out by Ibn Sa'ud (he died in exile, in Baghdad). 'Ali's son *'Abd-ul-Ilah (1912–58) was Regent of Iraq, 1939–53; 'Ali's daughter 'Aliya (d. 1950) married King *Ghazi of Iraq.

Two other sons of Hussein founded dynasties. *Feisal (1885–1933) reigned for a short time in Damascus, 1919–20, and was driven out by the French. In 1921, by an agreement with the British endorsed by a sort of referendum, he became King of Iraq and reigned there until his death. His only son *Ghazi (1912–39), who succeeded him, was killed in an accident. As Ghazi's son, *Feisal II (1935–58), was a small child, his uncle 'Abd-ul-Ilah acted as Regent; when Feisal came of age and was crowned in 1953, 'Abd-ul-Ilah became Crown Prince. They were both killed in the July 1958 coup d'etat in Baghdad, and the Iraqi branch of the H. came to an end.

Hussein ibn 'Ali's second son, *'Abdullah (1882–1951), was made by the British in 1921 Amir of Transjordan — a state they established for him in the framework of their Mandate for Palestine. In 1946 he obtained full independence, took the title of King, and changed the name of Transjordan to "The H. Kingdom of Jordan." He reemphasized the new name in 1948, when he occupied the Arab part of Palestine, the "West Bank" (formally annexed in 1950). 'Abdullah was assassinated in 1951 at the al-Aqsa Mosque in Jerusalem. His son *Talal (1909–72) succeeded him, but was deposed in 1952 when found to be mentally ill; he was hospitalized in Istanbul and died there. Talal's son *Hussein (b. 1935) has ruled Jordan since 1953 and has grown into one of the major statesmen of the Middle East. The Crown Prince is his younger brother Hassan (b. 1947) rather than his brother Muhammad (b. 1945). The eventual succession of Hussein's own sons might pose a problem, since only one of them — 'Ali (b. 1975) — was born from an Arab-Jordanian Muslim mother, while the mothers of two older and two younger sons were, though converted to Islam, of foreign origin. In 1978 'Ali was named (second) Crown Prince, after the King's brother Hassan.

The leadership of the H. dynasty stood at the cradle of Arab independence in the Fertile Crescent after World War I with British assistance. When H. plans to found a single kingdom, or a federation of kingdoms, failed and the region was divided into separate states under British and French tutelage, the H. found themselves reigning (apart from Hijaz, until 1924) in two countries: Iraq and Jordan. The idea of reviving the original scheme and establishing a H.-headed kingdom or federation, and mainly of bringing Syria, as well as Lebanon and Palestine (or at least its Arab part), under their domination, continued to animate some of them. 'Abdullah was the chief protagonist of this plan (for Greater Syria). The Iraqi branch had similar plans, in a different version, and its support for 'Abdullah's scheme was always in some doubt. Most Arab states always opposed both versions, particularly Egypt, Syria, Lebanon and Sa'udi Arabia, and their opposition prevailed. British support for these H. plans was doubtful and at best partial; yet the French, and many Arabs, always suspected British plots behind them. These revisionist-expansionist schemes of the H. faded away after the assassination of 'Abdullah in 1951 and that of Feisal II and 'Abd-ul-Ilah in 1958. Another aim of the H. was perhaps to return to Hijaz and rule it; though this idea was sometimes broached it never had serious prospects, and it was finally shelved in the late 1940s and the 1950s, when a H.-Sa'udi *rapprochement* took place.

The H. kings and princes were loyal allies of the British (perhaps with the exception of King Ghazi of Iraq, but he died too young to have much impact on the policies of his country). This loyalty, and the fact that the very rule of the H. was arranged by the British, made them suspect for many Arab nationalists, who regarded them as collaborators or stooges of Britain (and, after the eclipse of the British Empire, of the USA). Some of the H. were also prepared to envisage an agreement and cooperation with a Jewish-Zionist Palestine and later with Israel, and actively to work for it — from the Feisal-*Weizmann Agreement of 1919, through 'Abdullah's long-standing friendly contacts with the Zionist leaders, his secret understanding with them in 1946–47 and his negotiations and (abor-

tive) draft agreement with Israel in 1949–50, to Hussein's readiness, in principle, to accept peace and coexistence with Israel and his secret contracts with her several times. This attitude has made the H. further unpopular with radical Arab nationalists (and since the 1980s Hussein seems to have abandoned it).

The H. clan has several branches apart from the line of Sharif/King Hussein and his sons, and many of their members held state positions in Iraq. Thus Sharif **Sharaf** (1879/80–1955) was appointed Regent when the Rashid 'Ali *Kilani regime deposed 'Abd-ul-Ilah in 1941; when that regime fell, he was interned and after the war went to Jordan, where he was named a Senator. Many held or still hold, positions in Jordan — in the army, the Court, civil service and political posts. Among them, Sharif **Hussein ibn Nasser,** (1906–82), married to a daughter of King 'Abdullah, Ambassador, Chief of the Royal Court, and twice Prime Minister, 1963–64 and 1967. Sharif **Nasser ibn Jamil** (1927–79), born and educated in Iraq, an officer in the Iraqi army, later rose to a senior position in the Jordanian army; Minister of the Royal Court 1961–63, Commander in Chief 1969–70, dismissed upon the demand of the Palestinian guerrillas (his sister married King Talal and became the mother of King Hussein). Sharif **'Abd-ul-Hamid Sharaf** (1939–80), the son of the Iraqi ex-Regent Sharaf, Minister of Information, Ambassador to the USA and the UN, Prime Minister 1979–80; his brother **Fawaz** (b. 1938), Ambassador to the USA in the 1970s, Minister of Culture and Youth 1976–79; Sharif **Zeid ibn Shaker** (b. 1934), Commander in Chief of the Jordanian armed forces 1976–88, and since Dec. 1988 Chief of the Royal Court, except for eight months in 1989 as Prime Minister; **Ra'd ibn Zeid**, King Hussein's aide-de-camp, belongs to Sharif Hussein's direct line, being the son of the Sharif's youngest son **Zeid** (1898–1970), who never played a prominent role. King Hussein also took his first wife, Dina, in 1955, from the distant 'Awn branch of the H. clan (he divorced her in 1957).

AL-HASHEMI, TAHA (1888–1961)   Iraqi officer and politician, brother of Yassin al-*Hashemi. A Sunni Muslim, born in Baghdad, H. graduated from the Istanbul Military College and served as an officer in the Ottoman army, 1908–18. He participated in Arab nationalist societies, but in World War I remained loyal to the Ottomans. During Amir *Feisal's rule in Syria, 1919/20, he was Director of Defense. After Feisal's fall, H.

went to Iraq and joined the army. He retired in 1926 with the rank of Colonel and served in various civilian posts, but returned to the army and became its Chief of Staff, 1929–36; he was promoted to Lt.-General in 1936. During Bakr *Sidqi's coup of Oct. 1936 he was in Turkey, and remained there until the restoration of the old regime in 1937. He then became politically active. In 1937 he was co-founder and President of the Society for the Defense of Palestine in Baghdad. He also intrigued with the group of younger pro-German officers that later became known as the "Golden Square." In the governments installed under their pressure, H. was Minister of Defense and Interior 1938–40, and Minister of Defense 1940/41. In Feb. 1941, a semi-coup forced the Regent to appoint him Prime Minister, and in his two months in power he prepared the way for another semi-coup that brought the rightist, pro-German Rashid 'Ali *Kilani to power. When the British defeated Rashid 'Ali in May and restored the *Hashemite Regent, H. fled to Turkey, where he stayed until 1946. In autumn 1947 H. was mentioned as a possible Commander in Chief of the Arab forces preparing to invade Palestine, but the idea was dropped — probably because he was *persona non grata* with the Iraqi regime; he served, however, in 1948, as a military adviser to the all-Arab committee co-ordinating the Palestine struggle. In 1951–53, H. was active in attempts to form a right-wing opposition National Front. He was vice-chairman of the Development Board, 1953–58. After the coup of July 1958 his appointment was not renewed. H. published several books on geography and military subjects.

AL-HASHEMI, YASSIN(1884–1937)   Iraqi politician and officer. On the eve of World War I, H. was active in clandestine Arab nationalist societies, but in the war he remained loyal to the Ottoman army, in which he served as a colonel. After the establishment of the Kingdom of Iraq in 1921, he took an active part in political life and served several times as Finance Minister. In 1924–25 he was Prime Minister. H. was one of the leaders of the right-wing nationalist "National Brotherhood Party" (*Hizb al-Ikha' al-Watani*), 1931–35, which opposed the Anglo-Iraqi Treaty of 1930 as granting Britain excessive privileges. In 1935–36 he was again Prime Minister. His government was overthrown by an army officers' coup under Bakr *Sidqi and he went into exile to Damascus, where he died in 1937.

King Hassan II (IPS, Tel Aviv)

HASSAN II (b. 1929)   King of Morocco since 1961. The eldest son of *Muhammad V, Ibn Yussuf, the Sultan (from 1959: King) of Morocco, Prince H. (also bearing, according to Moroccan custom, the honorific *Moulay*), received a French and Arabic-Muslim education at a college founded in 1941 for his and his brother's schooling, and later studied law at Bordeaux University. He became a close collaborator of his father the Sultan, but was reputed to sympathize with the nationalists. In 1953 he accompanied his father into exile in Madagascar and returned with him to Morocco in Nov. 1955, on the eve of independence. In July 1957 his father appointed him Crown Prince; he also formally headed the armed forces as Chief of Staff. In May 1960 the King, assuming the Premiership himself, named Prince H. Deputy Prime Minister. In Feb. 1961 H. succeeded to the throne upon King Muhammad's death. He retained the Premiership until 1963 and resumed it from 1965 to 1967; after the coup attempt of Aug. 1972 he assumed the command of the armed forces and made himself Defense Minister (until 1973). King H.'s rule was conservative, but he introduced, after several attempts and experiments, a constitution of representative government and endeavored to keep leftist-nationalist factions within the establishment, sometimes as partners in coalition governments. He overcame two serious military coup attempts in July 1971 and Aug. 1972 and had to face a great deal of social tension and ferment, and sometimes subversion. Several times he resorted to harsh measures to suppress leftist factions and what he considered their subversive plots. His vigorous nationalist policy over the issue of Western (formerly Spanish) Sahara since the mid-1970s made him more popular even with leftist groups. In line with Moroccan tradition King H., a "Sharif," a direct descendant of the Prophet Muhammad, is also endowed with a certain religious-Islamic standing as head of Moroccan Islam.

King H.'s foreign policy was conservative — except for a brief demonstration of radical tendencies in the early 1960s (the "Casablanca Bloc"). He fostered close relations with France and the USA. In inter-Arab affairs, he kept Morocco within the moderate-conservative camp, and his relations with *Nasser's Egypt and the rest of the radical camp were sometimes tense; this applied particularly to Algeria where, in addition to Algeria's radical orientation, relations were troubled by border disputes and basic conflicts of interest (e.g., over Sahara), and to Libya (despite a brief abortive confederate union with that country, 1984–86). King H. demonstrated his independence of thought by secretly aiding the preparations for Egyptian President *Sadat's peace moves in 1977 (though he felt compelled to join the other Arab states in 1979 in severing relations with Egypt). He also showed his nonconformist moderation regarding the Arab-Israel issue by permitting a measure of relations between the Jews of Morocco and Israel, by allowing visits of Israelis to Morocco, including public figures, and inviting Premier *Peres of Israel to Morocco for talks in 1986. In the Persian Gulf crisis caused by Iraq's invasion of Kuwait, Aug. 1990, King H. sent a small contingent of Moroccan troops to help defend Sa'udi Arabia and join the U.S.-led international coalition against Iraq — despite largely pro-Iraqi public opinion and mass demonstrations.

HASSAN IBN YAHYA (b. 1896? 1897?) Yemeni prince and politician, Prime Minister of Yemen 1949–55, and of the Royalist Yemeni regime 1962–67/68. One of the sons of Imam-King *Yahya Hamid-ul-Din (bearing, like all the Imam's sons, the title *Seif ul-Islam*, "Sword of Islam"), H. was reported to aspire to the succession and thus

was a rival to his brother *Ahmad. This rivalry continued when Ahmad ascended the throne in 1948, after the assassination of Imam Yahya. But Prince H., who had filled quasi-ministerial posts before (Yemen then had no clearly defined council of ministers), continued serving the government in senior positions. From the late 1940s until 1955 he was described as Prime Minister. In 1955 he became his country's ambassador at the UN, a post he held until 1962. After Imam Ahmad's death and the coup of Sept. 1962, when Prince *Badr, the designated heir to the throne, was reported killed, H. proclaimed himself Imam-King, but stepped down when Badr emerged alive. From 1962/63 to 1967/68 he was Prime Minister of the Royalist Government that resisted the post-1962 Republican regime and was in limited control of some parts of northern Yemen. H.'s own position in the Royalist camp was precarious and involved in factional intrigues; he was also ailing and had to go abroad for treatment. With the Republican-Royalist settlement of 1969/70 that abolished the Imamate and excluded the royal family, H. went into exile and ceased all activity in public affairs.

HASSUNA, 'ABD-UL-KHALEQ (b. 1898) Egyptian administrator, diplomat and politician. Son of a leading Islamic scholar, H. studied law at Cairo and Cambridge Universities, and entered the foreign service, where he attained the rank of ambassador and became Under-Secretary of State. In 1942 he was appointed Governor of Alexandria. In 1949 he briefly served as Minister of Social Affairs, and in 1952 — as Minister of Education and, in the two governments formed by Nagib al-Hilali, Foreign Minister. After the revolution of July 1952, H. was elected Secretary-General of the Arab League, to replace *'Azzam; he held this position until June 1972, when he retired. H. was considered an administrator rather than a decision-making leader.

HATEM, 'ABD-UL-QADER (b. 1917) Egyptian officer and politician. H. graduated from the Military College, 1939, and Staff College, 1952, and also obtained degrees in Political Economy (B.A., London, 1947), Political Science (M.A., Cairo, 1953), and Information (Ph.D., Cairo). He was one of the "Free Officers" who staged the coup of July 1952 and became *Nasser's assistant for press and information. In 1957, he retired from the army with the rank of Colonel and became a member of the National Assembly. In 1959, he was appointed Minister of State for Information, and from 1962

'Abd-ul-Qader Hatem (AP Photo)

Na'if Hawatma (AP Photo)

coup, and when that failed, he escaped to Jordan with some of his supporters. In June 1967, during the Six Day War, he suddenly returned to Syria — to put himself, as he said, at the service of the army; but the regime maintained he had come to overthrow it, put him on summary trial and executed him in June 1967.

to 1966 was full Minister for Information, National Guidance and Culture, from 1964 also as Deputy Prime Minister; since 1963 he was also a member of the Secretariat of Egypt's single party, the Arab Socialist Union. From 1966 to 1971 he held no government position, owing to the factional struggles within Nasser's ruling group. In May 1971, when *Sadat ousted the 'Ali *Sabri faction, H. again became Deputy Prime Minister and Minister of Information, until 1974. When he left that post, he continued serving Sadat as an adviser. He also was, in 1974–75, for about a year, chairman of the board of the *al-Ahram* newspaper and publishing house. He was several times considered, in the 1970s, a candidate for the Premiership, but did not attain that office. Apart from numerous articles, H. wrote or edited several books on matters of information and propaganda.

HATUM, SALIM (d. 1967)   Syrian Druze officer. Heading Syria's commando units, with the rank of Major, then Colonel, H. was linked with the underground group of *Ba'th* officers. In Feb. 1966 he took a leading part in the coup that brought to power the "military" and extremist faction of the *Ba'th* under Salah *Jadid. Later, however, he plotted with the ousted *Ba'th* faction, the "National Leadership," and reportedly also with Jordan's secret services. In Sept. 1966 he attempted another

HAWATMA, NA'IF (b. 1934)   Palestinian-Jordanian guerrilla/terrorist leader. A Greek-Catholic Christian born in al-Salt, Jordan, H. is a Marxist-Maoist. He was active in the extremist Arab Nationalist Movement (*al-Qawmiyyun al-'Arab*) in the 1950s and 1960s and the Popular Front for the Liberation of Palestine (PFLP) that grew out of it after 1967, and headed their left wing. In 1969 H. seceded from the PFLP and set up his own organization, the Popular Democratic Front for the Liberation of Palestine (PDFLP) in constant leftist opposition to *'Arafat and the mainstream of the PLO.

HAZAN, YA'AKOV (b. 1899)   Israeli political leader. Born in Brest-Litovsk, Russia (later Poland). One of the founders of the *Hashomer Hatzair* youth movement. In 1922 he immigrated to Palestine and was one of the founders of Kibbutz Mishmar Ha'emek and the Kibbutz Ha'artzi. For many years he was a member of the executive secretariat of the *Histadrut*.

Together with Meir *Ya'ari, H. for many years headed the Kibbutz Ha'artzi and later *Mapam*. While Ya'ari's strength was primarily in thought and writing, H. was the representative figure, a brilliant orator and a charismatic leader.

In 1949, H. was elected to the First Knesset and

was a member of the Knesset continuously until 1973. He was the main spokesman of *Mapam* on topics of foreign and defense policy. He refused to join the government and had *Mapam* represented in the various governments by leaders of the second rank, not by him or Ya'ari. In 1969 he was one of the architects of the Alignment between the Labor Party and *Mapam* and for many years opposed tendencies to dissolve it and reestablish *Mapam* as a separate party. He was considered the leader of the right-wing faction in *Mapam*, and his positions on matters of national security were relatively hawkish. He was quite close to a number of Labor Party leaders, particularly Golda *Meir.

H. is widely respected, beyond the ranks of *Mapam*, the Kibbutz Ha'artzi and the Labor movement. In 1989 he received the Israel Prize for his contribution to Israeli society.

HERZOG, HAIM (Vivian) (b. 1918)   Israeli officer and politician, President of Israel since 1983. Born in Dublin, Ireland, son of Rabbi Isaac Halevi Herzog, then Chief Rabbi of Ireland. In 1936, when his father was named Ashkenazi Chief Rabbi of Palestine, he immigrated with him and studied at the Mercaz Harav and Hebron *Yeshivot*. Afterwards he studied law at the Palestine Law School and in London and Cambridge. During the Second World War he served as an intelligence officer in the British Army.

In 1948, with the establishment of the Israeli Defense Forces, he was appointed Director of Intelligence, and afterwards continued in army posts — military attache in Washington, 1950–54; Commander of the Jerusalem District and Head of the Southern Command, 1954–59; and Chief of Intelligence, 1959–62. He retired from the army in 1962 with the rank of Major-General.

After his demobilization he turned to private law practice. In 1965 he joined the *Rafi* faction which seceded from *Mapai* and was secretary of its Tel Aviv branch. In 1967, during the Six Day War, he was a leading and much appreciated military commentator for the Israel Broadcasting Authority, and after the war he briefly was Military Governor of the West Bank. During the Yom Kippur War of 1973 he resumed his military commentaries on the radio. From 1975 to 1978 he was Israeli Ambassador to the United Nations. Upon his return he became a member of the Bureau of the Labor Party and in 1981 was elected to the Knesset on the Alignment list. In 1983 he was elected as the sixth President of the State of Israel, narrowly

defeating the *Likud* candidate. He was reelected in 1988 for a second term.

HEYKAL, MUHAMMAD HASSANEIN (b. 1923) Egyptian journalist, writer and politician. After studying in Egypt (journalism, economics, law), H. worked as a reporter for several Egyptian newspapers (*Egyptian Gazette*; *Rose al-Yussuf*), reporting *inter alia* the desert campaign in World War II and the Greek civil war. He gained prominence reporting the Palestine War of 1948 for *Akhbar al-Yawm*. In the early 1950s he was editor of the *Akher Sa'a* weekly and later coeditor of the daily *al-Akhbar*, of which he became chief editor in 1956–57. After the revolution of 1952, he became close to *Nasser and his associates, and in 1957 was appointed chief editor of *al-Ahram*, Egypt's most prestigious daily, considered the semiofficial mouthpiece of the government. Gradually, H. became Egypt's most influential journalist and a close adviser and confidant of President Nasser. In 1970 he served for a few months as Minister of Information and National Guidance. H. was a loyal Nasserist, identified with the regime, but was permitted to retain a large measure of independent politicial thinking. According to his own account, he advised Nasser not to rely on an alliance with the Soviet Union exclusively but to cultivate better relations with the USA and the West, too, and also advocated a more liberal regime, a larger measure of democracy, press freedom, etc. In the factional struggles within Nasser's team he was thus considered a right-winger.

After Nasser's death, in 1970, he soon fell out with President *Sadat — despite their personal friendship. Remaining a Nasserist, he demounced Sadat's deviation from, or betrayal of, Nasser's heritage. He opposed Sadat's total alliance with the USA, and he disapproved of Sadat's peacemaking with Israel and the ensuing rift between Egypt and the Arab states. In 1974 he was dismissed as editor and chairman of *al-Ahram* and barred from publishing his articles in the Egyptian press. In 1977–78 he was subjected to interrogations by the police and the State Attorney, and for some months was denied the right to go abroad. In Sadat's Sept. 1981 purges he was detained, but was released later in the year by Sadat's successor, President *Mubarak. As he could not publish in Egypt, in 1975–76 he began publishing articles and regular columns in foreign newspapers, and from 1971 also published in the West several books on Egyptian and Middle East politics.

H. has not regained, under Mubarak's regime since late 1981, either his major influence on policy planning and decisions or his leading position in the Egyptian media, and maintains a stance of Nasserist opposition. But he enjoys considerable prestige as a leading intellectual and a gifted writer and journalist. He is sometimes mentioned as a possible mediator between Egypt and her adversaries among the Arab states (e.g., Libya).

HEYKAL, MUHAMMAD HUSSEIN(1888–1956) Egyptian writer, journalist and politician. Born to a wealthy landowning family in Lower Egypt, H. studied law in Cairo and Paris, where he obtained his doctorate (1912). In 1907 he joined the moderate and liberal *Umma* Party founded by Ahmad Lutfi al-Sayyid and contributed to the party's newspaper *al-Jarida*.

In 1913, a year after he returned to Egypt, under the pseudonym Misri Fallah ("Egyptian Peasant") — he published a novel, *Zaynab*, the first romantic Egyptian novel with a proper characterization and plot (the love of Zaynab who was forced to marry the friend of her beloved); it depicts peasant life in Egypt and defends women's freedom, social equality and Egyptian patriotism.

In 1915 H. established, with a group of young associates, the magazine *al-Sufur*, and in 1922 he became the editor of the newspaper *al-Siyasa* (and its literary and cultural supplement, added in 1926), the mouthpiece of the Liberal Constitutional Party.

In his journalistic, historical and biographical works H. propounded a modernist, rationalist liberalism strongly influenced by Western European liberal thought; later, in the 1930s, he turned to the

Muhammad Hussein Heykal (AP Photo)

Islamic heritage of the Arab world, writing biographies of the Prophet Muhammad (1935) and the first caliphs (1942, 1944) and sought a synthesis of Islamic and Western-liberal thought. In 1940 H. was elected as a member of the Academy of the Arabic Language.

H. was prominent in politics as well. He was one of the founders of the Liberal Constitutional Party (1922), served as Minister of Education from 1937 to 1942, and again in 1944. On the death of his party's chairman, Muhammad Mahmud, in 1941, he became party leader, at first jointly with 'Abdul-'Aziz Fahmy, and from 1943 served as the party's president. From 1944 to 1949 he was President of the Senate. After the "Free Officers" Revolution of 1952, H. was deprived, in Apr. 1954, of his political rights, along with other prominent politicians of the old regime. H.'s 21 books include three volumes of *Memoirs on Egyptian Politics* (1951, 1953 and 1978, posthumous), and Western orientalists have published several biographical studies of his thought.

AL-HILALI, (AHMAD) NAGIB (1891–1958) Egyptian jurist and politician, Prime Minister 1952. H. was Minister of Education, 1934–36, in Tawfiq Nessim's government close to the King's palace. He joined the *Wafd* party in 1937 and was Minister of Education in Mustafa al-*Nahhas' government, 1942–44. Yet he never belonged to the inner leadership of the *Wafd* and was at odds with the party apparatus. In 1951 he harshly criticized the party (mainly over the issue of corruption, which he wanted to make the main plank of the party and its governments), and was expelled. As an independent neutral, he was named Prime Minister in Mar. 1952, after the Wafdist government had involved the country in a violent conflict with Britain. He served for three months only, and was again Prime Minister for one day in July 1952, on the eve of the Free Officers' coup. H. was imprisoned for a while, and in Apr. 1954 he was one of 38 old-regime politicians deprived of their civil and political rights for ten years; he died before these rights were restored to the whole group in Jan. 1960.

HILOU, CHARLES (b. 1912) Lebanese politician. President of Lebanon, 1964–70. The son of a Christian-Maronite middle-class Beirut family, H. studied law and worked as a lawyer and journalist. In 1936, he was among the founders of the Phalanges, but later left that organization and joined

Bishara al-*Khouri's "Constitutional Bloc." From 1935 to 1946 he was managing editor of the daily *Le Jour*. In 1947, he served briefly as Minister to the Holy See. He was a member of Parliament from 1951 to 1961, elected on a list supporting President al-Khouri. H. was Minister of Justice and Information in 1949, and of Justice and Health in 1954/55, during Camille *Chamoun's presidency. In 1957 he joined Chamoun's opponents and founded, with Henri Far'oun, a "Third Force," mostly Christian supporters of Bishara al-Khouri who opposed Chamoun and his alleged efforts to win a second term as President, but stood aside and were neutral when the opposition adopted violent methods. This neutral stand, and his retirement from politics (he did not stand for Parliament in 1960), aided his election as President in 1964, as a neutral — and rather colorless — compromise candidate. As President, H. continued the policies of his predecessor, Fu'ad *Shihab, both in foreign affairs (with a slight shift towards stricter neutrality in inter-Arab affairs and less identification with the Nasserist bloc) and internally (cautious neutrality in communal and factional issues, administrative reforms); during his presidency, Shihab's strong personality continued to cast its shadow, with the army and secret services under Shihab's dominating influence. As President, H. approved the "Cairo Agreement" of Nov. 1969, by which Lebanon, bowing to *Nasser's pressure, allowed the Palestinian-Arab guerrillas of the PLO to operate, under certain conditions, in and from Lebanon.

After his presidential term expired in 1970, H. was no longer active in politics. However, during the civil war from 1975 on he was sometimes consulted as a respected former President who might assist in conciliation efforts. In July 1979 he agreed to serve as Minister of State for National Reconciliation in the government headed by Salim al-*Huss, but he resigned after three weeks. In the crisis of 1985/86 concerning Amin *Jumayyil's presidency H. did not wholeheartedly back Jumayyil; he made some feeble efforts to conciliate, but played no prominent role.

HINNAWI, SAMI (1898? 1904?–50) Syrian officer and politician. In Aug. 1949, a colonel, he staged a coup against President Husni *Za'im, executed both Za'im and his Prime Minister Muhsin al-*Barazi, and appointed himself Chairman of the Revolutionary Council and Chief of Staff. He allowed political activity to resume and in Nov.

1949 held elections. He was close to the People's Party (*Hizb al-Sha'b*) and encouraged its participation in the government. He initiated closer relations with the Hashemite kingdoms, Jordan and especially Iraq, and was suspected of planning a union of Syria and Iraq. H. was deposed, in another coup, by Adib al-*Shishakli in Dec. 1949, and arrested; but he was soon released and allowed to leave for Beirut. There he was murdered in 1950 — reportedly in revenge for the killing of al-Barazi.

HOROWITZ, DAVID (1899–1979) Israeli economist. Born in Eastern Galicia, he was one of the founders of *Hashomer Hatzair*. In 1920 he immigrated to Palestine and was one of the founders of Kevutzat Beitanya and Kibbutz Beit Alfa. He was a member of the *Gedud Ha'avoda* (the "Workers' Brigade") and a leader of its left wing. However, after the Brigade split in 1926, he did not join his associates who left Palestine for the Soviet Union.

In the late 1920s he joined the editorial board of *Davar*, the daily paper of the *Histadrut*. During the 1930s and 1940s he was one of the most prominent economists in *Mapai* and the Jewish *Yishuv* in Palestine. He was the chief assistant to Eliezer Kaplan, Treasurer of the Jewish Agency, and from 1935 to 1948 directed its Finance Department. In this capacity he was one of the architects of the economic policy of the Jewish Agency and presented it before the Anglo-American Committee of Inquiry and the United Nations during the deliberations which preceded the establishment of the State of Israel.

After the establishment of the state he was Director-General of the Finance Ministry until 1952. He then headed a committee which established the Bank of Israel and was chosen as its first Governor, a position he held until 1971. As governor of the national bank he played an important role in forming the country's fiscal and economic policy and was greatly respected by its economic leaders. After he retired from this position he headed the consultative committee of the Bank of Israel. In 1968 he was awarded the Israel Prize.

HOURANI, AKRAM (b. 1914) Syrian politician, lawyer and journalist. Vice-President of the United Arab Republic (UAR, Egypt-Syria), 1958–59. Born in Homs, H. was active in various nationalist organizations. During World War II, he went to Iraq and reportedly participated in groups preparing and assisting Rashid 'Ali *Kilani's seizure of power in 1941. In 1943 and 1947 he was elected to

Parliament, profiling himself as a campaigner for agrarian reform and a defender of the oppressed tenants against the big landlords. For some time he edited a newspaper, *al-Yakza*. In 1948 he volunteered for service with al-*Qawuqji's "Army of Deliverance" against emerging Israel and saw action in Galilee. In 1949 H. supported all three military coups — first Husni *Za'im's, then *Hinnawi's against Za'im, and finally al-*Shishakli's. Under Hinnawi, late in 1949, he was reelected to Parliament and served as a Minister in Hashem al-*Atassi's government. Under Shishakli, he was Minister of Defense in Khaled al-*'Azm's government. In 1949–50, he belonged to a loose "Republican Bloc" in Parliament, but in 1950 he founded his own party, the Arab Socialist Party. That party merged in 1953 with the Arab Renaissance Party (*al-Ba'th*) and H. became, with *'Aflaq and *Bitar, one of the top leaders of the united "Arab Socialist *Ba'th* Party." He fell out with Shishakli and went into exile to Lebanon. In 1954, after Shishakli's fall, H. was reelected, and in 1957 became President of Parliament. He was one of the architects of Syria's union with Egypt, 1958, and was named Vice-President of the United Arab Republic (UAR) and Minister of Justice, Syria's top representative in the new union's government. But, together with his *Ba'th* colleagues, he soon became bitterly critical of the new Egyptian-dominated regime and its chief leader, *Nasser, and late in 1959 he resigned. After Syria's secession and the disbandment of the UAR, 1961, H. opposed the *Ba'th* Party's efforts for renewed, federal union with Egypt. He left the party and, elected in Dec. 1961 on his own, local Homs list of candidates, he tried to reestablish his Arab Socialist Party.

During the *Ba'th* officers' coup of Mar. 1963 he was arrested, and when released he went into exile to Lebanon. He has not returned to Syria since, but has been cultivating his faction in exile, as a potential alternative to Syria's military *Ba'th* regime, joining, since 1968, with various like-minded factions in an exiled "National Progressive Front."

HOVEIDA, AMIR 'ABBAS (1919–79)   Iranian diplomat and politician, Prime Minister, 1965–77. Born in Tehran, H. graduated in political science and economics from Brussels (M.A.) and Paris (Ph.D.) universities. He joined the foreign service and gradually rose in rank, serving in France, Germany and Turkey. He also served with the UN Work and Relief Agency (UNRWA), at its Geneva office (1952–56), and was a member of the board of directors of the Iranian Petroleum Company (1958–64), and Secretary of the Treasury (1964–65). He was assistant secretary of the *Novin* Party, set up in 1963 to support the government.

H. served as Prime Minister longer than any other Iranian politican in the 20th century and symbolized the stability of Iran's political system under the Shah. His resignation, ordered by the Shah, as the regime faced growing economic difficulties and harsh public criticism, signaled the end of unrestricted economic growth and created the impression that public criticism was effective. In Feb. 1979, H. gave himself up to Ayatullah *Khomeini's government, and was tried and executed.

HOZ, DOV (1894–1940)   A leader of the Jewish Yishuv in Mandatory Palestine, active in the *Histadrut* and the Labor Party (*Mapai*) and one of the top commanders of the *Haganah*. Born in Warsaw, in 1905 H. immigrated to Palestine with his parents. He was in the first graduating class of the Gymnasia Herzlia high school in Tel Aviv.

During the First World War he was drafted into the Turkish army where he reached the rank of officer. Afterwards he joined the Jewish Battalions. He was one of the founders of the *Haganah* in 1920 and was one of its major activists. During the 1930's he initiated aviation training as an arm of the *Haganah*. He was also one of the leaders of the *Histadrut* during the 1930s, its representative in London and chief liaison with the British Labor Party (his contacts were instrumental in obtaining the "McDonald Letter" of 1931, which cancelled the restrictions imposed by the British on immigration and settlement). He was also a delegate to the Zionist Congresses representing *Ahdut Ha'avodah* and afterwards representing *Mapai*.

H. was elected to the Tel Aviv Municipal Council and in 1935 became deputy mayor. In the Second World War he was active in recruiting Jewish volunteers for the British army and their formation into a Jewish Brigade. In December 1940 he was killed in a road accident, along with his wife and daughter. *Sdeh Dov* (the airport on the outskirts of Tel Aviv) and Kibbutz Dorot are named after him.

HUSHI (original name: Shneller), **ABBA** (1899–1969)   Israeli politician, one of the leaders of the Labor Party. Born in eastern Galicia and one of the founders of *Hashomer Hatzair*, he was a founder of Kibbutz Beit Alfa and in 1927, after leaving the kibbutz, settled in Haifa. He joined *Ahdut Ha'avodah* and then *Mapai* and was one of its main activists in Haifa. From 1931 to 1951 he was secretary of the Haifa Workers' Council.

In 1949 he was elected to the Knesset and in 1951 became mayor of Haifa. He held this position until his death in 1969. H. was one of Israel's most prominent mayors. During his term, Haifa developed rapidly, including in the fields of education and culture; the Haifa municipal theater was founded and the foundations laid for Haifa University. Though he was a prominent leader of *Mapai*, he did not accept any national position, preferring to confine his activities to Haifa. As mayor he was associated with *Mapai* party "bosses" who were frequently accused of using harsh measures against political rivals.

HUSS, SALIM (b. 1929)   Lebanese economist and politician, Prime Minister 1976–80 and 1987–90. A Beirut-born Sunni Muslim, H. received his M.A. in business administration and economics at the American University of Beirut (AUB) in 1957 and his Ph.D. at the University of Indiana in 1961. He worked for some time as an accountant for the Transarabian Pipeline Co. and was a teacher of economics at the AUB. From 1964 to 1966 he was financial adviser to the Kuwait Development Fund. In 1966 he was named Chairman of the Lebanese Banking Control Commission, and in 1973 became Chairman and Director-General of the Industrial Development Bank. In both capacities he cooperated closely with Elias *Sarkis, the Governor of the Central Bank, and when the latter was elected President, in 1976, H. became one of his close advisers. Though he was not politically active and was considered a technocrat rather than a politician, he was chosen as Prime Minister during the civil war in Dec. 1976. His closeness to President Sarkis apparently was one of the reasons for that selection; another reason was the decline of the traditional Muslim-Sunni leadership and, as the Prime Minister had to be a Sunni, the need to groom new, younger leaders. H.'s premiership came at a time when central government control was disintegrating in the civil war and real power was in the hands of rival militas, each in its zone of control and battling each other. Though H. did his best to maintain a modicum of government control and security, his premiership remained weak and undistinguished. He resigned several times, but each time withdrew his resignation, and stayed on as Prime Minister until Oct. 1980.

When a "Government of National Unity" was formed in Apr. 1984, after protracted negotiations and under Syrian pressure, with Rashid *Karameh as Prime Minister, H. accepted the post of Minister of Labor, Social Affairs and Education. From that post, too, he resigned several times, but was always persuaded to stay. When Premier Karameh was assassinated on June 1, 1987, H. became acting Prime Minister. His new premiership, in fact hardly operative, with no real government control, was further frustrated by the establishment of Gen. Michel 'Awn's rival government in Sept. 1988. H. now became totally dependent on Syrian support and in fact a tool of Syria. After the Ta'if Accord of Sept.-Oct. 1989 and the election of Rene Mu'awwad as President, H. in Nov. 1989 formed a new government which stayed in office until Dec. 1990, but remained weak and only semi-operative.

H. has remained one of the chief representatives of the Muslim-Sunni community — but his political profile is rather colorless and his influence limited, and he has not been able to halt the decline in the weight and power of the Sunni leadership.

HUSSEIN, KAMAL-UL-DIN (b. 1921)   Egyptian officer and politician, Vice-President of Egypt 1961–64. H. graduated from the Military College in 1939. Reportedly a member of, or close to, the Muslim Brotherhood, he served with the volunteer force it organized to help the Palestine Arabs in early 1948, before Egypt's regular forces entered the war. In 1952, a major, he was one of the "Free Officers" who toppled King *Farouq and his regime. In 1954 he became Minister of Social Affairs and later the same year took the Education Ministry which he held until 1958. H. was also on the Executive Council, and for some time Inspector-General, of the National Union, the single political organization established in 1957; in 1959, under the Egyptian-Syrian UAR, he was named to reorganize its Egyptian chapter. In the UAR, from 1958, he served as Minister of Education (from 1960 concurrently Minister of Local Government in the Egyptian "Region"), and from Aug. 1961 briefly as one of seven Vice-Presidents. After the dissolution of the UAR, Sept. 1961, he became a Vice-President of Egypt, serving until Sept. 1962 concurrently as Minister of Housing and Local Administration. Having remained a right-winger and close to fundamentalist Islamic tendencies, he fell out with *Nasser in 1964, was dismissed from his government and party positions and placed under house arrest. This restriction was lifed after Nasser's death by *Sadat, but H. was not offered a government position. In 1976 he was elected, as an independent of Islamic-fundamentalist tendencies, to the People's Assembly. But in Feb. 1977 he published a memorandum sharply denouncing Sadat and his regime, particularly the harsh measures taken against dissidents and those held responsible for the riots of Jan. 1977, and was expelled from the Assembly and barred from presenting himself as a candidate in the by-elections; he won a court suit against that disbarment, but lost it, on government appeal, in the Supreme Court. H. became a staunch opponent of Sadat, and particularly his peace policy towards Israel, the 1978 Camp David Agreements and the 1979 Peace Treaty, and denounced them in public statements (jointly with the three other surviving former Vice-Presidents). In the 1979 elections he failed to win a seat in the People's Assembly. While he holds no position of institutional influence, he has remained, under *Mubarak's regime, a potential rallying point of opposition.

HUSSEIN, TAHA (1889–1973)   Egyptian scholar and writer admired by Arab readers as "the Dean of Arabic Literature." Born in Maghaghah in Upper Egypt to a poor peasant family, H. lost his sight at the age of two. He studied at the *kuttab* and knew the Qur'an by heart by the age of nine. In 1902 he joined his older brother to study at the al-Azhar mosque in Cairo, where he was influenced by Muhammad *'Abduh and other modernists, both religious and secular, such as Ahmad Lutfi al-Sayyid and his circle. Disappointed by his studies in al-Azhar, he started studying French and attending evening lectures at the Egyptian University (1908) given by eminent Orientalists such as Nallino, Littmann and Santillan. In 1912 he failed his *'alamiyya* examination, probably because of a grudge against his modernist attitudes.

In 1914 he was the first student to get his Ph.D. from the Egyptian University. From 1915 he studied at the Sorbonne and in 1919 earned a *doctorat d'Etat* on his thesis *La philosophie sociale d'Ibn Khaldoun*. In 1917 he married his French secretary and reader.

After his return to Egypt in 1919 he was Lecturer of Ancient History and in 1925 was given the Chair of Arabic Literature. In 1926 H. published a research *On Pre-Islamic Poetry* (*Fi 'L-Shi'r al-Jahili*), in which he maintained that great portions of pre-Islamic poetry are spurious, and doubted the historical reliability of some narrative chapters of the Qur'an. These theses led to angry protests by the conservatives; questions were asked in Parlia-

ment, legal charges were brought against him by al-Azhar and many scholars demanded his resignation from the university. He was forced to withdraw the book, and in 1927 published a revised version, *On Pre-Islamic Literature*.

In 1930 H. served as Dean of the Faculty of Humanities, but after one year he was dismissed by the Minister of Education. He joined the *Wafd* Party and became an editor of its newspapers. In 1944 he was appointed Acting Rector of the Farouq University. From Jan. 1950 to Jan. 1952 he was Minister of Education in the Wafdist government. After the Free Officers' Revolution of July 1952 he lost his public offices, but was respected in literary and cultural circles. He remained active in Arabic literature, published various books and articles and died in Cairo on 1973. His best-known book, translated into many languages, is his autobiography, *al-Ayyam*.

HUSSEIN (AL-TIKRITI), SADDAM (b. 1937) Iraqi politician, the strong man of Iraq since c. 1970, President since 1979. A Sunni Muslim born in the town of Tikrit, north-central Iraq, H. joined the *Ba'th* party underground organization as a youth and served it as an organizer of its strong-arm squads. He was involved in plots against the royal *Hashemite regime and was imprisoned in 1956. He continued subversive activities under the *Qassem regime after 1958. In Oct. 1959, he was involved in an attempt on the life of Qassem and escaped, first to Syria and then to Egypt (where he reportedly completed his secondary education). He returned to Iraq in 1963, after Qassem was toppled in a coup, and soon joined the *Ba'th* leadership, named in 1963 a member of its "regional," i.e., Iraqi, command and in 1965 also of the "national," all-Arab one; in 1966 he became Assistant Secretary-General of the Iraqi *Ba'th*. In 1964, after President *'Aref turned against the *Ba'th*, H. was arrested, but escaped in 1966; he was pardoned later the same year.

After the *Ba'th* coup of 1968, H. rose to a top position of power. In Nov. 1969, retaining his post as Assistant Secretary-General of the *Ba'th*, he became Deputy Chairman of the Revolutionary Command Council, the ruling body of the Iraqi state; and since the Chairman and President, A. H. al-*Bakr, was not a strong ruler, H. in fact ruled Iraq. In the factional struggles inside the Iraqi *Ba'th*, H. headed the "civilian" or "party" faction against the "military" one. Having grown within the party apparatus and, in contrast to many other

Saddam Hussein

Ba'th leaders, with no military background, he postulated the undisputed primacy of the party. From 1970 he built an armed party militia and a strong secret service under party control (in fact: his own). Helped by this *Ba'th* apparatus, H. from 1968 to 1971 systematically purged the state and party establishment, and public and political life, eliminating his rivals and adversaries one after the other — first non-*Ba'th* elements, "rightists" and "reactionaries" (whom he accused of plots and attempted coups in May 1969 and Jan. 1970), then *Ba'th* "extremists" (e.g., those opposing the agreement he reached in 1970 with Kurdish autonomist rebel leaders), and finally the *Ba'th* "military" faction and other rivals within the *Ba'th* (such as Hardan *'Abd-ul-Ghaffar, S. M. *'Ammash, 'Abd-ul-Karim al Sheikhli). In June 1973 he suppressed a coup attempt by Nazem Kazzar, the head of his own security apparatus. Reportedly he himself had instigated Kazzar to plot against Bakr, but abandoned him when the plot failed.

H. completed his takeover of total power in July 1979, when Bakr resigned for reasons of ill health or, in effect, was forced to abdicate, and H. was named Secretary-General of the *Ba'th*, Chairman of the Revolutionary Council and President of Iraq. H. accompanied the dismissal of Bakr with another bloody purge of the *Ba'th* command, executing, after a summary trial, 21 leading function-

aries, including five members of the Revolutionary Council, and jailing 33 more. As sole leader since 1979, H. is glorified by an incessant personality cult.

H.'s methods of struggle were thus particularly ruthless, even brutal. Yet in his policies, both internal and external, he was pragmatic, with frequent tactical shifts, a capacity to adapt to changing circumstances, and a propensity to take swift, ruthless action whenever he detected an opportunity. Despite his identification with the "party faction," he preserved, in the long run, a delicate party-army balance. He followed, sometimes, a remarkable moderate line towards the Kurdish autonomist rebels. It was H. who pushed through, in Mar. 1970, an agreement with the rebels conceding many of their demands and granting them a large measure of semi-autonomy. Yet when the Kurds rebelled again, he vigorously suppressed them in 1974–75 and used his 1975 accord with Iran to crush them cruelly, even using poison gas, and began "resettling" Kurds and replacing them by Arab Iraqis. Simultaneously, he continued implementing the Kurdish semi-autonomy as he perceived it. He tried to widen the political base of his regime, and in 1973 formed a "Progressive and Patriotic National Front" in which the Communists and a Kurdish faction collaborating with the government joined the *Ba'th*; but in 1977–78 he again suppressed the Communists. He supressed extremist-fundamentalist pro-Iranian Shi'i organizations, but managed to prevent a general uprising or widespread resistance of the Shi'i half of the population. He held, for the first time since 1958, elections for a National Assembly, in June 1980, with a single list of candidates endorsed by him and his apparatus, and again in 1984 and 1989.

H.'s pragmatism in his foreign policies as well were evident in Iraq's alliance with the Soviet Union; her *rapprochement* with the West, since the mid-1970s; her 1975 agreement with Iran; her secession from the "Rejection Front"; and her *rapprochement* with the mainstream and moderate Arab states and even with Egypt (under the pressure of her war with Iran). But this pragmatism was disrupted and turned into bursts of ruthlessly extremist action whenever he thought an opportunity presented itself. Thus he tore up his 1975 agreement with Iran in Sept. 1980 and waged a full-fledged war against Iran. From 1980 until 1988 he was wholly immersed in the war, which he personally led, assuming even the supreme military command (he had himself made a General in

1976). Iran held H. personally responsible for the war and for years demanded his dismissal and trial as a war criminal as a precondition for any peace or cease-fire negotiations. Yet, despite the hardships of the war, the large-scale destruction, the stupendous casualties (over 100,000 Iraqi soldiers killed), his leadership remained firm and uncontested — based on the gigantic military force he had built up.

In Aug. 1990, H.'s Iraq invaded the neighboring Arab Amirate of Kuwait and annexed it. A majority of the Arab states, led by Egypt, Sa'udi Arabia and Syria, demanded Iraq's withdrawal from Kuwait; a worldwide coalition led by the USA joined that demand and imposed an embargo; the UN Security Council endorsed it, set a deadline of Jan. 15, 1991, and approved the use of military force; even Iraq's allies and various mediators insisted that an Iraqi withdrawal from Kuwait must be the first step towards a solution. Yet, H. adamantly refused to withdraw. The only "concession" he offered was a commitment to "discuss" Kuwait (no promise of withdrawal) on condition all other "issues of occupation" in the Middle East would be resolved simultaneously — Syria in Lebanon, the USA in Sa'udia, and, most particularly, Israel in Palestine. He increasingly stressed the Israel/Palestine problem, threatening to attack Israel and destroy her, even if she did not involve herself in the Kuwait crisis. He also presented his struggle as an Islamic holy war (despite his and his *Ba'th* party's secularist past and doctrine), and denounced the campaign against him as an attack on Islam and the whole Arab nation — and as a huge U.S.-led multinational military force built up in Sa'udia, he gained much favorable public opinion and mass support in many Arab countries. In Aug. 1990 H. bought a reconcilation with Iran by reaccepting the agreement of 1975 (against which he had fought a bloody eight-year war) and unilaterally withdrawing from disputed border areas. The same month he outraged the world by barring the departure of scores of thousands of foreigners, treating them as hostages and placing some of them as "human shields" in places he considered potential targets for enemy attack (he allowed them to leave in Dec. 1990).

When the deadline expired and the U.S.-led multinational forces attacked, mainly by air bombings (Jan. 17 1991), H. refused to give in, relying on the huge land forces he had amassed. His counterattacks included the firing of missiles at Sa'udi cities (and at Israel — which had no part in the war, and

which refrained, on insistent U.S. advice, from retaliating).

As various peace and mediation efforts failed and H. rejected a final U.S. ultimatum — obviously miscalculating by either overestimating the real strength of his forces or doubting the resolve of the allies to mount a full-fledged offensive — the U.S. and her allies on Feb. 23 launched an all-out attack, and H.'s forces were defeated, expelled from Kuwait and pursued deep into Iraqi territory. On Feb. 26 H. ordered a total withdrawal from Kuwait; on Feb. 28 allied operations were suspended; on Mar. 2 the UN Security Council imposed harsh conditions for a cease-fire and far-reaching sanctions, and H. had to accept them; and on Mar. 5 H. annulled his annexation of Kuwait. Over the months following, H. had to accept a system of far-reaching UN inspections of his military build-up, including the destruction of his nuclear, chemical, biological and ballistic potential, and to agree to massive, UN-administered compensation payments.

Yet, thoroughly defeated, H. did not admit defeat — and did not fall or resign. The allies had not totally liquidated his army or his all-pervasive security apparatus, and though plots against him were reported (and never confirmed), he maintained his rule. Only the Shi'is in southern Iraq and the Kurds in the north broke out in rebellion; but these revolts, which the U.S. had encouraged but did not aid and support (fearing a disintegration of Iraq and an Iran-dominated Islamic-extremist regime in southern Iraq), remained limited local matters; H. defeated the rebellious Shi'is in the south and entered negotiations with the Kurdish rebels on the restoration of a Kurdish region with limited autonomy (similar to that he had negotiated in 1970). He also promised, in a Mar. 1991 broadcast, a new constitution based on full multiparty democracy. Iraq also gradually returned to the Arab family of nations, and Arab leaders went on record opposing the excessively harsh UN and allied sanctions liable to lead to the destruction of Iraq. Allied leaders, particularly those of the USA and Britain, insisted that no normalization of relations with Iraq and no lifting of UN sanctions were possible as long as H. stayed in power. But, by the fall of 1991, H. was still in power.

HUSSEIN BIN (IBN) NASSER, SHARIF (1906–82) Jordanian (formerly Iraqi) palace official, diplomat, politician, Prime Minister of Jordan, 1963 and 1967. A scion of the *Hashemite clan, H.

served his ruling cousins in Iraq — as a palace official 1929–35 and Assistant Chief of the Royal Cabinet 1944–46, and as a diplomat (in Ankara 1935–37, Assistant Chief of Protocol 1938–42, Consul-General in Jerusalem and Charge d'Affaires in 'Amman 1946–48). In 1949/50 he settled in Jordan and married a daughter of King *'Abdullah. He served as Jordan's Minister to Turkey 1949–50, and to France and Spain 1950–51, and as Ambassador to Spain 1953–61. From 1961 to 1963, and again briefly in 1967, he was Chief of the Royal Court, and in 1963 and 1967 Minister of the Court. Completely loyal to the King, his nephew, he was twice named Prime Minister — for one year in 1963–64, and for a few weeks in 1967. In 1969 the King appointed him a member of the Senate. Sharif H. did not wield political, decision-making influence, but was a loyal instrument of the King and the palace.

HUSSEIN IBN 'ALI, SHARIF (1852? 1853? 1854?–1931)

Sharif of Mecca; King of Hijaz 1916–24. A *Hashemite descendant of the Prophet Muhammad and hereditary bearer of the title Sharif of Mecca, H. was kept for years under surveillance in Istanbul by Sultan *'Abd-ul-Hamid. After the revolution of the Young Turks, 1908, he was allowed to return to Mecca and appointed Amir of Mecca. There was rivalry between him, *Ibn Sa'ud in Najd, and the House of *Rashid, the chiefs of the Shammar tribes in Ha'il.

In 1914, H. contacted the British High Commissioner in Cairo to enquire about British help for a revolt against his Turkish-Ottoman sovereign. These contacts were renewed in 1915, when the British, engaged in war with Turkey, had become more interested in such a revolt. Apart from military and financial help for the rebellion itself, H. demanded a promise of independence for "Arabia." The British agreed in principle, but had reservations concerning H.'s territorial demands; they also envisaged the future independent Arab state or states tied to some British tutelage. This discussion is documented in H.'s correspondence with Sir Henry McMahon, the British High Commissioner in Egypt, 1915/16. Without reaching a clear, written agreement, H. and his sons *'Ali, *'Abdullah and *Feisal in June 1916 launched the "Arab Revolt" — guerrilla operations against the Turks in Hijaz. He received British military and financial help, and his forces later advanced into Transjordan and Syria as the right wing of the British and allied forces under General Allenby.

At the end of World War I, H. sent his son Feisal to represent him at the Paris Peace Conference, where he was informally recognized as the chief spokesman for Arab nationalist claims. Since his demands were not completely satisfied, and in protest against inter-Allied imperial schemes, as embodied in the Sykes-Picot Agreement, and the imposition of "Mandates" instead of complete independence, H. refused to endorse the peace treaties and the arrangements made in Syria, Iraq and Palestine. He also rejected, in 1920/21, British proposals for an Anglo-Hijazi treaty, including British aid and guarantees against outside attack. As to Palestine and Zionism, H. at first endorsed Feisal's readiness to reach an agreement and cooperate with the Zionists, but later changed his mind. H. also refused to send delegates to a British-initiated conference in Kuwait, 1923, called to settle border problems in the Arabian peninsula. He thus threw away, step-by-step, Britain's vital support and protection and remained politically isolated.

In 1919/20, armed clashes erupted between Hijazi and Najdi-Sa'udi tribesmen, and H.'s Hijazis suffered defeat; H. was saved from a total debacle by British intervention with Ibn Sa'ud. After Turkey abolished the Caliphate in 1924, H. proclaimed himself Caliph. He had not obtained the agreement or support of any major Islamic leader, and the proclamation was unrealistic; it caused consternation and anger among many Muslims, and especially among his Sa'udi-Wahhabi neighbors. In Sept. 1924, the Sa'udis attacked, and H. was defeated. After the capture of Ta'if he abdicated in favor of his oldest son 'Ali, hoping thus to save the kingdom of Hijaz for his family, but in Oct. the Sa'udis took Mecca, and H. escaped to 'Aqaba ('Ali could not hold his kingdom and fled late in 1925). H. was taken by a British naval vessel to Cyprus and lived in exile there or with his son 'Abdullah in Transjordan. He died in 'Amman in 1931 and was buried in Jerusalem, in the precinct of the *Haram al-Sharif* (the Temple Mount).

HUSSEIN IBN TALAL (b. 1935)

King of Jordan. Born in 'Amman and educated at Victoria College (Alexandria) and in Britain, at Harrow and Sandhurst Military Academy. H. succeded his father *Talal in 1952, when the latter was dethroned because of a mental illness. As he was a minor, a Regency Council ruled for him until May 1953, when he came of age and was crowned.

H. ascended to the throne at a time of crisis and

had, in the first four years of his rule, to make important concessions to nationalist-Nasserist groups, concerning both internal and, mainly, foreign affairs. Thus he agreed in 1954 to an amendment of the constitution enabling Parliament to dismiss the government by a simple majority. In Dec. 1955 he had to withdraw a decision to adhere to the Western-sponsored Baghdad Pact, bowing to politicians of the opposition and popular demonstrations. In 1956 he dismissed General *Glubb, the British commander of his army, who was viewed by Arab nationalists as a symbol of Jordan's subservience to British imperialism. When a leftist-nationalist National Socialist Party won the elections of Oct. 1956, the King had to appoint its leader, Suleiman al-*Nabulsi, as Prime Minister. Under this new regime he approved Jordan's adherence to an Egyptian-Syrian Defense Pact and Joint Command, and early in 1957, the abrogation of the Anglo-Jordanian Treaty and the replacement of British aid, particularly for his army, by Egyptian, Syrian and Sa'udi subsidies.

In 1957, however, H. halted the integration of Jordan into a leftist-Nasserist bloc. He dismissed the leftist government — a step triggered by the government's decision to establish diplomatic relations with the USSR (which was then considered a "leftist" departure from traditional policies, though it later became normal, accepted policy). He averted, by a courageous personal confrontation, a subversive, apparently Egyptian-supported, officers' plot, reinstated conservative governments and army leaders and reestablished a *de facto* alliance with the West. In Feb. 1958, faced by the merger of Egypt and Syria, H. took a determined stand against what he conceived as a move to expand the power of the leftist-Nasserist Arab states and achieve domination of the Arab world. He created a Jordan-Iraq "Arab Federation" and became its Deputy-Head. When that Federation collapsed in July 1958, as a result of a coup in Iraq, and Jordan felt isolated and threatened by UAR intervention aided by subversion, H. asked Britain to send troops to protect Jordan; they stayed until Oct. He also complained to the UN Security Council against the UAR.

H. succeeded in preserving his throne in spite of numerous plots sponsored by Egypt or Syria. His relations with Nasser's Egypt fluctuated. Sometimes, in the course of vitriolic mutual propaganda attacks, Nasser called H. a traitor and imperialist stooge with whom progressive Arab leaders could not cooperate; at other times, when currents of

King Hussein (IPS, Tel Aviv)

inter-Arab unity were emphasized, H. was the noble king of an Arab sister country. In May 1967, in the frenzy of Nasser's escalating preparations for war against Israel, H. signed a defense treaty with Egypt — according to some reports under heavy pressure, and on terms imposed by Nasser, according to others on his own initiative — and symbolically placed his army under Egyptian command. He disregarded Israel's warning and promise not to attack Jordan and entered the Six Day War — misled, as he describes in memoirs (taken down and published by two journalists), by Nasser informing him of a victorious Egyptian advance.

Jordan's defeat in that war and the loss of the West Bank were a heavy blow to H. His position was also undermined by the Palestinian-Arab guerrilla organizations, their operations against Israel from Jordanian soil and their violation of Jordanian sovereignty, creating a state-within-a-state. The Jordan-PLO crisis culminated in 1970 in violent clashes, a veritable war ("Black September"). When H. completed the elimination of the PLO in Spring and Summer 1971, he was denounced and reviled in most of the Arab world and Jordan's relations with several Arab states were disrupted.

Syrian troops actually invaded Jordan in Sept. 1970, but were halted by Jordanian resistance — and the threat of U.S. and Israeli intervention.

Jordan's relations with the Arab States and H.'s standing in the Arab world were rebuilt only gradually in the 1970s. H. tried to resolve the basic contradiction between his claim to the Israeli-occupied West Bank as part of his kingdom and Palestinian-Arab claims to independence by proposing a federal or confederal structure for the future Jordan, after Israel's withdrawal, with a measure of autonomy for the Palestinian part of the kingdom. He first did so publicly in Mar. 1972, but the idea was not well received at the time; Egypt even severed diplomatic relations on account of it. During the October War, 1973, H. decided not to join Egypt and Syria in full-fledged war, a decision that was coordinated with and accepted by the two countries; but he sent an armored brigade to help Syrian forces — a contingent that arrived late, when the tide of war had already turned and Israeli forces were battling inside Syria. After the war, U.S.-mediated talks on a disengagement agreement with Israel, similar to those Israel concluded with Egypt and Syria, failed. The gap between what Israel offered in the way of a token withdrawal and what H. regarded as a minimum requirement even for an interim agreement was too wide. In Oct. 1974, H. had to acquiesce in a decision of the all-Arab summit at Rabat to reaffirm the Palestinian-Arabs' right to self-determination and to recognize the PLO as their sole legitimate representative.

H. was considered a moderate in international and inter-Arab affairs and concerning Israel. While he did but little to educate Arab public opinion and guide it towards coexistence, he had numerous secret meetings with Israeli leaders in the 1960s and 1970s, but the gap was always too wide to make an agreement possible. He insisted on complete Israeli withdrawal from the West Bank, including East Jerusalem, and even if he was ready to make some territorial concessions, those were far removed from whatever Israeli leaders demanded or proposed (e.g., the "Allon Plan"). He continued the *de facto* coexistence of Jordan and the occupied West Bank ("Open Bridges," controlled movement of West Bank Arabs to and from Jordan, economic and trade links, aid for West Bank Arab institutions, contacts with West Bank leaders, and not very intense efforts to influence West Bank public affairs); but even on interim arrangements — automony for the West Bank Arabs? joint Jordanian-

Israeli supervision? — he could reach no agreement with Israel.

While H. was considered pro-U.S., his relations with the U.S. were strongly influenced and often irritated by U.S. efforts to achieve progress towards Israel-Jordan peace and by H.'s hesitations and tactical shifts and his inability to take bold decisions and respond to America's pressing proposals. A particular irritant was the supply of American arms, several times decided upon and prepared by the U.S. administration but reduced or even blocked by a Congress responsive to Israeli objections and the influence of a pro-Israel lobby. In his irritation, H. several times indicated that he would acquire arms from the Soviet Union. He visited Moscow in 1967, 1976, 1981, 1982, and 1987, and in 1981 concluded an arms deal.

H.'s relations with the leaders of the Arab states remained complex and subject to tactical shifts. Since 1984 he fostered close relations with Egypt's President *Mubarak. He also achieved a growing *rapprochement* with the PLO, and in Feb. 1985 signed an agreement with *'Arafat on a future confederation of an Arab-Palestinian state (implied in part of Palestine) and Jordan, and a joint approach to negotiations on a Middle East peace settlement. This agreement was abrogated by the PLO in Apr. 1987, mainly because of the latter provision, but the idea of a future Palestine-Jordan confederation remained alive, and H.'s alliance with the PLO, though marred by tactical shifts and ups and downs, remained intact and deepened. H. was a chief architect of the "Arab Cooperation Council," an alliance of Jordan, Egypt, Iraq and Yemen set up in Feb. 1989, and within that group fostered increasingly close relations with Iraq.

H.'s relations with the U.S. were, in the 1980s, determined by the ups and downs of the negotiations about Middle East peace negotiations. H. informally accepted the "Reagan Plan" of Sept. 1982 and committed himself to negotiate a peace settlement jointly with a Palestinian-Arab delegation. He several times assured the U.S. that he could bring 'Arafat to agree to this course — but he was unable to live up to that assurance, and he made it clear that, contrary to U.S. and Israeli hopes, he would not negotiate alone, or with Egypt only, and without PLO endorsement.

In the Persian Gulf crisis caused by Iraq's invasion of Kuwait, Aug. 1990, H. tried to mediate, proposing compromise formulas and an "Arab solution." He claimed to have obtained Iraq's acceptance and blamed the anti-Iraqi camp —

Egypt, Sa'udi Arabia and the U.S.-led coalition —
for the failure of his efforts and the escalation of
the crisis into war. While he kept Jordan officially
neutral, his stance, perhaps under the pressure of
Jordan's public opinion, was stridently anti-U.S.
and pro-Iraqi.

In home affairs, H. succeeded, since the upheavals of 1957, and after overcoming in 1970–71 the
danger posed by the PLO to his kingdom, in maintaining a stable, orderly regime and impressive
economic development. His regime was liberal and
formally parliamentary — though Parliament was
suspended from late 1974 until Jan. 1984 because
no elections could be held in half of the kingdom,
the Israeli-occupied West Bank (from 1984 to 1988
H. reconvened the old Parliament, elected in Apr.
1967, with by-elections in the East Bank and Parliament replacing deceased West Bank members). In
July 1988 H. formally abolished all legal and
administrative links with the West Bank. Elections
in Nov. 1989 for a new Parliament representing the
East Bank only produced a strong bloc of Islamic-
fundamentalist members (c. 32 of 80), and H.
adapted his regime to the new trend; in Jan. 1991
several fundamentalists joined the government.

Despite these political-parliamentary shifts, it
was evident that H. alone led his country. Jordanian media foster a strong personality cult of the
King, but he seems to be genuinely popular. H. has
also been, at least until his *volte face* of 1990 internationally respected — a standing which, being an
excellent speaker, a master of public relations and
an attractive media personality, he has carefully
nourished.

H. married four times and has eleven children.
His wives: his distant relative Princess Dina 'Abd-
ul-Hamid (1955; one daughter; divorced in 1957);
Antoinette Gardiner, daughter of a British army
officer, converted to Islam and named Muna al-
Hussein (1961; two sons, two daughters; divorced
1972); 'Aliya Touqan, daughter of the prominent
official Baha-ul-Din Touqan (1972; one daughter,
one son; killed 1977 in an accident); Lisa Halabi,
daughter of a prominent American businessman of
Lebanese origin, converted to Islam and named
Nur al-Hussein (1978; two sons, two daughters)
(see genealogy table on page 252). H. in 1965
named as Crown Prince his younger brother Hassan (b. 1947) — and not the middle brother
Muhammad (b. 1945) or one of his own elder sons
(whose mother was of foreign origin) — with his
third son 'Ali (b. 1975) as Crown Prince after
Hassan.

AL-HUSSEINI   Prominent Arab family in Jerusalem, claiming descent from the Prophet Muhammad and therefore Sharifian standing (though its
members do not use the title *Sharif*). A member of
the H. clan was Mufti of Jerusalem in the 17th
century, and several bore the title *Naqib al-Ashraf*
("Chief of the Prophet's Descendants") of Jerusalem. Since the 18th century members of the family
have held high office, particularly that of Mufti.
Hassan H., Mufti 1789–1809, was succeeded by
Taher H. (d. 1866), Mustafa H. (d. 1868) by his son
Taher (1842–1908), Taher by his son Kamel (d.
1921), Kamel by his stepbrother Muhammad Amin
H. The H. clan also accumulated extensive landed
property, mainly in the villages northwest of Jerusalem and Ramallah. Its members held many
administrative posts in Ottoman-ruled Palestine,
including several times that of Mayor of Jerusalem: Salim H. in the 1880s and 1890s, his son
Hussein Salim H. (d. 1918) 1909–18, and his
younger son Mussa Kazim *H. 1918–20. Sa'id H.
(1878?–1945), Jerusalem Mayor 1902–06, was
elected in 1908 and again in 1914 as one of the three
deputies of the Jerusalem district in the Ottoman
Parliament.

The most prominent members of the H. family in
this century were **Hajj Amin*H., Mussa Kazim*H.**
and **Jamal*H.** Among many others active in public life, the following might be mentioned: **Ishaq
Mussa H.** (1904–90), one of the few Palestinian-
Arab writers who attained some all-Arab literary
prominence; his novel *Memoirs of a Hen*, 1943,
created some controversy because of its alleged political implications; one of his books described the
"Muslim Brotherhood" movement (also in English, 1958). **Munif H.** (1899–1983), active in
nationalist organizations, in the early 1930s edited
the organ of the H.s' political party; **Dr. Mussa
'Abdullah H.** (1904–51), also active in nationalist
organizations, went during World War II to Nazi
Germany. When apprehended after the war, he
was detained by the British in 1946 in Rhodesia;
after his return, he co-organized the assassination
of King *'Abdullah and was tried, found guilty and
executed. **Dr. Dawud H.** (b. 1904), active in
nationalist organizations and the rebellion of
1936–39, was captured by the British in Iraq in
1941 and detained in Rhodesia. After his return, he
was involved in the assassination of King 'Abdullah, put on trial but acquitted, and later became a
member of the Jordanian Parliament (1956, 1962).
In 1965 he was reported to be a member of the PLO
executive (?); in 1967 he stayed in East Jerusalem

and took part in efforts to organize the Arabs in the Israel-occupied areas and set up a Jerusalem Muslim Council; in 1968 he was expelled to Jordan; in 1970 he served briefly as Minister of the Economy in the Government of Jordan. **Rafiq H.** (b. 1909), **Amin Yussuf H.** (b. 1918?), **Muhyi-ul-Din H.** (b. 1930) also were Ministers in Jordanian governments. **Tawfiq Saleh H.** (1884–1952), a brother of Jamal H., was acting chairman of the H.'s "Palestine Arab Party," 1944–46, in the absence, abroad, of the top leaders, and from Nov. 1945 until Jamal H.'s return in Mar. 1946 a member of the renewed Arab Higher Committee. **Raja'i H.** (b. 1902) served from 1945 in the Palestine-Arab information offices established by Mussa al-*'Alami with a group of younger intellectuals; after the 1948 defeat he was a Minister in the abortive "Government of all Palestine" in Gaza, and later went to Sa'udi Arabia to become a senior official in her service. **'Abd-ul-Qader H.** (1907/08–48), a son of Mussa Kazim H., in the early 1930s organized a "Congress of Educated Muslims," to fight against discrimination in government service. He was one of the few scions of notable families actually to join guerrilla/terrorist squads and became a commander of the guerrillas in the Jerusalem area both in the rebellion of 1936–39 and in the guerrilla phase of the war of 1948. His son, **Feisal H.** (b. 1940), set up an "Arab Studies Center" in East Jerusalem in the 1980s; he has emerged as one of the chief spokesmen of the Palestinian Arabs in the West Bank. He usually takes a moderate position advocating peaceful coexistence with Israel by a Palestine-Arab state to be established; but, considered close to the PLO and al-Fatah, he is from time to time detained, and the Israeli right wing demands his imprisonment or deportation. **Fawzi Darwish H.** (1898–1946) was an exception to the usual political orientation of the H. clan; he advocated an accommodation with the Zionists and in 1946 set up an Arab "New Palestine" association to cooperate with the (Jewish) "League for Jewish-Arab Friendship and Cooperation"; he was assassinated in Nov. 1946.

From the 1920s to the 1940s, the name H. came to denote not only an influential clan, but — mainly owing to the dominating influence of Hajj Amin H. and the Supreme Muslim Council he headed — a political camp. The supporters of Hajj Amin and the Council were called *Majlisiyyin* — "Council Men," while the opposing camp was called *al-Mu'aridin* — "The Opposition"; but many simply called the *Majlisiyyin* "H.'s" (and their opponents "*Nashashibis*," after the prominent family head-

ing that camp). When the *Majlisiyyin* founded, in 1935, the "Arab Palestine Party" as their political instrument, it was also often called "the H.'s." The dominating influence of the H. clan, and the political camp it represented, declined and virtually disappeared after 1948 (as did the dominating influence of other clans among the Palestine Arabs and the perception of clan loyalty as a decisive political-factional determinant).

There is a prominent H. family also in Gaza; it is not related to the Jerusalem H.'s.

AL-HUSSEINI, HAJJ (MUHAMMAD) AMIN (1893? 1895? 1897?–1974)   Palestinian-Arab politician and religious leader. His education included a year at the Jewish-French "Alliance" school in Jerusalem, one year at the al-Azhar Islamic College in Cairo under Sheikh Rashid *Rida (without graduating), and some time at the Ottoman-Turkish school of administration in Istanbul. During World War I he served as a junior officer in the Turkish army. After the British and Allied forces took Palestine, 1917–18, he was recruiting officer for Amir *Feisal's army of the "Arab Revolt," and later an official in the provisional British military government. At the same time he became active in nationalist organization and agitation. He was president of the "Arab Club" (al-Nadi al-'Arabi) in Jerusalem, one of the two main associations of nationalist youth, which saw Palestine as part of an all-Syrian unity. He incited and headed anti-Jewish riots in Apr. 1920, was tried *in absentia* by a military court and sentenced to 10 years imprisonment, but escaped. In Aug. 1920 he was pardoned by the High Commissioner.

In Mar. 1921, the *Mufti* of Jerusalem, Kamel H., H.'s stepbrother, died. H. offered his candidacy, but was not among the three candidates nominated under Ottoman law by a small body of electors, one of whom the government was to appoint. However, after considerable pressure by the H. family and its supporters, as well as by some senior British officials, one of the three candidates nominated withdrew in H.'s favor, and in May 1921 the High Commissioner appointed H. as *Mufti*. The British apparently wished to keep a balance between the rival clans: the position of *Mufti* had long been held by the H. family, and that of Mayor of Jerusalem had just been taken from them and given to a notable of the rival *Nashashibi family. H. had also assured the High Commissioner that he would exercise his prestige and that of his family to keep Jerusalem quiet.

To the position of *Mufti*, a post carrying much prestige and spiritual and social influence, but no actual power, H. soon added another post with greater power potential. The British Mandatory Government deemed it inconvenient and improper to administer the communal and religious affairs of the Muslims, as the Ottoman Sultan, being Muslim, had done, and therefore in Dec. 1921 decreed the creation of a five-member "Supreme Muslim Council," to be indirectly elected, following Ottoman procedure. In Jan. 1922 the Council was elected — with H. as its president. His chairmanship of the Council, with its considerable income from and control of the *Waqf* (endowments) and its authority over all appointments of Muslim clerical functionaries and staff, gave H. much power. He used it to advance his clan's and his faction's influence and to fight his opponents among the Palestine Arabs, the Zionists, and the National Home policy of the Mandate and the Government. He fostered the Muslim character of Jerusalem and the position of its two great mosques, and injected a religious character into the struggle against Zionism. This was the background of his agitation concerning Jewish rights at the Western ("Wailing") Wall that led to the disturbances of Aug. 1929.

From the late 1920s, H. became the most important political leader of the Palestine Arabs, though he left the nominal chairmanship of the declining "Arab Executive" to Mussa Kazim *H., who died in 1934, and entrusted Jamal *H. with the day-by-day leadership of his faction. His politics were hard-line and extremist. In Apr. 1936, he formed an Arab Higher Committee and became its chairman. As such, he was the chief organizer of the riots of 1936 and the rebellion from 1937, as well as the mounting internal terror against Arab opponents. In Oct. 1937, H. was dismissed by the government from his position as President of the Supreme Muslim Council, which was disbanded, and the Arab Higher Committee was outlawed. He escaped to Lebanon and Syria, where he continued to direct the Palestinian-Arab rebellion. In 1939 he went to Iraq, where he was close to Rashid 'Ali *Kilani and the pro-Nazi army officers and assisted them in their revolt in 1941. When that revolt was put down, H. escaped to Italy and Nazi Germany, where he was welcomed as a leader of anti-British Arab nationalism, received by Hitler and accorded an honored position. He aided the Nazi war effort as a propagandist, mobilizing Muslim public opinion throughout the world, and recruiting Muslim volunteers for the German armed forces from Bosnia and Yugoslavia.

After the war, H. was detained by the French army but escaped and in June 1946 went to Egypt. He was not allowed to return to Palestine, but was appointed by the Arab League to be Chairman of the renewed Arab Higher Committee it set up for the Palestine Arabs (Jamal H. actually headed the Committee, but its presidency was kept "vacant" for H.). He began organizing the final struggle of the Palestinian Arabs against partition and the emergence of a Jewish state. Actually, the Arab states financed, equipped and directed that struggle. H. saw them only as providers of the help without which the fight could not be mounted, while claiming for himself supreme leadership, but the Arabs were unwilling to grant him that position, and a great deal of half-concealed tension ensued. In the final struggle, before the war of May 1948 and the invasion of Palestine by the regular Arab armies, H. exerted some influence on the fighting in the Jerusalem area, where his relative 'Abd-ul-Qadar H. commanded the guerrillas, but he was unable to gain control of the general battle, and even less so after May 1948.

After the defeat of 1948, H. tried to form a "Government of all Palestine" in Egyptian-occupied Gaza, but that body — welcomed at first by Egypt as an instrument to frustrate Jordan's annexation of the Arab half of Palestine — failed to gain any influence over the course of events and was dissolved after a few years of a shadow-existence. Attempts to create in Gaza some Palestinian-Arab autonomous entity under Egyptian rule also were not welcomed by Egypt. H., still residing in Cairo, established an alternative residence in Beirut and in 1959 went to live there permanently. He endeavored to keep alive, or revive, the Arab Higher Committee and to continue sabotaging the Jordanian annexation of the Arab part of Palestine, the West Bank, but the Committee, and H.'s own influence, continuously declined, particularly after the foundation of the Palestine Liberation Organization (PLO) in 1964 (which H. and his Higher Committee opposed). H. spent the last decade of his life as a respected refugee, hardly involved in political affairs and with no influence over them.

AL-HUSSEINI, JAMAL (1892? 1894?–1982) Palestinian-Arab politician. Educated at the Anglican St. George school in Jerusalem and the American University of Beirut, where his medical studies were interrupted when World War I broke out in

1914. After the war, H. served in the British military administration, as an official in the Health Department and assistant to the Governors of Nablus and Ramla. From 1921 to 1934 he was secretary to the "Arab Executive" headed by his uncle Mussa Kazim *H., and in this capacity joined, *inter alia*, the delegation sent to London for negotiations in 1930. In 1928-30 he was concurrently Secretary of the Supreme Muslim Council headed by Hajj Amin *H. After the disintegration of the Arab Executive he organized the political framework of the H. faction, the "Palestine Arab Party," founded in 1935, appeared as editor of its organ *al-Liwa'* and represented it on the Arab Higher Committee set up in Apr. 1936 to lead the rebellion; he was the right hand of its chairman Hajj Amin. When the Higher Committee was outlawed and some of its members were arrested in Oct. 1937, he escaped. In Feb. 1939 he was permitted to head the Palestinian-Arab delegation to the London Round Table Conference, despite an outstanding arrest warrant. In 1940-41 he was active among Palestinian-Arab exiles in Iraq and supported Rashid 'Ali *Kilani's anti-British revolt. When that revolt in 1941 was put down, he escaped to Iran, but was caught by the British and detained in Rhodesia. He was released in late 1945 — a measure that led his faction to agree to the establishment of a new Arab Higher Committee, though he himself was still barred from Palestine.

In Feb. 1946 H. was permitted to return to Palestine and assume the leadership of his party and set up a new Higher Committee (as "acting" Chairman, as the chairmanship was kept vacant for exiled Hajj Amin). His factionalism, however, and the packing of the Higher Committee with his supporters, caused resentment and a split, and his opponents formed a rival committee. In June 1946, the Arab League intervened, disbanding both committees and forming a new one. H. was again named Vice-Chairman, for the absent Hajj Amin. He acted as chief spokesman for the Palestinian Arab cause and represented it before the 1946-47 Committees of Inquiry. From 1946 he led the Arabs of Palestine towards violent armed resistance to the partition of the country and the foundation of a Jewish State. For that purpose he reorganized paramilitary youth squads, *al-Futuwwa*. During the war of 1948, he was in Cairo, Damascus and Beirut, endeavoring to direct the Palestinian-Arab fighting forces, but he and his party and his Higher Committee failed in their efforts to maintain their leadership. After the defeat, H. was Foreign Minister in the abortive "Government of All Palestine" set up in Gaza in Sept.-Oct. 1948. He continued his efforts to keep alive the Higher Committee, in exile, but had little success. He later went to Sa'udi Arabia and joined her service as a senior adviser, while in fact retiring from political activity. H. wrote many articles and also two political novels, *On the Hijaz Railway*, and *Thurayya*.

AL-HUSSEINI, MUSSA KAZIM (1850-1934) Palestinian Arab administrator and politician. The son of Salim H., Mayor of Jerusalem, H. was trained at the Istanbul School of Administration and joined the Ottoman service, rising to the position of governor (*Qaimaqam, Mutasarrif*) of various sub-districts in Palestine, Lebanon, Anatolia and the Arabian peninsula. He retired on the eve of World War I. In Mar. 1918, the British military administration appointed him Mayor of Jerusalem, to replace his brother Hussein who had died. He pledged to stay out of politics. He did not, however, honor that stipulation and was dismissed.

H. became a political leader when he was elected, in Dec. 1920, at the third Palestinian-Arab Congress, as President of the Arab Executive then formed — a position he held until his death. From 1921 to 1930 he headed all four Palestinian Arab delegations sent to London to negotiate with the British government and persuade it to abandon the Balfour Declaration and its commitment to the foundation of a Jewish National Home. He co-determined the Palestinian-Arab leaders' decision to reject British proposals for a Legislative Council and home rule institutions — until 1929, when he agreed to the formation of a Legislative Council (but the riots of Aug. 1929 prevented the implementation of that proposal). In the late 1920s and early 1930s his leadership weakened, and his Arab Executive declined; it faded away after his death. (For his son 'Abd-ul-Qader and grandson Feisal see above under H. family.)

I

IBN SA'UD (1876? 1880?-1953)   The name by which 'Abd-ul-'Aziz Ibn 'Abd-ul-Rahman Aal (i.e., of the House of) Sa'ud, King and founder of Sa'udi Arabia, was best known. His ancestors, of the 'Anaiza tribe, had ruled parts of Najd, but I.S. grew up in exile in Kuwait (see *Sa'ud dynasty). In 1902 he recaptured the town of al-Riyadh and reestablished the rule of the Sa'udi dynasty in Najd. In 1913 he conquered the al-Hassa region on the Persian Gulf, and his territory thus came within the sphere where Great Britain had negotiated a series of treaties imposing her protection on the rulers of the Arab coastal sheikhdoms. In a 1913 Anglo-Ottoman draft convention (never ratified) Britain still recognized the Sa'udi Amirate as part of the Ottoman Empire; but the outbreak of World War I changed the situation, and in Dec. 1915 Britain concluded a treaty with I.S. recognizing him as ruler of an independent Najd and Hassa (in fact under a veiled British protectorate; in 1916 Britain

King Ibn Sa'ud (Bar-David, Tel Aviv)

agreed to pay him a monthly subsidy of £5,000).

During World War I, Britain encouraged I.S. in his fight against the pro-Turkish Rashidis, but was content with his benevolent neutrality in the war. After the war, in 1920–21, I.S. defeated the Rashidis and incorporated their territory into his domain, calling himself, from 1921, Sultan of Najd and its Dependencies. In 1924 he defeated the *Hashemite Sharifs of Mecca, annexed Hijaz and began expanding and consolidating his rule, from Jan. 1926 as "King of Hijaz and Sultan of Najd, al-Hassa, Qatif and Jubail and their Dependencies," and from 1927 as "King of Hijaz and Najd." In 1932 he constituted his realm as "the Sa'udi Arabian Kingdom." In 1934 he fought a war with Yemen and completed his territorial expansion by the annexation of 'Asir.

In the 1930s I.S. was not very active in inter-Arab affairs. In 1936 he was, as arranged by the British, one of the Arab rulers who induced the Arabs of Palestine to end their general strike, promising them to aid their struggle, and in 1939 the British government officially involved him in the Palestine issue, by inviting him to send delegates to a British-Arab "Round Table Conference." Unofficial British go-betweens (e.g., H. St.J.B. Philby) also put him, in 1939, in indirect contact with Jewish-Zionist leaders, in search of a solution to the Palestine problem, but nothing came of these contacts. In World War II, I.S. kept Sa'udia neutral. He fostered growing ties with the USA, and U.S. oil interests (to whom he granted concessions from 1933); President Roosevelt, who met I.S. in Feb. 1945, was said to be much impressed by him. I.S. played an important role in the foundation of the Arab League, 1945; in inter-Arab politics he insisted on the acceptance of the territorial and political *status quo* and cooperation between the existing sovereign Arab states, rejecting all schemes for federal entities (such as a *Hashemite "Fertile Crescent" or "Greater Syria").

I.S. ruled his kingdom as an autocrat, consulting

the princes of his dynasty and the tribal sheikhs in the traditional manner, but reserving decisions to himself. He permitted no modern representative political institutions to develop and refrained from formalizing constitutional government, basing his rule on Islamic laws and traditions. He kept the unruly tribal chiefs — whom he had to suppress in the late 1920s by armed force — under strict control, by paying them subsidies, keeping their sons at his court and marrying their daughters to his sons. The tribal unrest was in part linked to a rebellion by Wahhabi "Brethren" (*Ikhwan*), suppressed by 1929. I.S. continued enforcing strict Wahhabi Islam, but discontinued his initial efforts to establish a nucleus of armed Wahhabi "Brethren" in settlements. I.S. permitted little economic or social modernization, except for the development of the oil industry by the American Aramco company — which began to make the country, and the royal family, immensely rich, and which triggered a process of development and modernization that came to fruition after I.S.'s days; he introduced, despite the rule of Wahhabi-Islamic law, increasingly luxurious ways of life which bred a measure of corruption among the dynasty and the ruling class.

I.S. had several wives and over 40 sons; 31 sons of legitimate full-status wives survive in the 1990s in line for the succession. I.S. strictly controlled the large royal family and determined his succession, appointing his eldest surviving son, *Sa'ud, in 1932, as Crown Prince and successor, with *Feisal next in line.

IDRIS, YUSUF (1927–91)   One of the outstanding and most prolific Egyptian writers and playwrights. Born in a village in the al-Sharqiyya district, I. studied medicine at the University of Cairo (M.D. 1951) and practiced as a doctor and health inspector. But he soon dedicated himself instead to literature and journalism. I. wrote on social problems, such as the overpopulation in Egypt — thus in his first collection of short stories (*Arkhas Layali, The Cheapest of Nights*, 1954), which gained much attention in the Arab world, and his play *Farhat Republic*, first performed in 1957. In the 1960s he became interested in modern Western pioneering theatre and tried to integrate its technique in his work. He aimed at the creation of an indigenous and popular Arabic drama derived from the medieval Arab shadow and puppet theater — thus in his plays *al-Farafir (The Small Birds)*, 1966, and in *al-Mukhattatun (The Striped)*,

1969 in which he criticised *'Abd-ul-Nasser's dictatorship and his restriction of the freedom of thought in Egypt. He later wrote psychological plays and drama of the absurd, and tried to develop a new Arabic style capable of expressing the most subtle and tender nuances of the soul. Some of his stories were translated into foreign languages, including English and Hebrew.

When Nagib Mahfuz was awarded the Nobel Prize in Literature in 1988, I. and his supporters in the Arab world were bitterly disappointed and argued that I. deserved the Prize more than Mahfuz.

IMAMI, SHARIF JA'FAR (b. 1908? 1910?)   Iranian politician, Prime Minister 1960–61 and 1978. Trained at the railway school in Germany and Boras Technical School in Sweden, he served in the Railway Administration (1943–46) and as director of the Irrigation Authority (1946–50). He was acting Minister of Transport 1950–51. In 1951, he became a member of the Planning Council and later its head. In 1955, he was elected to the *Majlis* (Parliament) and in 1963 its president. From 1957 to 1960 he was the Minister of Industry and Mines. He was close to the Shah and in Aug. 1960 was chosen to form a government, holding office until May 1961. I. also administered the Shah's Pahlevi Foundation and served as President of the Chamber of Industries and Mines (1962).

In Aug. 1978 he again became Prime Minister, with a mandate to continue a process of liberalization and to prepare the country for free elections in June 1979. He made concessions to Islamic religious circles, such as the prohibition of gambling and restrictions on alcohol consumption. His promise to fight corruption was ridiculed because he himself was considered tainted. His government survived for less than three months. Khomeini's Islamic revolution removed him from the political scene.

INÖNÜ, ERDAL (b.1926)   Turkish politician and scientist. Born in Ankara as the second son of Ismet *Inonu, he graduated from Ankara University and the California Polytechnic University, with a Ph.D. in theoretical physics. He began teaching at the Middle East Technical University in 1960, later serving as the Dean and President.

In 1983, he founded the Social Democratic Party (SODEP) and was elected chairman at its first convention. Turkey's military rulers, the National Security Council, barred him and his party from participating in the national elections of Nov. 1983. But SODEP was quite successful in the local elections of Mar. 1984, winning over 23% of the vote. In 1985 SODEP merged with the Populist Party to form the Social Democratic Populist Party (SODEPOP) and I. was chosen to lead the united party. From the elections of Nov. 1987 SODEPOP emerged as the largest opposition party, with 99 seats. In the local elections of 1989 it became, with over 28% of the vote, the largest party, but in national politics it stayed in the opposition, I. rivalling Bulent *Ecevit of the Democratic Left Party for the status of main opposition leader. Within his party I. faced internal power struggles, mainly between leftist and non-moderate factions.

INÖNÜ, ISMET (1884–1973)   Turkish statesman. Second President of the Republic 1938–50. Prime Minister 1923–24, 1925–37, 1961–65. Born in Izmir, I. graduated from the Military Academy of Pangalti in 1906 and served in various military assignments, including that of Commander of the Ottoman forces in Yemen, 1910–13. During World War I he was Commander of the Second Army and fought on the Russian, and later the Syrian and Palestinian fronts. After the War he joined the nationalist struggle led by *Ataturk against the remnants of the Ottoman regime, the Greek invaders and Western plans for the dismemberment of Turkey's Anatolian heartland. In 1920 he was elected to the Grand National Assembly. In 1921 he was appointed Chief of Staff and Commander of the Western Front, winning the two battles of Inonu (from which he took his family name). He became Foreign Minister in 1922 and led the Turkish delegation at the Lausanne Peace Conference, 1922–23.

On the proclamation of the Republic in Oct. 1923 he became Prime Minister, a post which he held until 1937. Upon Ataturk's death in 1938, I. was elected President of the Republic and leader of the Republican People's Party (RPP). He carried on Ataturk's policies and kept Turkey out of World War II, while maintaining close relations with the leaders of the Western Alliance — at first secretly and from Dec. 1943 openly. After the war he permitted the growth of a multiparty system; his RPP lost the elections of 1950 and he was replaced as President by Celal *Bayar, the leader of the Democratic Party. He led the fight against the democratic regime in the 1950s, and although he did not take part in the military coup of 1960 which toppled it, he exercised strong influence on the

Ismet Inonu (Bar-David, Tel Aviv)

coup's leaders. I. and his party emerged from the elections of 1961 as the strongest party, but without an overall majority, and until 1965 he led three successive coalition governments. In 1965 the Justice Party, the successor of the outlawed Democratic Party, won the election and I. again became leader of the opposition. In 1971 he gave his blessing — reluctantly and with reservations — to the ultimatum of the military chiefs that toppled the *Demirel government and to his party's participation in a new coalition. But he himself no longer took part in the government. From about 1964 I.'s RPP adopted, under his leadership, a left-of-center ideology (with a right-wing faction seceding) with an increasingly socialist slant. The dominant leftist faction, however, under Bulent *Ecevit, gradually adopted a line more radical than I.'s and disputed his leadership. At a May 1972 RPP Congress it won a majority against I., and he resigned as party chairman (in his late eighties); later in 1972 I. seceded from the RPP. He died in Dec. 1973.

In the 1980s I.'s son Erdal I. founded and led a new left-of-center party, the Socialist-Democratic Party.

IRMAK, SADI (1904–?)   Turkish politician and scientist. Born in Seydisekuc (in the Konya region), I. began studying law in Istanbul but switched to natural sciences and studied medicine in Berlin. He was appointed to a position in the state medical service in Ankara and from 1939 as a professor at the Istanbul medical faculty. From 1950 to 1952 he taught physiology at the University of Munich.

I. was elected to Parliament in 1943, for Konya. He was Minister of Labor 1945–47, and Prime Minister 1974–75. After the military coup of Sept. 1980 he was appointed to the Advisory Council.

I. published many books, among them *Physiology* (1938); *Surgery* (1942); *Lambroso* (1942); *Inheritance* (1945). He also wrote a novel, *Zerdist* (1940).

AL-IRYANI, 'ABD-UL-KARIM (b. 1935) Yemeni politician, Prime Minister 1980–83, Foreign Minister since 1985. I. had his secondary schooling in Egypt, then studied agriculture and biology in the USA, earning a BA and MA from the University of Virginia and a doctorate from Yale. He returned to Yemen in 1968 and, as one of the younger technocrats with a modern education, filled several senior positions in the civil service. From 1974 he was a member of the government, serving several times as Minister of Agriculture, Development or Education; he also chaired the Planning Commission for some time and served as Rector of San'a University. In the late 1970s, I. also was an adviser to Kuwait's Arab Development Fund. From Oct. 1980 until Nov. 1983 he was Prime Minister — considered a "technocrat" rather than a political decision-maker. In 1985 he joined 'Abd-ul-'Aziz *Abd-ul-Ghani's government as Deputy Premier and Foreign Minister. After the merger of Yemen and South Yemen, May 1990, I. became Foreign Minister in the new united government.

AL-IRYANI, AL-SAYYID 'ABD-UL-RAHMAN (b. 1905? 1910?) Yemeni politician, President of Yemen 1967–74. Member of a Zeidi family of *Sada* (pl. of *Sayyid*, i.e. descendants of the Caliph 'Ali and his son Hussein — the institutional elite of Zeidi Yemen), I. received a traditional Islamic education and became a *Qadi* (Islamic judge). He was involved in the abortive coup of 1948 and was imprisoned for six years. After his release, he remained an active opponent of Imam-King *Ahmad bin Yahyia and his regime and went into exile to 'Aden and Cairo, where he was among the founders and leaders of a "Free Yemen" movement. After the coup of Sept. 1962 he returned and joined the Republican camp in the civil war. I. was appointed Minister of Justice, 1962–63, and of Local Administration. 1964. In the factional struggles within the Republican leadership, I. was a conservative with close links to, and influence on, the Zeidi tribes (some of whom supported the Royalists, making it urgent for the Republicans to win them over). When the power of the Republic's

chief leader and President 'Abdullah al-*Sallal was restricted by the nomination of a Presidential Council (and Sallal was detained in Egypt), in Apr. 1965, I. became a member of that Council. During his tenure he was instrumental in convening a pro-Republican tribal conference at Khamir, May 1965, which tried to push the regime towards a conservative orientation and to curb Egypt's Nasserist influence. In Sept. 1966 Sallal returned, resumed power and purged his rivals; I. was sent to Egypt and kept there in semi-detention. When Sallal was toppled, in Nov. 1967, and a more conservative regime was established, I. became chairman of the new Republican (Presidential) Council, i.e., President of Yemen. Though the government was run by prime ministers, I. continued wielding a strong influence, maintaining his alliance with the conservative tribal leaders, especially Sheikh 'Abdullah al-*Ahmar of the Hashed federation of tribes, but keeping a balance between the various factions. I. was instrumental in ending the civil war through the Republican-Royalist settlement, 1970, and in Republican Yemen's reconciliation with and acceptance by Sa'udi Arabia, 1970. In 1972 he also mended relations with the USA and opened Yemen to Western technology and experts. In 1972 he helped end Yemen's war with South Yemen and reestablished a measure of cooperation, reaffirming the common aim of an eventual merger of the two countries. During the nearly seven years of his presidency, involved in constant factional struggles, he several times threatened, or even announced, his resignation, but was persuaded to retract.

I. and his regime were overthrown in June 1974 by Col. Ibrahim *Hamdi, and he went into exile, to Lebanon and later to Syria. According to unconfirmed reports, I. was allowed to return.

ISMA'IL (AL-JAWFI), 'ABD-UL-FATTAH (1936? 1938?-86) South Yemeni politician, President of South Yemen 1978–80. Of (North-) Yemeni origin, I. was employed in the 1950s in 'Aden by the British Petroleum Company and was active in the NLF, the most extremist among the various underground nationalist groups; by 1964 he was considered one of its chief leaders, in charge of its political and military/terrorist activities, and heading its leftist-Marxist wing. When South Yemen attained independence in Nov. 1967, he became Minister of National Guidance and Youth (and for some time also of Planning and Economy) in President Qahtan al-*Sha'bi's government. But in the factional struggle within the NLF and the government he took a radical-leftist line; in Mar.-Apr. 1968 he attemped a semi-coup that was suppressed, and lost his government post. In June 1969, his leftist faction overthrew al-Sha'bi and he became Secretary-General of the ruling NLF and a member of the Presidential Council, under Salem Rubai' *'Ali. He continued heading a leftist faction loyal to Moscow — together with 'Ali Nasser *Muhammad — and built up a strong armed party militia and secret services. In a coup of Aug. 1971 he and 'Ali Nasser Muhammad consolidated their position, and in June 1978 they overthrew (and killed) President Rubai' 'Ali, with Ali Nasser Muhammad becoming interim chairman of the Presidential Council; in December he ceded that post to I. During the nearly two years of I.'s presidency South Yemen followed his leftist-extremist policy in international, inter-Arab and home affairs. These policies, and constant factional struggle, brought I. into growing conflict with 'Ali Nasser

Muhammad, who began advocating a more pragmatic orientation, and in Apr. 1980 I. was forced to resign the presidency and go into exile. He spent the next five years in the USSR. Apparently the Soviet Union mediated between the factions and in 1985 I. was allowed to return, and his supporters were restored to party and government positions (in the Politbureau of the ruling party, reportedly, two of his men vs three of 'Ali Nasser Muhammad's); I. himself became Secretary-General of the party's Central Committee — a post seen by observers as mainly honorific and without real power. However, factional tensions increased during 1985, and it was reportedly only Soviet and PLO (?) mediation that prevented an eruption. That eruption came in Jan. 1986: a coup d'etat staged by I. and his faction led to bitter, confused fighting and the overthrow of 'Ali Nasser Muhammad. I. himself was killed (in 'Ali Nasser Muhammad's version: executed).

J

AL-JABERI Family of notables in Syria's northern city of Aleppo. Some of its sons were prominent in the Ottoman adminstration, and later in the Arab and Syrian nationalist movement. Most prominent in recent generations were Ihsan al-J. and Sa'ullah al-J.

Ihsan Active in the Pan-Arab nationalist movement in the 1920s, he for some years headed the Geneva office of the "Syrian-Palestinian Congress" and engaged in information work and political negotiation with diverse groups (including the Zionist leadership, pursuant to the *Feisal-*Weizmann agreement). The activities of the Geneva office faded out in the later 1920s. J. joined the "National Bloc," the mainstream of Syrian nationalism, in the 1930s, and from 1937, in the brief period of movement towards fuller independence under the Franco-Syrian agreement of 1936, served as Governor of the province of Lataqia. He did not live to attain high office after Syria became independent in 1945–46.

Sa'Dullah (1892–1947) An active nationalist since his youth, J. was one of the leaders of the "National Bloc" under the French Mandate. He was arrested several times during the years of struggle in the early 1930s. He served as a minister in several governments of the "National Bloc" in 1936–39, in the brief period of movement towards full independence in the late 1930s. When the "National Bloc" returned to power, in 1943, he was twice Prime Minister – in 1943–44 and 1945–46. In between, in 1944–45, he was President of the National Assembly.

JABOTINSKY, ZE'EV (VLADIMIR) (1880–1940) Zionist leader. The founder and head of the Revisionist movement. Born in Odessa, Russia. From 1898 he studied law in Switzerland and Italy. In 1901 he returned to Russia where he worked as a reporter for local newspapers. During the 1903 pogroms, he organized a group of Jewish youth for self-defense. These pogroms, and particularly that of Kishinev, heightened his Zionist consciousness and he joined the Zionist movement. In 1906 he participated in the Helsingfors (Helsinki) Congress of Russian Zionists which discussed the concept of "*Gegenwartsarbeit*" (work of the present) for Zionist activity in the Diaspora.

With the outbreak of World War I he went to Western Europe as a representative of a Moscow newspaper. During his travels he met Yosef *Trumpeldor in Alexandria, Egypt and the two initiated the establishment of "Jewish Battalions" which would fight alongside the British to capture Palestine. Jabotinsky joined the Battalion as an officer.

After his discharge from the army he settled in Jerusalem. On Passover 1920 he was arrested by the British for his part in organizing the Jewish defense of Jerusalem during the 1920 riots. He was sentenced to 15 years' imprisonment. In September 1921 he was released from Acre jail and left for London. He was elected to the Zionist Executive.

He resigned in 1923 in protest against its acquiescence in the policies of the High Commissioner, Herbert Samuel. He called for a harder line that would compel the British to fulfill their obligations to Zionism and to the "National Home." In order to fight for his views, he established and headed a new party called the "Revisionist Zionist Organization" (1925), as an alternative – both politically and ideologically – to the World Zionist Organization presided over by Chaim Weizmann. In the early 1930's, the Revisionists tried to take over the leadership of the Zionist movement; but they were defeated and the leadership was taken over by the Labor movement headed by David *Ben-Gurion. The Revisionists seceded from the Zionist Movement and in 1935 J. established a rival "New Zionist Organization" (NZO). He went to live in Palestine and became editor in chief of the *Doar Hayom* newspaper bought by his movement. When in 1930 he went abroad, the British refused to let him return to Palestine.

As president of the NZO J. advocated a mass evacuation of Polish Jews and negotiated with the anti-Semitic regime of Poland over his proposal. He also appeared before various bodies such as the Peel Commission. Parallel to his diplomacy, the Revisionist movement developed an underground military organization, the *Irgun Zevai Leumi* (IZL), from 1937. This body's line was much more militant and radical than J.'s. In the later 1930s his control over the movement weakened. Though he was formally the "Supreme Commander of the IZL," disagreements between him and the younger leaders of the IZL in Palestine and Poland deepened.

With the outbreak of World War II he endeavored to establish a Jewish army. For this purpose he went in early 1940 to the USA, where he died. He was buried in New York. His remains were brought to Palestine in 1964, as decided by the *Eshkol government.

The Revisionist movement considers J. as the founder and great leader of the movement and endeavors to blur the disputes and disagreements in which he was involved and the weakening of his control over the movement in the last years of his life. Even his adversaries agree that he was one of the outstanding political leaders of Zionism.

J. was active intellectually. Fluent in several languages, he was also a gifted writer, poet, playwright and translator.

JABR, SALEH (1896–1957)   Iraqi politician. Born in al-Nasseriyya of a Muslim-Shi'i family, J. graduated from Baghdad Law School and served as a judge, 1926–30. A member of Parliament since 1930, he was a minister in several governments (Education 1933–34 and 1938–40, Justice 1936–37, Social Welfare 1940, Finance 1942–43, acting Foreign Minister 1941–42 and 1943). In between he served as a provincial governor (Karbala 1935–36, Basra 1941–41) and Director of Customs (1937–38). From Mar. 1947 to Jan. 1948 he was Prime Minister — the first Shi'i to reach that position. Considered a moderate and pro-British, of Nuri al-*Sa'id's school (though not of his faction), J. negotiated with Britain the Portsmouth Treaty of Jan. 1948, designed to replace the Anglo-Iraqi Treaty of 1930 and reduce the privileges still enjoyed by Britain. The Treaty did not satisfy the more extreme nationalists and caused violent demonstrations, and J. had to resign (the treaty was scrapped by his successor). J. briefly rejoined the government in 1950 as Minister of the Interior. In 1951 he founded a short-lived conservative "People's Socialist Party." But his standing was impaired by the crisis of Jan. 1948, and he did not return to high office.

I.'s son, **Sa'd Jabr**, was in the 1980s active in opposition groups in exile (and underground?) and emerged in 1990/91 as one of their leaders, reportedly cultivated and supported by Sa'udi Arabia.

JADID, SALAH (b. 1929)   Syrian officer and politician. An 'Alawi born in Lataqia, J. became a professional officer. In the 1950s he joined a clandestine cell of the leftist Pan-Arab *Ba'th* party and soon played a leading role. He was among those who prepared and staged the coup of Mar. 1963 that brought the *Ba'th* into power. After the *Ba'th* group won in a bitter factional struggle with the Nasserists, J. became, later in 1963, Chief of Staff. In Oct. 1964 he was also made a member of the Presidential Council, and of both the "national" (i.e. all-Arab) and the "regional" Syrian high command of the *Ba'th* party. In the intra-*Ba'th* factional struggle in 1964–65, J. headed the "military" faction that was also more extreme-leftist and doctrinaire in its political orientation (besides having a more pronounced 'Alawi profile). When the "civilian" and more moderate wing, led by *'Aflaq, *Bitar and al-*Hafez won out, J. was dismissed in Sept. 1965 both from the Presidential Council and as Chief of Staff. However, in Feb. 1966 J. ousted the ruling 'Aflaq-Hafez faction in a coup and installed his military faction both in the Syrian government and army and in the Syrian-regional *Ba'th* command. As the 'Aflaq faction, now in exile, retained its leadership of the all-Arab *Ba'th* command, J. and his associates set up a rival all-Arab command in Syria.

In the new regime he established in 1966 J. took no formal post in either the government or the army but contented himself with the position of Deputy Secretary-General of the *Ba'th* Party, leaving the secretary-generalship to Nur-ul-Din al-*Atassi. In fact he was the strong man of Syria for over four years. His policy was doctrinaire and leftist both inside Syria and in foreign relations. Syria's increasing isolation within the Arab world caused by J.'s policies was one of the reasons for the widening of a further split within the *Ba'th*. Parts of J.'s own military faction, led by Defense Minister Hafez al-*Asad, coalesced in a "nationalist" faction and turned against J. In Feb. 1969 Asad, in a bloodless semi-coup, gained control of the government and the party command. He accepted a compromise: a coalition in which the J.

group kept some important posts. In 1970 Asad, in a second semi-coup, seized full control. J. and his associates were dismissed and detained — as it turned out, for over 10 years. J. was released in 1983 (according to unconfirmed rumors he had rejected an earlier offer to release him, as his conditions were not met). He is kept under close surveillance and not allowed to play any role in public-political life.

A brother of J., Major Ghassan J., also a professional officer, was politically active in a formation very much different from, and opposed to, J.'s *Ba'th*: the "Syrian Nationalist Party." He was murdered in Feb. 1957, in exile in Lebanon. Another brother, Fu'ad, was jailed in connection with the murder of Syria's leftist and pro-Egyptian Deputy Chief of Staff 'Adnan al-Maleki by the same "Syrian Nationalist Party" in 1955; J. released him from prison.

JALLUD, 'ABD-UL-SALAM (b. 1940/1? 1943?) Libyan officer and politician. Since 1969, Col. al-*Qadhdhafi's chief associate and Libya's "number two" leader under various official designations. A professional officer, commissioned 1965, J., then a

'Abd-ul-Salam Jallud (IPS, Tel Aviv)

captain, took part in al-Qadhdhafi's coup of Sept. 1, 1969. Promoted to major, he became a member, and informal deputy chairman, of the Revolutionary Command Council. In Jan. 1970 he joined Qadhdhafi's new government as Deputy Premier and Home Minister, becoming Minister of Economy and Industry in Sept. In Aug. 1971 the post of Deputy Premier was abolished, a measure interpreted by some as the dismissal of J. from that post; he retained his portfolios. In July 1972 he became Prime Minister, replacing Qadhdhafi – a shift again interpreted by some observers as the result of a factional struggle inside the junta and a restriction of Qadhdhafi's power (?). J. became increasingly responsible for the conduct of Libya's foreign relations, particularly from 1974, when Qadhdhafi decided to devote himself mainly to basic and ideological matters and leave daily government affairs to his associates. When, in Mar. 1977, Libya became a "*Jamahiriyya*" (Polity, or Republic, of the Masses) and changed the nomenclature of its governance, J. became a member (semiofficially: deputy chairman) of the "General Secretariat" which replaced the Revolutionary Council, i.e., in effect Deputy Head of State.

In Mar. 1979, both Qadhdhafi and Jallud resigned their positions on that Secretariat. They have since formally held no government posts — but their real power as Head of State and Deputy Head-of-State is undoubted, relying on the army, the all-pervasive secret service and the "people's committees" they have built up.

Frequent rumors of factional disputes, with J. allegedly heading a faction rivalling Qadhdhafi, have never been substantiated. But J. is undoubtedly very different from Qadhdhafi, both in personal character and politically. He does not have his leader's erratic firebrand charisma, and being rather more pragmatic, involved in management and power manipulation, he does not share Qadhdhafi's devotion to ideological doctrines with their revolutionary fervor in Islamic, social, political and international matters. He also reportedly has little part in Qadhdhafi's obsession with Pan-Arab unity and his relentless pursuit of mergers (such as Qadhdhafi's 1972–73 insistence on immediate union with Egypt), and favors an orientation towards closer Maghrib cooperation. Yet, he has never publicly challenged Qadhdhafi's doctrines or policies, nor his support for and use of international terrorism. J. is the architect of much of Libya's foreign relations, particularly those with the USSR, where he has been, since 1972, a frequent visitor.

JAM, MAHMUD (1890-?) Iranian politician. Born in Tabriz, and received his education in Tehran and Tabriz. Joining the government as a translator in the Ministry of Customs, J. eventually became the Minister of Customs. Later, he served as translator in the Iranian embassy in France. J. held many ministerial posts, including Foreign Affairs, Finance, Education, Interior, Justice, Posts and War. He was Deputy Prime Minister in the government of Sardar Sepah and governor of Kerman and Korassan. J. was Prime Minister in 1939. He was ambassador to Egypt and Italy and general governor of Azerbaijan. J. was also a senator.

JIBRAN (Jubran), JIBRAN KHALIL (1883–1931) Lebanese-American, Christian-Maronite writer, poet, and artist, known in English and American literature as Khalil Gibran. Born in the village of Bisharri in Mount Lebanon, J. was in 1894 taken by his mother to the USA; they settled in the Chinatown of Boston. In 1897 he returned to Beirut to study Arabic and French at the Maronite College al-Hikma.

Back in Boston in 1899, J. developed his talents as a writer and a painter. In 1904 he held the first exhibition of his drawings. At this exhibition he came into contact with his benefactress and friend Mary Haskell, who sent him in 1908 to Paris to study art.

In 1910 J. returned to Boston and in 1911 he formed a political society, The Golden Chain, for resisting Ottoman tyranny and for social and political reform in Lebanon.

In 1912 J. moved to New York where he published his novel *The Broken Wings* (in Arabic) — a romantic and naive novel criticizing the feudalists and clergymen in Lebanon who prevented the young and poor protagonist from marrying his rich beloved (a novel reflecting an unhappy love of J. himself).

Until 1918 J. continued writing books in Arabic, such as *A Tear and a Smile*, *The Storms*, and *The Processions*. In this period he was under the influence of Nietzsche, idolizing power. From 1918 he started publishing in English with *The Madman* as his first book. He now expressed an optimistic pantheism. In 1919 he published his *Twenty Drawings*, in 1920 his book *The Forerunner* and in 1923 *The Prophet* which brought him fame and wealth

(selling in 1959 the millionth copy); in this book he dealt with the relations of man to man he had previously discussed in his Arabic *The Processions*. Days before his death in 1931 he published *The Earth Gods*. His books *The Wanderer* and *The Garden of the Prophet* were published posthumously.

J.'s influence upon Arabic literature was significant. In Arabic he developed a new lyrical style based upon parallelism and Biblical metaphors suitable for his romantic and pantheistic ideas, a musically poetic prose that came to be known as "the Jubranian Style." In the English-speaking world, J. was considered sentimental and echoing familiar ideas.

JIBRIL, AHMAD (b. 1935? 1937?) Palestinian-Arab guerrilla/terrorist organizer. Born in Yazur near Ramla, J. left his home with his family in 1948, among the Palestinian refugees. He grew up in Jordan and Syria and until 1958 served in the Syrian army, reaching the rank of captain. In the 1960s he began organizing guerrilla/terrorist groups against Israel, and in 1967 his group joined the Popular Front for the Liberation of Palestine (PFLP) led by George *Habash. In 1968, however, the PFLP split, and J. seceded, forming his own organization, naming it "PFLP — General Command." This group, more extremist than even the PFLP in its policies and terror methods, is small, tightly knit and kept secret even from the leadership of the Palestine Liberation Organization

Ahmad Jibril (AP Photo)

(PLO). It perpetrated some of the worst terrorist attacks against "targets" both in Israel and in foreign countries (including daring ventures such as an attack by fighters flown in by hang gliders, Nov. 1987). J. also became known by a deal in May 1985 in which Israel granted him the release of 1150 detainees and convicted prisoners in exchange for three Israeli soldiers he had captured.

In intra-PLO politics, J. and his group form a most extremist faction, opposing *'Arafat and the mainstream leadership. In 1983 he joined a Syrian-supported armed rebellion of dissident PLO-*Fatah* squads against 'Arafat and his men in Lebanon that expelled the latter from east Lebanon and Tripoli, and from 1984/85 he adhered to a "National Alliance" and a "National Salvation Front" of anti-'Arafat groups within and without the PLO. In 1987 J. and his groups were suspended, and according to one version expelled, from the PLO. Though J. did not fully accept Syrian "guidance" and discipline, most of the time he was hosted and tolerated in Syria. In the late 1980s he reportedly developed strong links with Iraq and Iran.

JUMAYYIL, AMIN (b. 1942)   Lebanese politician, President of Lebanon 1982–88. A Christian Maronite from Beirut, J. is the elder son of Pierre *Jumayyil, the founder and leader of the "Phalanges," and the brother of Bashir *Jumayyil, elected President in Aug. 1982 and killed before assuming office. J. studied jurisprudence and worked as a lawyer and businessman with widely spread economic interests and activities. He was not very active in politics and little involved in the military activities and organization of the Phalanges; but as the son of the founder-leader and the brother of the emerging younger military commander he remained identified with them. J. entered Parliament in 1970, in a by-election. He was generally considered less determined, less hard-line, than his father and his brother in the defense of the Christian-Maronite predominance in Lebanese politics. He was more inclined to seek an accommodation with the non-Christian communities, with the radicals striving for constitutional reforms that would abolish the communal structure of Parliament and government, with Syria, and with the Palestinian guerrilla presence and operations in Lebanon (and he did not share his brother's inclination to cooperate with Israel). He therefore played no important part in the organization and defense of the Christian-conservative camp in the civil war since 1975 and in

the late 1970s maintained some contact with Syria and the PLO leadership. Despite all this, several attempts were made in the late 1970s to kidnap and/or assassinate him.

J. was propelled into the presidency when his brother Bashir, just elected President, was killed in the terror-bombing of the Phalanges headquarters, in Sept. 1982. Parliament elected him with an attendance and a majority larger than his brother's a month before, as he was seen less identified with the Maronite camp in the civil war, and as Syria did not oppose him (the only rival candidate, Camille *Chamoun, withdrew before the vote). He had pledged to continue the policies of his late brother, and the first, pressing point on his agenda was the conclusion of an agreement with Israel, in occupation of large parts of Lebanon, which would provide for security arrangements and a modicum of coexistence enabling Israel to withdraw. Though J. was not enthusiastic, and the agreement was whittled down in protracted negotiations to much less than Israel had hoped for, it was signed in May 1983. However, Syria and her Lebanese supporters, J.'s rivals with whom he strove to achieve an accommodation, were pressing to abrogate that agreement altogether as a precondition for any reconciliation. J. therefore procrastinated, delaying his final signature. He was at any rate incapable of assuring a coordinated transferral, as Israel requested, since he and his government and army had but little effective control (his standing was also hurt on the eve of his election by the massacre perpetrated by the Phalanges in the Palestinian camps of Sabra and Shatila: if, as he insisted, he bore no responsibility for that operation, it showed that he had no control over the Phalanges). When Israeli forces began unilaterally withdrawing, in Sept. 1983, bitter fighting broke out between Christians and Druze in the Shuf region, spreading to Beirut where Shi'i militias took over the Muslim western part and Druze ones the southeastern suburbs and approaches, and the power and control of President J. and his government were further reduced. The army disintegrated in 1984 into virtually separate Christian, Shi'i, Sunni and Druze parts. Repeated changes in the command of the Phalanges and their "Lebanese Forces" — changes over which J. had no control — were at least in part directed against his policies and deprived him in effect of any military base of support.

Efforts for a general pacification led to a National Reconciliation Conference in Geneva in Oct. 1983 and Lausanne in Mar. 1984, in the course of which

J. had to accept a large part of his rivals' and Syria's demands. He formally abrogated the agreement with Israel in Mar. 1984, before, and as the price for, the second Reconciliation Conference. He accepted far-reaching policy coordination with Syria. He agreed to the need for basic reforms in Lebanon's constitutional and political structure — giving more weight to Muslims, particularly Shi'i Muslims, and Druze, towards an eventual abolition of the communal system, with details and procedures to be worked out. And he set up a "Government of National Reconciliation" headed by his adversaries (Rashid *Karameh as Premier, the Shi'i leader Nabih *Berri and the Druze chief Walid *Junbalat among the Ministers). However, the hoped-for cease-fire and the beginnings of reforms and reconciliation proved illusive. A bloody, nearly incessant battle continued between a coalition of Druze and Shi'i militias and Christian ones, with the army ineffective and in fact split. Berri and Junbalat boycotted and sabotaged the government of which they were members and called for J.'s resignation or dismissal. Syria, now in effective military and political control, was pressing for a general agreement on lines acceptable to it, but was unable to enforce it (though J. was frequently summoned to Damascus). Negotiations, led mainly by the militia leaders, dragged on interrupted by bouts of bitter fighting and with the parties frequently reneging on points previously agreed. In Dec. 1985, Elie Hobeika, commander of the "Lebanese Forces," signed in Damascus an agreement with the Shi'i and Druze militia leaders that provided for the dissolution of all militias and for radical political reforms (abolition of the Christian majority in Parliament, steps towards the abolition of the communal structure of Lebanon's body politic, and a sharp reduction in the powers of the Maronite President), as well as total "coordination" of Lebanon's defense, foreign and inter-Arab policies, and her security services, with Syria's. Hobeika's rival, Samir Ja'ja', now rebelled, rallied to J. and those Phalange formations that had remained loyal to J., and defeated Hobeika's forces. J. himself did not reject the Dec. 1985 agreement openly and totally. But he clearly indicated that, while accepting the cease-fire and the military provisions, he had grave reservations concerning the political reforms dictated and the reduction of the President's powers. He insisted that any reform plan should be adopted through constitutional channels, and not be imposed by the militias; and,

while not daring to say so, he implied that the total subservience to Syria envisaged in the agreement was not acceptable. J. accepted the military alliance offered by Ja'ja', who was much more radical in his rejection of the agreement, and the ensuing military clash with Hobeika and his allies. Syria did not officially join Berri and Junbalat in demanding J.'s dismissal and maintained some relations with him, but its forces backed the Shi'i and Druze militias, as well as Hobeika and J.'s Maronite rival, former President Suleiman *Franjiyeh, and J.'s position remained precarious to the end of his presidency in Sept. 1988. As Parliament was unable to convene and elect a new president, J. appointed, in accordance with the Constitution, a temporary head of state to succeed him; he chose General Michel *'Awn, a hard-line Christian — an appointment that caused much strife and bitter battles. J. retired in 1988 and takes nearly no part in public affairs.

JUMAYYIL, BASHIR (1947–82)   Lebanese militia leader and politician. Elected President of Lebanon in Aug. 1982, killed before assuming office. A Maronite Christian born in Beirut, J. was the younger son of Pierre *Jumayyil, the founder and leader of the "Phalanges", and the brother of Amin *Jumayyil (who succeeded him as President). He studied law and political science at the Jesuit St. Joseph University of Beirut, but did not complete his studies. From his early youth he was active in the Phalanges. In the late 1960s, he organized student agitation against the presence and activities of the Palestinian-Arab guerrillas in Lebanon (1968). Considered ruthless and endowed with charismatic leadership, he rose rapidly in the organization's military command during the civil war from 1975 onward - stressing a youthful activism and a measure of disdain for the leaders of the older generation and their political deals and intrigues. In 1976, J. became the chief military commander of the Phalanges, and shortly afterwards also of the "Lebanese Forces" (at that time an umbrella formation of the Phalanges and other Christian-Maronite militias). He is credited with the bloody conquest, in Aug. 1976, of the Palestinian guerrilla camp-stronghold of Tel al-Za'tar in an East Beirut suburb.

From 1976–77, J. strove to impose on the Christian "Lebanese Forces" the complete primacy of his Phalanges, in effect the merger of all other Christian formations in the Phalanges - by force if necessary. He was held chiefly responsible for bitter intra-Maronite fighting - with *Franjiyeh's North-Lebanese militias (in the course of which Franjiyeh's son and heir was killed, with his wife and child), and with *Chamoun's National-Liberal Party "Tigers" (which he eliminated as a fighting force, absorbing their remnants into his Phalange-Lebanese Forces). J. thus got involved in bitter blood feuds and, while adored by his supporters, was hated by many, even within his own Maronite community. He and his relatives were also targets for terrorist attacks in the civil war; in one such attempt, in Feb. 1980, his baby daughter was killed.

J.'s political line was radical. No longer content with the elder Christian leaders' struggle to maintain the inter-communal equilibrium with a measure of Christian-Maronite primacy, he aspired to a Christian, Maronite-dominated Lebanon. In the first place he wanted to defend and strengthen Maronite control of the heartland of Mount Lebanon, he was not averse to the thought of transforming Lebanon into a federation of semi-independent communal cantons with the Maronite one as main and dominating part, and he seemed willing to consider even the cession of the Muslim-majority North, South and East, that had been added in 1920 to create "Greater Lebanon", and the recreation of a smaller, Christian Lebanon. He vigorously opposed Syrian intervention and the presence of Syrian troops in Lebanon, even if disguised as an "all-Arab" peace or deterrence force. He objected to all-Arab interference, and to the integration of Lebanon in an all-Arab power blocs. He fought the Palestinian guerrillas' use of Lebanon as a base for their operations, did not believe in co-ordination agreements with them and wanted them out altogether.

From about 1976 J. fostered clandestine links with Israel that the Phalanges had maintained, on and off, for many years. He received Israeli aid in arms and training and several times met (or sent his associates to meet) Israeli leaders. The invading Israeli forces in June 1982 made it possible for J. and his Phalanges to take control of Beirut and the key levers of government. But J. knew that he could not become an accepted leader of all Lebanon if he was borne to power on the coat-tails of an Israeli invasion and as Israel's collaborator; he therefore began, though clearly seen as cooperating with Israel to some degree, to shun a too visible collaboration with her.

When President *Sarkis' term expired, in Sept. 1982, J. was, in the political circumstances created by the Israeli invasion and the predominance achieved by the Phalanges, the only candidate for the Presidency. It proved difficult to convene Parliament, the more so as Syria did not permit the attendance of members from the areas she occupied. But eventually, 62 of the 92 members surviving were drummed together and on 23 Aug. 1982 elected J. President, with 57 votes, on the second ballot. On 14 Sept., before he was sworn in, J. was killed in the bombing of the Phalanges headquarters (a bombing revenged by the Phalanges, three days later, in a massacre of the Palestinian camps of Sabra and Shatila). J. was succeeded by his brother Amin *Jumayyil, elected President one week after Bashir's death.

JUMAYYIL, PIERRE (1905–84) Lebanese politician, Maronite Christian. Founder and leader of the paramilitary "Palanges" organization. Father of Presidents Bashir *Jumayyil and Amin *Jumayyil. A pharmacist, educated in Beirut and France, J. was active in sports and youth organizations, reportedly much impressed by European, and particularly German, organizations. In 1936 he founded the paramilitary "Phalanges Libanaises" (al-Kata'ib). Designed to protect the Maronites (though this was never explicitly spelled out), that organization soon took a political coloring, stressing Lebanon's independence and its Christian character and opposing its integration in Pan-Arab schemes. It gradually became more of a political party, making J. one of the leaders of the pro-Western Christian camp.

In the 1930s and 1940s, J. cultivated the Phalanges as a youth and paramilitary organization and was not active in politics. He took no prominent part in the struggle of those years between pro-French and anti-French factions (*Edde and his "National Bloc" vs *Khouri and his "Constitutional Bloc") or in the crisis of 1943. In the civil war of 1958 he was one of the leaders of the Christian-led resistance to the Nasserist, Muslim-led rebels. When that dispute was being settled, in Sept. 1958, he prevented, by threatening a coup, the formation of a government dominated by the Nasserist rebels and insisted on a more balanced group. In October, with the compromise that ended the crisis, he became one of the four members of the neutral government set up. He supported President *Shihab and was a cabinet minister during most of Shihab's presidency (to 1964) and that of his successor Hilou (to 1970) — Minister of Finance 1960–61, the Interior 1966, and 1968–69, and most of the time Public Works and/or Health. Since 1960 he was also a member of Parliament — elected as an independent, but gradually appearing as a representative of the Phalanges (with a handful of additional Phalangists in Parliament). J. did not take a strong stand on the basic Christian-Muslim issue, though his general attitude was well-known. He did not join other Christian factions to form a strong united Christian bloc, and engaged in much factional-tactical maneuvering. He did, however, form, in the 1960s, a loose "Triple Alliance" with Camille *Chamoun's "National Liberal Party" and Raymond Edde's "National Bloc." In 1970 he presented, with their support, his candidacy for the presidency, but withdrew in favor of a more "neutral" candidate, Suleiman *Franjiyeh.

J. took, since the late 1960s, a strong position against the use of Lebanon by the Palestinian-Arab guerrillas/terrorists as a base for their operations and against the growth of their separate and dominant establishment in South Lebanon. He did not follow the official Arab line of total hostility towards Israel, but neither did he associate himself with the willingness to coexist in peace and cooperate evinced by some other Christian politicians (such as Emile Edde), some leaders of the Maronite Church, and his own Phalanges. He certainly was aware of Israel's low-profile aid to, and cooperation with, the Phalanges since the 1950s, but he was not directly involved in this, and he took no part in the intensification of that cooperation in the 1970s and its culmination in June 1982. Of his two sons, he seemed closer to the positions taken by cautious, balancing Amin than to those of extreme, brash, militant Bashir.

Since the early 1970s, J. was not very active in Lebanon's public and political life. He did not play a prominent role in the marshalling of the Christian-conservative camp in the civil war since 1975, though he was, of course, identified with the Phalanges and his sons. In Apr. 1984 he agreed to serve in the Government of National Unity established by Rashid *Karameh and imposed on his son Amin, the President. In July 1984, he retired from the chairmanship of the Phalanges, appointing as his successor Elie Karameh (who was duly elected in Sept. 1984, soon after J.'s death).

JUNBALAT (also **JUMBALAT, JUMBLAT**) Prominent *Druze clan in Lebanon, one of the two clans struggling, since the mid-19th century, for the political leadership of the Druze community (the rival one: *Arsalan). The J.'s, of Kurdish origin, claim descent from Salah-ul-Din. Centered in Aleppo, they reportedly came to Lebanon in the 17th century at the invitation of the Druze ruler Fakhr-ul-Din, joined his Druze community, and established themselves as semifeudal lords of parts of the Shuf region, with Mukhtara as their center. In the clans' struggle for primacy they fought, in the 18th and early 19th centuries, against the ruling Shihab dynasty. After the decline of the latter, the J.'s emerged, from the mid-19th century, as one of the two leading clans and competed with the Arsalan or Yazbaki clan for the dominant position. While their political allegiance was shifting, they were generally allies of the French during the French Mandate. Prominent figures among them in the 1920s and 1930s were Fu'ad J. (assassinated in the early 1920s) and his widow Nazira, who became leader of the clan (d. 1951), and Hikmat J., who represented the clan in Parliament and was several times a government minister (d. 1943).

In independent Lebanon, since 1943, the J.'s have become increasingly assertive in their demands for the Druze community and have — under the leadership of Kamal *J. (the son of Fu'ad and Nazira), joined the leftist-Socialist, radical camp. As the Arsalans declined, the J.'s have become the chief leaders of the Lebanese Druze — and of the leftist camp and its military formations, allied with the Shi'is in recent years. While advocating the abolition of Lebanon's communal system of representation and, Kamal and Walid J. have in fact enhanced the strength of the Druze community and its weight in Lebanese politics and carved out a Druze "canton" in the Shuf and upper Matn areas that is *de facto* autonomous and under their control.

JUNBALAT, KAMAL (1917–77) Lebanese-Druze politician. The son of Fu'ad and Nazira J. (see *supra*), J. studied law and sociology in Beirut and Paris and became head of the J. clan in the late 1940s. Considered a highly cultivated man of wide horizons and original thought, J. was a skilled politician who had, in the complex community-party-clan politics of Lebanon, no permanent allegiance but played a power game of shifting factional alliances. A supporter of Emile *Edde and his "National Bloc" in his youth, he switched his support to Bishara al-*Khouri after 1943, but soon turned against him and joined Camille *Chamoun to bring about Khouri's fall in 1952. J. first became a government minister in Dec. 1945 (Economic Affairs) and was a member of Parliament from 1947 — except for the years 1957–64.

While J. drew his political strength from being the recognized leader of the Druze community, and later, of its armed militias — and not from the political-ideological views he propounded — he began turning left in the late 1940s and adopted increasingly radical Socialist, and gradually also Nasserist and Pan-Arab, views. In 1949 he founded a party of his own, the "Progressive Socialist Party," and began appearing as a Socialist leader, while keeping his position as a great landlord and semifeudal chieftain with various financial and business interests (though he distributed some of his land to his tenants). His party was mainly Druze, but claimed to be above communal interests; it advocated far-reaching social reforms and the abolition of Lebanon's system of communal representation.

In 1958, J. turned against President Chamoun and began organizing extra-parliamentary, Nasserist-inspired opposition that soon led to a violent insurrection and civil war. The ending of that crisis with the help of American military intervention confirmed him in his anti-Western, leftist-Nasserist views. Under the post-1958 regime of Presidents *Shihab and Hilou, J. several times held ministerial posts — Education 1960–61, Public Works 1961 and 1966, Interior 1961–63 and 1969–70. He was prominent, and as Home Minister instrumental, in his support for the Palestinian-Arab guerrilla operations and their establishment in Lebanon, and, as clashes erupted between PLO men and Lebanese, mainly Christian, formations, from 1970, he was involved in several crises on that issue. J. also fostered relations with the USSR and in 1972 was awarded the Lenin Peace Prize. But he also applied for membership for his party in the Socialist International, obtained observer status and was welcomed as a participant in several meetings of the International.

In the civil war since 1975, J. was one of the chief organizers of the leftist-Muslim camp, and his Druze (or "Progressive-Socialist") militias became one of the main military formations of that camp. He also cultivated, in the context of that civil war, close relations with Syria. Yet, when Syria's involvement became a full-fledged military intervention in 1976, and Syria tried to impose a comprehensive settlement and reform plan, J. adamantly opposed the plan (which, in his view, did not go far enough and made too many concessions to the Christian conservatives). He thus was jointly responsible for the strange constellation that found Syria, briefly, fighting against her allies of the Lebanese left and

cooperating with her adversaries of the Christian right. And when J. was assassinated, in Mar. 1977, it was generally assumed, though never proven, that Syrian agents had killed him.

J., who also taught for some years History of Economic Thought at Beirut University, wrote several books on Lebanese political issues (*The Truth about the Lebanese Revolution*, 1959; *Pour le Liban* — written down by a French associate — 1978, English edition, *I Speak for Lebanon*, 1982; *In the Current of Lebanese Politics*).

JUNBALAT, WALID (b. 1949)   Lebanese Druze politician and militia leader. The son of Kamal *J. (his mother was of the *Arsalan clan, the daughter of Shakib *Arsalan), J. studied at the American University of Beirut and in France. He was not very active in politics in his youth, and though he belonged to his father's militia, he was considered a playboy. When, however, Kamal J. was assassinated in Mar. 1977, Walid succeeded him — reportedly with some reluctance — as leader of the "Progressive Socialist Party" and its militias (in effect: Druze militias), and of the Druze community. At first it was thought that the community, and particularly its religious leaders, would not accept him (the more so as he broke Druze customs by marrying a non-Druze, a Jordanian of Circassian origin); but he soon asserted his leadership. At first considered moderate, he soon took his father's line of anti-Western leftism and a close alliance with the leftist-Muslim camp in the civil war; given to bold, somewhat erratic statements and much media exposure, he even took a more extreme position. Like his father, he advocated the abolition of Lebanon's system of communal representation and government, while he asserted in effect the power position of the Druze community. It fell to him to enhance that power to unprecedented strength after Sept. 1983. During the first months of the Israeli occupation, from June 1982, he stayed in his home at Mukhtara and kept a low profile; notwithstanding his extremist politics, he had, as the leader of the Druze in the Israel-occupied Shuf region, some contacts with the Israelis, and the latter hoped for cooperation with him in the pacification of the area, security arrangements and the coordination of their withdrawal. However, he preferred to leave his occupied home and spend some time in Syria, and returned to reassert his leadership and organize resistance to Israel (and to the *Jumayyils' Christian-dominated regime set up under Israeli auspices). In Aug.-Sept.

Walid Junbalat

In the efforts towards national reconciliation, 1984–85, J. took a hard, extremist line, insisting on speedy far-reaching reforms towards a non-communal constitution, and an immediate redistribution of power, with a larger share for the Druze (and Muslims) and a reduction of the powers of the Maronite President; he also repeatedly demanded the dismissal or resignation of President Amin *Jumayyil. He tightened his alliance with Syria, in effect becoming a client totally depending on her support, arms supplies, etc.; he sometimes agreed to compromise formulas worked out under Syrian guidance, but frequently reneged, shifted his tactical positions and burst out in new extreme pronouncements. He accepted the compromise formula of Mar. 1984 and joined *Karameh's "Government of National Unity" (as Minister of Public Works and Transportation), but boycotted and in effect sabotaged the government of which he was a member. J. supported the Fall 1989 Ta'if Agreement on a reformed Lebanese government and became Public Works Minister in the Nov. 1989 government of Salim *Huss, but again took no active part in the government. In Dec. 1990 'Omar Karameh made him (along with the other militia chiefs) Minister of State in his Government, but J. refused to take that seat and even announced his retirement from public affairs.

J. cultivated his alliance with the Shi'i *al-Amal* militias and their leader Nabih *Berri — though that alliance, too, was unstable and punctuated by crises and armed clashes. In the bitter fighting between *al-Amal* and Palestinian guerrillas since 1985, he took, despite his alliance with *al-Amal*, a rather neutral or even pro-Palestinian position, sometimes attempting to mediate. J. was instrumental in the foundation of several coalitions (a "National Salvation Front" in July 1983 — nine factions and militias of the civil war leftist camp; a "National Democratic Front" in Oct. 1984 — six parties, including the Communists and the pro-Syrian *Ba'th*). But these alliances did not turn into solid, living organisms, and J. remained a force causing instability, unreliable in his alliances and erratic in his policies, though firm in his aversions.

1983 he foiled all efforts to arrange a peaceful Israeli withdrawal from the Shuf and a coordinated takeover of the area vacated, and when Israeli forces withdrew without such coordination, he organized an immediate Druze onslaught on Christian forces in the Shuf (which had been allowed by Israel to set up strongpoints) and on Christian villages (which had coexisted with the Druze for centuries — though clashes and massacres had occurred before). The Druze won the bloody battle for the Shuf, and in 1984–85 extended their control farther south and west, to the Kharrub region, reaching the coast, and to the hills dominating Beirut and its southeastern suburbs. They also helped the Shi'i militias to take West Beirut and kept Christian East Beirut in a state of semisiege and under constant threat, with frequent battles in the hills to its east.

K

KAPLAN, ELIEZER (1891–1952)   Israeli econ-
omist and politician. Born in Minsk, Russia. One
of the founders and leaders of the socialist-Zionist
Ze'irei Zion movement. In 1920 he immigrated to
Palestine and became one of the leaders of *Hapoel
Hatzair* and its representative in the Tel Aviv
Municipal Council. He was also active in the Pub-
lic Works department (later *Solel Boneh*) of the
Histadrut.

In 1933 he was elected to the Jewish Agency
Executive as a representative of the Labor Party,
Mapai, and until 1948 was the treasurer of the
Jewish Agency and, in practice, the "Finance Minister" of the *Yishuv* and the central figure in all
matters dealing with finance and economy. From
1943 to 1948 he also headed the Settlement
Department of the Jewish Agency. His political
position was moderate. He was one of the leaders
of the *Mapai* faction which supported *Weizmann
and opposed the activist policies of *Ben Gurion.

After the establishment of the State of Israel, K.
was the first Finance Minister, until shortly before
his death in 1952. In June 1952 he became Deputy
Prime Minister. He was a member of the Knesset
from its establishment until his death.

K. laid the foundation for the financial and fiscal
structure of the new State and framed its first
budgets and taxation policy. He was responsible
for raising the first development loans from the
United States. His influence on financial policies
was decisive.

KARAMEH, RASHID (1921–87)   Lebanese politician, many times Prime Minister. Scion of a
Muslim-Sunni family of notables from Tripoli
whose sons held for a long time the office of *Mufti*
of Tripoli. K.'s father, **Abd-ul-Hamid K.** (1895–1950),
served as *Mufti* and was the political and religious
leader of the Muslims of Tripli and their chief
representative in Parliament; he also served briefly,
in 1945, as Prime Minister. K. studied law in Cairo,
graduated in 1947 and opened a law practice. Upon

Rashid Karameh

the death of his father, he succeeded him as leader
of the Muslims of Tripoli, and was elected to every
Parliament since 1951. He first joined the
Government in 1951, as Minister of Justice, served
as Minister of Economy and Social Affairs, 1953–55,
and first became Prime Minister in 1955.

In line with the traditions of the Muslim-Sunni
leadership in Lebanon, K. joined shifting parliamentary factions and several times formed such
groups himself, but never stabilized a permanent
party organization (or, later, a militia) of his own.
He belonged, like most of the Sunni leaders, to the
mainstream faction of Lebanese politics; but he
was on its "leftist" fringe: for far-reaching reforms,
and particularly for the abolition of Lebanon's
system of communal representation and government; against Christian predominance; strongly
nationalist and for a Pan-Arab, Nasserist orientation, radically anti-Israel and supportive of

Palestinian-Arab guerrilla activities. In his orientation he thus differed from most of the traditional, conservative Sunni leaders in Beirut (al-*Yafi, *Salam, al-*Sulh), his rivals for the leadership of the Sunni community. His Nasserist tendencies came to the fore in 1958, when he was one of the leaders of the resistance to President *Chamoun's regime that developed into a Nasserist rebellion and led to civil war. When that crisis ended with a compromise and the election of General *Shihab to the Presidency, K. headed a "Government of National Salvation," Sept. 1958, and remained Premier until May 1960. He was again Prime Minister in 1961–64, 1965–66, 1966–68 and 1969–70. However, owing to his extreme views and positions, his Premierships were controversial and he was involved in frequent crises, sometimes resigning and then withdrawing his resignation. In Apr. 1969, for instance, no other Prime Minister was appointed after his resignation and the country was without a government for several months until he resumed the Premiership. Many of these crises derived from K.'s extreme policies concerning the Palestine conflict. During the Six Day War, 1967, he reportedly ordered the army to enter the war — an order that was refused and countermanded by Gen. Boustani, the Maronite commander of the army. From the late 1960s, K. supported the Palestinian-Arab guerrilla establishment in Lebanon and its operations. As Prime Minister he tried to reach agreements with them on a measure of coordination, and foiled efforts to curb them by armed action. The government crisis of 1969 was related to this issue.

In the civil war since 1975 K. at first kept his image as a mainstream figure who could hold the country together and mediate. Therefore, after five years out of power, he was again made Prime Minister in June 1975. He was, however, unable to maintain an operating administration in control of the country, the government and the army disintegrated, and in Dec. 1976 he resigned. He now identified himself with the leftist-Muslim camp, but played no prominent role in its organization and leadership. He was handicapped, like the conservative Beirut Sunni leaders, by having no Muslim-Sunni militia at his disposal. Moreover, as Tripoli, his own bailiwick, was torn in battle between the fundamentalist *Tawhid Islami* and pro-Syrian, 'Alawi-dominated *Ba'th* militias, his leadership at his home base became ineffective.

After the Israeli invasion of June 1982, K. took an uncompromising anti-Israel line, rejected any security agreement with Israel and opposed the *Jumayyil administration that seemed prepared to sign such an agreement and collaborate with Israel. He strengthened his links with Syria and fostered an alliance with Syria's other clients in Lebanon — *Junbalat's Druze, *Berri's Shi'i *Amal* and Maronite ex-President *Franjiyeh. In July 1983, for instance, he set up, with Junbalat and Franjiyeh, a "National Salvation Front," which did not become an active organization. K. played a leading role in the negotiations over national reconciliation and reforms (the Geneva talks of Oct.-Nov. 1983 and the Lausanne conference of Mar. 1984) — representing, under Syrian guidance, those forces within the leftist-Muslim camp prepared to accept Syrian-devised compromise plans. In Apr. 1984 he formed a "National Unity Government." But this government could not really work: it was composed of forces diametrically opposed to each other; it was mostly boycotted by some of its key Ministers (Junbalat, Berri); and it was supposed to work with a President who had been compelled to appoint it and whom some of its own members strove to dismiss. It could not even meet for many months; and it had no means to impose its will and to administer and control the country while the army and police disintegrated into rival formations, and the country was in effect divided into separate cantons at the mercy of rival, battling militias. K., who remained Premier, though frequently threatening to resign, was Prime Minister *pro forma* only. From early 1986 he boycotted President Jumayyil and refused to convene the government. In May 1987 he finally resigned in frustration, but his resignation was not accepted by he President.

On June 1, 1987, K. was assassinated. A Muslim-extremist group and a "Lebanese Army" (Christian?) — both unknown — assumed responsibility for his murder; but a protracted official inquiry yielded no results.

K.'s brother **'Omar K.** succeeded him as head of the K. clan and its political faction. In Dec. 1990, after the defeat of Gen. 'Awn and the restoration of a unified regime, 'Omar K. formed a "National Unity Government".

KARRUBI, MEHDI (b. 1937)   Iranian politician, chairman of the *Majlis* (Parliament) since 1989. Born in Aligoodarz (Lurestan region). He studied Islamic theology at Tehran University.

K. taught theology and served as Imam during public prayers. He became involved in politics in

1962. In 1966–67 he was exiled to Gonbad Kavoos; he was jailed from 1973 to 1976 and arrested several times between 1976 and 1979. Following the 1979 revolution, K. served as director of the Imam's Relief Aid Committee.

Since 1987 K. has served as the superintendent of Iranian pilgrims to Mecca. In the summer of that year he headed the pilgrims whose aggressive demonstrations led to violent clashes with Sa'udi security forces resulting in over 400 deaths. In 1991 he was reportedly relieved of his responsiblity for the pilgrimage, to make possible a reconciliation with Sa'udia and the resumption of the pilgrimage.

Since 1980 K. has served as a member of Parliament, representing his home town, Aligoodarz, and later Tehran. He was a member of Parliament's Security Committee, Vice-President of the *Majlis* 1985–89, and since Aug. 1989 its President. In 1989 he was also appointed to the Constitution Review Panel.

K. was considered an Islamic radical, but according to 1990 reports he has become more moderate and pragmatic and moved closer to President Rafsanjani (some considered him a moderate even before). His wife, Fatimeh Hajji Sharifi, is the director of the Martyr Foundation Medical Center. His brother Hassan reportedly met Israeli representatives in July 1985 as part of secret contacts ("Irangate") — it was now assumed: with his approval; other reports (denied, but persistent) mention K. himself as a participant in these meetings.

KASHANI, AYATULLAH ABU'L QASSEM (1881? 1885?-1962)

Iranian Islamic cleric and politician, a member of the Islamic religious hierarchy hostile to the Shah and his establishment, and particularly to foreign (i.e., British) intervention. He was born in Tehran, but was raised in Iraq where he resided until the end of World War I. In the late 1940s K. encouraged the establishment of the *Fedayan Islam* ("Those who sacrifice themselves for Islam") a radical extremist group that did not recoil from assassinating key establishment leaders.

In 1946 K. was arrested and sent into forced exile in Qazvin until the end of 1947. Following the failed attempt on the Shah's life in Feb. 1949, he was again arrested and exiled to Lebanon. In June 1950 he was allowed to return. He was elected to the *Majlis* (Parliament) and in 1950–51 supported the radical Dr. *Mossaddeq's "National Front" and his election as Prime Minister. In 1952 K. was elected President of the *Majlis*. But he soon fell out with Mossaddeq (who was too leftist-secularist for K.'s taste), was ousted from the Presidency of Parliament in July 1953, joined the opposition and contributed to Mossaddeq's fall in Aug. 1953. Despite this brief collaboration with the Shah's policies, K., in his opposition to the Shah and his governments, continued fostering extremist Islamic organizations like the *Fedayan Islam*. Thus he was a predecessor and mentor of *Khomeini's Islamic Revolution of 1979.

KASZTNER, ISRAEL (REZSO) (1906–57)

Israeli journalist and lawyer, one of the leaders of Hungarian Jewry. Born in Cluj, Transylvania (then part of Hungary). From 1925 to 1940 he was a reporter for the Hungarian newspaper *Uj Kelet*. After Transylvania was reannexed to Hungary under German-Italian auspices (1940) and the newspaper was closed by the authorities, he moved to Budapest (1942), where he joined the local office of *Keren Hayesod* and became one of the main activists of the Labor Zionists in Hungary and Deputy Chairman of the Zionist Executive there. He was also one of the founders of a "Committee for Rescue and Assistance" which smuggled Jews into Hungary, then a relatively safe country. In 1944, after Hungary was invaded by the Germans, K. negotiated with the German authorities, and with Adolf Eichmann personally, on a German offer to release a million Jews in exchange for 10,000 trucks which the Allies would transfer to the German army for use against the Soviet Union. Joel Brandt, one of the members of the Committee, was sent to Istanbul to bring the offer to the attention of the heads of the Jewish Agency and the British Government. The "proposal" was not accepted; but the Germans allowed some Jews to leave and "rescue trains" with a total of 1685 Jews were sent from Hungary to Switzerland, their passengers chosen by K.

After the war, K. immigrated to Palestine. He was a candidate on the *Mapai* list for the Second Knesset (1951) and was spokesman for the Ministry of Commerce and Industry. In 1952 a Hungarian Jew, Malkiel Gruenwald, in a pamphlet accused K. of having collaborated with the Germans in the extermination of the Jews of Hungary by keeping the danger of extermination secret while saving "important" Jews (including his relatives and friends). Gruenwald was sued for libel.

The trial, from Jan. 1954, soon turned from a "Gruenwald trial" into a dramatic "K. trial." Moreover, Shmuel *Tamir, Gruenwald's defense attorney, succeeded in turning it against the leaders of the government, and particularly the *Mapai* leadership. The verdict, in June 1955, acquitted Gruenwald, regarding his collaboration charges as proven, and stated that "K. had sold his soul to the Devil." This verdict caused a grave political crisis, led to the resignation of the *Sharett government after a vote of no-confidence in June 1955 and damaged *Mapai* in the elections of July 1955. The verdict was overturned in Jan. 1958, after K.'s death, by a majority decision of the Supreme Court which ruled that K. had not collaborated with the Nazis.

K. himself was assassinated in March 1957 by three young extremists — Israel's first political murder. The whole "K. Affair" has remained highly controversial.

KATZIR (original name: Katchalsky), **EPHRAIM** (b. 1916)   Israeli scientist, fourth President of the State of Israel. Born in Kiev, Russia. In 1925 he immigrated to Palestine and in 1933 he graduated from the Gymnasia Ivrit high school in Jerusalem. He was an active member of the "Socialist Youth" affiliated with *Mapai*.

K. studied biochemistry at the Hebrew Univer-

Ephraim Katzir (GPO, Jerusalem)

sity of Jerusalem and then taught there. In 1949 he was one of the first scientists to join the Weizmann Institute of Science, where he headed the biophysics department. Under his chairmanship, the department became an important center for the study of proteins; K. himself was one of Israel's foremost scientists. In 1959 he was awarded the Israel Prize for Life Sciences. In 1966 he was the first Israeli to be elected to the American Academy of Sciences.

K. was also active in public life: from 1966 to 1969 he was the Chief Scientist of the Ministry of Defense. He was a member of *Mapai*, albeit not an active one. In 1973 he was named by the Labor Party's Central Committee as a candidate for the presidency of Israel (after a dramatic contest against Yitzhak *Navon of the former *Rafi* faction, which K. won by a narrow margin).

In Apr. 1973 the Knesset elected him as the fourth President of Israel. His term of office saw the Yom Kippur War, President Sadat's visit and the *Likud's* victory in the 1977 elections. In 1978 K. refused to present his candidacy for a second term. After completing his term of office he returned to scientific life and since then he has rarely been heard regarding contemporary political issues.

KATZNELSON, BERL (1887–1944)   One of the founders and top leaders of the Israel Labor movement. Born in Bobruisk, Russia, K. joined the Socialist Zionist organization and in 1908 immigrated to Palestine. He worked in settlements in Judea and Galilee.

He did not join one of the parties then active among the Jewish workers in Palestine, but devoted his efforts to establishing an Agricultural Workers Union in Judea and Galilee and central workers' institutions. Thus he was one of the founders of the workers' Sick Fund, (*Kupat Holim*), 1912. During the First World War he supported volunteering for the "Jewish Legion" within the British and American armies and was himself one of the first to volunteer.

After the war he was one of the founders of the "*Ahdut Ha'avodah*" Party, 1919; he formulated its platform and was the editor of its organ *Kuntres*. He also was one of the founders and leaders of the Trade Union Federation, the *Histadrut*, 1920. In 1925 he founded the daily newspaper *Davar*, the organ of the *Histadrut*, and edited it until his death. He led the efforts for the unification of the Labor movement, and in 1930 was one of the founders of the Labor Party, *Mapai*.

K. refused to accept any executive position in the *Histadrut*, *Mapai* or the Jewish Agency, though his associates urged him to do so. His influence and power were the result of his political-intellectual leadership, as a mentor of the Labor movement, and of his personal charisma.

In 1937 K. opposed the partition plan proposed by the Peel Commission, differing from the position taken by *Ben-Gurion, his colse associate. He actively supported "illegl" immigration. In 1942 he founded the *Histadrut's Am Oved* publishing company which became a leading book publisher, and served as its chief editor until his death. His death in 1944 was deeply mourned by the entire *Yishuv*, far beyond *Mapai* and the entire Labor movement.

K. wrote several political-ideological essays which had much influence. His letters were published in several volumes.

KECECILER, MEHMET (MUHAMMAD) (b.1944) Turkish politician. Born in Konya, he graduated in political science from Ankara University. K. joined the staff of the Ministry of the Interior and served as a governor of various districts. In 1975–77 he completed his graduate studies at the Sorbonne and the International Institute of Public Management.

After returning to Turkey in 1977, he was Mayor of Konya for the extreme-right Islamist "National Salvation Party." After the military coup in 1980 he was dismissed, but in 1983 he joined the new Motherland Party and stood for it in the Parliamentary elections. The military rulers, the National Security Council, vetoed his candidacy. However, after the party won the elections and formed the government, he became Deputy Chairman of the Motherland Party, heading a strong Islamic-fundamentalist faction — in opposition to the party's leader *Ozal and his associates. In Nov. 1989 he became Minister of State.

KHADDAM, 'ABD-UL-HALIM(b. 1932) Syrian Muslim-Sunni politician, since 1984 Vice-President of Syria. After studying law, Kh. worked as a lawyer in Damascus, 1954–64. He joined the *Ba'th* Party and from 1963, after the *Ba'th* assumed power, engaged in politics full-time. In 1967 he was appointed Governor of Damascus. In May 1969 he joined the government as Minister of Economy and Foreign Trade. In the intra-*Ba'th* factional struggle he was a follower of General Hafez *Asad, and when the latter assumed power, in Nov. 1970,

Kh. became Foreign Minister and Deputy Premier, and a member of the *Ba'th* high command. Considered knowledgeable, even brilliant, he has directed Syria's foreign relations ever since, interpreting President Asad's policies with suave, professional firmness. Kh. has for some years been particularly responsible for Syria's policies and operations in Lebanon, receiving Lebanese politicians and militia leaders in Damascus for countless consultations and briefings and trying to guide and instruct Syria's allies and clients, yet unable to translate Syria's undoubted domination into a full implementation of her plans. In the struggle for Asad's succession, Kh. is considered one of the potential contestants, possibly favored by Asad himself. He lacks the military background that has become traditional with Ba'thist Syria's top leaders, and being a Sunni, he perhaps does not belong to the inner leadership core dominated by 'Alawis; but he might be an acceptable compromise candidate. Since Mar. 1984, Kh. has been one of three Vice-Presidents, still mainly responsible for foreign and Lebanese affairs.

AL-KHAL, YUSUF (1917–87)   Lebanese poet, journalist and translator. Born in Tripoli, Kh. graduated in literature and philosophy from the American University in Beirut, where he then became a lecturer. In 1947 he edited *Sawt al-Mar'ah* (The Woman's Voice). From 1948 to 1952 he worked for the UN Press and Information Office in New York, and then edited the Lebanese Arabic newspaper *al-Huda* in the USA (1952–55). Back in Beirut, he established and edited the quarterly magazine *Majallat Shi'r* (Poetry Review) (1957–64, 1967). In 1962 he established a quarterly review of literature, thought and art, entitled *Adab*, and he later became an editor at *Dar al-Nahar* publishing house in Beirut.

In his poetry, modernist and free-verse, Kh. uses the image of Christ and the crucifixion as well as Syrian mythology to symbolize the Arab poet in his struggle to revive Arabic poetry and his refusal to abide by conventional poetic traditions. Kh. translated T.S. Eliot's *The Waste Land* and was influenced by its technique and ideas.

KHALAF, SALAH ("ABU IYAD") (1930? 1933?-91)   Palestinian-Arab politician and guerrilla/terror organizer. Born in Jaffa, Kh. with his family left his home for Gaza among the Palestinian refugees, when Israel became independent in 1948. He studied at a Cairo teachers' college and worked at

Gaza schools. In the 1960s Kh. was among the organizers of the *al-Fatah* guerrilla/terror group which from 1969 became the dominant faction in the Palestine Liberation Organization (PLO). In the 1970s and 1980s he emerged as one of the two-three top leaders of *al-Fatah* and one of *'Arafat's chief associates. He was a member of *al-Fatah*'s Executive Council, but as a mainly "military" man was not on the PLO Executive. Kh. was co-responsible for most of *al-Fatah's* military/terrorist operations; moreover, he was rumored to be in charge of several secret branches of *al-Fatah* for special operations, such as the beginnings of Black September — or one section of that group (in which more extremist, dissident elements soon became dominant). Kh.'s image was that of a hard-liner. In the late 1980s, however, he seemed gradually to become more moderate. He fully supported 'Arafat's new policies proclaimed in Nov. 1988, opting for a political-diplomatic solution of the Palestinian-Arab issue and the future peaceful coexistence with Israel by a Palestinian state in part of Palestine. He was therefore hated by the more extremist groups within and without the PLO, the more so as he was thought to be in charge of the mainstream's violent suppression of dissident groups (such as *Abu Nidal's men in South Lebanese camps in 1990). Kh. was seen by many as a possible successor to 'Arafat as PLO Chairman. He was assassinated in Jan. 1991 at his headquarters in Tunis by bodyguards identified by the PLO as Abu Nidal's men. Kh. published his life story and views in a book, *Palestinien sans Patrie*, 1978, ghostwritten by the French journalist Eric Rouleau.

AL-KHALIDI Prominent Palestinian-Arab family in Jerusalem. Many of its sons served in senior positions in the Ottoman-Turkish administration and in public life. Among prominent members of the clan in the 20th century: **Yussuf Dia Kh.** (1842–1906) — after serving in various administrative and consular posts, he represented Jerusalem in the newly-established Ottoman Parliament, 1876; Mayor of Jerusalem in the 1890s; also a writer and translator. **Ruhi Kh.** (1861–1913) — an administrator, writer and essayist, Ottoman Consul in Bordeaux 1898–1908, represented Jerusalem in the Ottoman Parliament from 1911 until his death. **Dr. Hussein Fakhri Kh.** (1894–1962) — Mayor of Jerusalem 1934–37 (elected, against Ragheb *Nashashibi, with the support of the *"Husseini" faction — though he was no adherent of that faction — and most of the Jewish vote). He

founded, in 1935, a Reform Party and joined, as its leader, the Arab Higher Committee, 1936, which directed the Arab rebellion. Dismissed as Mayor in 1937 and exiled to detention in the Seychelles, he was released in 1938 and allowed to take part in the Feb. 1939 Anglo-Arab Round Table Conference. He returned to Palestine in 1943 and joined the renewed Arab Higher Committee in 1945, and when it split — the rival "Higher Front"; reappointed to the Arab League-nominated Higher Committee Kh. was the only Higher Committee member to stay in Palestine during the fighting, 1947–48, but had no influence on the course of events. After the war he briefly joined the "Government of All Palestine" set up in Gaza, but soon left it to join the service of Jordan. From 1953 he was several times a Cabinet Minister (1953–54 and 1956 — Foreign Minister), and in Apr. 1957, when King *Hussein reasserted his power in a royal semi-coup, he was Prime Minister for some ten days. **Mustafa Kh.** (1879–1944) served in the Palestine Mandate judiciary and in 1937 was appointed to replace his dismissed relative Hussein Fakhri Kh. as Mayor of Jerusalem. **Ahmad Sameh Kh.** (1896–1951), Hussein Kh.'s younger brother, was a well-known educator and writer, in the Mandate government's education service, from 1941 Deputy-Director of Education; for some time, Kh. was also Principal of the Arab College of Jerusalem. His son **Walid Kh.** (b. 1925) is since the 1940s an outstanding representative of a new generation of Palestinian-Arab intellectuals: in 1945 — one of Mussa al-*'Alami's team of young intellectuals in his Information Offices; in the 1960s one of the founders and directors of the PLO's Institute of Palestine Studies, Beirut, and a professor at the American University of Beirut; since the 1970s at Harvard. Kh. is close to the PLO, though as an academic he maintains a measure of independence, and is a leading exponent of Palestinian-Arab political thought. He has frequently been mentioned as a potential Palestine Arab representative in future peace negotiations.

AL-KHALIFA, AAL ("House of") The dynasty of sheikhs (since 1970: Amirs) ruling Bahrain. The beginning of their rule is put by some in 1782–83, when the Bahrain islands were taken from Persia by raiding-invading Arab tribes from the mainland; some put it at c. 1816. From the 1920s until 1971 the Sheikhs were under a British protectorate. The rulers in this century were Sheikh **'Issa ibn 'Ali Kh** (1869–1923), who was deposed in 1923 by his son, with British encouragement; Sheikh **Hamad ibn 'Issa** (1923–42); Sheikh **Salman ibn Hamad** (1942–61); and Sheikh **'Issa ibn Salman** — since 1961. Other sons of the House of Kh. usually serve in key positions of government and administration, and as Ministers since the establishment of a Council of Ministers in 1970. Since 1970–71 the head of that Council, or Prime Minister, has been the ruler's brother, Sheikh **Khalifa ibn Salman Kh.**

KHALIL, 'ABDULLAH (1888? 1892?–1970) Sudanese officer and politician. Prime Minister 1956–58. Kh. served in the Egyptian army 1910–24, and in the Sudanese Defense Forces from their establishment in 1925 until his retirement in 1944 as Brigadier-General, the first Sudanese to attain that rank. In 1945 he founded the Nation Party (*Hizb al-Umma*) which advocated independence for Sudan (as opposed to union with Egypt) and was closely linked to the *Mahdiyya* sect's leadership; Kh. served as the party's Secretary-General, 1945–47. When a Legislative Assembly was created in 1948, in the gradual transition to self-rule, he became its chairman. Later the same year he was appointed to the Governor-General's Executive Council, serving as Minister of Agriculture, until 1953. Upon the attainment of independence, on Jan. 1, 1956, and the establishment of a coalition government under Isma'il al-*Azhari, the leader of the rival National Unionist Party, Kh. joined that government as Minister of Defense. In July his own *Umma* Party took over the leadership of a new coalition without the National Unionists, and he became Prime Minister, retaining the Defense portfolio. During his premiership his party emerged as the strongest party in the elections of Feb.-Mar. 1958. Kh. followed a moderate, conservative, pro-Western policy. He was overthrown by Gen. 'Abbud's military coup of Nov. 1958, and retired. In 1960–62 he was suspected of subversive activities against the 'Abbud regime and was put under house arrest. He may have had some influence on the formation of the "National United Front" that overthrew 'Abbud in Oct. 1964, but did not resume an active political role.

KHALIL, MUSTAFA (b. 1920) Egyptian politician. Prime Minister 1978–80. Son of a middle-class family, he graduated in engineering from the University of Cairo, and obtained a doctorate at the University of Illinois (1951). He joined *Nasser's government as Minister of Communications and Housing, 1956–65, and of Industry and Energy,

Mustafa Khalil (AP Photo)

1965–66; from 1964 he was also Deputy Premier. Kh. was a technocrat rather than a member of the decision-making political core; but as he opposed the increasing leftist turn of Nasser's team, under the growing influence of 'Ali *Sabri, he resigned from the government in 1966 and retired from active politics. After Nasser's death in 1970, and *Sadat's purge of the Arab Socialist Union (ASU), Egypt's single party, in 1971, he resumed a leading role in the party and the National Assembly; in June 1976 he became Secretary-General of the party — in effect: to wind it up, as it was dividing into recognized "platforms" or streams that turned from 1977–78 into full-fledged parties. Kh. accompanied Sadat on his historic visit to Jerusalem in Nov. 1977 and took part in Egypt-Israel negotiations that led to the Camp David Agreements of 1978 and the Peace Treaty of 1979. From Oct. 1978 to May 1980 he was Prime Minister, and from June 1979 also Foreign Minister. When he left the Premiership, in May 1980 — because Sadat himself took it over — Kh. became Deputy Chairman of Sadat's new National Democratic Party (the ASU being formally dissolved). In that capacity he continued playing a certain role in the execution of Sadat's policies, as a member of the President's team. Since 1981 Kh. seems to have lost some of his standing and influence under President

*Mubarak; he was, for instance, dropped from the NDP list for the National Assembly elections of 1984. But he continues as Deputy Chairman of the NDP, the government party, and a respected member of the President's circle of advisers; he is also one of the few Egyptian political figures who maintain relations with Israeli leaders.

KHALKHALI (SADEQI), MUHAMMAD SADEQ

(b. 1926)   Iranian Islamic cleric and politician. Born in Khalkhal (Eastern Azerbaijan region), Kh. studied theology in Tehran and Qom. He has written books and articles about both religious and secular issues.

In the late 1940s, he was affiliated with the radical *Fedayan-e-Islam* organization, and since the early 1960s he was a follower of Ayatullah *Khomeini. He was in hiding following the execution of the *Fedayan-e-Islam's* leaders, 1956, and was later arrested several times, after Khomeini was exiled from Iran (1963).

Following the 1979 Islamic Revolution, Kh. for a few years headed the Islamic Revolutionary Court which tried members of the Shah's regime, and the Anti-Drug Islamic Revolutionary Court; he became known for his cruel sentences sending hundreds to the gallows (the "Hanging Judge"). He was a founding member of the Tehran Council of Militant Clerics and served on its Central Committee. Kh. was elected to the *Majlis* (Iranian Parliament) for three terms from 1980 and was a member of its Foreign Affairs Committee. He was also a member of the Islamic Experts Council and the Council of the Islamic Revolution. He belongs to the radical extremist faction advocating an unrelenting struggle against "counter-revolutionaries." In May 1991, according to unconfirmed reports, a writ was issued for his arrest and trial for illegal executions, embezzlement and corruption.

KHAMENEI, AYATULLAH SAYYID 'ALI (b.

1939)   Iranian religious leader and politician, President of Iran 1981–89, supreme spiritual leader since June 1990. Born in Mashhad to a family of Islamic clerics, Kh. studied theology in Najaf, Iraq, and returned to Qom in 1958 to study under the Ayatollahs Borujerdi, Ha'eri and *Khomeini amd obtain a degree in Islamic jurisprudence and the title *Hojat-ul-Islam* (a lesser rank than Ayatullah). He took part in the struggle against the Shah led by Khomeini (1962–63) and was arrested, but later resumed activities against the government. For some time he cooperated with the leftist-Islamic

Mujahidin Khalq (which later turned against the Islamic regime). He co-founded an organization of militant clergymen. He reportedly received guerrilla training in camps of the Palestinian Liberation Organization (PLO) in Lebanon.

In 1978, Kh. joined Islamic Revolution activists in Mashhad, and in Feb. 1979, with the victory of the Revolution, he was among the founders of the Islamic Republic Party (IRP). A leading member of the Tehran Militant Clergy Association and the Foundation of the Oppressed, he was appointed by Khomeini to the Council of the Islamic Revolution. In Aug. 1979 he became Deputy Minister of Defense and in Dec. was appointed Commander of the Revolutionary Guards. He resigned from these two posts in Feb. 1980, and in May became Khomeini's representative on the Supreme Council of Defense. In 1980, he was elected to the *Majlis* (Parliament).

In June 1981, while speaking in a Tehran mosque, he was wounded by a bomb set off by the *Mujahidin Khalq* and his right hand was paralyzed. In Sept. he was elected general secretary of the IRP, a day after his predecessor, Muhammed Javad Bahonar, was assassinated. One month later he was elected President by a 95% majority of the popular vote.

Kh. was also named to the Council of Experts (1982) and was reelected as General Secretary of the IRP (1983) and for a second term as President (1985). Between 1985 and 1989 he was also appointed to several other official institutions, such as the Council of Cultural Revolution, the Supreme Defense Council and the Supreme Council for the War Effort.

With the completion of his second term as President in the summer of 1989, he was barred by the Constitution from running for a third term.

After Khomeini's death, in June 1990, he was named Khomeini's successor as supreme spiritual leader.

Kh. was greatly trusted by Khomeini, though they had differences of opinion. In the past Kh. had been considered a leader of the radical faction, but as President he followed a pragmatic and moderate line, endeavoring to keep the rival factions united: he viewed hostility toward both the USA and the USSR as a main component of the philosophy of Iran's revolution; but in the late 1980s he supported pragmatic relations with both countries. He endeavored to improve Iran's relations with the pro-Soviet Arab countries - Syria, Libya, and South Yemen. He visited Syria, Libya, India, Yugoslavia, Romania, Pakistan, Algeria, China, and North Korea and spoke before the United Nations General Assembly (1987).

Kh. has written several books (in Persian), including *The Role of Muslims in the Liberation of India*, *The General Outline of Islamic Thought in the Qur'an*, *Life of Imam Sadeq*, *From the Depth of Prayers*, and *The Waiting*. He has also translated a few Western books.

AL-KHATIB, AHMAD (b. 1920? 1928? 1930?) Syrian politician. A teacher by profession, Kh. was active in the *Ba'th* Party, and in the 1960s became a member of the Party leadership, though he never joined the first echelon. He also headed the Syrian Teachers' Union. In Dec. 1965 he became a member of the Presidential Council — for three months, until the Mar. 1966 coup of the military faction. When Hafez *Asad in his Nov. 1970 coup deposed the President, government and party leadership and became Prime Minister, Kh. was appointed President, in a provisional arrangement not submitted to a referendum. In Feb. 1971, when Asad decided to take the Presidency himself, Kh. stepped down. He then became President of the newly-appointed National Assembly ("People's Council") and a member of the *Ba'th* "regional" (Syrian) command. In Dec. 1971 he was appointed Prime Minister of the newly created "Federation of Arab Republics" (Syria-Egypt-Libya) which did not in effect materialize.

KHAZ'AL, SHEIKH (d. 1934)   Semi-independent Arab tribal chief who controlled Muhammara (Khorramshahr) in the southwest Iranian province of Khuzistan from 1910, subsidized and protected by Britain in return for his pledge not to interfere with oil exploration and drilling in the area (begun in 1909). His rebellious semiautonomy was crushed by *Reza Shah in 1924–25.

KHOMEINI, AYATULLAH SAYYID RUHUL-LAH MUSSAVI (1902?-89)   Iranian Muslim-Shi'i spiritual and political leader of the Islamic Revolution of 1979, founder of the Islamic Republic of Iran. Born in Khomein in the Isfahan region to a clergyman (who was murdered when Kh. was five months old). At the age of six, he knew the Qur'an by heart; in 1917 he began studying theology with his eldest brother, the Ayatullah Murteza Rasandideh, and from 1921 he studied in Qom. He completed his studies in 1926 and began his career as an Islamic cleric. He soon gained a reputation as a brilliant teacher of theology.

In the early 1940s, he published his first book, *The Key to Secrets*, and continued to teach at the Greater Fayzieh Seminary. Kh. was drawn into Islamic political activities, e.g., campaigns against a law allowing non-Muslims to run for local councils and women to vote. That law was cancelled, but the Shah's reforms, known as the "White Revolution," caused further protests from the clerical leadership, escalating, from about Mar. 1963 and after harsh measures to suppress it, into a violent anti-Shah movement. After the death of the top Shi'i leader Ayatullah Borujerdi in 1962, Kh. became the main leader of this movement. He was arrested and in 1964 was exiled; he went to Turkey and then to Iraq, directing the struggle against the Shah from his exile.

Late in 1977, Kh. began calling himself Imam — the highest, sacred appellation for Shi'i Islam, not applied to anyone for many centuries — and ordered an escalation of the Islamic revolution. The Iraqis considered his activities dangerous and expelled him. In 1978 he was given refuge in France and set up headquarters near Paris. The Shah's regime collapsed in late 1978 –early 1979, and Kh. triumphantly returned to Tehran in Feb. 1979 and

Ayatullah Khomeini (IPS, Tel Aviv)

took over the supreme leadership of Iran. At first he set up a provisional government headed by Mehdi *Bazargan. The following month, Kh. proclaimed the foundation of the Islamic Republic — which would be based on the ideology of pure Islam, as interpreted by him and his followers, and which would provide remedies to all of society's ills. The Republic would be led by the masters of Islamic religious law and jurisprudence (*Wilayat al-Faqih*); according to Kh.'s book *Islamic Governance* (*Hokamat-e-Islami*, 1970), the clerical leaders, whom he saw as the legitimate rulers, should guide the affairs of state (e.g., lay down guidelines in their Friday sermons). A new Constitution reflecting their principles was drafted under Kh.'s guidance and endorsed by plebiscite in Dec. 1979. Kh. himself was the undisputed "Savant Guide" (*Wali Fagih*) or "Revolutionary Leader" (*Rebber*), above the institutions of state and government.

Kh. and his regime ruthlessly and bloodily suppressed any opposition — actual or potential — and Kh. himself was the ultimate arbiter of all issues in doubt or dispute (e.g., the constant factional wrangle between hard-liners and "moderates" within the new political and religious establishment, the division of powers between the various government institutions and Councils of "Guardians" and "Experts," and the problem of determining his successor). In June 1981 he dismissed President *Bani-Sadr (he formally "guided" Parliament to vote him unfit) and saw to it that the new Head of State would be a man fully loyal to him (*Raja'i, *Khamenei). Kh. also decided on matters of foreign policy — Iran's hard aggressive line against the USA ("the Big Satan"), her refusal to yield to Iraq's demands and invasion, even at the price of a cruel eight-year war in his quest for supranational Islamic unity; overriding the separate existence and interests of different Muslim nations, he viewed nationalism as an "imperialist plot" to divide the Muslim world, and advocated and initiated the export of his Islamic revolution, his model of an Islamic society, to other countries — even by force or subversion. Kh.'s ten-year rule immersed Iran in a grave crisis — internal and external—international; yet, the country stood firm and until his death in June 1989 no one, except for some revolutionary guerrillas and exiles, dared question the supreme guidance and leadership of the Imam.

AL-KHOURI, BISHARA (1890? 1892?-1964) Lebanese, Christian-Maronite politician. President of Lebanon 1943–52. Educated in Beirut Jesuit schools, Kh. studied law in Paris, and in 1911 opened a law practice in Beirut. During World War I he escaped to Egypt. He returned in 1918–19 and, after a brief spell as secretary of a government which Lebanese politicians tried to set up before the French Mandate administration was established, he reopened his law practice. He then joined the judicial administration, becoming a judge in 1923. When in 1927 the first Lebanese government was formed under the French Mandate, he became Minister of the Interior, and in 1927–28, and again in 1929, Prime Minister. In 1932 he was a candidate to succeed Charles Debbas as President, but the French suspended the Constitution. Kh. now led a group fighting for the restoration of the Constitution, formalizing it in 1934 as a party, the "Constitutional Bloc," considered anti-French and favoring the integration of Lebanon in the Arab nationalist movement (against Emile *Edde with his "National Bloc," who was pro-French and, stressing Lebanon's Christian-pluralistic character, did not see her way to independence as part of the Arab nationalist struggle).

In 1936 Kh. was a candidate for the Presidency, against Edde, and lost by a small margin. But in Sept. 1943, with the resumption and intensification of the struggle for independence, he was elected President of the Republic — unanimously, as Edde had not formally presented his candidacy and Edde's supporters absented themselves from Parliament. His election was due in no small measure to the alliance he had made with Riyad al-*Sulh, the leader of the Arab-nationalist Sunni Muslims. The unwritten agreement he had reached with Sulh and the Muslim leaders, the "National Covenant" of 1943, laid down the details of Lebanon's communal political system, i.e., the distribution of power among the communities.

In 1948–49, Kh. sponsored a change in the Constitution to allow his reelection in 1949 for a second Presidential term. This breach of the Constitution raised a storm; it had been preceded by irregularities in the Parliamentary elections of 1947 and charges of corruption. A campaign of mounting opposition culminated in Sept. 1952 in a semi-coup led by his leading rival, Camille *Chamoun; Kh. was forced to resign, and his public career was ended. His brother Salim and later his son Khalil (b. 1921) succeeded to the leadership of his "Constitutional Bloc," but the party did not regain its leading position; until 1968 various Parliamentary candidates still used its name.

AL-KHOURI, FARES(1877–1962)   Syrian politician. A Protestant Christian, Kh. was one of the very few Christians who rose to first-rank leadership in nationalist Syria and the only one to serve as Prime Minister. A graduate in law of the American University of Beirut, Kh. represented Damascus in the Ottoman Parliament before World War I. During the war he was suspected of Arab nationalist subversion, and was arrested. In 1920 he joined Amir *Feisal's short-lived Damascus administration. He took part in the Syrian-Druze rebellion of 1925–27, and was arrested and exiled to Lebanon. After returning to Syria in 1928, he lectured at the Damascus Law School. In the 1930s Kh. was one of the leaders of the Syrian "National Bloc," and when it came to power following the Franco-Syrian treaty of 1936, he became President of Parliament (1936–39). In 1939 he served briefly as Foreign and Finance Minister. When the "National Bloc" returned to power, in 1943, Kh. again became President of Parliament; in 1944–45 he was Prime Minister, and from 1945 to 1949 again President of Parliament. He also led Syria's delegation to the UN several times. When the "National Bloc" disintegrated, Kh. was one of the leaders of the successor group, the "National Party" (which did not develop into a strong, permanent organization). After the overthrow of Adib *Shishakli and his regime in early 1954, Kh. again served as Prime Minister, 1954–55, and then he retired. In the crisis of 1957–58 that led to Syria's union with Egypt, he was no longer active or influential.

KILANI (also **KAILANI, GILANI, GAILANI**), **RASHID ʿALI** (1892–1965)   Iraqi politician. Prime Minister 1933, 1940, 1941. Born in Baghdad, a scion of a leading Muslim-Sunni family, K. graduated from the Baghdad Law School. After briefly serving as a judge, he soon became active in politics. He first joined the government in 1924 as Minister of Justice and Minister of the Interior, 1925–28. In 1931 he co-founded the nationalist *al-Ikha' al-Watani* (National Brotherhood) Party which rejected the terms of the Anglo-Iraqi Treaty of 1930. In 1933 he became Prime Minister for the first time, for half a year. He then served as Minister of Interior in 1935–36, and in Dec. 1938 became Chief of the Royal Cabinet. Strongly nationalist and anti-British, K. saw World War II as an opportunity to complete Iraq's independence by fully emancipating her from British influence. He was at first cautious and hesitant as to the means to oust

Britain and deny her the facilities which Iraq was obliged, under the Treaty of 1930, to put at her disposal. The ex-*Mufti* of Jerusalem, Hajj Amin al-*Husseini, then in Baghdad, encouraged him, and the group of anti-British and pro-German colonels then *de facto* ruling Iraq behind the scenes (the "Golden Square") saw him as a potential instrument of their policies and projected him into the premiership in Mar. 1940, with the help of some of the older politicians of other factions. In Jan. 1941 he had to cede the Premiership, because of factional intrigues; but in Apr. 1941 he was reinstated as Prime Minister in what amounted to a semi-coup by the colonels. In the grave crisis that followed — an attempt to deny facilities and services to the British that led to military operations against Britain; a call for German help; the dismissal and replacement of the pro-British Regent and a purge of his supporters and the *Hashemite-loyal and pro-British political establishment — K. was little more than a puppet. When his rebellious government and its forces were defeated by the British, at the end of May, he fled with those who had placed him in power. He went to Germany, where he served the Nazi war effort as a leading Arab collaborator and propagandist.

After the war, K. lived as an exile in Saʿudi Arabia and Egypt. After the Iraqi coup of July 1958 he hoped that Gen. *Qassem's revolutionary regime would turn Pan-Arab-nationalist and Nasserist and offer him an honored place among its leaders, so he returned to Iraq in Sept. 1958. His hopes were, however, soon disappointed, and he was also concerned by what he saw as the "leftist" turn of the new regime. He became involved with Nasserist plotters, or gave his name to their attempts, and was arrested. In July 1959 it was announced that he had been sentenced to death in a secret trial in Dec. 1958. He was, however, granted a reprieve, and in July 1961 he was released from prison. He played no further part in public life.

KOC, VEHBI(b.1901)   Turkish industrialist and philanthropist. He was the first of the powerful businessmen of the republican era. K. began his business career in 1926 and today owns KOC Holding Company, which incorporates 224 firms controlled by his family. The company's sales totaled more than 3.6 billion Turkish *lira* and its assets total 350 million Turkish *lira*. He was a founding member of the Turkish Industrialists' and Businessmen's Association (TUSIAD) in 1971. As a philanthropist he has contributed significant funds to social projects such as hospitals and public libraries. In 1977, he published an autobiography, *My Life Story: The Autobiography of a Turkish Businessman.*

KOLLEK, TEDDY (b. 1911)   Israeli civil servant and politician. Born in Vienna, in 1934 he immigrated to Palestine and in 1936 was one of the founders of Kibbutz Ein Gev on the shores of the Sea of Galilee. During the 1940's he was active in matters of foreign policy and intelligence, during the Second World War as the Jewish Agency's Political Department representative in the *Yishuv's* delegation in Istanbul, which dealt with the rescue of European Jews, and as liaison with British and US intelligence in Cairo. From 1947 he headed the *Haganah* delegation in the United States, dealing, *inter alia*, with the acquisition of arms and military supplies.

After the establishment of the State of Israel he was appointed Minister at the Israeli embassy in Washington. Upon his return to Israel he was appointed Director-General of the Prime Minister's Office. He served in this position between 1952–64 and was one of *Ben Gurion's closest advisors. In this capacity he initiated the Government Tourist Corporation and a number of cultural activities, such as the Israel Festival. He was the co-founder of the Israel Museum and headed it after resigning from his government position. In 1965 he was one of the founders of the *Rafi* Party which seceded from *Mapai* and which was led by Ben Gurion.

In 1966 K. was elected mayor of Jerusalem, heading a list supported by *Rafi*. He holds this position until today and has become a figure most closely associated with Jerusalem, not only in Israel but worldwide. After the Six Day War and the unification of Jerusalem, 1967, he was responsible for policies striving to create a *modus vivendi* between Arabs and Jews in the city. Through his many international contacts K. succeeded in raising large sums to aid the city's development. In 1988 he was awarded the Israel Prize for his activities for Jerusalem. He also received several international honors.

KÖRPRÜLÜ, FUAT MEHMET (1890–1966) Turkish scholar and politician; pioneer of modern Turkish studies in Turkey. Born in Istanbul to a family descended from the sister of the Ottoman vezir Korprulu Mehmet Pasha, K. attended law school (1907–10), but was to a great extent an autodidact. He was a poet and literary critic, and in

Fuat Mehmet, Körprülü

1913 published *Method in the History of Turkish Literature.* Influenced by Ziya *Gokalp and his movement, K. contributed many articles to the movement's newspaper, *Turk Yurdu.* With Gokalp's help he was named to the chair of Turkish literature at Istanbul University, a position he held until 1939, and also taught Ottoman history and institutional history in Ankara. A prolific writer, he published many poems, articles, and books, and founded journals. Among his writings are the *History of Turkish Literature* (1920–21), *The History of Turkey* (1923), *Anatolian Folk Poets* (4 vols., 1928–30), and *History of Islamic Civilization* (1940).

K. entered government service in 1924 as Undersecretary in the Ministry of Education. He was elected to Parliament in 1935/36, representing Kars. In Jan. 1946, he was among the founders of the Democratic Party — the first large opposition party in Kemalist Turkey, which won the elections of 1950 and formed the Government. From 1950 to 1955 K. was the Minister of Foreign Affairs and, in 1956, he became Minister of State. However, as he opposed the repressive policy of Adnan *Menderes, K. resigned in 1956 from the Democratic Party and the Government. After the coup of May 1960, K. was arrested and tried at Yassiada, with the other leaders of the Democratic Party. He was, however, acquitted.

In 1961 he founded the short-lived New Democratic Party. Immediately after, he resigned from political life.

KORUTÜRK, FAHRI (1903–87)   Turkish officer and politician, President of Turkey 1973–80. Born in Istanbul to an aristocratic family from eastern Anatolia, K. graduated from the Naval Academy in 1923 and was sent to Germany for further study; he was greatly impressed by Germany and her officers' corps. Upon his return to Turkey, he graduated from the War College (1933) and served in the Navy, *inter alia* as naval attache in Germany (1937, and again 1943), Greece, Italy, and Sweden. In 1957, he became the Commander of the Navy and in 1959, was promoted to the rank of Admiral. After the military coup d'etat of 1960, he resigned from the armed forces, to serve the new regime in political and diplomatic posts. He was ambassador to the USSR, 1960–1964, and to Spain, 1965–66 (resigning due to poor health). In 1968 he was appointed to the Senate as an independent. In Dec. 1971 he agreed, after much pressure, to become Prime Minister, but on condition that parliamentary elections be postponed for several years and the Prime Minister's authority be enlarged — conditions that were unacceptable to the parties.

When in Mar. 1973 the election of a new President ran into an impasse, K., as a highly respected independent, emerged as a compromise candidate and was elected President. After serving his seven-year term, he retired in 1980.

KÜÇÜK, FAZIL (b. 1906)   Turkish-Cypriot politician. Vice-President of Cyprus 1960–64. K. studied medicine in Istanbul and Luzern. In 1945, he organized the Cypriot-Turkish National Union Party (later known as the Turkish Party). From 1956 to 1960 he served as the chairman of the *Evkaf* (Muslim Religious Endowments High Council Foundation). Between 1960 and 1964, K. represented the Turkish community as Cyprus' Vice-President. He resigned in 1964, when after a violent crisis between the Greeks and Turks of Cyprus the Turks seceded from the joint Greek-and-Turkish Cypriot administration agreed upon in 1960. From 1968 to 1975 he was President of the Provisional Cyprus-Turkish administration.

KURD-'ALI, MUHAMMAD (1876–1953)   Syrian historian, writer, journalist, an ardent advocate of Arab national and cultural revival. Born in Damascus, of Kurdish origin, K.-'A. received religious education in Damascus. He dwelt in Egypt in 1901, attending Muhammad *'Abduh's lectures and co-editing a biweekly journal, and again in 1905–1908, when he edited the daily newspaper *al-Zahir*, established his own monthly, *al-Muqtabas*, and joined the editorial board of the monthly *al-Muqtataf* and the Muslim journal *al-Mu'ayyad*. Back in Damascus he continued to publish his monthly *al-Muqtabas*. During World War I, he edited with Shakib *Arsalan *et al* the magazine *al-Sharq* (1916–1918) published by the Turkish Governor, Gen. Ahmad *Cemal (Jamal) Pasha, for the Turkish army, and later on established the daily *al-Qabas*.

Under the French Mandate he served as Syria's Minister of Education in 1920 and 1928. Together with some Syrian scholars he established the "Arab Academy" in Damascus (1919) and served as its head (1920–53) and the editor of its journal (1921–53). He edited several classical works and published a 6-volume *History of Syria* in *Khitat al-Sham*, (1925–28).

KUZBARI, MA'MOUN (b. 1914)   Syrian jurist

Fazil Kucuk (Bar-David, Tel Aviv)

and politician. Born in Damascus, K. studied law in Beirut and Lyons and became a professor at the University of Damascus. He also served the government in various judicial posts, 1948–53. During the rule of Adib *Shishakli, K. was President of Parliament, 1953–54, and headed the "Arab Liberation Movement" founded by Shishakli as Syria's single party. When Shishakli was overthrown, in Feb. 1954, K. tried to take over as acting President, but failed. Later that year he was reelected to Parliament and served as a minister in several governments, 1955–58, but withdrew from politics after Syria's merger with Egypt and the formation of the United Arab Republic. After Syria seceded from the UAR, in Sept. 1961, through a coup in which his relative Col. Haidar al-K. played a leading role, K. became Prime Minister, serving also as acting President. But he resigned in Nov. 1961, to present his candidacy for the Parliamentary elections of Dec. 1961. He won a seat and was again elected President of Parliament. With the abolition of Parliament after the military coup of Mar. 1962 he withdrew from politics and did not return to high office.

L

LAVON (original name: Lubianiker), **PINHAS** (1904–76) Israeli politician; a leader of the Labor Party. Born in East Galicia, in the mid-1920s he founded and led the pioneering youth movement *Gordonia*. In 1929 he immigrated to Palestine and acted to affiliate his movement to *Hever Hakevutzot*. In 1938–39 he served as secretary of *Mapai* together with Yitzhak *Ben-Aharon. During the 1940s he was a member of the Executive Secretariat of the *Histadrut* and in 1949–50 its General Secretary.

L. was elected to the First Knesset and served as a Knesset member until 1961. He was Minister of Agriculture, 1950–51. In Jan. 1954, after *Ben Gurion's first resignation and retreat to Sdeh Boker, he was appointed Minister of Defense. This triggered a change in his political views — he turned from dove to radical hawk. This change affected his functioning as Minister of Defense — his relationship with Moshe *Sharett, the Prime Minister to whom he was responsible, was shaky and he tried to impose a hard-line policy upon the army. His term was marked by the capture of an Israeli spy network in Egypt which attempted to ruin Egypt's relations with the West (later called the "Lavon Affair"). It is almost certain that L. did not give the direct order which put the network into action, but his general attitude made its functioning possible, and in any case he was responsible. In Feb. 1955 he was forced to resign as Minister of Defense, accompanied by a crisis of confidence with the army and with his friends in the government.

In June 1956 he was again elected Secretary of the *Histadrut*. He held this position for five years and was considered to be a powerful and very influential secretary. During his term he succeeded — through a difficult political struggle — in bringing about the dissolution of *Solel Boneh*. During the Summer of 1960 the issue of the "Lavon Affair" arose once again, turning into possibly the most serious and traumatic political scandal in the history of the State of Israel. The struggle over the question of "Who gave the order?" dragged the entire country in general, and the ruling party in particular, into a political whirlpool which lasted for five years. It caused Ben Gurion's political decline, and in the long run, the decline of *Mapai*.

L. himself was forced, by an ultimatum of Ben Gurion, to resign as secretary of the *Histadrut*. He formed a political group called *Min Hayesod* (From the Foundation), which was primarily composed of intellectuals and members of *kibbutzim* who had seceded from *Mapai* in Nov. 1964. After the Six Day War he advocated Israel's withdrawal from the occupied territories, thus reverting to a dovish position. In Jan. 1976 he passed away after a long, grave illness.

L. was an outstanding, influential and enigmatic figure on the Israeli political scene. He was the respected leader of a youth movement, a brilliant intellectual and orator. But he failed the major test he had to face — that of being Defense Minister. To a great extent L. may be summed up by a statement used to describe Berl Katznelson: "a brilliant brain within a troubled soul."

LAWRENCE, THOMAS EDWARD (1888–1935) "L. of Arabia." British archaeologist, officer, intelligence agent, Middle East expert and writer. Following travels and some archaeological expeditions in Syria and Egypt from 1909 on, L. was sent, after Turkey entered World War I against Britain and her allies, to join the British "Arab Bureau" in Cairo, under D. G. Hogarth. He participated in the preparation of the "Arab Revolt" mounted by Sharif *Hussein of Mecca in June 1916, was sent with a small British expeditionary force to assist it, and took part in its sabotage and guerrilla operations. He served as chief British liaison officer, handling British subsidies and aid, from 1918 attached to General Allenby's staff, and in Oct. 1918 entered Damascus with the Arab forces. He described the Revolt, and his part in it, in his book

Seven Pillars of Wisdom (privately printed 1926, published 1935; an abridgment, *Revolt in the Desert*, was published 1927). It has remained controversial whether his book, considered a creation of literary value, is a fully truthful report of the events he described.

L. was a member of the British delegation to the Paris Peace Conference in 1919, chiefly as liaison to the Arabs and acting as adviser to Amir *Feisal; he was an intermediary in the Feisal-*Weizmann Agreement. Later L. served, in 1921–22, as an adviser on Arab affairs to the Colonial Office. His views on the post-World War I Middle East settlement were complex and torn by doubts. He sometimes felt that the Arabs had been let down by Great Britain, but several times stated that Britain had honorably fulfilled her commitments to the Arabs. He supported the Balfour Declaration and advocated (and saw prospects for) a Jewish-Arab settlement along the general lines of the Feisal-Weizmann Agreement he had helped to conclude.

AL-LAWZI, AHMAD (b. 1925)   Jordanian politician. Trained as a teacher, L. worked in his profession for some years in the early 1950s. He joined the civil service in 1953, working at the Royal Court and the Foreign Ministry. In 1961 he was elected to Parliament. In 1964 L. became Minister without Portfolio, attached to the Prime Minister's Office, in 1967 Minister for Municipal Affairs, and late in 1970 Minister of Finance in Wasfi al-*Tall's cabinet. When al-Tall was assassinated, in Nov. 1971, L. became Prime Minister, until May 1973. In 1974 he was appointed to the Senate, and in 1978 to the Consultative Council which for nearly three years replaced Parliament. From Dec. 1979 to Jan. 1984 he was Chief of the Royal Court. In Jan. 1984 he was reappointed Senator and elected President of the Senate, a position he has held ever since. L. is an administrator, conservative and loyal to the King and his inner circle, but not a decision-making political leader.

LEIBOWITZ, YESHA'YAHU (b. 1903)   Israeli scientist and philosopher. Born in Riga, L. studied philosophy in Berlin and medicine in Basel. In 1935 he immigrated to Palestine and from 1936 taught biochemistry and philosophy of science at the Hebrew University of Jerusalem. For several years he was the chief editor of the *Encyclopedia Hebraica*.

L. became widely known for his unique dissident position on religion and politics. While strictly Orthodox and insisting that every Jew must keep

Thomas Edward Lawrence (Bar-David, Tel Aviv)

the commandments, he sharply opposed the religious political parties and advocated the separation of religion and state. After the Six Day War he called for Israel's withdrawal from all occupied territories even without negotiations, warning that Israeli rule over a million and a half Arabs would cause the degeneration of the Jewish State and its eventual destruction. These positions, voiced with sharply intellectual rhetoric, were unpopular and totally unacceptable to the establishment. Yet L. was highly respected as a lone, dissident intellectual and frequently invited to debates and interviews.

LEVY, DAVID (b. 1937)   Israeli politician. Born in Morocco, L. immigrated to Israel in 1957. After some time in an immigrants' camp (*Ma'abara*) he moved to the development town of Beit-She'an. At first he was a construction worker. In the 1960s he became politically active and became deputy mayor of the Beit-She'an Municipal Council.

In 1969 he was elected to the Knesset on the *Herut* list, the first new immigrant from North Africa to be elected on that list. He was also active in the *Histadrut* where he served as joint chairman of the *Herut* "*Tchelet Lavan*" faction in the *Histadrut* (the other chairman was Yoram *Aridor).

In 1977, after the *Likud*'s election victory, he joined the government, initially as Minister of Absorption. In 1979 he also became Minister of Housing and in 1981 Deputy Prime Minister. At the outset of his career he was the butt of many derogatory jokes; the attitude towards him changed in 1982 during the Lebanon War when he was one of the main opponents of Minister of Defense Ariel *Sharon's policies. Still, he is frequently criticized for his excessive ambitions and his desire to be honored.

In 1983, after *Begin's resignation, L. contested Yitzhak *Shamir to become the *Likud*'s candidate for Prime Minister, but lost. In 1990 he was named Foreign Minister. He is considered one of the central figures in *Herut* and a potential candidate for the premiership, deriving his political strength from being seen as a representative of the immigrants of Oriental, North African origin. His political positions are not quite consistent: in 1989 he fiercely opposed the peace plans proposed by Yitzhak Shamir and Yitzhak *Rabin; but in 1990, after he became Foreign Minister, he greatly moderated his positions.

M

MAGNES, JUDAH LEIB (1877-1948) American-Israeli rabbi and Zionist leader. Born in Oakland, California, M. studied at the Hebrew Union College in Cincinnati and was ordained as a (Reform) rabbi, and continued his studies in Berlin and Heidelberg where he was awarded a Ph.D. In 1903 he returned to the USA and was a lecturer and librarian at Hebrew Union College. He served as rabbi of a Reform congregation in Brooklyn, 1904-1906, and of Temple Emmanuel, one of the largest Reform congregations in New York, 1906-1910.

At the beginning of the century he joined the Zionist movement, under the influence of Jewish students from Eastern Europe. After a visit to Eastern Europe he founded a "Community" (*"Kehillah"*) in New York, 1908, to form a bond between the different groups of Jews in the city and to assist the absorption of Eastern European immigrants. In 1907 and 1912 he visited Palestine. During the First World War he co-founded a committee which assisted Jewish victims of the war in Europe.

During the war he formulated, together with Chaim *Weizmann, a program to found a Hebrew university in Palestine with research and scientific institutes. In 1922 he immigrated to Palestine and devoted all his energies to establishing that university, which he saw as a spiritual center of the Jewish people. When it was opened in 1925, he was appointed Chancellor of the Institute for Jewish Studies. In 1935 he was chosen as the University's first President and was active in fund raising and in establishing the Hadassah Hospital on Mt. Scopus.

In the political sphere, M. held independent views largely unacceptable to the leadership of the *Yishuv* and the Zionist movement. He believed in the possibility of Jewish-Arab coexistence and advocated restraint in the face of Arab violence. He was connected with *Brit Shalom*, although he was not one of its members. During the 1930s he was a member of a group of five Jewish leaders who attempted to create a dialogue with Arab leaders at the height of the 1936-39 riots. During the 1940s he was a founder of *Ihud* — a body which supported an Arab-Jewish compromise. Since he was willing to compromise cardinal principles of Zionism, such as free immigration, his position was rejected and bitterly resented by the mainstream, and his influence on the Jewish population was slight.

MAHDAVI-KANI, MUHAMMAD REZA (b.1931) Iranian Islamic cleric and politician. Prime Minister Sept. to Oct. 1981. Born in the village of Kan to a religious family, M.-K. began studying theology in Tehran. He moved to Qom in 1947, where he studied under Ayatullah *Khomeini and other clergymen until 1961. In 1949, he cooperated with Nawab Safavi, the founder of the *Fedayan-e-Islam*. In 1953, during the revolt against the nationalist government of Muhammad *Mossaddeq, he was arrested in Isfahan.

He returned to Tehran in 1962 and resumed his political activities. In addition, he taught theology and led public prayers in mosques. M.-K. was one of the founders of the Tehran Militant Clergy Association, which promoted the anti-Shah protest movement in 1978. Arrested several times prior to the Islamic Revolution, M.-K. was appointed by Khomeini to the Council of the Islamic Revolution, 1979. As Interior Minister (1980-81) he manipulated the 1980 election in favor of Khomeini and — participated in the regime's propaganda campaign which aimed to preserve an image of popular support for the government. He served on the committee mediating between President *Bani-Sadr and Prime Minister *Raja'i, 1980.

Following the assassination of Prime Minister Bahonar, 1981, M.-K. served as an interim Prime Minister for two months. Shortly before Khomeini's death, he appointed M.-K. to the Constitution Review Panel. Since 1982 M.-K. has been involved with the establishment of the Islamic University.

He is rarely seen in public and has opted to act as a behind-the-scenes adviser.

In Oct. 1989, President *Khamenei awarded him the influential position of Director of Iranian Mosques.

AL-MAHDI   The M. (Arabic: the Guided One) is in Islamic theology chosen by God at the end of time to fill the earth with justice and equity (and sanctioned to overthrow the existing regime). In 1881, in Sudan, **Muhammad Ahmad ibn 'Abdullah** (c. 1840–85) claimed to be the M. and Imam (the head of the Muslim community). His followers established a religious order, the *Mahdiyya*, with a body of activists called *al-Ansar* (Arabic: the Helpers; the original *Ansar* were the "Helpers" of the Prophet Muhammad in Medina).

The M. called for a holy war against the infidels, including Muslims who did not acknowledge his mission. His fanatical followers, whom Europeans incorrectly called "Dervishes" (a term usually applied to members of the mystic Sufi orders strongly opposed to and by the M.), defeated the Egyptian troops sent against them and conquered the provinces of Kordofan, Darfur and Bahr al-Ghazzal. The British advised the Egyptians to evacuate these territories and sent Gen. Gordon, former Governor-General of Sudan, to organize the evacuation. But the M. besieged Gordon in Khartoum, took the town in Jan. 1885, killing Gordon, and established his rule over Khartoum and most of Sudan. The M. died in 1885 and was succeeded by **'Abdullah Ibn Muhammad**, the *Khalifa* (successor). The order lost much of its vigor and failed to establish a well-ordered state. An Anglo-Egyptian force commanded by Gen. Kitchener reconquered Sudan, 1896–98. The *Khalifa* was killed in battle. Continuing resistance was quelled at the beginning of the 20th century.

The *Mahdiyya* gradually changed from a fanatic-military revolutionary force into an ordinary sect or order which, in time, gained great political influence. It later became generally pro-British and anti-Egyptian and was in favor of Sudanese independence (as opposed to union with Egypt).

From the 1950s it was a focus of opposition to the military-revolutionary regimes controlling Sudan. It played an important role in the overthrow of *Numeiri, Apr. 1985, and in the new regime estalished after the elections of Apr. 1986 (see al-Sadeq al-*Mahdi).

The *Mahdiyya* order (*al-Ansar*) was led by Sir **'Abd-ul-Rahman al-M.** (1885–1959), the posthumous son of the M. (al-M. gradually was used as the family name). During World War I he helped the British combat the Pan-Islamic propaganda of the Ottomans. He gradually took a pro-British line and was knighted in 1926. In the 1940s he became the patron of the *Umma* Party. Efforts to elect him President of independent Sudan did not succeed.

Sir 'Abd-ul-Rahman's son, **Siddiq al-M.** (1911–61), succeeded him in 1959 as head of the order. Under him the *Mahdiyya* became the spearhead of resistance to Gen. *'Abbud's military rule.

Siddiq was succeeded as leader of the order, in 1961, by his brother **al-Hadi al-M.** (1915–70). He caused a schism in the *Umma* Party, 1966, by patronizing its conservative right wing. He was a strong candidate for the presidency, but his ambitions were thwarted by the Numeiri coup of May 1969. After the coup he retired to the order's stronghold on the Nile island of Aba. He was considered to be a leader of the opposition to the new regime, and in Mar. 1970 was accused of fomenting a rebellion. When the rebellion was crushed, the Imam al-Hadi was killed, reportedly while trying to escape to Ethiopia. Since al-Hadi's death his brother **Ahmad al-M.** has been considered leader of the order, but he was not formally proclaimed Imam.

AL-MAHDI, AL-SADEQ (b. 1936)   Sudanese politician, a member of the *Mahdiyya* sect; the son of its *Imam* Siddiq M., grandson of the *Imam* Sir 'Abd-ul-Rahman *M., and great-grandson of the Mahdi himself. M., an Oxford graduate, held no position in the religious establishment of the order, but became a leader of its political arm, the *Umma* Party, which advocated independence rather than union with Egypt and was considered anti-Egyptian. He became Prime Minister in July 1966, heading a coalition government, but was forced out in May 1967 by a split in his *Umma* Party, his uncle the *Imam* Hadi M. sponsoring the semi-secession of a more conservative faction. *Numeiri's coup of May 1969 put an end to his legal political activities, and he was in and out of prison or under house arrest. After the alleged *Mahdiyya* rebellion of Mar. 1970 he was deported to Egypt. He returned in 1972, was again arrested, and in May 1973 went into exile in England, Sa'udi Arabia and Libya. He was one of the leaders of a "National Front," semiclandestine in Sudan and mainly in exile, increasingly with Libya as a base of operation, and was in the forefront of the fight against Numeiri culminating in July 1976 in an attempt to overthrow him. After a reconciliation with Numeiri he returned to Sudan in Aug. 1977 and cooperated with the regime for a while, but soon fell out with Numeiri and resigned his position on the ruling single party's Politbureau (*inter alia*, because he objected to Numeiri's approval of Egyptian President *Sadat's peace moves towards Israel). In Sept. 1983 he publicly denounced Numeiri's decrees imposing the Islamic law (*Shari'a*) code of punishments. He was again arrested and kept in detention until Jan. 1985.

In Apr. 1985 M. was among the leaders of the coup that overthrew Numeiri. A year later he led his *Umma* Party to victory in the Apr. 1986 elections and formed a coalition government. He sought a *rapprochement* and a normalization of relations with Libya, while somewhat cooling down those with Egypt. While under his government Numeiri's *Shari'a* decree was no longer followed in practice, M. did not feel able to abrogate it altogether. Nor did he devise a formula to end the rebellion of the African tribes of South Sudan. While he vacillated on both these vital issues, he was also involved in nearly constant crises with his coalition partners, the Democratic Unionist Party and from 1987–1989 the Islamic Front, and several times reshaped his government. The governance of Sudan deteriorated in the three years of his rule.

M. was overthrown in Apr. 1989 by a military coup under General 'Omar H. Bashir. He has since been detained or kept under house arrest and surveillance.

MAHER, AHMAD (1886? 1889?–1945)   Egyptian politician. After graduating in law (Montpellier, France), M. taught at the Law College. In 1918–19 he joined *Zaghlul's *Wafd Party and soon rose to prominence. He was elected to Parliament from 1924, but served in Wafdist governments only once — for a few weeks in 1924, as Education Minister. He was president of Parliament in 1936. After the accession of King *Farouq in 1936–37, he strove for a reconciliation between the *Wafd* and the King and his court — deviating from the line adopted by the party, and in 1937 he was expelled from the *Wafd*. Together with M. F. *Nuqrashi, he then founded the Saadist Party, which claimed to represent the true traditions and ideology of Sa'd Zaghlul, the late founder-leader, and his original *Wafd*. In fact, the Saadist Party came to collaborate with the royal court against the *Wafd*. In the elections of 1938 it emerged as the second-largest faction, after the Liberal Constitutional Party, its

ally. M. became Finance Minister, and in 1940 again President of Parliament. In Oct. 1944, when the King dismissed the *Wafd* government that had been imposed on him in 1942 by the British, M. became Prime Minister and Minister of the Interior. Elections he held in Jan. 1945 returned his Saadist Party as the largest by far parliamentary faction. In Feb. 1945 he obtained parliamentary endorsement for a declaration of war on Germany and Japan (he and his party had advocated an Egyptian declaration of war since 1939). He was assassinated the same day in reprisal for that declaration. The murderer, a young lawyer, according to some reports belonging to the extremist, pro-Fascist "Young Egypt" (*Misr al-Fatat*) group, was tried and executed.

MAHER, 'ALI (1883–1960)   Egyptian politician. A wealthy landowner and a graduate of the law school, M. in 1919 joined the *Wafd*, then emerging as the main and representative nationalist organization, but he soon seceded to join the conservative, royalist camp. A member of Parliament since its foundation in 1924, he served as Chairman of the Constitution Committee. M. was many times a minister (Education 1925–26; Finance 1928–29; ustice 1930–32) and Head of the Royal Cabinet in 1935 and 1937. On the death of King *Fu'ad, 1936, he was a member of the Regency Council until King *Farouq came of age in 1937. M. became Prime Minister from Jan. to May 1936, heading, as a respected independent, a transitional government slated to prepare the return to a constitutional regime and arrange elections. He again formed a government in Aug. 1939, serving (as in 1936) as his own Foreign and Home Minister. He was forced to resign, under British pressure, in June 1940, because he displayed marked pro-Axis sympathies, obstructed the services and facilities Egypt was obliged under the Treaty of 1936 to put at Britain's disposal in time of war and was suspected of secret contacts with Axis agents; from 1942 to 1945 he was kept under house arrest. He again became Prime Minister (and Foreign and War Minister) in Jan. 1952, after the *Wafd* government had involved Egypt in a violent struggle with the British that led to bloody clashes and riots against British troops as well as foreigners and minorities ("Black Saturday"); he was in office for only five weeks. After the July 1952 revolution of the "Free Officers," M., as a respected and nonconformist, though right-wing, independent, was asked to form the new government; he again served as his own Foreign, Home and War Minister. He resigned in Sept. 1952, as he was not willing to go along with the agrarian reform and the general reformist-revolutionary tendencies of the officers, and withdrew from political activity.

MAHFUZ, NAGIB (b. 1911)   Eminent and prolific Egyptian novelist and playwright, the first Arab writer to win the Nobel Prize (1988). Born in Cairo, M. graduated in philosophy from Cairo University in 1934 and was employed at the University Secretariat from 1936.

In 1939 he was transferred to the Ministry of Religious Foundations. In 1954 he was appointed Director of Technical Supervision at the Ministry of Culture, and then Director of the Cinema Organization.

M. published his first short story in 1932 and his first novel in 1939. He received the Arabic Language Prize of the Egyptian Academy. Contrary to many other Arab writers, M. used only literary Arabic, even in dialogue.

M. wrote three historical novels on Pharaonic times, but soon turned to more realistic trends. Between 1945 and 1949 he published five novels depicting the life and *milieu* of past generations in Cairo. His trilogy bearing the names of three districts of Cairo, *Bayn al-Qasrayn, Qasr-ul-Shawq, al-Sukkariyya* (1956–57), portrays three generations of a Cairo family and the changes in social, political and intellectual life at the end of the nineteenth and the beginning of the twentieth centuries; this trilogy contains elements of his own intellectual biography, represented by Kamal, the youngest son of the family. In later phases of his literary development, M. dealt with more subjective themes, the search of individual protagonists for their identity and the meaning of life.

In 1966 M. joined a delegation of writers and journalists sent by the Egyptian government to Yemen to explain to the Egyptian public the necessity of 'Abd-ul-Nasser's war against the Royalists. But after the Six Day War, 1967, he tended towards mysticism (Sufism), symbolism, allegory and the absurd and in that way criticized 'Abd-ul-Nasser's regime, his haphazard wars and his lack of solutions to Egypt's problems.

In 1972 M. retired from his government posts but continued writing. He joined the editorial board of the daily *al-Ahram*, publishing short stories and serialized novels. Among such novels is his allegorical and philosophical novel *Awlad Haratna* (English translation: *Children of Gebelawi*), 1959, in which the three religions of Judaism, Christianity and Islam and the idea of God are treated allegorically with modern science being the only hope for humanity.

After the October 1973 War M. and Tawfiq al-*Hakim were the first Egyptian writers to advocate peace with Israel.

Many of his 52 novels, plays and stories were translated into foreign languages, including Hebrew. In Israel, four scholars of modern Arabic literature specialized in M. works (Profs. M. Milson, M. Peled, R. Snir and S. Somekh).

MAHMUD, MUHAMMAD (1877–1941)   Egyptian politician. A wealthy landowner, Oxford-educated, M. was a follower of Sa'd *Zaghlul, the founder of the nationalist *Wafd* Party (1919), but soon seceded and joined the conservative, royalist camp. In 1922 he was among the founders of the Liberal Constitutional Party, the main adversary and rival of the *Wafd*, and from 1929 served as its president. He became a minister in 1926, and a senior government figure from 1927–28, when he served as Finance Minister. In 1928–29 he was Prime Minister, and also Minister of the Interior. In the elections of 1937 he led to victory an anti-*Wafd* coalition headed by his Liberal Constitutional Party, and again became Prime Minister, until Aug. 1939.

MAIMON (FISHMAN), YEHUDAH LEIB (1875–1962)   Rabbi and Israeli politician. Born in Bessarabia, one of the founders of the *Mizrahi*, the religious Zionist movement, 1900 (Vilna) and soon one of its main leaders. M. was a delegate to most of the Zionist congresses, beginning with the Ninth Congress in 1909.

In 1913 M. immigrated to Palestine, settled in Tel Aviv and established an office of the *Mizrahi* in adjacent Jaffa. During the First World War he was deported to Egypt and went to the United States, where he organized the *Mizrahi* movement of America. In 1919 he returned to Palestine and settled in Jerusalem, where he set up the world center of *Mizrahi*. He advocated the full participation of the religious Zionist movement in the life of the *Yishuv* in Palestine and its participation in the elections to the "Elected Assembly," the representative body of the Jews in Palestine (while the non-Zionist Orthodox boycotted it, because women had the vote). He also campaigned for the creation of a Chief Rabbinate in Palestine.

In 1935 M. was elected to the Jewish Agency

Executive. Thus becoming a leader of the *Yishuv*, he began the longstanding "historical partnership" of the religious Zionist movement with the Labor Party, *Mapai*. His position on political matters was hawkish; in 1937, for example, he opposed the partition plan proposed by the Peel Commission. During the "Black Sabbath," in June 1946, he was imprisoned in the Latrun detention camp, together with the rest of the *Yishuv*'s leadership, but he was released due to his age and state of health and went to Paris. In 1947, at the Jewish Agency Executive meetings, he supported the partition plan proposed by the United Nations Special Commission on Palestine (UNSCOP).

With the establishment of the State of Israel he joined the Provisional Government as Minister of Religion. In the elections to the First Knesset, 1949, he headed the United Religious Front. In 1951 he resigned, retired from political activity and devoted himself to religious scholarship. In 1958 he was awarded the Israel Prize.

AL-MAJALI   Jordanian family of notables, a large clan of Bedouin descent centered in al-Kerak and influential in southern Jordan. The M. clan is closely linked to the king, and most of its members are considered deeply loyal to the regime. Many of them have served in senior positions in the government, the armed forces and the civil service. The following were prominent in the last decades: **Hazza' M.** — see entry. **'Abd-ul-Wahhab M.** — several times minister (Interior 1962 and 1965–66, Education 1962–63, 1966–67, Finance 1967, Defense 1970, Deputy Premier and Education 1985). Field Marshal **Habes M.** (b. 1913) — one of the top commanders of the Jordanian army, now retired; Chief of Staff 1957–65, Commander in Chief 1965–67 and again 1970–76, Minister of Defense 1967–68, Military Governor in 1970 during the struggle with the Palestinian-Arab guerrillas. **'Abd-ul-Salam M.** — several times minister (Health 1969–70 and 1970–71; Prime Minister's Affairs 1971–72; the same and Education 1976–79); since 1980 President of the University of Jordan. **'Abd-ul-Hadi M.** — a senior army officer, in the 1970s Assistant Chief of Staff for Operations and Planning, 1979–81 Chief of Staff, 1981–83 ambassador to the USA. **Saleh M.** — several times minister (Posts and Telegraph 1956–57; Interior 1963–64). **Nasuh M.** — Minister of Information 1989. **Amjad M.** — ambassador.

AL-MAJALI, HAZZA' (1916–60)   Jordanian politician, of a south Jordan clan of notables. He served as a minister in several governments (Agriculture 1950–51; Justice 1951 and 1954–55; Interior 1953–54 and 1955) and became Prime Minister in Dec. 1955. His (and the King's) intention was to finalize Jordan's joining the Baghdad Pact — but following protest riots he resigned, and the decision to join the pro-Western pact was scrapped. In May 1959 he again became Prime Minister and Foreign Minister. Early in 1960 he denounced Egyptian agents for plotting against Jordan's regime and her leaders and predicted an attempt on his own life. He was assassinated in Aug. 1960 — it was generally assumed by Egyptian agents.

MAKKAWI, 'ABD-UL-QAWWI (b. 1918)   South Yemeni politician. Born to an 'Aden middle-class family, M. graduated in law and worked as a company manager in Eritrea and 'Aden. He had nationalist sympathies, and upon being nominated to the Legislative Council he became in the early 1960s leader of the opposition in the Council. When the British attempted to work out a gradual, agreed transition to independence and to appease the nationalists, whose struggle had turned since 1963 into a violent insurrection, they appointed M. in Mar. 1965 Chief Minister. But as his views remained nationalist and pro-revolutionary and he was suspected of collaboration with the insurgents, he was dismissed in Sept. 1965 and went into exile (and the government and Legislative Council were dissolved and the Constitution suspended). When in Jan. 1966 various rival nationalist and insurgent groups formed a united "Front for the Liberation of Occupied South Yemen" (FLOSY), M. joined it and became the head of its Political Bureau with headquarters in Ta'izz in Yemen. After the main insurgent group, the NLF, seceded, M. stayed with FLOSY. As the NLF won a violent struggle against FLOSY and took over the emerging independent South Yemen, 1967, M. remained in exile, in Yemen and later in Egypt. Since 1967 he has been organizing exiled opposition and resistance groups, and a potential alternative government of South Yemen — since 1978 as a "United National Front" or "Rally of National Forces," with headquarters in Cairo, but does not seem to have been very successful.

AL-MAKKI, HASSAN (b. 1933)   Yemeni politician and diplomat. A Hodeida-born Shafe'i Muslim, M. studied economics at Rome University, 1953–56, and took a doctorate at Bologna in 1960.

After some years as a civil servant in the Ministry of Economy, he was appointed to political, ministerial posts — and since, as a Shafe'i, he was not identified with any of the rival (mostly Zeidi) factions, he could serve various presidents and governments. He was Minister of the Economy in 1963/64, Communications in 1965, Foreign Minister in 1964, 1966 and 1967/68 (each time for less than a year), and Ambassador to Italy, 1968–70, and West Germany, 1970–72. M. became Deputy Prime Minister for Economy and Finance, 1972–74, and again later in 1974; in between, he was Prime Minister for four months in 1974. He was Ambassador to the UN in 1974/75, and again to Italy 1976–79. In 1975 M. was named President of San'a University. In July 1979 he was again Deputy Premier — until Oct. 1980 for Foreign Affairs, and from 1980 to Nov. 1983 for Economic Affairs. With the merger of Yemen and South Yemen, May 1990, M. became Deputy Premier in the united government. M. is a technocrat rather than a decision-making leader.

AL-MAKTUM   The clan or dynasty of sheikhs ruling the small principality of Dubai, in Trucial 'Oman — since 1971 the United Arab Emirates (UAE). Sheikh Rashed ibn Sa'id M. (1914–90) succeeded his father, Sheikh Sa'id, in 1958, upon the latter's death. He served also as vice-president of the UAE since its inception in 1971, and from July 1979 also as its Prime Minister. His sons also occupy top positions in the UAE: the elder son, Maktum Rashed M., was Dubai Crown Prince and Prime Minister of the UAE from its inception in 1971 until July 1979, when he stepped down in favor of his father and became Deputy Prime Minister. In Oct. 1990 he succeeded his father as ruler of Dubai and Vice-President and Prime Minister of the UAE. Muhammad Rashed M. has been Defense Minister of the UAE since its creation, and Hamdan Rashed M. Minister of Finance and Economy. Reports speak of rivalry and friction among the brothers.

The M. clan, as rulers of Dubai, have been in constant rivalry with the rulers of Abu Dhabi, of the al-*Nuhayan clan — both over primacy in the UAE, and over its shape and constitutional structure. The M.'s insist on the retention of stronger and wider powers by the individual sheikhdoms (mainly Dubai) and oppose the creation of too powerful federal institutions (with the Sheikh of Abu Dhabi as President of the UAE). The positions held by the M. clan in the federal government are the result of a careful balance worked out in nearly constant struggle.

MALEKI, KHALIL (1910–69)   Iranian politician. Born in Tabriz, M. completed undergraduate studies in chemistry in Germany and also informally studied philosophy and social sciences. He was one of Iran's most veteran Communists, after he joined the Communist Party during his studies in Germany and cooperated with the founders of the underground Communist *Tudeh* Party. In 1936, M. was arrested and sentenced to five years in prison. Following the Allied occupation of Iran, 1941, he was released and joined the *Tudeh* Executive. But in 1946/47, opposing Soviet involvement with the party and interference in Azerbaijan, he left the Party and tried to found a more moderate Socialist *Tudeh* League; he dissolved that group after a few years. He was politically inactive until 1951 when he and Muzaffar Baqai founded a Toilers Party. He soon fell out with Baqai and in 1953, tried to organize a Third Force Party. He cooperated with Prime Minister *Mossaddeq until the latter's fall in 1953. M. was arrested, but did not serve time in jail. In 1961, he founded and led the Socialist League Party. He was again arrested several times in the 1960s. M. failed in his efforts to establish a non-Communist left in Iran.

MANSUR, ANIS (b. 1924)   Egyptian writer and journalist. Born in Mansura to a wealthy family, M. studied in the *Kuttab* Qur'an school and graduated in philosophy from Cairo University; he mastered several European languages. He was appointed lecturer in philosophy at 'Ain Shams University; he wrote the first book in Arabic on Sartre's existentialist philosophy. His more than 75 books include essays, research, an autobiography and travel books. M. also translated several books, especially plays, from Italian, French and English.

After the Six Day War, 1967, his articles vehemently denounced Israel; he also bitterly criticized *'Abd-ul-Nasser on account of his defeat in 1967, and the latter and the regime harassed and persecuted him. After Nasser's death, M. was a close associate of *Sadat. He persisted, however, in his anti-Israel attitude even after the Peace Treaty of 1979, and published anti-Israeli articles and several books.

M. edited several magazines such as *al-Jil*, and in 1971 he was appointed editor of the weekly *Akhir Sa'a*. In 1976, guided by Sadat, he founded and edited the political weekly *October*, which soon became quite influential. Since 1989 he edits the ruling National Democratic Party's weekly *Mayo*.

M. was awarded several literary prizes in acknowledgement of his literary and journalistic talents. He was also named to the "Consultative Council" (Senate).

MANSUR, HASSAN 'ALI (1923–64)   Iranian politician, Prime Minister 1964–65. The son of 'Ali Khan Mansur, who was Prime Minister in 1940/41 and 1950, M. was educated in Tehran and Paris and earned degrees in economics and political science. In 1945 he joined the diplomatic service and was posted to France and Germany and in the Vatican. In 1959 he was appointed Minister of Labor with the rank of Deputy Prime Minister and in 1960 Minister of Commerce.

In 1961 M. established a Progressive Center of reform-minded intellectuals and civil servants. In 1963 he was elected to the *Majlis* (Parliament) and transformed his Center into a political party, *Iran Novin* (New Iran), which soon gained control of the *Majlis*. In Mar. 1964 the Shah appointed him Prime Minister. Though at first perceived as an overly cautious newcomer to politics, M. soon proved himself active and energetic as he launched a progressive program of economic reform, in line with the Shah's plans. His cabinet included many intellectuals from his Progressive Center.

M.'s pro-West attitude, his modernization projects and his opposition to Islamic fundamentalism angered extremist Muslim groups. In Jan. 1965 he

Hassan 'Ali Mansour (IPS, Tel Aviv)

was shot by a religious fanatic and died five days later.

MARDAM, JAMIL (1888–1960)   Syrian politician. Damascus-born, M. was active in the Arab national movement from its beginnings. He was one of the founders of the *al-Fatat* nationalist association (Paris, 1911) and the organizer and secretary of the first Arab nationalist congress (Paris, 1913). He was a member of a Syrian-Arab delegation to the Paris Peace Conference of 1919 — which was not fully in line with Amir *Feisal's plans, but tried to promote independent Syrian national policies and maintained contacts with France. In the 1920s M. took part in the nationalist resistance to French rule and the rebellion of 1925–27. He was, in the late 1920s and early 1930s, one of the founders of the National Bloc, Syria's mainstream nationalist organization; but as he advocated cooperation with France, he did not belong to its inner leadership core. He took part in the negotiations which resulted in the Franco-Syrian treaty of 1936 (not ratified by France) and was Prime Minister and Minister of the Economy in Syria's first national government, 1936–39. When Syria approached full independence, in 1943, he became Foreign Minister and from 1944 also Defense Minister, until 1945; and after full independence was achieved, he was Prime Minister from Dec. 1946 to Dec. 1948 (in 1947 also Minister of the Interior, and in 1948 Minister of Defense). With the disintegration of the National Bloc, M. was among the founders of a National Party; but after 1948–49 he was no longer politically active.

MAR'I, SAYYID (b. 1913)   Egyptian politician and agrarian economist. Son of a landowning family of notables in Sharqiyya province, M. studied agriculture and agro-engineering at Cairo University, graduating in 1937. Besides developing his own estate, he was keenly interested in, and wrote about, agrarian problems, including land reform and planning. He also took an interest in politics and, like other members of his family before him, represented his district in Parliament, first elected in 1944 (on the ticket of the Saadist Party). After 1952, he was attracted by the reform plans of the new officers' regime, and particularly those for land reform; he became close to *Nasser and his associates and began advising them on agrarian reform and took part in its planning and formulating, until he became largely identified as its leading exponent. In 1956 M. first joined the goverment, as

Minister of State for Agrarian Reform. In the Egyptian-Syrian Union (UAR) he was Minister of Agriculture and Land Reform from Oct. 1958 to Aug. 1961, when the Land Reform portfolio was given to a Syrian; he continued as UAR Agriculture Minister until the dissolution of the UAR a month later. In June 1967, he resumed the office of Agriculture and Land Reform Minister in Egypt, acquiring the status of Deputy Prime Minister in Nov. 1970 after Nasser's death. He continued in office under *Sadat, until the end of 1971.

M. was also on the executive of Egypt's single party — the National Union 1956–62 and the Arab Socialist Union from 1962, and from late in 1971 to Mar. 1973 served as Secretary-General of the latter. His appointment to that political post caused some controversy, since despite his dedication to land reform his life-style had remained that of a wealthy landowner and member of the ruling class, and he was regarded by leftists and the younger generation as a "feudalist" (he had also reportedly been involved in some unsavory affairs involving corruption and abuse of power).

M. remained close to Sadat and became one of his trusted advisers — to a degree that he was sometimes mentioned as a possible heir and successor. There were also family ties, as M.'s son married Sadat's daughter. In 1974 M. was proposed as Director General of the UN Food and Agriculture Organization (FAO), but was not elected. Later the same year he was elected President of Egypt's National Assembly (People's Council), a post he held until Oct. 1978. Upon the end of his term, he was formally appointed presidental assistant and adviser. This appointment was terminated in Jan. 1982, when President *Mubarak abolished former President Sadat's "kitchen cabinet."

AL-MASRI   Palestinian-Arab family of notables and business leaders, centered in Nablus. The family does not seem to be very old-established in the area (its name indicates its Egyptian origin), does not control a network of client clans in the villages surrounding Nablus, is fully urbanized, and has reached its wealth and prominence mainly in commercial and industrial enterprise. It is closely linked to Jordan and many of its sons live there, partly or permanently. Among its prominent sons: **Hikmat M.**, (b. 1905? 1907?) — linked, in pre-1948 Palestine, with the non-*Husseini Opposition (and, in 1948, with its paramilitary organization, *al-Najjada*). He was elected to the Jordanian Parliament 1950, 1951, 1954 and 1956, and its Speaker in

1952–53 and 1956–57. M. was Minister of Agriculture in 1952–53; in 1956 he joined the leftist-Nasserist National Socialist Party and in Oct. 1957, in opposition to the king's policies, resigned from Parliament, but later reverted to a more conservative position. He was appointed to the Senate in 1963 and (though staying, under the Israeli occupation, on the West Bank) in 1967, and again in 1984, when he became Deputy President of the Senate. He led efforts, in the 1970s, to develop the Nablus al-Najah College into a full university and became chairman of its board. He was considered a potential leader of a new moderate, pro-Jordanian Palestinian-Arab political elite in the West Bank, but did not take action to realize that potential. **Ma'zuz M.** — active in Nablus municipal affairs, member of the Municipal Council, Mayor 1969–76. **Munib M.** — Jordanian Minister of Public Works, 1970–71. **Zafer M.** (1941–86) — Chairman of the Nablus Chamber of Commerce from 1973, member of the Municipal Council, Deputy Mayor from 1976; Acting Mayor in 1980, he resigned in 1981. Late in 1985 he accepted an appointment by the Israeli Military Governor as Mayor — a move interpreted as the beginning of a process of devolution towards local, municipal autonomy. He was assassinated in Mar. 1986. **Taher N. M.** (b. 1942) — resident in Jordan, headed the Office for the Occupied Territories in the 1970s; 1984–88 and 1991, Deputy Prime Minister and Minister of State 1989, Prime Minister and Minister of Defense 1991.

AL-MASRI, 'AZIZ 'ALI (1878–1965)   Egyptian officer and politician. Born in Cairo into an Arab-Circassian family, M. studied at the Military Academy in Istanbul and from 1901 served in the Ottoman Army. He was a member of the Young Turks' "Committee for Unity and Progress." After the Young Turks' revolution, 1908, his hopes for Arab independence or autonomy with the Ottoman Empire and a joint Turkish-Arab kingdom were disappointed, and he joined Arab nationalist activities. M. was a co-founder of the clandestine *al-Qahtaniyya* association (1909) and of *al-'Ahd*, a secret society of Arab officers in the Ottoman Army (1913). He was arrested, tried and sentenced to death, but was released and permitted to leave for Egypt. Despite the rift between him and the Turks, he at first refused to join the British in World War I. But when Sharif *Hussein of Mecca proclaimed his "Arab Revolt" in 1916, with independence envisaged in his correspondence with the British High Commissioner, McMahon, M. joined the Revolt as Chief of Staff of the Sharif's army. He resigned the same year — reportedly after he attempted in vain to mediate between the Sharif and the Turks.

In the 1920s and 1930s M. was sporadically active on the fringes of Egyptian politics, taking part in several associations that advocated an Arab orientation and active Egyptian involvement in efforts for all-Arab unity (an orientation that became dominant in Egypt only in the late 1930s). He was close to right-wing circles and in the 1930s fostered pro-Fascist and particularly pro-German sympathies (he had always admired Germany and had tried before World War I to enlist her influence with Turkey in favor of Arab autonomy within the Ottoman Empire). In 1939 he was appointed Chief of Staff of the Egyptian Army by Premier 'Ali *Maher, who was also considered pro-German; but as the British considered him hostile and suspected him of sabotaging Egypt's treaty-envisaged contribution to the war effort, they compelled the government to dismiss him in Feb. 1940. He thereupon deserted and tried to reach the Axis forces in the Western Desert. He was caught and put on trial in May 1941, together with several other officers (his protector 'Ali Maher had been dismissed in June 1940 and was under surveillance). The trial dragged on, bogged down in legal complexities, and M. was released early in 1942 by the new *Wafd* government, without a verdict.

M. had some links with the "Free Officers" preparing the coup of 1952 and, being regarded as a symbol of nationalism and resistance to foreign occupation, had some influence on their thinking; some of the officers, such as Anwar *Sadat, had been party to his anti-British activities in 1939–40. In 1953 the new regime appointed him ambassador to the USSR; but he retired after only one year, in 1954.

MATIN-DAFTARI, AHMAD (1897? 1898?–) Iranian politician and lawyer; Prime Minister of Iran, 1939–40. Born in Tehran, M.-D. studied law and political science in Tehran, Paris, Berlin and Lausanne, receiving his doctor's degree in 1930. He was professor of law in Tehran (1933) and lectured in Geneva, Berlin, and the Hague.

M.-D. joined the Foreign Ministry as Chief of the Department of Treaties and the League of Nations. In 1927 he began to work in the Ministry of Justice, where he reached the post of Director General and Administrative Undersecretary. He was a judge in Tehran, legal counselor to the Iranian delegation

to the League of Nations (1930–31), and chief of the Iranian delegation to the International Penal and Penitentiary Congress of 1935. M.-D. was named to the International Arbitration Court, the Hague, in 1939.

He was Minister of Justice, 1938 and Prime Minister, 1939–40. During World War II, he was detained by the British for a year (1941) and was then held in the Russian prison camp in Resht. After his release, he was elected in 1945 to the *Majlis* (Parliament). He was elected to the Senate in 1950 and again in 1957. He was a member of the parliamentary committee that controlled the nationalization of the Anglo-Iranian Oil Company and was part of the Iranian delegation to the Security Council of the United Nations. In 1952, he headed the Iranian delegation to the International Economic Conference (Moscow). He chaired the Iranian United Nations Association. M.-D. was Vice-President of the Executive Committee of the Interparliamentary Union (1963–64).

MEIR (original name: Meyerson), **GOLDA** (1898–1978)   Israeli political leader. Born in Kiev, Russia, M. was profoundly influenced by the 1903 pogrom. In 1906 she immigrated with her family to Milwaukee, Wisconsin, where she was trained as a teacher. In 1921 she immigrated to Palestine and joined the *kibbutz* Merhavia. After leaving the *kibbutz* in 1924 she was active in the *Histadrut* and the Labor Party (from 1930: *Mapai*); she was a member of the *Histadrut* Executive and its Secretariat and from 1936 headed its Political Department. She belonged to the "activist" group in *Mapai* and in 1937 was one of the opponents of the partition plan proposed by the Peel Commission.

In 1946 M. replaced Moshe *Sharett (Shertok), who had been arrested by the British, as the head of the Jewish Agency's Political Department. On the eve of the establishment of the State of Israel she met secretly with *'Abdullah, the king of Jordan, in Nov. 1947 and May 1948, in an effort to persuade him not to join the Arab countries threatening to invade nascent Israel, but to remain loyal to the secret understanding reached in 1946/47. In 1948–1949 she was ambassador to the Soviet Union.

In 1949 M. was elected to the Knesset, where she held a seat until 1974, and the same year she was appointed Minister of Labor. In this position, which she held until 1956, she was co-responsible for creating employment for masses of immigrants who reached Israel. One of her achievements was

Golda Meir (GPO, Jerusalem)

the creation of the National Insurance Institute. In 1956 she became Foreign Minister in place of Moshe Sharett, who was forced by *Ben-Gurion to resign. She held this position for ten years, until 1966, loyally executing Ben Gurion's policies. As Foreign Minister she devoted much effort to developing and advancing relations with the new nations of the Third World, primarily in Africa. During those years she became one of the central leaders of her party.

In 1966 she resigned from the government and was elected General Secretary of the Labor Party. When she left this position during the summer of 1968, it appeared that her political career was coming to an end. However, in March 1969, after Levi *Eshkol's death, she became Prime Minister as a compromise candidate, in order to avoid a split between the supporters of Moshe *Dayan and Yigal *Allon. M. was a popular Prime Minister, and her hard-line policies were accepted by most of the Israeli public. On the social scene, during her term in office, demonstrations of the "second Israel" began (e.g., the creation of a "Black Panther" movement).

The Yom Kippur War, 1973, broke out during her term in office. Many see this war as the result of her hard-line policies, but even her opponents respected her courageous leadership during the war. After the war, though exonerated of responsibility by the Agranat Commission, she felt compelled to accept her part of the overall responsibility and resigned; there had also been demonstrations against her and her government. During her final months as Prime Minister she signed the disengagement agreements with Egypt and Syria. In 1975 she was awarded the Israel Prize for her contribution to Israeli society. She passed away in December 1978, a year and a half after the election defeat of her party.

M., though considered rigid, was highly respected and held in awe throughout the world, particularly the Jewish one. Yet many consider her term as Prime Minister to be a time of missed opportunities to reach a political solution to the Arab-Israeli conflict.

MELEN, FERIT (1906–88)   Turkish politician (reportedly of Kurdish origin), Prime Minister 1972–73. Born in Van, M. attended Ankara's School of Political Science. He served in various civil service posts — Lieutenant Governor of Bursa province 1931, inspector and later Director-General in the Treasury Department 1932–50. He was Defense Minister 1971–72 and again 1975–77 and Prime Minister for a short period in 1972–73.

M. represented Van in Parliament, but changed his party loyalties, leaving the Republican People's Party, joining various factions opposing it and co-founding the Republican Reliance Party, 1972.

MENDERES, ADNAN (1899–1961)   Turkish politician, Prime Minister 1950–60; executed in 1961. Born in Aydin to a landowning family, M. studied law at Ankara University. In 1930 he was active in the Liberal Republican Party, an opposition group permitted to function for a short time; but when it was dissolved the same year, he returned to the ruling Republican People's Party and was elected to the National Assembly for that party. In 1945 he resigned from the party, together with *Bayar, *Koprulu and Koraltan, demanding a far-reaching liberalization, including a multiparty system. When competing parties were permitted, M. and his group in 1946 formed the Democratic Party. They lost the first elections they contested, in 1946, but won those of 1950, and M. became Prime Minister.

During the ten years of his premiership he greatly strengthened Turkey's Western alignment by send-

Adnan Menderes (Bar-David, Tel Aviv)

ing a Turkish brigade to Korea, 1950, joining Nato, 1951–52 and the Western-sponsored Baghdad Pact, 1955, and fostering economic, technical and military cooperation with the USA. He also embarked upon an ambitious program of economic development, and adopted a permissive attitude towards Islamic education and organization, contrary to Kemalist secularism. These policies earned him the trust of Turkey's peasant majority; but he was rejected by the intellectuals, and later the army, because of his allegedly irresponsible economic policy, his repression of the opposition, and his deviation from Kemalist principles. He was ousted by an army coup in May 1960. M. was tried with other leaders of the Democratic Party and the government on Yassiada Island on charges of violating the constitution and corruption; he was sentenced to death and hanged.

MESSALI HAJJ, AHMAD (1898–1974)   The most prominent leader of Algerian nationalism from the late 1920s to the early 1950s. Born in Tlemcen into a working-class family, M. served with the French army in World War I and stayed in France after the war, marrying a Frenchwoman. He became an Algerian nationalist, rejecting the conception then prevailing of Algeria's integration in France. In 1924–25 he co-founded an organization called *L'Etoile Nord-Africaine*, which was at first linked to the Communists. M. himself was reportedly for some time a member of the Communist Party; he later severed these links and increasingly adopted Islamic tendencies, also maintaining ties with Fascist and extreme right-wing groups. *L'Etoile* was banned in 1929 and M. was arrested. The organization was reformed in 1933 but was soon outlawed again and M. was rearrested. In 1936–37 he founded the *Parti du Peuple Algerien* (PPA), which soon had to go underground. M. was rearrested in 1939 and sentenced in 1941 to 16 years in prison. He was released in 1943, after the Allied landing in North Africa, but was exiled into forced residence. In 1946 M. founded a new party, the *Mouvement pour le Triomphe des Libertes Democratiques* (MTLD), advocating full independence for Algeria; the MTLD merged later with what remained of the PPA. In the early 1950s it sponsored a new *Mouvement National Algerien* (MNA), seen by some as a new party replacing the MTLD and by some as the military arm of the MTLD. M. himself, in and out of prison (he reportedly spent 30 years of his life in prison), was again imprisoned in 1952. From the late 1940s he was increasingly out of touch with a younger generation of nationalist leaders (*Ben-Bella, Belkacem Krim, Hussein Ait-Ahmad, Muhammad Khidr), who went underground and set up a "Special [*or Secret*] *Organization*" for *armed struggle* — against M.'s wishes or without his knowledge, though M. was still respected as the grand old man of Algerian nationalism. When that *Organisation Speciale* set up a *Conseil Revolutionnaire pour l'Unite et l'Action* (CRUA) in 1953 and a *Front de Liberation Nationale* (FLN) in 1954, and launched an armed revolt on Nov. 1, 1954, the break was complete. M. denounced the revolt and the new leaders, and was denounced by them. Since the 1950s he was completely alienated from what had become the mainstream of Algerian nationalism. Though still imprisoned as a nationalist, he had no part in the final struggle, the negotiations of 1961–62 that led to Algeria's independence, or the establishment of the new state. Released in 1962, he stayed in France as an exile. Though he had feeble links with attempts to organize groups in opposition to the Algerian regime, mainly in France, he played no major role in them and died after a decade of isolation and alienation, a relic of earlier times.

AL-MIDFA'I, JAMIL (1890–1958) Iraqi politician. Born in Mosul, a graduate of the Istanbul School of Engineering, M. became an officer in the Ottoman Army and served in the Balkan wars (1912–13) and World War I. A member of Arab nationalist societies, he deserted in 1916 and joined Sharif *Hussein's "Arab Revolt." In 1918–19 he acted as military adviser to Amir *Feisal, then ruling in Damascus. Returning to Iraq in 1920, M. took part in the anti-British rebellion and had to flee to Transjordan, where he remained until 1923, serving Amir *'Abdullah from 1922 as a provincial governor. After returning to Iraq he was governor of several provinces. M. belonged to the *Hashemite-loyal, pro-British camp headed by Nuri al-*Sa'id (though not to the latter's faction), and became one of the group of politicians among whom ministerial office and the premiership rotated. 3He was Minister of the Interior 1930–33, Prime Minister 1933–34, 1935, 1937–8. During Rashid 'Ali *Kilani's semi-coup and rule, 1941, he fled with the Regent and Nuri Sai'id to Transjordan and Palestine, returning after the restoration of the regime the same year and becoming again Prime Minister for four months. In 1944–45 M. was President of the Senate, in 1948 Minister of the Interior. He resumed the Premiership in 1953 for eight months, and was President of the Senate 1955–58.

MODAI (original name: Mederowitz), **YITZHAK** (b. 1926) Israeli businessman and politician. Born in Tel Aviv. From 1948 to 1953 M. served in the Israeli Defense Forces, reaching the rank of Lieutenant-Colonel. After his demobilization he went into business. From 1961 to 1977 he was manager of the Revlon cosmetics firm.

In 1961 he joined the Liberal Party and in 1962 was elected chairman of the party's Young Guard. In 1969 he headed the candidates list of the Liberal-Herut bloc (*Gahal*), to the Herzliah municipality, but lost against the Alignment candidate, Yosef Nevo. In Dec. 1973 he was elected to the Knesset where he has since held a seat.

After the *Likud's* election victory in 1977 he served as Minister of Energy in *Begin's government, a position which he held until 1981 and again from 1982 to 1984. In 1979–81 he was Minister of Communications, and in 1981–82 Minister without Portfolio. His appointment to the government as one of three Liberal Party men showed he held a strong position in that party. In 1980 he was elected Chairman of his party's Presidium and thus became number two in the party. After the head of the party, Simcha *Ehrlich, died in 1983, he became the party's main leader although his leadership was not accepted by all party activists.

In the national unity government of Sept. 1984 he was Minister of Finance. He was one of the architects of a plan to stabilize the economy: to drastically reduce the rate of inflation threatening to ruin the country. The plan succeeded owing to the strong support it received from Prime Minister Shimon *Peres. In April 1986, after offending the Prime Minister by disparaging remarks, he was removed from his post and became Minister of Justice. He held this position for a short time (and caused controversy by firing Attorney-General Yitzhak Zamir).

In July 1986 M. again publicly insulted Prime Minister Peres and he was forced to resign from the government. But in Oct. of that year, after *Shamir became Prime Minister under the rotation agreement, he returned to the government as Minister without Portfolio. In December 1988 he was appointed Minister of Economics and Planning, a mainly honorific post with little actual power. Inside the *Likud*, M. for some time took extremist positions and took part in factional intrigues against the *Likud's* leader, Prime Minister Shamir. In the Spring of 1990, after the dissolution of the National Unity Government, he left the *Likud* and formed a new political body, "The Party for Furthering the Zionist Idea." As the Knesset votes of that party were deemed necessary to form a new government, Prime Minister Shamir felt compelled to appoint him Finance Minister — unwillingly and against his preferences. The antagonism between Shamir and M., his Finance Minister, has remained strong.

M. is considered a shrewd, knowledgeable and intelligent politician, but is seen by many as capricious, unstable and unpredictable.

MOHTASHEMI, HOJATUL-ISLAM 'ALI AKBAR (b. 1946) Iranian Islamic cleric and politician. Born in Tehran, he studied theology in Qom under Ayatullah *Khomeini. In 1966, he moved to Najaf, Iraq, where he continued his education. M. was among the founders of the Council of Tehran Militant Clerics and of Militant Clergy Abroad. He worked in Khomeini's offices in Paris, Tehran, and Qom, managed the delegation in the "Foundation of the Oppressed *Mustazafan*" in the name of Khomeini and served as his representative in the national radio.

M. received military training from Palestinian

terror/guerrilla organizations and helped to establish *Hizbullah* in Lebanon. He served as ambassador to Syria (1981–85), where he lost an arm and an ear in an explosion in Damascus. From 1985 to 1989 he was Minister of the Interior. He has been a member of the *Majlis* since Dec. 1989. M. is a leading radical hard-liner.

MONTAZERI, AYATULLAH HUSSEIN 'ALI (b. 1922)

Iranian Islamic cleric and theologist. Born in Najafabad in the district of Isfahan, M. studied Islamic theology and jurisprudence in Qom, *inter alia* under the Ayatullahs *Khomeini and Borujerdi. By the age of 30, M. was accorded the rank and title of *Hojat-ul-Islam.*

In the early 1960s he joined the Islamic resistance and took part in demonstrations against the arrest of Khomeini. In 1964 he visited Khomeini in his exile in Najaf, Iraq. He was arrested in 1966, along with other clergymen, and sentenced to 18 months in prison. After his release he secretly went to Iraq and resumed contacts with Khomeini. Upon his return he was arrested once more and exiled into forced residence. In 1975, he was again arrested and sentenced to ten years' imprisonment for conspiring against the Shah. He was released in Nov. 1978 when the escalating Islamic resistance erupted in riots.

Before the Islamic Revolution of 1979, M. concentrated on teaching philosophy, theology and science in the Islamic Seminary in Qom. He also wrote several books on Islam. He was considered Khomeini's representative in Iran and Khomeini appointed him to the Council of the Islamic Revolution before the Revolution began. In the summer of 1979, after the victory of the Revolution, he was named to the Council of Experts guiding the new regime and became its chairman. He was considered the natural successor to Khomeini as spiritual leader, though he lacked Khomeini's personal charisma and political sophistication. When in Nov. 1985, Khomeini named him as his deputy, this was seen as equivalent to an appointment as his successsor.

But M. gradually took moderate positions dissenting from the regime's leadership. He criticized the regime's harsh attitude toward political prisoners and advocated the return of exiles, especially professionals, without calling them to account for their past opinions and actions. He was willing to allow a measure of opposition and recommended a more liberal economy. He reportedly opposed the war against Iraq, but did not express this opinion

publicly. He expressed support for Islamic liberation movements abroad.

Differences between M. and Khomeini deepened in 1988/89, as M. developed contacts with semiliberal critics of the government and called on the government to confess and redress the mistakes committed during the ten years of the revolution. In Mar. 1989 M. resigned from his public posts in response to a letter from Khomeini advising him to stay out of politics and to concentrate on religious subjects. Since then he has kept a low profile and refrained from intervening in political and government affairs. When Khomeini died in June 1990, M.'s candidacy as his successor and the new spiritual leader was no longer mentioned.

MOSSADDEQ, MUHAMMAD (1881–1967)

Iranian politician, Prime Minister 1951–53. He was educated in Paris (*Ecole des Sciences Politiques*) and Switzerland (Neuchatel University).

Elected to the *Majlis* (Parliament) M. served as Minister of Justice, Foreign Minister, and was the governor of a province. In 1949, he became the leader of a National Front of opposition parties, which gained power in 1951, and in May 1951 he became Prime Minister. The same month he nationalized the Iranian oil fields, which led to a grave crisis and an international embargo by oil importers. The effectiveness of the embargo resulted in decreased public support for M. and the loss of his majority in Parliament.

As he was determined to continue his nationalist policies and rid Iran of the conservative Shah, he dissolved the *Majlis* in July 1953. But his Islamic allies deserted him and popular unrest erupted. The following month the Shah ordered M.'s removal from his post, and appointed General Fazlullah *Zahedi prime minister. M. refused to accept his dismissal and rebelled, and the Shah left Iran. The revolt failed, however, when the army continued to support the Shah. General Zahedi arrested M., suppressed the unrest and enabled the Shah to return to Iran (supported by the American CIA, which feared the turn to the left under M.).

Accused of treason, M. was jailed (1953–1956) and banned from participation in political activities. However, he enjoyed widespread popularity, and government attempts to silence him actually increased his political status.

M. died while under house arrest in Ahmadabad.

MU'AWWAD, RENÉ (1925–89)

Lebanese politician, President in Nov. 1989, assassinated after 17 days. A Maronite Christian born in Zaghorta, northern Lebanon, M. graduated in law from St. Joseph University, Beirut, in 1957. He was elected to Parliament in 1960 and reelected in 1964, 1968 and 1972. He served as Minister of Telecommunications (PTT) 1961–64, of Public Works and Transport 1969 and of Education 1980–82. M. was a follower of Suleiman *Franjiyeh, the main Maronite leader in North Lebanon (President 1970–76), who opposed the mainstream Maronite stress on Christian-Maronite predominance and a Lebanese nationalism distinct from Pan-Arab concepts and policies, and advocated instead a far-reaching accomodation with Arab-Muslim aspirations and Syrian policies. M. was thus considered pro-Syrian, and when in 1988/89 efforts were made under Syrian guidance to reestablish a regime that would stand against Michel *'Awn's rival government, he became, though not a major leader, an acceptable Presidential candidate (who had to be, according to a firm tradition of almost constitutional standing, a Maronite). He was elected President, by the rump Parliament of 1972 convening in Ta'if, Sa'udia, on Nov. 5, 1989. He was killed on Nov. 22, 1989, by a roadside bomb (no one claimed responsibility: Syria and her supporters accused 'Awn's rival regime: the perpetrators were not apprehended).

MUBARAK, (MUHAMMAD) HUSNI (b. 1928)
Egyptian officer and politician. Vice-President of Egypt 1975–81, President since Oct. 1981. Born in Kafr al-Musaliha village in the Menufiyya district northeast of Cairo, the son of a petty official of peasant stock, M. graduated from the Military College in 1949 and the Air Force Academy in 1950. After serving as a fighter pilot, he was an instructor at the Air Force Academy, 1954–61. He attended several training courses in the USSR, including a full year, 1961–62, at the Soviet General Staff Academy. In 1967 he became Commander of the Air Academy, with the rank of Colonel, in 1969 — Chief of Staff of the Air Force, with the rank of General (Air Vice-Marshal), and in 1971–72 — Commander in Chief of the Air Force. In that capacity M. played a key role in the preparations for the October War of 1973; its conduct, and the successful manner in which the Air Force fulfilled its task in that war, are usually seen as M.'s personal achievement. In 1974 he was promoted to the rank of Air Marshal.

In Apr. 1975 President *Sadat appointed M. as his only Vice-President. M. had never been active

Husni Mubarak (IPS, Tel Aviv)

or prominent in politics and was seen as a professional rather than a political leader; he had no political base of his own. As Vice-President, M. followed Sadat's lead and policies, without much independent action. He served as the President's envoy on many missions to the Arab countries and the world, including the USSR and China. Observers thought that even as Vice-President M. did not create a political base for himself — though some saw his hand in the elimination of several potential rivals (such as War Minister and Deputy Premier *Gamasy in Oct. 1978, or Mansur Hassan, Minister for Presidential Affairs and Information, in Sept. 1981). M. was fully associated with Sadat's moves towards peace with Israel, from Nov. 1977 to the Camp David Agreements of 1978 and the Peace Treaty of 1979, though he did not participate in the actual negotiations.

When President Sadat was assassinated in Oct. 1981, M. immediately took over as President — and within a week was nominated by the National Democratic Party and confirmed by a referendum (with no rival candidate). For some months he also took the Premiership, but in Jan. 1982 he reverted to the practice of having the government headed by an associate. M. also became the head of the National Democratic Party.

M. proclaimed that he would continue Sadat's policies — and in general did so. Yet, his Presidency was different from Sadat's in style and mode of operation, and gradually in some of its policies. M. was not a charismatic, flamboyant leader as both his predecessors, Sadat and *Nasser, had been, and put much less stress on his own personality and leadership. He appeared as a solid, hardworking, somewhat dour administrator, honest and cautious, rather than a brilliant tribune. He also emphasized, in contrast to his predecessors, an unusual modesty in his personal life-style (and so did his wife, who in contrast to Mrs. Jihan Sadat, did not appear much in public). In his policy, M. somewhat toned down the liberalization, the "Opening" and free enterprise of Sadat's regime, reimposed stricter state control, and tried to eliminate the excesses and negative side effects and the measure of corruption and nepotism that had sprouted under Sadat. In the face of growing Islamic fundamentalist movements he continued Sadat's policy of forcibly suppressing their extremist excesses, while emphasizing Egypt's Islamic elements in public manifestations of his own regime. His ability to halt the Islamic fundamentalist threat to Egypt's modern regime was, after a decade of his rule, still in some doubt, as was the ability of his regime to solve Egypt's socioeconomic problems.

In foreign affairs, M. made no basic changes in Sadat's policies, but certain shifts of emphasis became apparent. M. continued and developed Egypt's close alliance with the USA (while trying to maintain some outward manifestations, such as cooperation in the fight against terrorism, or the military facilities granted to the U.S., under wraps, and rejecting — until 1990 — suggestions of publicly visible joint action, e.g., against Libya) and continued reliance on ever-increasing U.S. military and economic aid. But he also made efforts to restore and improve relations with the USSR. He also endeavored to strengthen relations with the European community. M. kept the peace treaty with Israel and rejected all Arab attempts to entice him into abrogating it. But he appeared to turn that peace into a "cold" one and in effect to freeze relations — he withdrew Egypt's ambassador in Sept. 1982 (after Israel invaded Lebanon); he allowed a border dispute on the possession of a small area at Taba near Eilat to grow into a major issue; he refrained from effectively countering anti-Israel manifestations in the Egyptian media (especially those of the opposition) and public opinion; and he virtually halted most cooperation in various fields. In Sept. 1986, when the Taba issue

was submitted to agreed arbitration, relations improved somewhat, a new Egyptian ambassador was appointed and M. held a summit meeting with Israel's Premier — the first since 1981, and his own first.

M.'s handling of relations with Israel was related to his desire to effect a reconciliation with the Arab states and see Egypt resuming her leadership of the Arab world. For, while refusing to renege on the peace treaty with Israel, as they demanded, and insisting that it was not for Egypt to ask the Arab states for a resumption of relations but for them to propose it, M. was actively interested in mending Egypt's relations with the Arab world — and the complete success he attained on his terms was one of his most impressive achievements. Jordan, the first to break the all-Arab front against Egypt, resumed official relations in Sept. 1984 (whereupon very close relations began developing). M. also fostered *de facto* ties to the moderate Arab states (Sa'udi Arabia, Morocco, Tunisia, the Gulf principalities); he vigorously aided Iraq in her war against Iran, despite the absence of diplomatic relations; he cultivated Egypt's special relations with Sudan; and he supported and aided the PLO (*'Arafat's wing) — despite ups and downs in Egypt's relations with it. He also tried — unsuccessfully — to promote, in conjunction with Jordan, U.S.-guided moves towards a comprehensive Middle East (i.e., Arab-Israel) peace settlement and to get 'Arafat's PLO to join it. In Feb. 1989 he led Egypt into a close alliance, an "Arab Cooperation Council," with Jordan, Iraq and Yemen — though he did so, as he later revealed, reluctantly and with reservations.

In the crisis of 1990/91, caused by Iraq's Aug. 1990 invasion and annexation of Kuwait, M. took an uncompromising, vigorous stand against Iraq's aggression. He headed the Arab camp demanding Iraq's immediate and unconditional withdrawal; and, responding to Sa'udi (and U.S.) requests, he dispatched troops to Sa'udia, to join a multinational U.S.-led force assembling to defend Sa'udia, oust Iraq from Kuwait and restore Kuwait's independence — though he made it clear that his troops would not attack Iraqi territory (and their part in military operations was indeed restricted). M.'s strong stand on these issues gravely disturbed Egypt's relations with the pro-Iraq Arab states (Jordan, Yemen) and in fact spelled the end of the "Arab Cooperation Council"; Iraq severed official relations in Feb. 1991. On the other hand, it strengthened Egypt's alliance with Sa'udia and with

Syria (which took a position similar to M.'s). M. also had to contend with a domestic public opinion segments of which sympathized with Iraq and rejected his policy.

AL-MUFTI, SA'ID (1898? 1903?–89)   Jordanian politician, of Circassian origin. Educated in Turkish schools in Damascus, M. joined the Transjordanian civil service in the mid-1920s, rising to senior posts (Governor and Mayor of 'Amman 1924, 1927, 1938; director of government departments). He was a member of the pre-parliamentary Legislative Council, 1929–31, and of Parliament from 1947. M. was first appointed a cabinet minister in 1944, and from that time frequently held ministerial positions (1944 — Interior, 1945 Finance and Economy, 1947/48 Economy, Communications, 1948–50 Interior). He became Prime Minister in 1950; but as he displayed a tendency to oppose the King's policies he had to leave this post in Dec. 1950 (he advocated a hard line against Israel, reportedly objected to King *'Abdullah's 1950 plan to conclude a nonaggression pact with Israel, and during 1950 was co-responsible for two border crises). At the same time he was nominated President (Speaker) of the Chamber of Deputies, warmly supported by the radicals because of the nationalist stand he had taken. He did not, however, fully join the anti-regime camp and remained a member of the King's team, though in good standing with the opposition. From July 1951 (after the murder of King 'Abdullah) to May 1954 he was Deputy Premier, and until May 1953 also Minister of the Interior. He was again Prime Minister in 1955, resigning in Dec. 1955 (again because he opposed the King, this time over the plan to join the Baghdad Pact), and for a few weeks in 1956. In 1957 and 1963 he served again as Deputy Prime Minister, each time for only a few weeks. M. lost his parliamentary seat in 1954, but in 1955 was appointed to the Senate. He served as a Senator until 1974, and was President of the Senate in 1958/59, from 1961 to 1963, and again from late 1963 to 1974. His son **'Azmi al Mufti,** who married an English woman, became a Jordanian diplomat. He was murdered in Dec. 1984, while serving as *chargé d'affaires* in Bucharest, by the Palestine-Arab terrorist group Black September.

MUHAMMAD, 'ALI NASSER (b. 1939/40) South Yemeni politician, Prime Minister 1971–85, president 1980–86. Of tribal background, M. was trained as a teacher in 'Aden, graduating in 1959, and became a school principal in his Dathina tribal area. In the 1960s he was one of the founders and leaders of the National Liberation Front (NLF), the nationalist faction considered most anti-British and extreme, and especially of its fighting squads. During the decisive struggle of 1967, he commanded the NLF's guerrilla formations in the Beihan area. When South Yemen became independent under the NLF, late in 1967, he was appointed governor of several provinces successively. In 1969, when President Qahtan al-*Sha'bi was ousted by a more leftist-extremist faction, he joined M. 'A. *Haitham's government, first as Minister for Local Government and later the same year as Minister of Defense. Though active in the victorious leftist faction, M. was not yet a Member of the five-man Presidential Council, but some observers already saw him as one of an emerging ruling "triumvirate" (with Salem Rubai' *'Ali and 'Abd-ul-Fattah *Isma'il). In Aug. 1971 that triumvirate ousted Haitham and took over as a new Presidential Council. M. also became Prime Minister, retaining the Defense Ministry for some time.

In June 1978 Salem Rubai' 'Ali was overthrown by 'Abd-ul-Fattah Isma'il and M., and was killed. M. became president, but ceded the Presidency to Isma'il after a few months, contenting himself with the Premiership and membership in the Presidential Council. Within the ruling leftist faction and the duumvirate at its head an unrelenting struggle now began to escalate; it was generated by personal rivalry between M. and Isma'il and each one's desire to wield full power, by tribal-factional interests, and by some political differences: Isma'il was a doctrinaire extremist, guided by a strict Moscow loyalist party line, which led South Yemen into near-complete isolation within the Arab world, while M. gradually tended to more pragmatic policies, aspiring to a measure of reintegration in the Arab mainstream and an improvement in South Yemen's relations with her Arab neighbors, particularly Sa'udi Arabia. In Apr. 1980 M. won and Isma'il was ousted, going into exile to Moscow.

M. as President, in full power, gradually implemented his more pragmatic line and achieved some improvement of South Yemen's inter-Arab relations. The factional struggle, however, continued even in Isma'il's absence, as other members of the ruling team turned against M. (particularly Defense Minister 'Ali 'Antar, made Vice-President in 1981, and Deputy Premier 'Ali Salem al-Beid). After several attempts at mediation and reconciliation, and apparently some Soviet pressure, Isma'il was allowed to return in 1985. His return reintensified the factional struggle. The course of the final showdown in Jan. 1986 has remained confused, reported in conflicting versions, with each side claiming that the other had attempted to stage a coup and assassinate its rivals. In the fighting, Isma'il, 'Antar and several others were killed. But M. was defeated and ousted. He escaped death and went into exile in Yemen. He continued speaking of rallying his supporters and resuming the fight. In Dec. 1986 he was put on trial, *in absentia*, with about 140 others; no verdict was reported. Partial amnesties and reported tendencies to allow a multiparty system, 1989/90, in preparation for South Yemen's union with Yemen, did not include M. and his faction.

MUHAMMAD V, IBN (BEN) YUSSUF (1909? 1911?-61) Sultan of Morocco 1927-57, King 1957-61. Sultan M., addressed according to Moroccan custom also as "*Sidi* M." or "*Moulay* M.," succeeded his father, Sultan Yussuf, in 1927. Under the French protectorate, his authority was very restricted; in fact, his administration, the *Makhzen*, was limited to the "native" sector of life and economy. Even in that restricted sphere he was repeat-

King Muhammad V (IPS, Tel Aviv)

edly forced to take measures or sign decrees he disapproved of, such as the "Berber *Dhahir*" (Decree) of 1930, and sometimes he resisted the French dictate. In general, Sultan M. was considered an instrument of the French, and the incipient national movement turned in some measure against him, too. During World War II, under France's Vichy regime, he protected his Jewish subjects to some degree (the degree is in dispute). As the nationalist movement intensified, from the late 1940s, Sultan M. increasingly sympathized with it, and on account of that he entered into growing conflict with the French, while the nationalists and popular opinion began to appreciate him. In Aug. 1953 the French exiled him to Madagascar and replaced him with his relative *Moulay* Muhammad Ben-'Arafa (though he did not abdicate or renounce his claim). But mounting unrest, virtually a nationalist uprising, compelled them to rescind that measure and to reinstate Sultan M. In Nov. 1955 he returned to Morocco and his throne, and it was during his reign that Morocco became independent, in 1956. In Aug. 1957, Sultan M. assumed the title of king. In May 1960, in one of Morocco's government crises, he assumed the Premiership himself, and held it until his death. He died in Feb. 1961 and was succeeded by his eldest son, *Moulay* *Hassan.

MUHAMMAD REZA SHAH (PAHLAVI)(1919-80) King or Emperor (Shah) of Iran 1941-79. Educated in Switzerland and at Tehran Military Academy, M.R. ascended the throne in Sept. 1941, upon the abdication of his father, *Reza Shah, who was deposed by the Allied powers. Unlike his father, whose refusal to cooperate with the Allies resulted in Britain and the USSR occupying Iran in 1941, M.R. permitted the Allies to use Iranian territory as a supply route to the USSR, cooperated with them and after the war strengthened Iran's ties with the West. In 1946 he appealed to the UN and the West for help in getting the Soviet occupation forces out of Iran. In 1955 he brought Iran into the Western-sponsored Baghdad Pact. From the mid-1960s the Shah, while maintaining his pro-Western orientation, followed a more balanced policy between East and West and led Iran to a *rapprochement* with the USSR. In the 1970s M.R., tightening his links with the USA, set up a large military establishment, displaying growing ambitions to turn Iran into the major military power in the Middle East. He also maintained strong semisecret relations with Israel.

Muhammad Reza Shah (AP Photo)

In 1950–51 M.R. began the distribution to farmers of over 2,000 villages of the Crown estates; but he had to shelve his plans for agrarian reform, owing to the opposition of the landowners. In 1951 M.R. had to appoint Muhammad *Mossaddeq, a leftist anti-Shah oppositionist, Prime Minister and allow him to nationalize the oil industry, creating a grave crisis between Iran and Great Britain and the West. When Premier Mossaddeq refused to obey the Shah's order dismissing him, in Aug. 1953, M.R. even left Iran. But he returned a few days later after Mossaddeq was ousted by Gen *Zahedi in a coup supported by the Army and the Shah's followers (and reportedly aided by the American CIA). M.R. then consolidated his position. From 1959 he implemented a far-reaching land reform, which was further extended in 1962. In 1963 he put his social and economic reforms (known as "the White Revolution") to a plebiscite and won an overwhelming majority. He kept tight control of the government, relying on an obedient conservative majority in Parliament and an ubiquitous Secret Service (the *Savak*); in fact, his government, like that of his father before, was a one-man rule.

Opposition to M.R.'s government came from the radical left, Communist and non-Communist, and, in a continuously mounting crescendo, from the Islamic clerical establishment. He suppressed both these forces — e.g., a serious Islamic upheaval in 1963. However, as the Islamic establishment was deeply rooted and powerful, the Shah was in the long run unable to fully suppress it; its resistance continued fermenting, and in the later 1970s its violence, egged on by exiled leaders abroad, in Iraq and Europe (such as, first and foremost, Ayatullah Ruhullah *Khomeini) — turned into a mounting rebellion and destabilized the country. The Shah's attempts, on American advice, to save his rule by liberalizing his regime and handing the government to leaders of the liberal-leftist opposition failed, and on Jan. 16, 1979, he left his country and his throne (without formally abdicating). He wandered, seeking asylum as a refugee, which no one was ready to grant him (Mexico, the USA, Panama), until President Sadat allowed him, in Mar. 1980, to stay in Egypt. He died of cancer four months later.

M.R. was divorced twice (from Princess Fawzia, the sister of King *Farouq of Egypt, and Soraya Esfandiari, neither of whom produced a male heir), and in 1959 he married Farah Diba, who in 1960 bore him a son, Crown Prince Reza.

Apart from several books written about M.R., the Shah himself authored three books: *Mission for My Country*, 1961; *The White Revolution*; and *Answer to History*, 1980.

MUHYI-UL-DIN, FU'AD (1926–84)   Egyptian politician, Prime Minister 1982–84. Born into a middle class, landowning family, M. studied medicine, graduating in 1949 from Cairo University. He specialized in radiology and for some time taught at the University. However, he soon became interested in politics and gradually turned into a full-time politician. When *Nasser's officers' regime held its first elections, in 1957, he became a member of the National Assembly and was subsequently reelected five times. In 1965 he joined the secretariat of the single-party Arab Socialist Union. From the same year until 1972 he served as governor of several provinces. M. first joined the cabinet in 1972, as Minister of Local Administration, until 1974, when he was given the Health portfolio. In 1976 he became Minister for Parliamentary Affairs, until Oct. 1978, serving in 1977/78 also as government spokesman in the National Assembly. In 1978 he lost his ministerial post and became Chairman of the National Assembly's Foreign Affairs Committee. In May 1980, when President *Sadat himself took the Premiership, M. became Deputy Prime Minister, and from Sept. 1981 also

Minister of Information. From Jan. 1982 to his death he was Prime Minister — serving President *Mubarak as a technocrat rather than a policy-shaping leader and loyally executing the President's policies, as he had previously done under Nasser and Sadat.

MUHYI-UL-DIN (usually transcribed Mohieddin), **KHALED** (b. 1922)   Egyptian officer and politician, leader of Egypt's left. Born into a middle-class, landowning family with medium-sized holdings, M. studied at the Military Academy and became a professional officer, reaching the rank of Major. He also took a B.A. in Economics at the University of Cairo. He was a member of the "Free Officers" group that staged the coup of July 1952, and of the Revolutionary Command Council established after the coup. However, as he displayed marked leftist tendencies (the "Red Major"), and also supported *Nagib against *Nasser in the Feb. 1954 showdown between these two (which Nasser won), he was expelled from the Revolutionary Council and was under arrest for some time. Since the 1950s, M. has been the leader of the Egyptian non-Communist but Communist-leaning left (some maintain that he was a member of the Communist Party for some time). He has been Chairman of the Egyptian Peace Council and since 1958 a member of the World Peace Movement's Presidential Council — fostering, in that capacity, many international contacts. He received the Lenin Peace Prize in 1970.

Despite M.'s leftist "heresy" he remained inside Nasser's establishment and no harsh action was ever taken against him. He was a member of the Central Committee of the regime's single party, the National Union, and from 1957 a member of the National Assembly on behalf of that party. In 1956–57 he was made editor of a new daily, *al-Massa'*, but was dismissed in 1959; in 1964 he was appointed chairman of the board of the *al-Akhbar* mass-circulation paper, but this post, too, he held only for about a year. In the new single party, the Arab Socialist Union (ASU), M. rose to membership in the Secretariat in 1964, but failed in 1968 in his efforts to be elected to the Supreme Executive. For some time he was chairman of the Aswan High Dam Committee.

After Nasser's death, under *Sadat, M.'s links with the regime became more precarious. He opposed Sadat's liberalization, his policy of "Opening" for free, capitalist enterprise, and his growing alliance with the USA, and maintained a leftist "Nasserist" line. In 1979 he was formally charged with anti-state activities and security offences — but no trial was held. M. deviated from the regime's position also concerning the conflict with Israel. Conforming to the line taken by the international left, he took part in abortive attempts to organize a conference with the Israeli left in 1971–72, while insisting that no "Zionist" leftists should be allowed to attend. In 1976 the ASU disavowed him and called off his attempts to organize ASU volunteers to join the leftist-Muslim camp in Lebanon's civil war. He opposed Sadat's peace moves, from 1977.

When in 1975–77 various trends or "platforms" were allowed to crystallize within the ASU, and finally to become separate, independent parties in 1976–77, M. headed the leftist "platform" that became the "National Progressive-Unionist Rally." In 1978 he founded the NPUR's organ, the weekly *al-Ahali*, and has remained its editor. The NPUR has not, however, developed into a strong organization and seems to have little influence. M.'s weekly, too, has remained a marginal periodical with little impact (its publication was suspended several times). Under the Sadat-*Mubarak regime, M. kept his parliamentary seat in 1976 — because of his family's standing in his constituency rather than his ideology and politics — but lost it in the elections of 1979, 1984 and 1987 when his NPUR won no seats: he won it back in the elections of Nov. 1990.

MUHYI-UL-DIN, ZAKARIYYA (b. 1918) Egyptian officer and politician, Vice-President 1961–68, Prime Minister 1965–66. Born into a middle-class landowning family with medium-sized holdings in the Dakahliyya province, M. became a professional officer, graduating from the Military Academy in 1938 (together with *Nasser and *Sadat). He was close to the "Free Officers" group and joined them on the eve of their coup of July 1952, as a Lieutenant-Colonel, becoming a member of the Revolutionary Command Council. From 1953 to 1962 he was Minister of the Interior, including the three years of the Egyptian-Syrian United Arab Republic (UAR); he was also responsible for security and the secret service. From 1961 he was also a Vice-President — for one month, of the UAR, and then of Egypt. In Sept. 1962 he gave up the Interior Ministry, but continued as Vice-President (one of five, from 1964 — one of three). In Oct. 1965 he became Prime Minister, serving also as his own Minister of the Interior; there were conflicting reports as to whether he was also considered a Vice-President during his Premiership. In any case, he resumed the Vice-Presidency when he had to resign the Premiership in Sept. 1966. When Nasser resigned on June 9, 1967, after the Six Day War, he nominated M. as President in his place — but the resignation and the appointment were withdrawn following mass demonstrations. In Nasser's reconstituted government of June 1967, with Nasser himself as Premier, M. served as Deputy Prime Minister (again with contradictory reports as to whether he was also regarded as Vice-President). He was dropped from the government in Mar. 1968 and since then has not held any government position, though he is held in high respect as a former Vice-President and longtime pillar of the regime.

M. was considered, in Nasser's days, as the chief proponent, within the ruling junta, of "right-wing" tendencies, being pro-West and opposed to the tightening alliance with the USSR. He advocated a mitigation of the state socialism in practice, a wider scope for free enterprise, a slower pace of devel-

Zakariyya Muhyi-ul-din (Bar-David, Tel Aviv)

opment and cuts in the budget. M. formed his 1965 government with the intention of implementing these policies, but he was unable to push them through, and his resignation (or dismissal) in 1966 was an indication that leftist trends were gaining the upper hand in Nasser's team.

On the death of Nasser in Sept. 1970, M. was seen as a possible candidate for the Presidency, and according to some reports he did indeed struggle to win power, but failed; rumors said that Nasser himself, on his deathbed, had proposed him, but the USSR had vetoed the proposal. In the crisis of May 1971 he supported Sadat against the bid for power of the leftist-Nasserist faction. Some of Sadat's new policies of liberalization, "Opening" and alliance with the West were quite similar to what M. had proposed in the 1960s. Yet no close alliance between M. and Sadat developed; Sadat seemed to regard M. as a possibly dangerous rival and kept him under surveillance. M. opposed Sadat's peace policy towards Israel, and though he did not resume political activities, he publicly denounced — together with the three other surviving former Vice-Presidents — both the Camp David Agreements of Sept. 1978 and the Peace Treaty with Israel of Mar. 1979.

AL-MUKHTAR, 'UMAR (OMAR) (c. 1862–1931) A leader of Libyan resistance against the Italians. Born in Cyrenaica and educated in Sanussi *Zawiyyas* (lodges, retreats), M. took part in Ottoman Turkey's war against Italy, 1911/12, after the Italian invasion of Libya, and in guerrilla resistance activities afterwards. In 1922 he followed Sayyid Idris al-*Sanussi into exile in Cairo, but returned to Cyrenaica in 1923 to lead the guerrilla war against the Italians for the next eight years. He was captured in Sept. 1931 and hanged in public. He became a national hero and a symbol of Libya's struggle for independence. When young Libyans organized after World War II to resume their struggle for independence, they called their association the "'U. M. Society."

AL-MULQI, FAWZI (1910–62) Jordanian politician and diplomat. M. studied chemistry at the American University of Beirut, graduating in 1932, and continued his studies in Cambridge and Edinburgh, taking a doctorate. He joined the Jordanian civil service, and later the diplomatic service. In 1944 he was named Consul-General in Egypt, and in 1946 when Jordan became independent and established diplomatic relations, he became Minister to Egypt. In Jan. 1948 he joined the government as Foreign Minister, and later the same year became Defense Minister, until late 1950. In this capacity he co-initialed the secret draft Non-Aggression Pact with Israel of 1950 which King *'Abdullah had negotiated and which remained abortive. In 1951–52 he served as Minister to France (and nonresidentially Italy, too), and in 1952–53 — to Britain. In 1953/54 he became Prime Minister, taking also the Defense portfolio. During the crisis over the Baghdad Pact, Dec. 1955, he briefly was Minister of Defense and Education, but soon went abroad again, as Minister to Egypt, 1956–57 — a service he briefly interrupted in May 1956 to become Deputy Prime Minister and Minister of Foreign Affairs and Education. He resumed his diplomatic post after a few weeks. During the crisis of Apr. 1957 he was Minister of Education and Public Works for ten days. From 1961 to his death he served as ambassador to the UN. Dr. M. was a technocrat and civil servant, loyal to the King and executing the King's policies, rather than a decision-making political leader.

MUSSAVI-ARDEBILI, AYATULLAH 'ABD-UL-KARIM (b.1926)

Iranian cleric and politician, Chief Justice and head of the Supreme Judicial Council, 1981–89. Born in Ardebil (eastern Azerbaijan), M.-A. studied theology in Qom under the Ayatullah *Khomeini, and from 1948 to 1950 in Najaf, Iraq.

In 1960, M.-A. and other clergymen in Qom published an Islamic newspaper, Maktab-E Islam (Islamic School). Between 1962 and 1971 he founded religious centers in his hometown, maintaining close ties with Khomeini. He moved to Tehran in 1971, became a prayer leader and preacher (Imam) in the Amir al-Mu'minin Mosque and founded the Amir al-Mu'minin School. His close ties with Iranian youth and his forceful preaching earned him high praise from Tehran's religious leaders.

Following the Islamic Revolution of 1979, he was one of the founders of the Islamic Republic Party. Khomeini appointed him Prosecutor-General (1980–81) and member of the Council of the Islamic Revolution. After Ayatullah Beheshti was killed in an explosion in the headquarters of the Islamic Republic Party (Summer 1981), M.-A. was appointed Chief Justice. He often served as Friday Imam, giving sermons. In the elections of 1982 for the "Council of Guardians" he received (together with *Khamenei and *Rafsanjani) the largest number of votes in the Tehran region. He was one of Khomeini's closest advisers. In the factional struggles of Islamic Iran he was generally considered a moderate.

MUSSAVI, KHO'EINIHA MUHAMMAD (b.1941)

Attorney-General of Iran. Born in Qazvin, M. studied theology in Qom under Ayatullah *Montazeri and in the late 1960s in Iraq under Ayatullah *Khomeini. He returned to Qom in 1967, participated in the struggle against the Shah and was arrested. M. did not hold an official position during the initial period following the Islamic Revolution of 1979, but later was appointed Khomeini's representative in the national radio and television. As the students' political leader and their liaison to Khomeini, M. played a major role during the occupation of the American Embassy in Tehran in Nov. 1979 and the seizure of American hostages. In 1980 he was elected to the Parliament (Majlis), for Tehran, and appointed to the Second Assembly of Experts; he did not stand for a second parliamentary term in 1984. In 1986, Khomeini appointed him Attorney-General.

M. is a radical, advocating a drastic reduction of ties with the West and a strengthening of relations with radical opposition groups in the West, as well as extreme measures of nationalization and expropriation and extensive government control of the economy.

MUSSAVI, MIR HUSSEIN (b.1941)

Iranian politician, Prime Minister 1981–89. Born in Khamaneh near Tabriz (Azerbaijan), graduated in architecture (1969). M. worked in private companies and was politically active in the Islamic Movement against the Shah's regime. He was arrested in 1973. After the Islamic Revolution of 1979 he was for some time a member of the Council of the Islamic Revolution and formed close ties to the Ayatullahs *Beheshti and *Khamenei. He became a member of the Central Council of Beheshti's Islamic Republic Party and editor of the party's organ Jumhuri Islami.

After the fall of the Provisional Government headed by Mehdi *Bazargan in Nov. 1979, M. was named Minister of Foreign Affairs by the new Prime Minister, *Raja'i, but was rejected by President *Bani-Sadr. After Bani-Sadr's dismissal, 1981, M. became Minister of Foreign Affairs, and in Oct. 1981 was appointed Prime Minister. During his eight-year term he was under pressure from various factions, but as he had Ayatullah *Khamenei's support, he won three votes of confidence.

M. presented himself as a patron of the lower classes and supported bills restricting private capital and land ownership and imposing government control on trade. M. was a hard-liner. He frequently explained his policies in press conferences and public speeches. Though he hardly intervened in foreign affairs, he made several visits abroad.

MUTRAN, KHALIL (1872–1949) Lebanese writer and journalist, a pioneer of modern Arabic lyric, epic and narrative Romantic poetry. Born in Baalbek to a Greek-Catholic family, M. studied in Zahla and in Beirut at Catholic schools. To escape Ottoman persecution, M. departed to Paris for two years and in 1892 emigrated to Egypt where he spent the rest of his life as a journalist, translator and poet. In 1900 he established a biweekly cultural and literary magazine, *al-Majalla al-Misriyya*, and left his work in the daily *al-Ahram*. In 1903 he founded his own daily *al-Gawa'ib al-Misriyya* (1903–4). In 1908 he published his anthology of poems, *Diwan al-Khalil*, of which a new 3-volume edition was published in 1948–49 (with a fourth volume added 1975–77). In 1935 he was appointed director of the National Theatre Troupe, for which he translated various plays of Shakespeare, Corneille and Victor Hugo. After the death of the poet Ahmad *Shawqi, M. was elected President (1932–34) of the *Apollo* Poetic Society established by Dr. Ahmad Zaki Abu-Shadi. M. was deeply influenced by French Romantic literature and tried to introduce its criteria into Arabic poetry. He revolutionized Arabic poetry and established a school of followers and admirers who continued his methods of treating new themes of epic, dramatic and romantic poetry, introducing new poetic techniques and using images, symbols and mythology.

N

AL-NABULSI, SULEIMAN (1908–76) Jordanian politician. Born in al-Salt and a graduate in law and social studies of the American University of Beirut (1932), N. held several civil service posts, including those of Secretary to the Government and, until 1946, Director of the Agricultural Bank. He first joined the government in 1947, as Minister of Finance and Economy and held the same post in 1950–51. In 1953–54 he was Ambassador to Britain. He gradually became a spokesman for a nationalist, anti-British and hard-line anti-Israel opposition and in 1954 was exiled from 'Amman to a provincial town. The same year he co-founded the National Socialist Party as a mainstay of the leftist-nationalist, pro-Egyptian-Nasserist, anti-British and anti-Hashemite opposition, and became its main leader. In the elections of Oct. 1956, N. himself was defeated, but his party emerged, with 11–12 of 40 seats, as the largest single group in Parliament, and he became Prime Minister and Foreign Minister. His government put Jordan on a leftist course, linking her to Egypt and Syria in a close alliance and terminating her treaty with Britain. When he decided to establish diplomatic relations with the Soviet Union — an act then still considered a bold move to the left — the King in Apr. 1957 dismissed the government and took steps to reassert his power and put Jordan back on her traditional political course. N. was placed under house arrest, and his party disintegrated. The restrictions on N. were gradually eased and finally lifted in 1963, but he never again held a governmental position, nor was he elected to Parliament. He continued heading an extra-parliamentary leftist opposition, which did not, however, develop into a strong, effective movement. In the showdown of 1970 between Jordan and the Palestinian-Arab guerrillas, he supported the latter and opposed the King's and the army's policies. In the 1970s he was Secretary-General of the Jordanian Peace Council, the Jordanian branch of the Afro-Asian Peoples' Solidarity Organiza-

tion and the Jordan-Soviet Friendship Society. In his later years he was reconciled to a degree with the Jordanian establishment, and in Feb. 1976 the King appointed him a member of the Senate. He died soon afterwards.

NAGIB, MUHAMMAD (1901–84) Egyptian officer and politician, President of Egypt 1953–54. Born in Khartoum, the son of an Egyptian army officer, N. graduated from the University of Cairo (law) and the Military Academy, 1921. He joined the regular army and slowly rose in rank, becoming a colonel in 1948, a general in 1950. He was wounded as a brigade commander in the Arab-Israel war of 1948. Later he became Commander of the Frontier Force and, in 1951, of the Land Army.

Among army officers, N. was admired for his integrity; he frequently voiced demands for army reforms and the elimination of corruption. He apparently was not a member of the "Free Officers" group, but was in touch with them through his operations officer, 'Abd-ul-Hakim *'Amer. In 1952 he was their candidate for the presidency of the Officers' Club, and his election, against the wishes of the King and the senior establishment, caused a minor crisis. N. himself claimed that he joined the Free Officers from the start, 1949–50, and was their leader in the coup of July 1952. However, according to the later official, generally accepted version, he did not take an active part in the coup but was asked by the young revolutionaries to represent them as a sort of figurehead, while *Nasser was the real leader.

After the revolution of July 1952, N. was made Commander in Chief of the Armed Forces and Chairman of the Revolutionary Command Council. When the civilian government formed after the coup resigned in Sept. 1952, N. became Prime Minister and Minister of War. On the proclamation of the Republic in June 1953, the Revolutionary Council appointed N. President and Prime Minister, but relieved him of his military post. From about that time, a deep rupture evolved between him and Nasser, which led to a grave crisis in Feb. 1954. N. held that his high office should carry real authority and a decisive share in the formulation of policies, while Nasser regarded him as a mere figurehead. N. thought, contrary to Nasser, that the army should return to its barracks and political-parliamentary rule should be restored — a view supported by right-wing circles, the *Wafd*, the Muslim Brotherhood, and the left. N. seemed, in general, to hold more moderate views — in foreign affairs, too, such as relations with Sudan, and a settlement of the Anglo-Egyptian dispute — and wished to restrain the revolutionary fervor of the young officers. The differences came to a head when it was decided, in Feb. 1954, without N.'s knowledge, to ban the activities of the Muslim Brotherhood. N. resigned in protest, but some of the ruling Free Officers, led by the leftist Khaled *Muhyi-ul-Din, supported him, used their army units to threaten a violent showdown, and forced N.'s return as President in Feb. and as Prime Minister in Mar. Nasser now mobilized counterdemonstrations of workers and army units — and gained the upper hand. In Apr. N. was relieved of the Premiership, and while he retained the Presidency, its powers were much reduced. In Nov. 1954 he was dismissed from the Presidency, too (which remained vacant until 1956, when Nasser assumed it), and placed under house arrest. It was even hinted that he was involved in a Muslim Brotherhood plot. His supporters, too, were purged.

N. was released from house arrest only in 1971, after Nasser's death. But, while *Sadat accorded him respect as a retired elder statesman, he was offered no post and never regained any real influence. In the few interviews and articles he published, N. strongly supported Sadat — both in his internal and general policy and concerning his moves for peace with Israel. He also voiced harsh criticism of Nasser and his regime — going in one interview so far as to regret the revolution of 1952, and his part in it, and to claim that had it not been for Sadat's efforts to "save what could be saved," Egypt "would have gone to the dogs."

N.'s memoirs (as told to a Western journalist) were published in English in 1955, under the title *Egypt's Destiny*; he later partly dissociated himself from this book, and a Lebanese weekly serialized new memoirs by N. in 1973.

AL-NAHHAS, MUSTAFA(1879–1965) Egyptian politician. After law studies at the University of Cairo, N. opened a law practice, and from 1904 to 1919 was a judge. In 1918 he joined Sa'd *Zaghlul in his nationalist agitation, became a member — and soon a leader — of Zaghlul's *Wafd* Party, and was exiled with Zaghlul to the Seychelles. Since Egypt's first elections under a new constitution, 1924, he was a member of Parliament. In 1924 he was Minister of Communications in Zaghlul's shortlived government. On Zaghlul's death in 1927, N. was elected head of the *Wafd* Party, and remained its leader until his death. In 1928 and 1930 he was for short periods Prime Minister (keeping the Home Ministry for himself) — each time dismissed or forced to resign by the political manipulations of the King and the politicians close to him. In 1935 he led — and won — a campaign of agitation for the reinstatement of the parliamentary constitution that had been replaced since 1930. He led the *Wafd* to victory in the elections of May 1936 and formed a new Wafdist government. In Aug. of the same year he headed the all-party delegation which negotiated and signed the Anglo-Egyptian Treaty giving Egypt nominal full independence. In Dec. 1937 King *Farouq dismissed N., and the *Wafd* again went into opposition.

In Feb. 1942 the British, convinced that only a *Wafd* government would fully cooperate with them and fulfill Egypt's obligations towards the war effort, forced the King to dismiss the government and appoint N. Prime Minister (he again also took the Interior portfolio). In the elections of Mar. 1942, N. again led the *Wafd* to victory. As Prime Minister, N. chaired the talks towards the establishment of the Arab League, 1943–44, and the League's preparatory Alexandria Conference, Oct. 1944. The day after the conference — with the British no longer so blatantly intervening in Egypt's internal affairs — King Farouq dismissed him. The *Wafd* boycotted the elections of Jan. 1945, but won the next ones, in Jan. 1950, and N. once again formed a government. He now followed a nationalist, anti-British policy. As negotiations on the termination of the presence of British troops and bases and the amendment or abrogation of the treaty of 1936 made no progress, N. in Oct. 1951 unilaterally abrogated the treaty and proclaimed the incorporation of Sudan under the Egyptian crown. He also rejected a Western invitation to cosponsor a Western-led Middle East Defense Pact (and seek a solution to the problem of British bases in the framework of such a pact). He started a popular struggle to eject the British troops that led to mounting violence and clashes, culminating in battles between Egyptian and British troops, the eruption of mob violence ("Black Saturday," Jan. 1952), and the fall of his government. Corruption charges voiced against N. and his colleagues also contributed to that fall.

In the purges conducted by the "Free Officers" regime after the coup of July 1952, N. did not face trial (as many politicians of the pre-coup regime did), but the *Wafd* Party was compelled to dismiss him from its leadership. His wife was tried on several charges of corruption, and was sentenced to heavy fines and the confiscation of most of her property. N. himself was in 1954 deprived of his civil and political rights; they were restored to him in 1960, but he did not return to political activity.

AL-NASHASHIBI Palestinian-Arab family in Jerusalem which became prominent in the last century of Turkish-Ottoman rule and provided many administrators and public figures. At the beginning of the 20th century, 'Uthman N. was considered head of the clan; he was elected to the Ottoman Parliament in 1912 and 1914. After his death the same year, **Ragheb N.** became head of the family and its most prominent figure.

A colorful member of the N. clan was **Fakhri N.**, a political organizer and, from the late 1920s, the family's strong-arm man. For some time he served the Mandate government — as aide to the Governor of Jerusalem, 1920, and later *Aide-de-Camp* to High Commissioner Herbert Samuel. During Ragheb N.'s term as Mayor of Jerusalem, Fakhri was his chief aide. He later became one of the chief organizers of opposition to the Mufti of Jerusalem, his Supreme Muslim Council and his *Husseini faction, and one of the founders and organizers of the N.'s Defense Party, 1934. He also organized trade unions. In the first stage of the Arab rebellion, 1936, he was active in the recruitment of guerrilla bands, but when the Husseini-led rebellion turned against the Opposition and embarked upon internal terror (including several attempts on his life), Fakhri N. in 1938 became a chief organizer of counter-bands for the protection of the Opposition leaders, the so-called "Peace Gangs" (in secret cooperation to some degree with branches of the British military and the Jews). He was reportedly prepared to accept the 1937 plan for the partition of Palestine and to seek an accommodation with the Jews, and tried to revive the Defense Party as a moderate political force. In World War II, he promoted the recruitment of Palestinian-Arab volunteers for the British Army. Detested by the Husseini-led nationalists as a traitor (accused also of corruption in his business activities) and sentenced to death by secret terrorist courts, Fakhri N. was assassinated in Baghdad in 1941.

Among other notable members of the N. family in the last generations: **Muhammad Is'af N.** (1882?-1948), the son of the family's head 'Uthman N., was a known writer, one of the few Palestinian-Arab writers with all-Arab renown. 'Ali N. was among the founders, in 1912, of a Decentralization Party for the Arab parts of the Ottoman Empire; in 1915 he was suspected of subversive activites, tried and executed in 1916. **Anwar N.** (b. 1913) was an official in the Palestine government, *inter alia* as adviser to the Arabic section of the Palestine Broadcasting Service, and later a French-trained lawyer. He was also active as a journalist and wrote many articles. In 1945 he joined Mussa al-*'Alami's Palestine-Arab propaganda offices. He then entered the service of Jordan, becoming an ambassador and, in the late 1950s, several times a cabinet minister. 'Azmi N. (b. 1903) — a journalist, and from the 1930s an official of the Palestine Mandate government, *inter alia* director of the Arab section of the Palestine Broadcasting Service (1944–48); from 1948 in the service of Jordan — as director of the Broadcasting Service, cabinet minister and diplomat. **Nasser-ul-Din N.** (b. 1924) — a well-known journalist, living mostly in Egypt, served for some years as Arab League emissary in Europe, mainly for information/propaganda work; N. published a book of memoirs (*Roving Ambassador*, Arabic, Beirut 1970). **Muhammad Zuhdi N.** has been active in the PLO leadership, as a member of its Executive Committee from the mid-1970s to the mid-1980s and again in Sept. 1991.

In the 1920s and 1930s, and to a decreasing extent in the 1940s, the term "the N.'s" in common usage also denoted the political group which the family headed, *viz.* the faction of the Opposition (*al-Mu'aridin*) to the Supreme Muslim Council and its Husseini leadership. The official program of the N. faction and its Defense Party, founded in 1934, was not very different from that of the other nationalist parties and the mainstream. In practice, however, they were ready to cooperate with the British Mandate authorities, maintained close relations with Amir *'Abdullah of Transjordan and in the 1940s advocated and prepared his takeover of the Arab part of Palestine; they were also more moderate with regard to the Jews. In 1936, the N.'s joined in organizing the Arab rebellion in its early stages; but when guerrilla formations launched a campaign of assassinations directed against the N.'s and their Opposition faction, they seceded and organized counterguerrillas, "Peace Gangs'" (see above, Fakhri N.).

During the later 1930s and the 1940s, the family and its political faction declined in influence, many of their members took public and political positions conflicting with the family tradition and their leaders displayed no assertive activity. To a degree, this was part of a general decline of the role of the prominent families and their function in determining the political affiliation of their members and clients.

AL-NASHASHIBI, RAGHEB (1875? 1880? 1881?–1951) Palestinian-Arab politician, head of the N. family of Jerusalem (see above). A graduate in engineering of Ottoman-Turkish universities, N. was Jerusalem District Engineer and from 1914 one of the representatives of Jerusalem in the Ottoman Parliament. In World War I he was an officer in the Turkish army. After the British occupation of Palestine (1918), with the first steps of Palestinian-Arab political organization, he was among the founders of the "Literary Club" (*al-Muntada al-Adabi*), which competed with the "Arab Club" (*al-Nadi al-'Arabi*) dominated by the rival *Husseini family.

When Mussa Kazem al-*Husseini was dismissed as Mayor of Jerusalem in 1920, N. was appointed to that post, which he held until 1934. He cooperated with the British authorities and advised the Arabs to participate in representative, self-governing bodies which the British proposed and the nationalist Arab mainstream rejected. In 1923, his adherents formed a National Party (*al-Hizb al-Watani*) — which in appearance and extremist slogans hardly differed from the Husseini nationalist faction, but under the surface tried to promote more moderate policies and cooperation with the government, and to a degree with the Jews. The party did not last long. In his efforts to organize the camp opposing the Supreme Muslim Council and the rival extremist Husseini faction dominating that Council, N. now turned to local, municipal interests and succeeded, despite the failure of his party on the national level, in recruiting many mayors to his camp of "the Opposition" (*al-Mu'aridin*). In the first municipal elections, held in 1927, he won in Jerusalem, and his supporters triumphed in all towns except Gaza. In 1934, however, he was defeated in the Jerusalem elections.

In 1934 the N.'s founded a "Defense Party" with Ragheb N. at its head. In that capacity he became a member of the Arab Higher Committee formed in Apr. 1936 to lead the general strike that turned into a rebellion. He supported the strike and the first stage of the "disturbances," but when in 1937 they deteriorated into internal terror, he resigned from the Higher Committee and turned against the Husseini leadership.

In 1937, N. was inclined to accept the proposals for the partition of Palestine then announced by the British, though publicly he opposed it. He supported Amir *'Abdullah of Transjordan and was one of his confidants — but this position, too, found little public expression. Nor did N. publicize his reported moderation on the Arab-Jewish issue. He accepted and supported the new British policy under the White Paper of 1939 (which other Arab leaders publicly rejected as conceding too little). But in the late 1930s and the 1940s he was politically inactive — depressed by the Palestinian-Arab internecine terror and the impasse into which the Husseini leadership had led the Palestine Arabs, and disappointed that the British, after the suppression of the Husseini rebellion, did not actively promote his alternative leadership. He thus allowed his faction to decline.

In 1948, N. actively promoted the Jordanian annexation of the Arab part of Palestine (to become the "West Bank" of Jordan) and organized Palestinian-Arab support for that move. He was appointed as the first governor of the West Bank — but did not take active charge, seemed to regard that post as a symbolic position of honor and kept it for a short time only. In 1950 he joined the Jordanian Cabinet as Minister of Agriculture, and later of Transport, and in 1951 he became Minister without Portfolio in charge of *al-Haram al-Sharif* (the Jerusalem Temple Mount), and Guardian of the Holy Places. He died the same year.

NASSER see *'Abd-ul-Nasser, Gamal.

NAVON, YITZHAK (b. 1921)   Israeli politician. Born in Jerusalem to a Sephardi family which had lived in Palestine for generations. During the 1940s he was active in the Intelligence Service of the *Haganah*, and after the establishment of the State of Israel, he joined the Foreign Ministry. At first he was Second Secretary at the Israeli Legation in Argentina and afterwards Foreign Minister Moshe *Sharett's political secretary. In 1952 he was appointed secretary to Prime Minister David

Yitzhak Navon (GPO, Jerusalem)

*Ben-Gurion and he held this position until 1963, when Ben-Gurion resigned. In this capacity he garnered a great deal of influence.

In 1963 he was appointed Director of the Culture Division of the Ministry of Education and Culture. In 1965, after the split within *Mapai*, he joined *Rafi* and was elected to the Sixth Knesset as a member of that party. He was a Member of Knesset until 1978 and acted as Deputy Speaker of the Knesset (1966–1973) and as Chairman of the Committee for Foreign Affairs and Defense (1974–1977). During these years he was called a political "loser" — in 1972 he lost to Yisrael Yeshayahu in the elections for Knesset speaker; in 1973 he lost to Ephraim *Katzir in the elections to the Presidency; in 1974 he was not named as a representative of his faction in the Cabinet.

In 1978, after the political victory of the right, he was elected by a large majority as President of the State of Israel and held this position for one five-year term (until 1983). These years were the pinnacle of his public activity. In 1982, after the Sabra and Shatila massacres, he threatened to resign if a Commission of Inquiry would not be formed.

After ending his term as President he returned to political life. It was expected that his popularity as President would lead his party to a sweeping victory in the elections and back to power. However, his fall was very quick. He did not compete for his party's leadership and after the 1984 elections he was appointed Deputy Prime Minister and Minister of Education and Culture. He held this position until 1990 and was considered to be a colorless, conservative minister.

NISSIM, MOSHE (b. 1935)   Israeli politician. Born in Jerusalem to a religious family of note. His father, Rabbi Yitzhak Nissim, was for many years the Sephardi Chief Rabbi. In 1959, at the age of 24, N. was elected to the Fourth Knesset, the youngest man ever elected to the Knesset. He was elected on the General Zionist list which chose him due to his Sephardic origins and his family standing. He was not elected to the Fifth Knesset in 1961. He completed his military service, studied law and opened a law office.

In 1969 he was again elected to the Knesset on the *Gahal* list and has since served in the Knesset. In 1978 he was appointed to the government as Minister without Portfolio and in 1980, after Shmuel *Tamir resigned, became Minister of Justice. He was considered a capable Minister of Justice who accepted the recommendations of his senior staff, and his considerations were usually professional, not political. In 1986, after the dismissal of Yitzhak *Moda'i, he became Minister of Finance. He accepted this Ministry with a marked lack of enthusiasm, but was a capable Finance Minister. His considerations were primarily businesslike and he accepted the advice of his professional advisers. After the 1988 elections he refused the Justice portfolio and became Minister without Portfolio. In January 1990, after Ariel *Sharon's resignation, he became Minister of Trade and Industry. In the political climate existing after the Shamir government was formed in the summer of 1990 and as a result of the political weakness of the Minister of Finance, Yitzhak Moda'i, N. became a central economic figure wielding a great deal of political influence, a senior and experienced politician, considered very close to the Prime Minister and to the religious parties. His personal ideology is national-conservative.

AL-NUHAYAN (also **NAHAYAN, NIHAYAN**) The clan or dynasty of sheikhs ruling Abu Dhabi in Trucial 'Oman, since 1971 the United Arab Emirates (UAE). The ruler and head of the clan in recent decades is Sheikh Zayed ibn Sultan al-N. (b. 1918). He was Governor of the sheikhdom's al-'Ain district, with the oasis of al-Buraimi at its center, 1946–66. In Aug. 1966 he overthrew — reportedly with the encouragement of the British, then still the protecting power — his brother Sheikh Shakhbut ibn Sultan (who had ruled the sheikhdom since 1928 and was considered an obstacle to development and progress) and became the ruler of Abu Dhabi. He played a major role in the negotiations towards the federation of the Trucial Coast sheikhdoms as the UAE and in efforts to overcome the rivalries and disputes between the various sheikhs (chief among which was his own clan's near-permanent rivalry with the al-*Maktum sheikhs, the rulers of Dubai). With the foundation of the UAE, 1971, Sheikh Zayed became President of the Federation, remaining also ruler of Abu Dhabi. He was reelected by the Supreme Council of Rulers in 1976, 1981 and 1986 for five-year terms. Sheikh Zayed has been pressing, with gradual, slow success, for stronger federal institutions — with the main resistance coming from the ruler of Dubai. Other members of the clan occupy various positions in government and business — chief among them Sheikh Zayed's sons Khalifa ibn Zayed and Sultan ibn Zayed.

NU'MAN, AHMAD MUHAMMAD (b. 1905? 1910?) Yemeni Sunni-Shafe'i politician. Educated at the Islamic University of al-Azhar, Cairo (graduated 1941). In the later 1940s N. was linked to the clandestine Free Yemen movement and accused of involvement in the abortive coup of 1948. He was pardoned in 1949 and tried to cooperate with the Imam-King and the government, urging them in vain to move towards modernization and liberalization; in 1955 he went into exile, joining the Free Yemen exiles in Egypt and 'Aden. His support for the revolution of Sept. 1962 was halfhearted, as he saw hope in the promises of liberalization made by Muhammad al-*Badr, the new Imam. But he served the new Republic for two years as its representative to the Arab League. In 1964 he was named to a newly formed Council, or Politbureau, and soon became its Deputy Chairman. In Apr. 1965, when under Egypt's guidance the Republic embarked upon more moderate policies, N. became Prime Minister. He was allied with the Zeidi tribal leaders and though a Shafe'i, co-organized a Zeidi tribal conference at Khamir, May 1965, intended to win the tribes' support for the Republic. Soon

afterwards he had to resign, but later in 1965 became a member of the Presidential Council. In Sept. 1966, when the Egyptians reinstated 'Abdullah al-*Sallal and his more radical policies, N. was dismissed and exiled to Egypt, where he was kept in semidetention until Oct. 1967. He did not return to San'a, though he was offered his place on the Republican (Presidential) Council, but went to Beirut and continued calling for a Republican-Royalist reconciliation. When such a reconciliation was achieved in 1970, following the decline of the Royalists, N. returned and rejoined the Presidential Council. In Apr. 1971 he was not reappointed, but was made Prime Minister from May to Aug. 1971. Late in 1973 he again became a member of the Presidential Council, until Ibrahim *Hamdi's coup of June 1974. Since then, N. has not held any governmental political position. He was in exile for some years, but was reported to have returned, and retired, in 1985.

N.'s son, **Muhammad Ahmad al-N.** (1928? 1933?–74), was active with his father in the Free Yemen movement and later joined the diplomatic service of the Republic, becoming Ambassador to West Germany 1963, the Arab League 1964, France 1971. He was Foreign Minister in his father's shortlived government, 1971, and again from Dec. 1972 to Dec. 1973. Considered pro-West and anti-Nasserist, he stayed abroad, in Beirut, in the late 1960s (though keeping the title of a roving Ambassador), and again took refuge in Beirut in 1974. He was assassinated in Beirut in June 1974.

NUMEIRI, (MUHAMMAD) JA'FAR (b. 1930) Sudanese officer and politician, ruler of Sudan 1969–85. After graduation from the pre-independence Military College of Khartoum in 1952, N. served in infantry and armor units. He was suspected of participating in antigovernment instigation and heading subversive cells, including a "Free Officers" group from 1963, and was suspended and arrested several times (1957, 1959, 1965), but reinstated. After his rehabilitation of 1966 he completed a course at an American military college and later attained the rank of Brigadier-General.

In May 1969 N. seized power in a military coup. He dismissed the Presidential Council and the government, dissolved Parliament and banned all political parties, and formed a Revolutionary Council as the supreme state organ, with himself at its head. He also appointed himself Commander in Chief and Defense Minister, and in Oct. 1969 also

Prime Minister. N. had to balance between conservative groups (such as the two great orders, the *Mahdiyya* and the *Khatmiyya* — both of which had little sympathy for his regime), the army (on which he relied), and the Communists (whose main faction he half-suppressed, while letting other factions participate in his government). In Mar. 1970 he suppressed *al-Ansar*, the militant organization of the *Mahdiyya*. In July 1971 he was overthrown in a coup headed by leftist officers whom he had purged in 1970; but a counter-coup returned him to power three days later (reportedly with Egyptian and Libyan help). He then savagely suppressed the Communists.

In Sept. 1971 N. was elected President, the only candidate in a plebiscite. He was reelected in 1977 and 1983. As President he also retained the Premiership. In 1972 he founded a single party on the Egyptian pattern, the Sudan Socialist Union, and headed its Politbureau. From 1972 he also convened a "People's Council" or National Assembly. In Mar. 1972 he reached agreement with the South Sudan African rebels by conceding a wide local-regional autonomy — his major achievement. But his regime did not attain real stability — the single party did not take roots; he frequently changed his Vice-President and the heads of the defense establishment; a National Front, comprising both the *Mahdiyya* with its *Umma* Party and its adversary, the National Unionists supported by the *Khatmiyya*, harassed his regime, partly from bases in Libya; the settlement with the South Sudanese rebels turned sour and he began to renege on it; and the economic situation continuously deteriorated. N.'s foreign policy was also somewhat erratic. In 1969–70 he planned to join a Federation with Egypt and Libya; but in 1971 he opted out. He fostered, however, close relations with Egypt, signing a Defense Agreement with her in 1976–77 and an accord on gradual integration in 1982 and instituting a joint "Nile Valley Parliament." The USA and the West came to regard him, in his later years, with sympathy.

N. gradually cultivated an alliance with fundamentalist Islamic groups, chiefly the Muslim Brotherhood. In Sept. 1983 he decreed the full implementation of the code of punishments of Islamic law, the *Shari'a* — a measure that aroused strong opposition. A new rebellion of the South Sudanese Africans also erupted. These two developments hastened N.'s fall. He was overthrown in Apr. 1985 in a coup mounted by the Army in collaboration with his political foes. N. escaped to

Ja'afar Numeiri (AP photo)

Egypt and received political asylum there — despite the new regime's repeated demands for his extradition. A decision to try him *in absentia* was reported, but not implemented.

NUQRASHI, MAHMUD FAHMI (1888–1948) Egyptian politician, Prime Minister 1945–46, 1946–48. An engineer by profession, N. was active in the *Wafd* Party. After the *Wafd*'s victory in the elections of 1936, he was Minister of Transport. In 1937 he left the party, mainly because he sought an accommodation with the King, as against the intransigent position taken by al-*Nahhas. Together with Ahmad al-*Maher, he founded the Sa'adist Party, which claimed to represent the true traditions of the *Wafd* and its late leader Sa'd *Zaghlul, but became an anti-Wafdist ally of the King and his court. N. was a minister in anti-Wafdist cabinets — Interior 1940, Foreign Affairs 1944–45. In Mar. 1945, after the assassination of Ahmad Maher, he became Prime Minister (taking also the Interior portfolio), until Feb. 1946. When Isma'il *Sidqi's government fell, in Sept. 1946, N. again formed a government, again serving as Interior Minister and until Nov. 1947 also as Foreign Minister. In 1947, while Premier and Foreign Minister, he took the

Anglo-Egyptian dispute over Sudan to the UN Security Council, but failed to obtain the Council's support.

During his tenure, Egypt went to war with nascent Israel in May 1948. After the failure of this venture, the army leaders claimed that it was N. who had decided against their advice to intervene in Palestine with the regular army. N.'s associates (he himself was dead by then) claimed that the decision had been imposed on him by King *Farouq. When the Muslim Brotherhood, stepped up its terrorist activities, N. outlawed the organization in Dec. 1948 and ordered measures to disband and suppress it. He was assassinated the same month by members of the Brotherhood.

NUSSEIBA   Prominent Muslim Palestinian-Arab family in Jerusalem. The family keeps the keys of the Church of the Holy Sepulchre, entrusted to it, according to tradition, by the Caliph 'Omar, the Muslim-Arab conqueror of Jerusalem in AD 138. In the struggle for supremacy among Jerusalem's leading Arab families in the last few generations the N.'s have played but a minor role. Among members of the family prominent in recent times: **Hazem M.** (b. 1922), a graduate in political science, since 1948 in the service of Jordan in senior positions — Foreign Minister 1962–63 and 1965–66, Minister of Reconstruction and Development

1967–68, Ambassador to Egypt 1969–71, to Turkey 1971–73, to Italy 1973–75, and to the UN 1976. **Anwar N.** (1913–86), a lawyer trained in Beirut and Cambridge, and for some years a magistrate in the courts of British-mandated Palestine. In 1945 he joined Mussa al *'Alami's information/ propaganda office in London, but returned to Palestine in 1946 and was named by the Arab League to a new Palestinian-Arab Higher Committee (as a "neutral" between the rival factions). In 1948 he was made Secretary-General of the abortive "Government of all Palestine" set up by the *Husseini faction in Gaza, but soon resigned and returned to Jordan-occupied East Jerusalem. In 1950 he was elected to the Jordanian Parliament and later became a Minister in Jordan's government (Development 1952–53), Defense and Education 1954–55) and Ambassador to Britain, 1965–67. After the Six Day War, 1967, he stayed in Israel-occupied East Jerusalem and was prominent, among its Arab residents, but not very active in public-political affairs. Of Anwar N.'s sons. **Zaki N.** (b. 1946), a Cambridge-trained economist, is a senior adviser to the government of the United Arab Emirates (Abu Dhabi); **Sari N.** (b. 1951), a professor of philosophy at Bir Zeit University, has since the late 1980s been vocal as a spokesman for the Palestinian Arabs in the search for a settlement with Israel.

O

OKYAR, ALI FETHI(1880–1943)   Turkish officer and politician, Prime Minister (1923–25). O. graduated from the Istanbul Military Academy (1903), served as a military attache in Paris (1909–11) and fought in North Africa in the war against Italy (1911–12). After resigning from the army he served as ambassador to Bulgaria and, in 1918, he was appointed Minister of the Interior. Due to his active opposition to the British occupation after World War I, he was exiled to Malta (1920).

Upon his return to Turkey in 1921, he became a member of the Grand National Assembly in Ankara and was appointed Interior Minister. O. was Prime Minister for two short terms in 1923 and 1924/25. He had to step down after a vote of no confidence due to his opposition to action against the rebelling Kurds. He was ambassador to France (1925–30).

In 1930, believing that to ensure proper, democratic political life an opposition party was needed, O. founded a Liberal Republican Party (*Servest Cumhuriyet Firkasi*), permitted and encouraged by President *Ataturk and the government. But that party showed very weak results in the elections and objections were raised to its very existence, and O. dissolved it the same year. He became ambassador to England (1934–39). In 1939 he was again elected to Parliament, and from 1939 to 1941 was Justice Minister.

ORBAY, HUSEYIN RA'UF (1881–1964)   Turkish politician, Prime Minister 1922–23. Born in Istanbul, O. studied in the Naval College, served in the Ottoman Navy and on diplomatic missions, and became Minister for Naval Affairs in 1918. A deputy in the first Grand National Assembly from 1920. At first he cooperated with *Ataturk during the nationalists' struggle in Anatolia, and in 1922–23 served briefly as Premier. His conservatism, however, led him to break away. In 1924 O. was among the founders of the short-lived opposition Progressive Republican Party, and in 1926 he took part in a plot on Ataturk's life. He fled and lived abroad for ten years, but returned to serve as Ambassador to London 1942–44.

OZ (original name: Klausner), **AMOS** (b. 1939) Israeli writer, prominent among the younger Israel-born writers. Born in Jerusalem to a family of right-wing, Revisionist leanings (his father's uncle was the historian Joseph Klausner), O. was a member of Kibbutz Hulda from 1957 until the mid-1980s. His first stories, collected in *Artzot HaTan* (*Lands of the Jackal*), 1965, received great acclaim. His second book, *Makom Acher* (*Another Place*) (1966), describes *kibbutz* society. Further novels were *My Michael*; *Touch the Water, Touch the Wind, Hill of Evil Counsel*; *Just Report*; *Black Box*. His books were translated into many languages. His later books received controversial reviews.

O. has also been politically active. In 1960s he was a member of Pinchas *Lavon's "*Min Hayesod*" group and was personally close to Lavon. After the Six Day War he was one of the first to oppose the "Greater Israel Movement" and expressed his position in many articles and speeches. During the 1970s he was one of the founders of the left wing dovish *Moked* (1973) and *Sheli* (1977) groups. Before the elections to the Tenth Knesset, 1981, he returned to the Labor Party and participated in its election campaign. He was also active in various institutions of the *kibbutz* movement. Throughout the years he published many articles on political and ideological topics. These articles were collected in two books.

ÖZAL, TURGUT (b. 1927)   Turkish politician, Prime Minister 1983–89, President since Oct. 1989. Born in Malatya in eastern Turkey, O. graduated from Istanbul Technical University in 1960 as an electrical engineer; he also studied economics and engineering in the USA. After working in power station and electrification projects, and (as his military service) on the Scientific Committee of the

Defense Ministry, from 1965 to 1967 he was technical adviser to Prime Minister *Demirel. From 1967 to 1971 he was the manager of the State Planning Organization. He was an adviser to the World Bank, 1972–73. Returning to Turkey, he joined the private sector. In 1975, he was appointed Undersecretary to Prime Minister Demirel and acting Undersecretary of the State Planning Organization. O.'s first attempt to win a seat in Parliament, 1977, failed.

After the military coup of Sept. 1980, O. was appointed Deputy Prime Minister in charge of economic affairs. In this position he enforced economic measures recommended by the International Monetary Fund which brought down inflation from 120% p.a. to 45% and increased production, but caused a high increase in interest rates and a decline of investment. O. along with the Minister of Finance, resigned in July 1982.

When in 1983 the military regime again permitted political and party activity, O. co-founded the Motherland Party (MP). In the elections of Nov. 1983, the MP won a majority of 211 seats, defeating the Nationalist Democracy Party favored by the military, as well as the left, and O. formed the government.

In 1987, the MP again won a majority of seats (though its share of the vote declined to 36%), and O. continued as Prime Minister.

In his foreign policy, O. was considered a moderate. He endeavored to improve relations with Greece and met with Greek Prime Minister Andreas Papandreou in 1988, the first Turkish statesman to visit Athens in a quarter of a century. He tried to strengthen Turkey's relations with Western Europe, and in 1987 formally requested to change Turkey's status in the European Community to full membership. He also strengthened Turkey's relations with the Arab and Islamic countries.

O.'s economic plans suffered a setback in the late 1980s when inflation rose again to 80%, the economy showed signs of crisis and the gap between the rich and the poor grew. His leadership was challenged by Demirel's right-wing True Path Party and Erdal *Inonu's left-wing Social Democratic Party, as well as by rival factions in his own Motherland Party, whose standing in public opinion declined in the late 1980s.

When in Oct. 1989 Kenan *Evren ended his term as President, O. presented his candidacy — though opinion polls gave him a low rating and the opposition parties, as well as some in his own Motherland Party, rejected him, regarding him as a party politician unable to become an independent head of state above politics and parties. He was elected in the third vote only, with the opposition boycotting the vote. As President he tries to rule Turkey with a strong hand and is frequently accused of having remained a party politician, as well as of interfering in political decisions and imposing his will on his ministers.

Ö. suffered a severe setback when his Motherland Party lost the Oct. 1991 elections, coming second after Demirel's True Path Prty.

ÖZALP, KAZIM (b. 1882?)   Turkish officer and politician. Born in Koprulu, he was educated in the Military Academy in Istanbul. His military career began in 1905 and he fought in the war in the Balkans in 1912, in World War I, and in the Turkish War of Independence 1919–1922. O. was Vice-President of the Grand National Assembly (Parliament). He was Chief of Staff and served as Minister of Defense, 1922–25 and 1937–39.

P

PACHACHI (in written Arabic: **AL-BAHJAJI**) Prominent Iraqi Muslim-Sunni landowning family, from whom have come several men active in public life. Among them: **Hamdi P.** (d. 1948) — a right-wing politician, Minister of Social Welfare 1941–44, Prime Minister 1944–46 (resigned or was dismissed when it was decided to liberalize political life), Foreign Minister in M. al-*Sadr's right-wing cabinet (appointed after the riots against the Anglo-Iraqi draft Treaty of Portsmouth), from Jan. 1948 to his death. **Muzahim P.** (1891-?) — active in the pre-World War I Arab nationalist movement; member of the committee drafting the Iraqi constitution, 1924; Minister of Public Works and Communications 1924–25, of Interior 1931–33 (though he had joined the right-wing opposition to the Anglo-Iraqi Treaty of 1930); in the diplomatic service Minister to Britain 1927–28, Representative to the League of Nations 1933–35, Minister to Italy 1935–59, France 1939–42 (stayed in Switzerland 1942–45 after the German occupation of France); active in the Committee for the Defense of Palestine, 1946–47. P. was Prime Minister and Foreign Minister from June 1948 to Jan. 1949; taking an extreme position during the Palestine War, he rejected a UN-ordered truce, refused to negotiate an armistice, and recognized the abortive Gaza "Government of all Palestine." Briefly again Foreign Minister and Deputy Premier, Dec. 1949 to Feb. 1950, he later in 1950 led the right-wing opposition to the law allowing the Jews of Iraq to leave the country. In 1951, after failing to establish a pro-Egyptian party, he left Iraq and stayed abroad. He returned after the coup of 1958, but did not resume political activity.

'**Adnan P.** (b. 1923, the son of Muzahim P. and the son-in-law of the veteran politician 'Ali Jawdat al-*Ayyubi) — a graduate of American universities in political science (Ph.D. 1949), he quickly rose to high rank in the foreign service, serving as Iraq's Ambassador to the UN 1959–65; he was Minister of State for Foreign Affairs in 1965/66, under al-*Bazzaz, and full-rank Foreign Minister, under Naji Taleb from 1966–1967. However, he could not, apparently, find a place under the Ba'th regime, since 1968; he left Iraq and since 1974 has been in the service of Abu Dhabi.

PEKER, RECEP (1888–1950) Turkish officer and politician, Prime Minister 1946–47. Born in Istanbul, P. received a military education, served in the First World War and took part in Turkey's war of independence as a staff major (1920–22). He was elected to the National Assembly and served as a minister in several posts — e.g., Minister of Defense 1925–27, Public Works 1928–30, the Interior 1942–43. He was Secretary-General of the ruling Republican People's Party and, from 1935 to 1942, lectured on the Turkish Revolution at the Universities of Ankara and Istanbul. After World War II, he headed the faction of his party that resisted a change to a multiparty system (as was eventually decided and implemented in 1950). In Aug. 1946 he became Prime Minister. However, as a hard-line party man who opposed the winning trend towards a multiparty system he clashed with the opposing group dominating his party and with President Ismet *Inonu, and in Sept. 1947 he resigned and retired from political activity.

PERES (original name: Persky), **SHIMON** (b. 1923) Israeli political leader. Born in Poland, P. immigrated to Palestine with his family in 1934. He studied at the Ben-Shemen agricultural school and later joined Kibbutz Alumot. From his youth he was active in public life: from 1941 to 1944 he was secretary of the *Hanoar Haoved* (Working Youth). In 1947 he joined the *Haganah* staff where he dealt, *inter alia*, with the purchase of arms. At the end of the War of Independence he was the head of the naval arm of the IDF. From 1950 to 1952 he headed the Ministry of Defense delegation to the United States.

From 1953 to 1959 he was Director-General of

Shimon Peres (GPO, Jerusalem)

the Ministry of Defense. During these years he was responsible for many projects; he initiated and developed the Israel Aircraft Industries; strengthened and deepened military ties with France; initiated the establishment of the nuclear research center in Dimona. But he also created much antagonism, e.g., with Moshe *Sharett and Golda *Meir, who claimed that he "ignored" the Foreign Office.

In 1959 P. entered political life. He was elected to the Knesset for the Labor Party and has been a member of Knesset ever since. From 1960 to 1965 he was Deputy Defense Minister under David *Ben Gurion and Levi *Eshkol. He became increasingly close to Ben Gurion, supported him in his struggles against Eshkol (whose Deputy Minister he was) and in 1965 resigned from the Ministry of Defense and was one of the founding members and General-Secretary of the *Rafi* party seceding from the Labor Party. On the eve of the Six Day War he was among those who forced Eshkol to resign as Minister of Defense. After the return of *Rafi* to the Labor Party, 1968, he was Deputy Secretary-General of that Party.

In 1969 P. joined Golda Meir's government as Minister without Portfolio. In 1970–1974 he was Minister of Transport and Communications and in 1974, Minister of Information. After Meir's resignation, 1974, he contested Yitzhak *Rabin for the Prime Ministership; he lost and was appointed Defense Minister. As Defense Minister (1974–1977) he was responsible for strengthening the army after the Yom Kippur War and for the Entebbe raid. He was also responsible for the compromise with *Gush Emunim* in Kadum, a step which paved the way for Jewish settlement in the heart of the West Bank, in opposition to his party's policies.

In 1977, after Rabin's resignation from the Prime Ministership, he was chosen as his party's candidate. But in the 1977 elections his party was defeated and P. became the leader of the opposition.

After the elections of 1984 he signed a coalition and rotation agreement with the *Likud* and from 1984 to 1986 he was Prime Minister. His chief achievements were the withdrawal of the army from Lebanon and the stabilization of the economy, which was plagued with inflation of 400%. In 1986 he became Deputy Prime Minister and Foreign Minister. In this capacity he reached an informal agreement with King *Hussein on the modalities of a peace process (London 1987); but it was rejected by Prime Minister *Shamir. From 1988–90 he was Finance Minister in Shamir's new government. In 1990 he led his party to withdraw from the coalition government and again became leader of the opposition. Inside his party, P. endeavored to balance dovish and hawkish factions and keep the party united; but his leadership was constantly challenged by his rival Rabin.

P. is a controversial figure. Some consider him a wise, moderate statesman with vision; others, like Yitzhak Rabin, denounce him as a troublemaker who brought his party to an unprecedented low. While his talents are undoubted, many see him as a shifty politician and have no confidence in him. Some think the Labor Party could have better election prospects under another leader. Yet P. remains the chairman of his party and its candidate for the Premiership.

P. authored several books of political thought and analysis.

Q

QABBANI, NIZAR (b. **1923**)   Syrian poet and writer. Born in Damascus, Q. graduated in law from the University of Damascus (1945). He joined the Syrian diplomatic service (1945–66) and served in various capitals such as Cairo, Ankara, Beirut, London, Peking and Madrid.

In 1966 he resigned and settled in Beirut, where he established a publishing house bearing his name and devoted himself to poetry and journalism.

After publishing several anthologies of free verse poetry, mostly love and erotic poetry which often violated the taboo against frank descriptions of love and sex in Arabic literature, Q. turned to political and social concerns. He showed much sympathy for the Palestinian-Arab struggle and wrote anti-Israeli and political poetry, denouncing the conservative regimes in the Arab world. But when his wife was killed in an explosion at the Iraqi Embassy in Beirut in 1982, he accused Palestinian-Arab terrorists and turned against the PLO. That year he left Lebanon for Egypt.

Q.'s poetic diction is simple and clear, similar to a journalistic style and echoing spoken Arabic. His complete poetic works were issued in two volumes by his publishing house in Beirut.

QABUS IBN SA'ID (b. 1940? 1942?)   Sultan of 'Oman since 1970. Educated in England (Sandhurst Military Academy, one year with a Scottish regiment, social studies at a British university), Q. returned to 'Oman in the mid-1960s. He was kept in total seclusion at the Salala palace by his father, Sultan Sa'id ibn Taimur (1910–72), who objected to, and prevented, the modern development of the country and maintained an autocratic regime. In July 1970, Q. overthrew his father, with active British encouragement, and became Sultan (his father went into exile in England and died there in 1972). As Sultan, Q. fostered gradual economic and social development and a measure of reform, while maintaining a strictly conservative regime. He followed low-profile moderate policies in both

international and inter-Arab affairs and continued a close alliance with Britain and the USA. He also maintained fairly good relations with Iran and acted as liaison between that country and the Arab principalities on the Persian Gulf (most of whom feared Iran and tended to support Iraq in her war with Iran, 1980–88). In the crisis of 1990/91 following Iraq's invasion of Kuwait, Q. joined the U.S. and Sa'udi-led alliance against Iraq and dispatched a small contingent of troops.

AL-QADHDHAFI, MU'AMMAR (b. 1942 — or, in other versions, 1938? 1935?)   Libyan officer and politician, since his coup of 1969 Libya's top leader. Born in the Sirte desert into a poor family of the Qadhadhifa tribe originating in the Fezzan region of southern Libya and adhering to the Sanussi sect, Q. was imbued with a fighting tradition: his grandfather was reportedly killed in 1911 while resisting the Italian conquest, and his father and uncle fought in the resistance and were imprisoned. Q. was sent to a secondary school in Sabha, Fezzan, but was expelled for organizing a demonstration, and continued his secondary studies in Tripoli and Misurata. He enrolled at the University of Benghazi to study history and geography, but transferred in 1963 to the Military Academy, from which he graduated in 1965. In 1966 the army sent him to further officers' training in Britain.

A fervent revolutionary nationalist deeply influaenced by Egypt's *Nasser, Q. agitated and organized revolutionary cells within the army and was reportedly imprisoned, but reinstated. In Sept. 1969 he took a leading part in a military coup d'etat which overthrew the monarchy. He was promoted to the rank of Colonel and made Commander in Chief of the Armed Forces and chairman of the Revolutionary Council that headed the new regime. In Jan. 1970 he made himself also Prime Minister and Minister of Defense and held these posts until July 1972. In 1973, Q. proclaimed a "Popular Revolution" and began building a network of

"People's Committees" topped by a general "People's Congress." In Mar. 1977, Q. declared Libya a *Jamahiriyya* — a new term he coined to mean "Republic of the Masses" — changing the structure, and mainly the terminology, of government institutions. He made himself chairman of the "General Secretariat" that replaced the Revolutionary Council as the supreme institution of the state. In Mar. 1979 he gave up this post of Head of State and retained only that of Commander in Chief. However, Q. has remained the sole and supreme leader and continues being treated as the Head of State.

Q. is a fervent Arab nationalist, actively aspiring to Pn-Arab union. He has relentlessly proposed Libya's merger with other Arab countries: Egypt 1969–70 and 1972–73; Sudan 1969–70; Syria 1970–71 and since 1980; Tunisia 1974; Morocco 1984 — and included in his quest for union even non-Arab countries such as Malta (1971) and Chad (1981); none of these mergers has materialized — and while no one doubts Q.'s fervent Pan-Arab sincerity, his frequent merger offers are not taken quite seriously. Q. does not shun revolutionary plots and subversion to force his plans on other Arab countries and most of them have repeatedly denounced that subversion and sometimes severed relations with Q.'s Libya. In his overt inter-Arab policy Q. took a radical-extremist line and was the mainstay of the Rejection Front, including the most uncompromising hostility towards Israel and support for the most extreme Palestinian-Arab terrorist groups. He was at odds with the Arab consensus by supporting Iran in her war with Iraq.

Q.'s revolutionary-subversive activities were directed also against most of his non-Arab African neighbors, and most of them complained bitterly and repeatedly; in Chad he has conducted actual warfare. His relations with the Organization for African Unity were troubled; in 1982 the Organization delayed for a year its summit, scheduled to take place in Tripoli, because a majority of its members refused to go to Libya and to grant Q. the status of its President until the next summit. Q.'s relations with the group of nonaligned nations also were troubled because the group did not accept either his policies or his claims to leadership.

Q. has supported and aided revolutionary or subversive movements in many foreign countries — from the Irish IRA, independence movements in the Canary Islands and Corsica, the Red Army terrorists in Italy and Germany, to groups in the Philippines and the South Pacific. He is violently

Mu'ammar al-Qadhdhafi (IPS, Tel Aviv)

anti-Western, in near-constant conflict with the USA and several European countries, mainly Britain, and with no official relations with the USA (since 1981) and Britain (since 1984); his dispute with the USA erupted several times in armed clashes (1981, 1983, 1986). One of the reasons for his dispute with European countries is his involvement in terrorist activities there — including the systematic assassination of Libyan dissident refugees in Europe. With the USSR and the Soviet Bloc, on the other hand, he has maintained, despite his strict anti-Communism, a close *de facto* alliance. In recent years, Q. seems to have moderated his inter-Arab policies. Thus he has restored relations, previously often disturbed, with Egypt and Sudan. In the crisis of 1990/91 following Iraq's invasion of Kuwait he has, while opposing the U.S.-led military operations, refrained from taking an extreme position.

Q.'s doctrine is also fervently Islamic — though his revolutionary Islam is unconventional and seen as heretic by many orthodox Muslims, e.g., the Sa'udi establishment, while he has denounced orthodox Sa'udi Arabia and fundamentalist Islamic trends (such as the Muslim Brotherhood). Q. himself presents his nationalist-Islamic populist-revolutionary ideology and practice as a "Third Universal Theory," neither communist nor capitalist, offering a solution to the basic problems of modern mankind. He formulated his doctrine in a *Green Book*, published in 1976, with two more parts in 1978 and 1979.

Q. has been described by his Arab foes (e.g., Egypt's *Sadat), in public as mentally disturbed and a madman, and Western observers have also seen him as suffering from a personality disorder. But others, while conceding that his policies are often erratic and his fervor tends to lead him into wild excesses of extremism, dispute this "diagnosis." Q.'s oil policies, which are hard-line but restrained, certainly show that he is capable, when he so chooses, of cool, rational calculation.

QASSEM, 'ABD-UL-KARIM (1914–63)   Iraqi officer and politician, ruler of Iraq 1958–63. Born in Baghdad of a Sunni-Muslim lower middle-class family, Q. became a professional army officer,

'Abd-ul-Karim Qassem (GPO, Jerusalem)

commissioned in 1938. He served as a battalion commander with the Iraqi expeditionary forces in the Palestine War of 1948. In about 1956, by then a brigade commander, he became head of a group of "Free Officers" plotting to overthrow the monarchy and end Iraq's special relationship with Britain. On July 14, 1958, the group carried out their coup or revolution, led by Q. and his confederate Col. 'Abd-ul-Salam *'Aref, and proclaimed a republic. Contrary to his fellow-conspirators' plans and expectations, Q. declined to form a Revolutionary Command Council, but appointed himself Commander in Chief, Prime Minister and acting Minister of Defense. He did not assume the title of President but in effect became dictator and "Sole Leader" (which was for some time his semiofficial title).

Though there were affinities between Q.'s revolution and that of Egypt's *Nasser, Q. did not wish to formalize closer ties to Egypt (then united with Syria as the UAR) and strove to keep Iraq independent of Nasser's dominating influence. Bitter hostility between the two men ensued. Q.'s associate 'Aref wanted much closer coordination with Egypt (and also nurtured ill-disguised ambitions to become the top leader); he was deposed in Sept. 1958, and later tried and sentenced to death, but reprieved by Q. Nationalist-Nasserist disaffection soon culminated in a mutiny and coup attempt staged in Mar. 1959 in Mosul by Col. Shawwaf. In the suppression of that mutiny Q. was aided by the Communists. This cooperation soured when the Communists began clamoring for a real share in power; when they increasingly infiltrated the administration in the summer of 1959, Q. suppressed them.

In Sept. 1958 Q. enacted a major land reform law. Early in 1960 he tried to revive political parties; but the attempt was halfhearted and failed. Q. became increasingly erratic — to an extent that he was nicknamed "the Mad Dictator." Endowed with an exalted sense of his own mission, he had not created a political base for his rule, and by 1961 he had no remaining supporters among the political groupings and was in serious political difficulties (a rebellion of the Kurds; his attempt of 1961 to realize Iraq's claim to Kuwait by military means was defeated by British and all-Arab intervention; his breach with the oil company).

A combination of civilian *Ba'th* activists and nationalist anti-Communist officers toppled Q. on Feb. 8–9, 1963. Q. and his closest collaborators were shot.

QAVAM AL-SALTANEH, AHMAD (1874–1960) Iranian politician. Prime Minister 1922–23, 1923–24, 1942–43, 1946–47 and July 1952. Q. was private secretary to Shah Muzaffar-ul-Zin, who ruled from 1896 to 1907. He was a Minister many times. As Prime Minister from Feb. 1946, Q. was Iran's chief negotiator with the USSR during the Azerbaijan crisis of 1945–46. In order to appease the Russians and persuade them to withdraw from Iranian Azerbaijan, he included three *Tudeh* (Communist Party) ministers in his cabinet and signed an oil agreement with the USSR; however, this was never ratified by the *Majlis* (Parliament) — and rumor had it that Q. himself had "arranged" that. When in July 1952 Prime Minister *Mossaddeq resigned over the Shah's refusal to appoint him also as Minister of War, Q. was appointed in his stead; but he had to yield, four days later, to violent pro-Mossaddeq demonstrations in Tehran; he resigned and retired from political life.

AL-QAWUQJI, FAWZI (1890–1976) Syrian-Lebanese soldier, guerrilla leader and politician. Born in Tripoli, Lebanon, Q. served in the Ottoman-Turkish army. His early life has remained obscure, but he took part in the Syrian-Druze revolt, 1925–27, and escaped to Iraq. There he taught at the military academy. In Aug. 1936, he recruited several hundred volunteers, mainly from Iraq and Syria, to assist the Arab rebels in Palestine, and entered the country at their head, without being hindered by government troops and police. His force, centered in the Arab-populated areas, mounted a number of attacks on Jewish settlements and communications, but had no major military impact or successes and his efforts to organize a revolutionary army under his own centralized command failed. The *Husseini-led command of the rebellion suspected him of being close to rival factions. When the first stage of the rebellion ended in the Fall of 1936, through the British-arranged mediation of the Arab rulers, the Palestine government permitted Q. to escape across the border with his troops. In 1941, he took part in the Rashid 'Ali *Kilani rebellion in Iraq, and when it was quelled, he fled to Germany, where he headed an Arab Office for Propaganda, the recruitment of volunteers and secret services. After World War II, he returned to Syria.

In Jan. 1948, he again recruited and commanded an army of volunteers — the "Army of Deliverance" (*Jaish al-Inqadh*) — that entered Palestine to assist the Palestine-Arab guerrillas. His force again attacked, unsuccessfully, several Jewish settlements and roads and communications, but had no major impact on the military situation; nor had the officers he sent to various Arab and mixed towns to organize the defense of these towns. He also failed, as in 1936, in his efforts to impose a unified command on all the Arab guerrilla groups. Many units of Q.'s forces were withdrawn from May, when the regular Arab armies took over and ordered volunteer formations to cease separate, independent activities. The remnants of the "Army of Deliverance" were forced by the Israel army in Oct. 1948 to withdraw to South Lebanon.

Q. retired and took no further part in public affairs. Some of his officers later became prominent in Syria's army and politics, particularly in her numerous military coups.

AL-QUDSI, NAZEM (b. 1906) Syrian politician. Prime Minister 1949 and 1950–51, President 1961–63. Born in Aleppo, Q. studied law at the Universities of Beirut and Damascus and took a doctorate in international law in Geneva. After practicing law, 1930–43, he was Minister to the USA, 1944–46. From the late 1940s Q. was one of the leaders of the Aleppo-based People's Party and was several times elected to Parliament; but as his party was frequently in opposition to the Damascus-based main faction, the National Bloc and its successors, he was usually not included in the government team. He became Foreign Minister under Hashem al-*Atassi, after Colonel *Hinnawi's coup, Aug.-Dec. 1949, and in Dec. 1949 was Prime Minister for a few days, until Col. *Shishakli's coup. From June 1950 until Mar. 1951 he was again Premier and Foreign Minister. He was elected by Parliament as its President 1951–53 and 1954–57. When Syria united with Egypt to form the UAR, Q. withdrew from political life. After the dissolution of the UAR in 1961, he was elected President of the Republic. He was deposed in a military coup in Mar. 1962, but when the plotting officers were unable to form a government, entangled in internal dissension and with no program of their own, he resumed the Presidency in Apr. Q. was again deposed in the *Ba'th* coup of Mar. 1963 and retired from public life, residing in Lebanon and France. His son Fawwaz is with the foreign service of the United Arab Emirates.

AL-QUWWATLI, SHUKRI (1886–1967) Syrian politician. President of Syria 1943–49 and 1955–58. Born in Damascus, Q. was active in the Arab nationalist movement from his youth and was one of the leaders of the secret *al-Fatat* society. During World War I, he was arrested by the Turks and, according to some reports, sentenced to death. Under Amir *Feisal's brief rule in Syria, 1918–19, Q. was Governor of Damascus. In the years 1920–31 he was in exile in Egypt and Europe, active on behalf of the Syrian nationalists; the French reportedly condemned him to death *in absentia*. Q. returned to Syria in 1931 and became a leader of the National Bloc, the main faction of the nationalist movement struggling for independence. He was a member of the delegation that negotiated the Franco-Syrian treaty of 1936 (never ratified by France) and became Minister of Defense and Finance in the first nationalist government, 1936–39.

From 1941 Q. was out of Syria. He returned in 1943 as leader of the National Bloc. That same year he was elected President of Syria and led the final struggle for complete independence from France, 1943–46. He was reelected President in 1948, but was deposed in Mar. 1949 by Gen. Husni *Za'im in Syria's first military coup. After spending five years in exile in Egypt, he returned to Syria in 1954, after the fall of Adib *Shishakli. In Aug. 1955, Q. was elected President of Syria for the third time. He promoted closer links with the Soviet Union and actively supported the conclusion of the first cooperation and aid agreements with that country. He also followed a pronounced pro-Egyptian policy,

Shukri al-Quwwatli (Bar-David, Tel Aviv)

and when a union with Egypt was considered, in 1957–58, he vigorously supported the idea — though he was no longer in the confidence of the younger officers working for that aim, and was gradually losing influence. With the consummation of the union and the establishment of the UAR, Q. resigned and proposed Gamal *'Abd-ul-Nasser as President of the new united republic. He then retired.

R

RABIN, YITZHAK (b. 1922)   Israeli military and political leader. Born in Jerusalem to parents who were central figures in the Palestine workers movement. His mother, Rosa Cohen, represented the workers in the Tel Aviv City Council for many years. He studied at the Kadouri Agricultural School before joining the *Palmah*. During the War of Independence he commanded the Harel division, which fought on the Jerusalem and Negev Fronts. He was also the Operations Officer on the Southern Front.

Unlike his friends in the *Palmah*, after the war he continued to serve in the army in high-ranking positions. Between 1953 and 1956 he was head of the Training Department, holding the rank of General. From 1956 to 1959 he was Commander of the Northern Command. From 1959–1964 he was Chief of Operations and in 1961–1964 Deputy Chief of Staff. From 1964 to 1968 he was Chief of Staff. One of his more important successes in this position was building a general staff composed of men with original military thought. Among them were Yisrael Tal, Matti Peled and Ariel *Sharon. He commanded the army during the Six Day War.

After completing his term as Chief of Staff, R. was appointed Ambassador to the United States. He held this position until 1973. He was close to Prime Minister Golda *Meir and maintained contact with her behind the back of Abba *Eban, then Foreign Minister. In 1970 he advised bombing the interior of Egypt, during the height of the War of Attrition.

Upon his return from Washington, he entered political life within the framework of the Labor Party and was put on the list for the Eighth Knesset. The Yom Kippur War and the downfall of the political leaders made him a candidate for key positions. In the government assembled by Golda Meir in March 1974 he was appointed to a minor position — Minister of Labor. However, when this government fell in April 1974 he was the outgoing leaders' candidate for Prime Minister. When he

Yitzhak Rabin (GPO, Jerusalem)

contested Shimon *Peres for this position in the Labor Party's Central Committee, he won 55% of the votes and in June 1974 presented his government before the Knesset. He called this a "government of continuity and change."

R. served as Prime Minister for three years. During his term of office he had a number of successes — the August 1975 agreement with Egypt which paved the way for the peace treaty, income tax reforms (the Ben-Shachar Commission), the rebuilding of the army and the economy after the Yom Kippur War, putting equality before the law into effect, a move which caused a number of prominent personalities, including some in his own party such as Asher Yadlin, to be put on trial. However, his government had a poor image. This was caused by R.'s lack of experience, his introversion and difficulties in communication, his poor relationship with Defense Minister Shimon Peres and the general feeling that the *Mapai* leadership had reached the end of the road.

In April 1977, R. resigned from his party's leadership as a result of the discovery that his wife had a bank account in the United States (illegal under Israeli law). Thus, he also caused his party's downfall in the ensuing elections. In 1984, with the establishment of the National Unity Government, he was appointed Defense Minister and served in this capacity until 1990. Together with Shimon Peres, he has consecutively served as leader of the Labor Party since 1974.

R. is the first, and so far the only, member of the Israel-born generation to become Prime Minister.

RABINOWITZ, YEHOSHUA (1911–79)   Israeli politician. Born in Poland, he immigrated to Palestine in 1934 and began to work for the *Histadrut*, and was active also in the Tel Aviv branch of *Mapai*. In 1955 he was elected to the Tel Aviv City Council and in 1959, following *Mapai's* victory in the municipal elections, became deputy to Mayor Mordechai Namir, with responsibility for the municipality's finances.

In 1969 he was elected Mayor of Tel Aviv. He initiated and supported many activities in the spheres of culture and quality of life, among them the Yarkon Park and the Tel Aviv Museum, and was considered a successful mayor. But in 1974 he lost the elections to the *Likud* candidate Shlomo Lahat.

In March 1974, R. was appointed Minister of Housing in Golda *Meir's last government, and three months later, he became Finance Minister in Yitzhak *Rabin's government. He held that position during a very difficult period, with the aftermath of the Yom Kippur War and the worldwide energy crisis laying a heavy burden on the Israeli economy. Yet he successfully steered the Israeli economy through these crises. He was responsible for a number of important reforms, such as an income tax reform and the institution of a value-added tax. During his term, inflation was pushed down from 55% to 25%, foreign currency reserves increased greatly and a rein was kept on salaries and wages. These successes were properly appreciated by the public only after his term of office.

R. was a Member of Knesset from 1977, after the political right wing rose to power, until his death. During these years he received much public recognition. Some considered him to be the best Finance Minister the State of Israel ever had. Politically, he held moderate views.

RAFSANJANI, 'ALI AKBAR HASHEMI (b. 1934) Iranian politician, President of Iran since 1989. Born in Behraman in the province of Kerman, R. studied Islamic theology in Qom. In the 1950s he joined in *Mossaddeq's struggle against the Shah. Later he became a militant activist in *Khomeini's Islamic resistance and was close to the future leaders of the revolution, such as *Beheshti, *Khamenei, Bahonar. When Khomeini was exiled to Iraq in 1964/65, R. was one of his contacts in Iran. He was arrested and suffered torture at the hands of the *Savak* (secret police).

R. was one of the founders of the Tehran Association of Militant Clergy. In 1978/79 he was appointed to the Council of the Islamic Revolution; he co-founded the new regime's Islamic Republic Party (IRP) and was a member of its central committee.

When the Revolutionary Council took over the government, R. became Minister of the Interior. He organized the referendum on the new constitution, Dec. 1979, and the first presidential elections, Jan. 1980. He resigned from his ministerial post to stand for the *Majlis* (Parliament) in Mar. 1980. He was duly elected and was soon named President of the *Majlis*, wielding considerable influence and power; he was reelected in 1984 and 1988. He was also Khomeini's representative in the Supreme Council of Defense and the Council of the Cultural Revolution. He was a co-founder of an Open Islamic University.

In July 1989, R. was elected President. While completely devoted to the principles and ideals of the Islamic Revolution, R. was considered a realist and a pragmatist. As President he endeavored to preserve unity and maintain the balance between the rival factions, but he opposed and reined in the extremists. Reportedly it was he who persuaded Khomeini to agree to an armistice with Iraq in Aug. 1988.

As President he ruled without a Prime Minister. He dismissed most of the radical ministers. He also endeavored to improve Iran's foreign relations and conduct a pragmatic foreign policy. He tried to enlarge Iran's oil exports, signed economic cooperation agreements with the USSR and expressed a willingness to improve relations with the USA. Extremist-radical factions tried to weaken his position by denouncing his pragmatism in foreign affairs (i.e., by leaking reports on his part in secret arms deals with the USA and Israel); so far he has kept them in check.

R.'s writings (in Persian) include *The Story of Palestine, Revolution or a New Resurrection* and *Champion of the Struggle Against Colonialism.*

RAJA'I, 'ALI (1934–81)   Iranian politician, Prime Minister 1980–81, President July-Aug. 1981. Born in Qasvin to a family of poor shopkeepers, R. left school at the age of 16 and worked as a bricklayer. A few years later he enlisted in the Iranian Air Force as an orderly. R. resumed his studies in the evenings and in 1960 received a degree in mathematics from Tehran Teachers College. In 1963 he joined Mehdi *Bazargan's Iran Liberation Movement and was arrested for anti-Shah activities. In 1973 he was again arrested after planting a bomb outside the Tehran offices of El Al, Israel's airline; he was lamed by secret police torture in prison.

R. was released from prison in 1978 and returned to teaching, joining the Council of the Islamic Teachers' Association, a fundamental Islamic group. During the Islamic Revolution of 1979, he led demonstrations in Tehran. When the Islamic Republic's first government, headed by Bazargan, was joined by the Revolutionary Council, in July 1979, R. was named Minister of Education. In this position, which he held for 10 months, he instituted a program of Islamization in Iran's educational system, banned the teaching of English and other subjects he deemed "non-Islamic," dismissed teachers found unsuited to the Islamic regime and closed universities.

In 1980 R. was elected to the *Majlis* (Parliament). In June he was appointed to the Commission for the Cultural Revolution to purge the universities of non-Islamic tendencies. In Aug. 1980 the *Majlis*, dominated by Islamic fundamentalists, forced President *Bani-Sadr to appoint R. Prime Minister. As Prime Minister he opposed Bani-Sadr's call for the early release of the American hostages seized in Nov. 1979 and advocated putting them on trial. Yet later R. arranged, with Algerian mediation, for the release of the hostages in Jan. 1981. When Iraq invaded Iran in Sept. 1980, R. presented Iran's case to the UN Security Council, claiming the invasion was due to the instigation of the USA (during the session, he removed his shoes, baring his feet to show the members of the Council the scars he had acquired as a political prisoner of the Shah).

After Bani-Sadr was dismissed in June 1981, R. was in July elected President by an overwhelming majority, with the other candidates withdrawing and endorsing his candidacy. A month later he was killed in an explosion in the Prime Minister's office, together with Prime Minister Javad Bahonar.

RAJAVI, MAS'UD (b. 1948)   Iranian politician; leader of the *Mujahedin Khalq* Organization (MKh). Born in Tabas, Khorassan, R. joined MKh, an extreme Islamic reformist revolutionary organization, upon its foundation in the mid-1960s. He was a member of its Central Committee from 1970 and reportedly was sent for military training with the Palestinian Liberation Organization. In 1971, R. was arrested and sentenced to death, but his sentence was commuted and in 1978 he was released.

After the Islamic Revolution of 1979, R. was a candidate for the First Assembly of Experts (1979), but failed to get elected. In Jan. 1980, the Ayatullah *Khomeini disqualified him from running for President of the Islamic Republic of Iran, because R. and the MKh had not supported the new Islamic constitution. R. denounced these elections, and those for Parliament in Mar. 1980, as controlled and manipulated by the Revolutionary Guards, and the MKh's opposition to the Khomeini regime hardened.

In the second round of the Parliamentary elections, in May 1980, Khomeini allowed R. and the MKh to run for office, but denounced them as leftist and anti-Islamic, and prevented their election. R., now the main leader of the MKh, went into exile in Paris and, together with former President *Bani-Sadr, founded a National Resistance Council. Meanwhile, in Iran, the MKh was suppressed and driven underground, and many of its leaders were killed or arrested. R. and the underground MKh moved the center of their activity to Kurdistan and collaborated with Iraq, then at war with Iran. Bani-Sadr opposed the MKh's growing cooperation with Iraq and by 1984 the alliance between him and R. had broken down. In 1986, Iran prevailed upon France to expel R., and he moved his headquarters to Iraq.

RASHID, AAL (House of)   A clan of sheikhs of the Shammar tribe in northern Najd, centering on al-Ha'il. In the late 19th century the R.'s became rivals of the House of *Sa'ud — see there for their struggle. In World War I, the R.'s were loyal to the Ottoman Sultan-Caliph. After the war, the Sa'udis were victorious in renewed fighting, and in the fall of 1921 the R.'s surrendered and renounced all claims to power. After winning out, Ibn Sa'ud followed a policy of reconciliation: he kept the leaders of the R. clan as guests (and hostages?) in his quarters and married one of their daughters (who bore him his son *'Abdullah — Crown Prince and First Deputy Prime Minister since 1982).

RASHID 'ALI see *Kilani, Rashid 'Ali.

RAZMARA, 'ALI (1901–51)   Iranian officer and politician. Prime Minister 1950–51. A graduate of the French Military Academy at Saint Cyr, R. held several military commands in Iran. As Chief of the General Staff, 1946–50, he was responsible for the successful entry of Iranian troops into secessionist Azerbaijan, Dec. 1946. R. was Prime Minister from June 1950 to Mar. 1951. He received strong support from the Shah and tried to initiate land reform measures, but was opposed by the powerful group of landowners in the *Majlis* (Parliament). He was assassinated in Mar. 1951 by a member of the fanatical *Fedayan Islam* because he had stated in Parliament that Iran was not ready for oil nationalization.

REMEZ (original name: Drabkin), **DAVID** (1886–1951) Israeli politician. One of the leaders of the Labor movement. Born in Byelorussia. After studying law at Constantinople (Istanbul), he immigrated to Palestine in 1913. During his first five years in the country he was an agricultural worker, primarily in Zikhron Ya'akov. He was one of the founders of *Ahdut Ha'avodah* and one of the founders and central figures of the *Histadrut*. In the 1920's he headed the *Histadrut*'s Department for Public Works (later *Solel Boneh*). From 1935 to 1945 he was the Secretary-General of the *Histadrut*, responsible for a remarkable expansion of the workers' economy (including the establishment of enterprises like the *Zim* shipping company and the *Hasneh* insurance company). From 1945 to 1948 he headed the National Council of the *Yishuv* (*Va'ad Hale'umi*). He was a prominent leader of the *Yishuv* and of *Mapai*. Inside Mapai he was a leading member of a moderate faction and supported the continuation of relations with the British authorities even after the White Paper of 1939.

With the establishment of the State of Israel he was named Minister of Transport in the Provisional Government. He kept that office until 1950, and from then until his death was Minister of Education and Culture. He was a member of the

Knesset from its establishment until his death.

In addition to his public and political activities, R. was also a linguist and a poet. He coined many new words in the Hebrew language. Two books of his poems were published posthumously.

REZA SHAH (PAHLAVI) (1878–1944)   Shah of Iran 1925–41, first of the Pahlavi dynasty. He was born in Alusht in the province of Mazanderan, the son of an army officer. He joined the army at a young age and quickly moved up the ranks, becoming the commander of the Cossack Brigade. In Feb. 1921, R. — then "R. Khan" — staged a military coup (aided by British officers). He appointed himself army Commander in Chief and Minister of War and in 1923, Prime Minister as well. In 1925 he had Ahmad Shah, last of the Qajar dynasty, deposed by the *Majlis* (Parliament), and in 1925 was himself proclaimed Shah, choosing the name Pahlavi for his dynasty.

After restoring order and suppressing separatist tribes and regions, R. initiated bold Westernizing reforms, inspired, *inter alia*, by *Ataturk's reforms in Turkey. In 1935, he changed the country's name from Persia to Iran. He developed a modern transportation system, completing the Trans-Iranian Railway in 1939, laid the foundation for a modern system of education and established the Iranian Academy for Literature to reduce the influence of foreign languages, especially Arabic. His industrialization efforts were less successful, except for the textile industry. He adopted the French legal system instead of the Islamic system, but recognized Islam as the country's religion, in order not to antagonize the religious establishment.

R.'s reforms did not include a democratic system of government. He did not believe that democratic institutions would work in Iran but rather built a centralized semiauthoritarian government supported by a large army. He admired the effective centralized regime established by the Nazis in Germany.

Impatient in his efforts to modernize and secularize Iranian society, he banned traditional clothing in public, including that of religious leaders, and ordered men and women to wear modern Western-style clothing. These attempts at Westernization led to serious conflicts, especially with the Muslim clergy.

In his foreign policy, R. maneuvered between the USSR and Great Britain, trying to balance relations with both countries while enjoying the royalties paid by the Anglo-Iranian Oil Company. He also strove for a *rapprochement* with Iran's Muslim neighbors and concluded the Saadabad Pact of 1937 with Turkey, Iran and Afghanistan. He was especially close to Germany; German generals helped to train the Iranian army, and the German ambassador became R.'s close adviser. In 1941, Britain and the USSR pressed him to expel the German "technicians," but he refused, insisting on Iran's sovereign right to make her own decisions. As he also refused to let Western war supplies for the USSR pass through Iran, Britain and the USSR invaded and occupied Iran in Aug. 1941 and forced R. to abdicate in favor of his eldest son *Muhammad Reza (Sept. 1941). The Allies exiled R. to Mauritius and then to South Africa, where he died. He is buried in a mosque in Cairo.

RIAD, MAHMUD (b. 1917)   Egyptian diplomat and politician, Foreign Minister 1964–72, Secretary-General of the Arab League 1972–79. A graduate of the Military College (1939) and a career officer, R. represented Egypt on the Egypt-Israel Mixed Armistice Commission from 1949–1952 and headed the Foreign Ministry's Department for Arab Affairs, 1954–55. He was Ambassador to Syria, 1955–58 (until the Egypt-Syria merger of 1958 as the United Arab Republic [UAR]), and Presidential Adviser on foreign affairs during the time of the UAR, 1958–61. In 1961 he became Deputy Head of Egypt's Permanent Mission to the UN, and in 1962 its Head and Ambassador. From 1964 to 1972 he served as Foreign Minister — from 1970 with the rank of Deputy Premier — considered an expert rather than a policy-making leader, but wielding considerable influence. R. was not as close a collaborator and confidant of President *Sadat as he had been under 'Abd-ul-*Nasser, and Sadat removed him from his cabinet in Jan. 1972, appointing him Special Adviser to the President with the rank of Deputy Premier (a nominal honorific rather than an actual function). In June 1972 R. was appointed Secretary-General of the Arab League. He held that post for nearly seven years, standing for the mainstream (as his predecessors had done) and working to keep the League together and mediate between rival blocs. He resigned in Mar.-Apr. 1979, as Egypt's membership of the League was suspended and her relations with the Arab states were severed in the wake of her peace treaty with Israel.

R. did not go along with Sadat's peace policy, largely agreed with the Arab states' denunciation of that policy and himself publicly criticized it

Mahmud Riad (Bar-David, Tel Aviv)

(which was bitterly resented in Egypt); but when the League began preparing steps against Egypt and the latter ceased attending its meetings, in 1978, he was torn by his conflicting loyalties. He absented himself from the Foreign Ministers' Council in Oct. 1978, but attended the summit of Nov. and its follow-up meetings in Mar. 1979. Eventually, he saw no way to resolve his loyalty conflict and continue as League Secretary. Since 1979, R. has not been politically active. He has published his political memoirs (*The Struggle for Peace in the Middle East*, 1981).

RIDA, (MUHAMMAD) RASHID (1865–1935) Muslim-Arab thinker and writer. Born in a village near Tripoli (Lebanon) and educated in traditional Qur'anic and Turkish government schools, R. became an influential Islamic scholar. From 1897 he lived mostly in Egypt, where he was a leading disciple, and to some extent a successor, of the Islamic reformer and scholar Muhammad *'Abduh, continuing and developing 'Abduh's teachings of Islamic revival and reform and of Pan-Islamic unity. In 1898 R. founded a periodical, *al-Manar*, in which he expounded his thought. He wrote many books, some of them collections of his essays in *al-Manar*, including a *Qur'an* commentary and a biography of 'Abduh. He founded

(1912) and directed for two years a seminary for Muslim scholars and missionaries based on his doctrine. R.'s teachings of a revitalized and reformed Islam were in conflict with the official Islamic establishment, but his reformism was deeply conservative. He sought to revive the pristine, simple Islam of the founding fathers (*Salafiyya*), and was thus close to the Hanabali school (*Madhhab*) and to *Wahhabism*. He was suspicious of Western values and thought and antagonistic to their penetration and increasing domination. In the Ottoman period, until the end of World War I, he sought to keep Arab nationalist tendencies within the limits of loyalty to and support of the Ottoman Islamic Caliphate, advocating a decentralization of the empire rather than Arab secession; in 1913 he was among the founders of the Decentralization Party.

Yet, R. was a nationalist, seeing the Arabs as the nation bearing Islam and the core of the Muslim world community (*umma*), and sought to combine the struggle for their national revival with that for an Islamic renaissance and Pan-Islamic unity. He was close to a group of Arab activists, mostly Syrian, who during World War I had talks with British officials in Cairo on future Arab independence. He was named President of the first Syrian-Arab Congress in 1920. In 1921–23 he was a member of a Syrian-Palestinian delegation in Geneva (which had talks and contacts also with Zionist leaders — though R. was deeply suspicious of and hostile to Zionism). In 1925–26 he represented the Syrian nationalists, then rebelling against France, in Cairo and agitated for them. At the same time he continued his activities for Islamic issues — such as the abortive efforts to revive the Caliphate, and took part in the Islamic congresses of Mecca, 1926, and Jerusalem, 1931. In many of his literary and political activities he was closely associated with Shakib *Arsalan — another influential but marginal figure of Arab-Islamic nationalism.

R. was never fully associated with any specific political endeavor, never joined a particular political group or party, and despite the considerable intellectual and moral influence he wielded, he remained a marginal figure in the actual political struggle of Arab nationalism and the emergence of Arab statehood.

AL-RIFA'I, 'ABD-UL-MUN'IM (1917–85) Jordanian diplomat and politician, Prime Minister 1969/70. Born in Safad, Palestine, the brother of Samir al-*Rifa'i. A graduate of the American University of Beirut, R. joined the Jordanian civil and

'Abd-ul-Mun'im al-Rifa'i (Bar-David, Tel Aviv)

diplomatic service in 1938. He was Minister to Iran 1951–53 and to the USA 1953–57, Ambassador to Lebanon 1957–58, Great Britain 1958, the UN 1962–65, the Arab League 1966. In Oct. 1967 he became Minister of State for Foreign Affairs and in Apr. 1968 Foreign Minister. From Mar. to Aug. 1969 R. was Prime Minister, from Aug. 1969 to Apr. 1970 Deputy Premier and Foreign Minister, and from June to Sept. 1970 again Prime Minister. Loyal to the King, but respected by the Palestinian guerrillas, he was expected to achieve a compromise with the latter, after the protracted Jordan-PLO crisis had erupted in June 1970 in serious clashes; but he was unable to work out an effective settlement, and as the confrontation escalated, he was replaced by a military governor in Sept., and did not return to a Cabinet position. In 1973/74 he briefly served as Ambassador to Egypt. R. was named a member of the Senate late in 1974, resigned in 1976, and was reappointed in Jan. 1984; but he did not regain much influence. R. was also a poet and wrote a number of patriotic songs, including the Jordanian national anthem.

AL-RIFA'I, SAMIR (1899? 1901?1–965) Jordanian politician, Prime Minister in the 1940s and 1950s (and briefly in 1963), and many times Minister, a staunch supporter of the Hashemite dynasty, a conservative and a moderate. He took a comparatively moderate attitude towards Israel, too (but King *Abdullah did not take him fully into his confidence concerning his negotiations and agreements with the Zionist leaders). His brother 'Abd-ul-Mun'im *R. was a senior diplomat, a Minister, and Prime Minister in 1969/70.

AL-RIFA'I, ZEID (b. 1936)   Jordanian politician, Prime Minister 1973–76 and 1985–89. The son of Samir *Rifa'i (married to the daughter of Prime Minister and Senate President Bahjat *Talhouni), a confidant of King *Hussein, whose classmate he had been at college. A graduate of American universities (Columbia, Harvard) in political science and international relations, R. joined the diplomatic service and that of the Royal Court, also attending to the family's ramified business interests and landed property (e.g., in the Jordan Valley development zone). He served at Jordan's embassies in Egypt, Lebanon and at the UN, and in 1967 was appointed Private Secretary to the King, promoted in 1969 to be Head of the Royal Cabinet, a post he held during the Jordan-PLO crisis of 1970. In 1970 he was named Ambassador to Britain, until 1972–73. From 1973 to 1976 R. was Prime Minister, also taking the Foreign Affairs portfolio. While the PLO considered him to be hostile, a remarkable improvement in Jordan-Syria relations was ascribed largely to his efforts. From 1985 R. was again Prime Minister — and some commentators again considered a noticeable *rapprochement* with Syria to be a result of his policies. From 1978, R. was a member of the Senate, in 1979–80 and 1984 its Deputy-President.

ROKAH, ISRAEL (1896–1959)   Israeli politician. Born in Jaffa, R. studied electrical engineering in Lausanne, Switzerland. In 1922 he was elected to the Tel Aviv Municipal Council and from then on devoted most of his years to public activity in that city. In 1929 he became Deputy Mayor and Mayor Meir *Dizengoff's aide.

In 1937, after Dizengoff's death, R. was elected Mayor. During his 16-year term, until 1953, the city developed rapidly and became the main and largest city in Palestine (and from 1948 in Israel), its population growing from 130,000 to 350,000. He was known as a harsh, honest mayor, involved in every aspect of the city's life. As one of the leaders of the *Yishuv*, he was among those arrested on the "Black Sabbath" in 1946, and spent four months at the Latrun detention camp.

R. was one of the heads of the conservative right and a prominent leader of the General Zionists. In 1949 he was elected to the Knesset on their list and served continuously until his death. From 1952 to 1955 he was Minister of the Interior in the *Ben Gurion and *Sharett governments. His final years were years of political decline. After the General Zionists resigned from the government, 1955, he

was not reelected as Mayor of Tel Aviv, and his stature within his party also diminished.

ROSEN (original name: Rosenbluth), **PINHAS** (1887–1978)   Israeli jurist and political leader. Born in Germany, R. was one of the founders of the Zionist youth movement *Blau-Weiss* and a leader of the Zionist Federation in Germany. From 1926 to 1931 he was a member of the Zionist Executive in London and head of its Organization Department. In 1931 he immigrated to Palestine, opened a law office and was active in the Organization of Immigrants from Germany. During the 1940's he founded and headed the *Aliyah Hadashah* (New Immigration) Party, speaking for new immigrants, mainly from Germany.

After the establishment of the State of Israel he headed a new party — the centrist, moderate Progressive Party. He was its representative in the Provisional Government, in which he served as Minister of Justice. He was elected to the First Knesset and served as a Member of Knesset until 1968. He was Minister of Justice (with the exception of 1951–52) until 1961 and made an important contribution to the formation and independence of the legal system. His honesty and lack of favoritism were admired. His political views were moderate. When there was a conflict between *Ben Gurion and Moshe *Sharett, he backed the latter. In 1960 he headed a Ministerial committee — "the Committee of Seven" — which exonerated Pinhas *Lavon from having ordered the Secret Service operation in Egypt that was discovered and caused the Lavon Affair. After Ben Gurion reversed the Committee's findings, a split occured between the two which was never bridged.

In 1961 his party, the Progressives, merged with the General Zionists as the Liberal Party and he became its President. When that party and the *Herut* party in 1965 set up the right-wing *Gahal* block, R. seceded and became President of an Independent Liberal Party. He retired in 1968. In 1973 he was awarded the Israel Prize for his contribution in shaping the legal system.

RUPPIN, ARTHUR (1876–1943)   Architect of Zionist settlement in the Land of Israel. Born in East Prussia, R. studied law and economics at the University of Berlin. In 1907, when the Zionist Organization began practical work in Palestine, he agreed to manage its office in Jaffa. From then until his death he was the central figure in planning and establishing agricultural settlements in *Eretz*

Yisrael. In his first years he founded "national farms" in Kinneret, Hulda and Ben-Shemen, where Jewish workers were trained for agricultural work, and founded the *Hahsharat Hayishuv* Company which played a central role in purchasing land. Though he was not a member of the labor movement he understood the potential of collective settlement and assisted in founding the first *kvutzot* in Degania and Kinneret. He also assisted urban settlement, arranged for loans to buy the land upon which Tel Aviv, the "first Hebrew city," was established, and aided in building modern Jewish neighborhoods in Jerusalem and in Haifa.

During the First World War he was exiled to Istanbul. There, with the assistance of the German consulate, he led efforts to assist the Jews of Palestine suffering famine, persecution and exile by the Ottoman rulers. In 1919 he returned to Palestine and was chosen as head of the Zionist Organization's Settlement Department. During the early 1920s he supported the purchase of land in the Jezreel Valley — against the wish of the heads of the the Jewish National Fund who considered this purchase financially unsound — and aided pioneering settlements in the valley. In 1927 he resigned in protest against the policy of the Zionist Organization, which for budgetary reasons opposed the development of further settlements. In 1929 he returned to his post, and during the 1930s guided the settlement of immigrants from Germany (including a new form of settlement: the *Moshav Shitufi*, a combination of small-holder cooperative and collective). From 1933 he was a member of the Jewish Agency Executive.

R. was also a scientist and theoretician. He founded and headed the Institute for Economic Research of the Jewish Agency, and lectured on the sociology of the Jewish people at the Hebrew University in Jerusalem. He also published books and articles on settlement, sociology, economics and demography. Politically, he opposed the Zionist leadership on the Jewish-Arab issue: he was a co-founder of *Brit Shalom*, which advocated far-reaching concessions to the Arabs and a binational state; but resigned in 1929 after the Arab riots.

R., who was not a member of a political party, was highly respected both for his activities and his noble personality. He requested to be buried in Degania, the "mother of the *kvutzot*." His memoirs, *Chapters of my Life*, were published in 1968.

RUTENBERG, PINHAS (1879—*1942*) *A leader of the Yishuv* during the Mandate, founder of the Palestine Electric Company. Born in the Ukraine, R. graduated from the Technological Institute of St. Petersburg (Leningrad). He was active in the 1905 revolution as one of the leaders of the march to the Czar's palace, which ended in bloodshed. After the revolution he moved to Italy where he worked as a water engineer and invented a new hydroelectric system. There he also began to evince an interest in Jewish affairs. During the First World War he cooperated with Ze'ev *Jabotinsky in establishing Jewish Battalions within the Allied armies. In February 1917, after the Menshevik revolution, he returned to Russia and was appointed Deputy Governor of St. Petersburg. After the Bolshevik October revolution he was arrested. In 1919 he was released and immigrated to Palestine.

In Palestine he began researching water sources in preparation for a plant generating electric power from the waters of the Jordan River. In 1923 he established the Palestine Electric Company, which established the first power plants (thermal) in Tel Aviv, Haifa and Tiberias and received a concession, finalized in 1926, for a plant to use the waters of the Jordan and the Yarmukh to generate electricity. The plant, located in Naharayim at the confluence of the two rivers, was built from 1928 to 1932 and all of Palestine, with the exception of Jerusalem, was connected to a central electrical network.

R. was not a member of any political party. This impartiality and the great prestige he enjoyed as the founder of the Naharayim power plant, earned him the respect of many sectors in the *Yishuv*. After the riots of 1929 he headed the *Va'ad Leumi* for a short time. In 1933 he tried to mediate between Jabotinsky and *Ben Gurion, to lessen the tension created between the two largest political camps in the *Yishuv* by the murder of *Arlozoroff. During the Arab rebellion of 1936–1939 he was one of five Jewish leaders who attempted (in vain) to create a dialogue with Arab leaders. In 1939 he was again co-opted into the *Va'ad Leumi* and made its president, but soon had to retire due to ill health.

S

SA'ADEH, ANTOUN(1902–49)   Lebanese politician. Son of a Christian, Greek-Orthodox doctor who emigrated to Brazil, S. was brought up there. He returned to Lebanon in 1930 and taught German at the American University of Beirut. In the 1930s, he propounded a Syrian nationalism, based on the idea of a specifically Syrian nation — as against both Pan-Arab aspirations to all-Arab unity (and Lebanon's integration in its framework) and a separate Lebanese national entity as propounded by one wing of Christian-Lebanese mainstream opinion — and proposed the creation of a "Greater Syria." He was strongly influenced by German Fascism. He called for the immediate independence of Syria-Lebanon and the eviction of the French. In 1932, he founded a "Syrian Nationalist Party" (*al-Hizb al-Suri al-Qawmi*). His party was banned and S. was harassed by the authorities, until he left in the late 1930s — reportedly first to Italy and Germany and then to South America. He returned to Lebanon, now independent, in 1947 and resumed his political activity, adding the word "Social" (*al-Ijtima'i*) to the name of his party; but he was kept under surveillance and arrested on several occasions. After Husni *Za'im's coup in Syria, 1949, S. hoped for his support, but was disappointed. In June 1949, clashes erupted between his party and the Christian Phalanges in what was described as a coup attempt by S. He escaped to Syria, but he was extradited to Lebanon, sentenced to death by a summary military court and executed in July. His SSNP was suppressed and many of his associates were imprisoned. In revenge for his execution, his men in July 1951 assassinated Riyad al-*Sulh, who had been Prime Minister in 1949. The SSNP, which remained on the margins of Lebanese politics, later joined the "leftist," pro-Syrian camp in the civil war since the late 1970s.

AL-SABAH   The ruling dynasty of Kuwait since 1756, the ruler using the title *Sheikh*, or in recent decades *Amir*. The dynasty is divided into two branches, the Jaber S. and Salem S. branches, alternating since 1915 as Heads of State. The Jaber branch ruled 1915–16 (Sheikh Jaber), 1921–50 (Sheikh Ahmad ibn Jaber), and since 1978 (Sheikh Jaber ibn 'Ahmad), the Salem branch — 1916–21 (Sheikh Salem) and 1950–77 ('Abdullah ibn Salem 1950–65, Sabah ibn Salem 1965–77). Since 1965 the head of the branch not holding the position of *Amir* has served as Crown Prince and Prime Minister (Jaber ibn Ahmad 1967–77, Sa'ad ibn 'Abdullah since 1977). Other members of the dynasty hold the main ministerial and other executive positions (e.g., Salem ibn Sabah — Defense and since 1988 Interior Minister; Nawwaf ibn Ahmad — Interior and since 1988 Defense Minister; Sabah ibn Ahmad — Foreign Minister since 1963, and also Deputy Prime Minister since 1978).

SABRI, 'ALI (1920–91)   Egyptian officer and politician, Prime Minister 1962–65, Vice-President 1965–67. S. was trained as a professional officer, graduating in 1939 from the Military Academy. He was not among the ten founding members of the "Free Officers" group that staged the coup d'etat of July 1952, but was close to them and reportedly acted as their liaison to the U.S. Embassy before and during the coup. He began his climb to power as Director of President 'Abd-ul-*Nasser's Office. When Egypt merged with Syria in 1958 to form the UAR, S. became Minister for Presidential Affairs in the UAR government. When the UAR was dissolved in 1961 he kept this post in the Egyptian government. As he had become one of President Nasser's closest associates, he was appointed Prime Minister in Sept. 1962, heading the government until Oct. 1965; as Prime Minister he was also a member of the Presidential Council named in 1962. From 1965, when he had to give up the Premiership, until 1967, he was one of the Vice-Presidents. In 1967–68 he served briefly as Deputy Prime Minister and Minister of Local Government.

'Ali Sabri (Bar-David, Tel Aviv)

From 1965 S. held, concurrently with his Vice-Presidency, the chairmanship of the Arab Socialist Union, Egypt's single party and the mass basis of her regime. He endeavored to reorganize that party into cadres, on the Soviet model, and turn it into an effective mass organization — and a base for his own climb to power. In the 1960s, S. headed the left wing of Egypt's ruling junta — advocating ever closer relations with the Soviet Union and a speedier and more intense advance towards state socialism, the expansion of the state sector of the economy, more vigorous nationalizations and a stricter regime. As he came to be considered "Moscow's man," his position in the leadership team was seen as an index of the regime's shifting relations with the USSR. In June 1967 he was credited with the organization of the mass demonstrations that persuaded Nasser to withdraw his resignation. After 1967, however, when Nasser felt compelled to moderate his policies in the internal, inter-Arab and international arenas, S.'s influence declined. He remained, except for a few months in 1967–68, without a government position, and in 1969 he was dismissed as chairman of the ASU — apparently both because of his leftist radical tendencies and because of his power ambitions.

After Nasser's death, in Sept. 1970, he was seen by many as a leading candidate for the succession — the one preferred by the Soviet Union. He lost out to *Sadat, but was included in the new government as one of Sadat's two Vice-Presidents. However, a power struggle continued behind the scenes, and in May 1971 he was accused, together with a group of other leaders and administrators from Nasser's days, of plotting, treason, and abuse of power in his pre-1970 positions. He was dismissed from all government and party posts and put on trial. In Dec. 1971 he was sentenced to death, but the sentence was commuted to life imprisonment. He was pardoned and released by Sadat in May 1981 but has not resumed political or public activity.

AL-SADAT, (MUHAMMAD) ANWAR (1918–81) Egyptian officer and statesman. President of Egypt 1970–81. Born in Mit Abu'l-Kom in the Delta province of Minufiyya into a peasant family (his father was a clerk with the army, his mother — Sudanese), S. graduated from the Military Academy in 1938 and became a professional officer. A keen nationalist of conservative Islamic tendency, he was close to, and for some time a member of, the Muslim Brotherhood and the right-wing, pro-Fascist *Misr al-Fata* (Young Egypt) party. In 1941–42 he was active in a pro-German underground group, and in Oct. 1942 he was expelled from the army. He was detained for about two years: in 1944 he escaped and went underground until the detention order was lifted in 1945. He was arrested in 1946 and charged with complicity in the murder of the former Finance Minister Amin Osman ('Uthman) and also suspected of involvement in an attempt to assassinate ex-Premier al-*Nahhas. In prison for over two years during the trial, he was acquitted in Dec. 1948. He then worked as a journalist, but in Jan. 1950 he was readmitted to the army.

Restored to his officer's rank and position, S. soon joined the secret group of "Free Officers" headed by Gamal *'Abd-ul-Nasser and took part — then a Lieutenant-Colonel — in that group's coup of July 1952. He became a member of the 12-man Revolutionary Council heading the new regime and remained, in various capacities, one of the leaders of the new team throughout the years of its rule — though he held no ministerial positions except for one term as Minister of State, 1954–56. In the first years of the new regime, S. served as liaison with the Muslim Brotherhood and right-wing groups. After the Brotherhood was banned and suppressed (1954) and the regime began turning to the left, he was no longer in Nasser's inner circle (his appointment as Minister of State was a token appointment with no real power). For some time he was editor of the regime's daily, *al-Gumhuriyya*. S. was a member of the Council of the regime's single party and served as its Secretary-General from 1957; this post did not carry much influence, particularly after Egypt's merger with Syria as the UAR (1958–61). From 1959 to 1969 S. was chairman of the National Assembly, including one year, 1960–61, of that of the UAR. As he was, among the "Free Officers," the closest to Islamic tendencies, he was sent on several missions to Muslim countries and represented Egypt at Islamic conferences. He was also Egypt's chief liaison with Yemen.

In Dec. 1969 S. was appointed Vice-President of Egypt, as Nasser's only deputy — an appointment seen as a step to balance rightist and leftist tendencies within the ruling team and particularly to check the advance of the left, led by the power-hungry 'Ali *Sabri. On Nasser's death in Sept. 1970, S. was chosen as President of Egypt, and also of the single party, the Arab Socialist Union (ASU); he was duly elected, as the only candidate, in Oct. 1970. His selection by the ruling team was apparently intended to avoid a struggle for the succession by rightist and leftist candidates — it was assumed: Zakariyya *Muhyi-ul-Din vs. 'Ali Sabri — and S. himself was seen as a rather colorless compromise candidate, a weak *primus inter pares*. However, he soon formed his own policies and established his personal leadership with a firm grip on power. In May 1971 he suppressed a leftist-Nasserist plot and eliminated his rivals.

Firmly in power, S. began changing Egypt's regime and policies. At first he did so cautiously and without admitting that he was abandoning at least some of the principles of Nasserism; he insisted that his measures were merely a "corrective revolution," restoring the true principles of the 1952 revolution. Gradually, and mainly from 1973, he introduced a liberalization of the economic regime. This liberalization was accompanied by a gradual change in foreign policies. He practiced moderation in inter-Arab affairs, abandoning attempts to impose Egyptian domination on other Arab states and moving closer to the moderate ones, especially Sa'udi Arabia. He went along with the plan for a "Federation of Arab Republics" (FAR), with Libya and Syria — a scheme that did

not really get off the ground — but resisted Libyan pressure for a full merger of Egypt and Libya (to which he had at first formally agreed), putting up with the resulting deterioration in Egypt's relations with Libya.

S.'s main policy change concerned relations with the great powers. He initiated a significant *rapprochement* with the USA and sought closer relations with Western Europe and the EEC. And he cut back Egypt's alliance with the USSR (which had never cultivated S. and would probably have preferred in 1970 to see 'Ali Sabri elected). In 1971 he still hosted President Podgorny and signed a Treaty of Friendship with the Soviet Union; but this was seen by observers as an effort to shore up crumbling relations rather than a sign of mutual confidence. S. visited Moscow in Oct. 1971 and Feb. 1972 to settle differences. But in July 1972 he unilaterally terminated the services of an estimated 15–20,000 Soviet experts, including all the military ones. He later explained that the main reason for that drastic step was the Russians' unwillingness to give him a free hand and unlimited support in his preparations for war against Israel and to remove their involvement in, or even control of, Egyptian decision-making. But later in 1972–73 relations

Anwar al-Sadat (Bar-David, Tel Aviv)

were improved, and the USSR resumed full military aid towards and during the war of 1973.

S.'s main concern, indeed, was with the continuing Israeli occupation of Sinai and other Arab territories since 1967 — a matter of priority and national honor. He was ready to move towards peace negotiations — as he told UN envoy Jarring in Feb. 1971 and U.S. representatives many times; but his precondition was Israel's total withdrawal to the pre-1967 lines and a "just settlement" of the refugee problem. As Israel could not accept these conditions, S. resolved that the occupation could be ended and Egyptian territory restored only by military action, and from 1971–72 prepared for war. In military terms the October War of 1973 was not an Egyptian victory; but in a wider political perspective, and in Egyptian and Arab perception, it was a great achievement: Egyptian forces had won battles, displayed impressive capabilities of military planning and leadership and thus restored their pride and honor; and they had forcibly recovered part of occupied Sinai, including the vital eastern shore of the Suez Canal, and broken the deadlock. This was S.'s victory, and his prestige was at its peak, both in Egypt and in the Arab countries.

S. now sought to resume, on the basis of the new situation created, negotiations with Israel, and he did so increasingly and almost exclusively with U.S. mediation. However, after two major Interim Agreements reached in 1974 and 1975 following protracted, U.S.-mediated negotiations, no further progress was achieved. The deadlock was broken in Nov. 1977 by S.'s dramatic surprise visit to Israel (which had in fact been prepared by secret diplomatic contacts). In his meetings with Israeli leaders and his public address to a special meeting of the Knesset, S. offered complete peace and normal relations in return for a total withdrawal from all territories occupied in 1967 and an agreed, negotiated solution to the problem of the Palestine Arabs. In substance, his proposals were thus not different from previous positions held by Egypt and other moderate Arab states. His great achievement was the psychological breakthrough of meeting the "enemy" face-to-face and talking to him, spelling out what before had at best been implied: a preparedness to coexist in peace with Israel once she agreed to Arab demands and conditions, and his willingness to negotiate for Egypt alone, without waiting for an all-Arab consensus. He made it clear, though, that he would not conclude a *separate* peace with Israel but would consider an eventual agreement as a first step towards a general Arab-Israel settlement.

The negotiations that followed — protracted and difficult, conducted by S. himself with Israel Premier *Begin, with U.S. President Carter playing a major mediatory role — yielded the Camp David Agreements of Sept. 1978 and the Egypt-Israel Peace Treaty of Mar. 1979. The official normalization of relations went into effect in Jan. 1980 and ambassadors were exchanged in Feb.; S. did not live to see the completion of Israel's withdrawal in Apr. 1982. He had received the Nobel Prize, jointly with Begin, in Dec. 1978 (after the Camp David Agreements, before the Peace Treaty), as well as several European and American medals and prizes, some of them posthumously. S.'s relations with Israel's leaders soon cooled and went through several crises. Negotiations on an autonomous regime for the Palestinian Arabs, as the first stage towards an agreed solution of their problem, soon stalled and were discontinued. Israel's formal annexation of East Jerusalem, in July 1980, was resented by S. So were her air raid on an Iraqi nuclear reactor, in June 1981, and several raids on PLO positions in Lebanon. (The cooling-off, or freezing, of Egypt-Israel relations deepened after S.'s death, but the peace established by S. held fast).

S.'s moves towards peace with Israel led the Arab world to denounce and ostracize Egypt, and him personally. S. bore this severance of Egypt from the Arab family of nations — which was never complete, relations in many fields continuing unofficially — and the personal defamation accompanying it with angry disappointment and a show of pride. He refused not only to abrogate his agreements with Israel, but declined to actively seek the restoration of Egypt to her natural place within the Arab world, and at its head, asserting that since the Arab states had severed relations it was they, not Egypt, that should seek a reconciliation (as they did in 1987 — long after his death).

After 1979, S. continued enhancing close relations with the USA and encouraged her to play a crucial, near-exclusive, mediating role in the peace process. During his rule Egypt also became increasingly dependent on U.S. aid. S. received U.S. Presidents Nixon and Carter in Egypt and himself visited the U.S. in Oct. 1975 and several times later. In 1979–80 he became a partner to wider U.S. strategy plans and agreed to provide low-profile facilities for a planned U.S. "Rapid Deployment Force" (that was not fully implemented). His relations with the USSR declined. In

1976 S. abrogated the Treaty of Friendship. In 1977 he recalled Egypt's Ambassador, leaving her represented at a lower level; later he expelled several Soviet diplomats, and in Sept. 1981 requested the withdrawal of the Soviet Ambassador and the closure of the Military Attache's office.

At home S. continued his policy of liberalization and de-Nasserization. He gradually dismantled the single-party system, allowing in 1975 the formation of "platforms," i.e., organized factions, within the ASU, and late in 1976 their transformation into full-fledged parties. In 1978 he formed a party of his own, the National Democratic Party, which soon became the government party and absorbed the ASU. He took measures against the Communists and supported a growing emphasis on Egypt's Islamic character while curbing, and later suppressing, Islamic extremist organizations (it was one of these groups that assassinated S. in Oct. 1981). In the executive, no further major upheavals occurred. S. served as his own Prime Minister in 1973–74 and thereafter appointed loyal second-rank associates to that post. He dismissed Vice-President al-*Shafe'i in 1975 and replaced him with the commander of the air force, Husni *Mubarak. He changed his Defense Minister (considered the most important man after the President) several times. S. himself was reelected President in 1976, with no rival candidate.

The main issue that clouded S.'s last years — and his record and memory — was the complex of Egypt's economic and social problems, the inability of his liberalization to fulfill the high-pitched expectations pinned on it and solve the country's basic problems. The growing disappointment with S.'s policies was aggravated by their negative side effects: an increasing relapse into the inequalities of a free enterprise society, the emergence of a new class of profiteers flaunting their wealth in visible contrast to the poverty of large parts of the population, and a great deal of spreading corruption and nepotism. S. and his policies, both socioeconomic and concerning Israel, were denounced by the Communists and the left, the Nasserists, the extreme Islamists, and many intellectuals. S. himself, aware of his inability to solve the socioeconomic problems facing Egypt, turned mainly to foreign affairs. In the latter years of his Presidency he tightened his regime, taking harsher measures against his adversaries on the Communist and Nasserist left and the Islamic right, including an extensive purge in Sept. 1981.

The impression was that S.'s charisma, his pater-nalistic leadership and his ebullient command of popular support were declining during his last years. He had also gradually abandoned the simple life-style that had made him popular and adopted a more imperial style of grandeur. Ramified activities of his family were disliked. His wife, Jihan, of partly English origin, whom he had married in 1951 after divorcing his first wife, seemed personally popular — but her increasing involvement in active public life was not.

S. was murdered in Oct. 1981, during a parade on the anniversary of the October War of 1973, by Islamic extremists — and there were few signs of genuine mourning. His memory as a leader and a statesman who had shaped Egypt's history seems to be dimmed and not very actively cultivated.

S. wrote a book on the revolution of 1952, with autobiographical features (*Revolt on the Nile*, 1957), and an autobiography (*In Search of Identity*, 1977–78).

SADEH (original name: Landoberg), **YITZHAK** (1890–1952)   Israeli military leader, among the founders and commanders of the *Haganah*, with much influence on the development of its defense doctrine. Born in Lublin, Poland (then Russia), to a rabbinical family, S. served in the Russian army in the First World War, winning much praise for his courage and receiving a medal of valor. After the October revolution he was a commander in the Red Army.

After his demobilization he began studying philosophy. There he met Yosef *Trumpeldor in the Crimea and assisted him in forming Hehalutz. In 1920 S. immigrated to Palestine and was one of the founders and leaders of the *Gdud Ha'avodah* ("Work Brigade"). During the 1921 Arab riots he took part in defending the Jews of Jerusalem and from then on devoted most of his time and energy to matters of defense and security. After the *Gdud Ha'avodah* was disbanded, he worked in the electric plant at Naharayim and the Atlit quarry.

During the 1936–1939 Arab rebellion he played a central role in turning the *Haganah* from a local defense group within the settlements into an active country-wide organization. He initiated many innovations in the fighting doctrine of the *Haganah* and formed the *Plugot Hasadeh* (field squads) and *Plugot Meyuhadot* (special squads) which for the first time initiated active steps against the Arab guerrilla bands. He was among the founders of the *Palmah*, the regular force and elite unit of the *Haganah*, and was its first commander (1941–1945).

From 1945 to 1947 he was acting Chief of Staff of the *Haganah*. As commander of the *Palmah*, S. was an admired model for his soldiers and trained a generation of commanders, such as Yigal *Allon and Moshe *Dayan.

During the 1948 War of Independence S. established the first armored brigade of the IDF and commanded it during some of the decisive battles, such as the capture of Lydda, Ramle and the country's airport and the battle to open the road to the Negev. After the war he was removed from the army by David *Ben Gurion — for political reasons. During his later years he was an active member of the *Mapam* Party.

AL-SADR, MUSSA (1928–78?)   Lebanese-Iranian Shi'i religious and political leader. Born in Iran to a family reportedly of Lebanese origin, S. received both a traditional Islamic and a secular education, graduating from Tehran University in 1956. In 1959 he moved to Tyre, Lebanon, where he began mobilizing the Shi'i population with the aim of reducing the political influence of both the traditional leadership and the leftist parties. In 1967 he established, for the first time in the modern history of Syria-Lebanon, a Supreme Islamic-Shi'i Council. These activities won him wide support among the rank and file of Lebanon's Shi'is, and he was often referred to as Imam. Politically, S. supported the integrity of the Lebanese state and its basic structure, but he demanded modifications to accommodate the growing needs of the Shi'i community and raise its status. He was pro-Syrian and anti-PLO. In the early 1970s he founded and led a movement for the advancement and defense of the Shi'i community, originally conceived as mainly social and nonpolitical and called "the Disinherited" (*al-Mahrumin*). In the mid-1970s this movement grew increasingly political and turned into the Shi'i *al-Amal* organization, of which S. became the first and main leader.

In Aug. 1978 S. disappeared while on a mission in Libya. The Libyans claim that he departed for Italy, but Lebanese Shi'is do not believe that and are convinced that S. was either detained (and is still imprisoned in Libya?) or killed by the Libyans. His disappearance has caused a grave crisis between Libya and Lebanon in general, and the Lebanese Shi'is in particular. The latter venerate S.'s memory, regarding him as a martyr.

AL-SADR, SHEIKH AL-SAYYID MUHAMMAD (1882? 1887?–1958)   Iraqi Shi'i-Islamic dignitary

and politician. Of a family claiming descent from the Prophet Muhammad (hence the title *al-Sayyid*) and the son of the head of the Shi'i savants in Iraq (*Kabir al-'Ulama'*), S. received a traditional Islamic education. On the eve of World War I he was active in the Arab national movement. In 1919/20 he founded a nationalist party, the National Guard (*al-Haras al-Watani*), and was among the organizers of the nationalist rebellion against British rule. He escaped arrest by fleeing to Najd, but returned after Amir *Feisal became King. As he continued agitating against the British Mandate and the Anglo-Iraqi treaties concluded to replace it, he again went into exile in Persia, returning after a few years. He was appointed a member of the Senate and in the 1940s became its President. He also headed the Regency Council several times during absences of the Regent *'Abd-ul-Ilah. A right-wing conservative, he opposed the alternating teams heading Iraq's pro-British governments, but was considered a moderate. When Saleh *Jabr's government fell in Jan. 1948, in the crisis over the abortive Portsmouth Treaty, considered excessively pro-British, S. was called to form a new government which abrogated that treaty — the second Shi'i ever to become Prime Minister. He headed that government for five months and did not return to executive office afterwards. However, he served again as President of the Senate from Jan. 1953 to Dec. 1955.

AL-SA'ID, AMINA (b. 1914)   Egyptian novelist, journalist and translator. Born in Cairo, S. graduated from Cairo University in English literature (1953). In 1954 she became the Editor in Chief of the women's magazine *Hawa'* ("Eve"). She was active in the Arab women's movement, joined the "Women's Union" founded by the leading feminist Huda Sha'rawi (1879–1947), and established its magazine *al-Misriyya*. Later on she joined the editorial board of *al-Hilal*, a leading literary magazine, and from 1976 chaired the board of the *al-Hilal* publishing house. S. also served as Secretary of the Council of the Egyptian Journalists' Union.

S'AID, W. EDWARD (b. 1945?)   American-Palestinian-Arab scholar, literary critic and politician. Born in Jerusalem to a Christian family, S. studied English literature in Palestine, Egypt, and the USA, where he settled. He has become very active speaking for the Palestinian case in the West. S. is identified with the Palestine Liberation Organization (PLO), a member of the Palestine National

Council and is its spokesman in the USA. He was Visiting Professor in Comparative Literature at Harvard and Fellow of the Center for Advanced Study in Behavioral Sciences at Stanford and serves as Parr Professor of English and Comparative Literature at Columbia University and Coeditor of *MERIP (Middle East Report)*, and Music Editor for the *Nation*. He is the author of many books such as *Orientalism; Joseph Conrad; The Fiction of Autobiograhy; Beginnings; Intention and Method; The Question of Palestine; The Last Sky; Culture and Imperialism*. In some of his books — especially *Orientalism* — he strongly criticized Western Orientalists, denouncing them as instruments of Western imperialism who denigrate and falsify Oriental, and particularly Arab, history and civilization.

AL-SA'ID, NURI (1888–1958)   Iraqi officer and politician, the most prominent of a group of pro-*Hashemite and pro-British Iraqi leaders, many times Prime Minister. Born in Baghdad to a Muslim-Sunni family of mixed Arab-Kurdish descent, S. graduated from the Istanbul Military Academy and became an officer in the Ottoman army. Active, but not prominent, in pre-World War I Arab nationalist associations, S. deserted from the Ottoman army during World War I, joined Sharif *Hussein's Arab revolt in 1916 and became Chief of Staff in Amir *Feisal's army (commanded by his brother-in-law, Ja'far al-'Askari). He remained attached to Feisal after the war and became the first Chief of Staff of the Iraqi army in 1921. He was Minister of Defense 1922–24 and 1926–28. In 1930 he became Prime Minister for the first time, founding a party — *al-'Ahd* ("the Covenant") — to support him in Parliament. He negotiated the treaty of 1930 with Britain which terminated the Mandate. S. was Prime Minister 1930–32, 1939–40, 1941–44, 1946–47, 1949, 1950–52, 1954–57, 1958, heading 14 governments, and often held other or additional ministerial offices, particularly Foreign or Defense Minister. After the defeat of the Rashid 'Ali *Kilani movement in 1941, S. was Iraq's leading statesman, whether in or out of office, and the chief representative of the Hashemite establishment. In Feb. 1958 he became Prime Minister of the short-lived "Arab Federation" of Iraq and Jordan. S. was murdered in Baghdad during the coup of July 1958.

S. believed in the need for a firm alliance with Britain and loyally supported the Hashemite dynasty — though in the late 1930s he was allied for some time with the anti-British and anti-Hashemite junta of officers ruling Iraq behind the scene, and apparently tried to insure himself by undercover contacts with Germany in 1940. He feared and hated communism and distrusted the USSR. In Arab affairs he was keenly conscious of Iraq's age-old rivalry with Egypt. He favored a Federation of the Fertile Crescent under Iraqi leadership (with a measure of automony for the Jews of Palestine and the Christians of Lebanon); late in 1942 he submitted a scheme along these lines to the British and the Arab states — but it met with strong Arab opposition, particulary Egyptian, and he did not pursue it. In domestic affairs S. promoted administrative efficiency and economic planning. He was a conservative, even an autocrat, and did not believe that parliamentary democracy was a suitable form of government for Iraq. In his heyday Iraq was in effect a police state — though his regime seems mild and rational in the light of more recent developments. During his last years S. was not in tune with the social and political forces sweeping the Arab world.

SAKA, HASAN (1885–1960)   Turkish politician, Prime Minister 1947–49. Born in Trabzon, S. graduated from the School of Public Service (*Mulkiye*) and studied economics and finance in Paris. He was a deputy in the last Ottoman parliament and was elected in 1920 to the first Grand National Assembly. He served in several ministerial posts and was Foreign Minister from 1943 to 1947. In Sept. 1947 he took over from Recep *Peker as Premier and held office until Jan. 1949.

SALAM, SA'EB (b. 1905)   Lebanese politician. Born into a influential Muslim-Sunni family in Beirut, and a graduate of the American University of Beirut and the London School of Economics, S. was a leader of the conservative-moderate bloc of Beirut Sunnis and served several times as Prime Minister, alternating with other leaders of the same bloc (al-*Sulh, 'Abdullah al-*Yafi, et al). He was also an industrialist and a landowner and had ramified business interests (he was cofounder, for instance, of Middle East Airlines in 1943–45). S. was a member of all Parliaments since 1943 except that of 1957–60 (when he was defeated by the supporters of Camille *Chamoun and his government). He was Minister of the Interior in 1946 and Prime Minister briefly in 1952 and again for a few months in 1953. In 1956 he was Minister of State and Deputy Premier, but resigned in Nov. 1956, together with Premier Yafi, in protest against President Chamoun's pro-Western policy, becoming one of the leaders of the Nasserist opposition (it was then that he was defeated in the elections). In the civil war of 1958 he backed the Nasserists/Muslims, but as a prominent moderate he was active in reconciliation efforts. In 1960–61 he again became Prime Minister. Later, in the 1960s, he led the Beirut bloc of Muslim politicians who opposed Premier *Karameh of Tripoli. From Oct. 1970 to Apr. 1973 he again headed the Government. Whenever Prime Minister, he usually kept the Ministry of Interior for himself. Throughout these years he did not establish a party of his own, nor did he permanently join any other political formation, though the Beirut Muslim-Sunni group he headed (alternating with, and rivalling, Yafi) enjoyed much influence in Parliament and in the shifting factional struggle for power. In 1975, he was a member of a "Dialogue Committee" set up to prevent the civil war then erupting. In the later 1970s, with the civil war raging, the Sunni leadership, and S. personally, lost much of their power-brokering influence, since they had never established a militia of their own and had little influence over the Muslim-Sunni armed groups, which were weak in any case. S. remained a respected elder statesman. He regained some influence in 1982, when he helped mediate the evacuation of the Palestinian-Arab guerrillas from Beirut and worked for a national reconciliation with the new regime of Bashir *Jumayyil (whose election as President he had opposed) and later of Amin *Jumayyil, and in 1983 when he again took part in efforts to achieve a reconciliation and a government of national unity. But he was no longer fully active in politics.

SALEH, 'ALI 'ABDULLAH(b. c. 1942)   Yemeni officer and politician, President of Yemen since 1978. A son of the Hashed tribes, S. was a professional army officer who came into prominence in 1977–78. A battalion commander with the rank of Major, and from 1977 military commander of the Ta'izz region, he helped A. H. al-*Ghashmi, the Chairman of the Military Council after the assassination of President Ibrahim *Hamdi in Oct. 1977 and President from Apr. 1978, to consolidate his power and suppress a rebellion of rival officers in Apr. 1978. When Ghashmi was assassinated in June 1978, S. became a member of the Presidential Council as well as Chief of Staff and Deputy Commander in Chief; he was also promoted to the rank of Lieutenant-Colonel. A month later he was made President. He purged the officers' corps, escaped several assassination attempts, and succeeded in consolidating his power and giving Yemen, torn for years by factional rivalries and internecine violence, a period of comparative stability, keeping a balance between the conservative tribal federations and leftist urban factions. (In his first year or two he tried to reconcile the underground leftist National Democratic Front, and even invited it to join the government, but no final agreement was reached, and S. soon felt secure enough to drop the offer and continue on a more median course.) He was reelected in 1983 and 1988. In May 1990 he led Yemen into union with South Yemen and became President of United Yemen.

At first considered dependent on and subservient to Sa'udi Arabia, and faced in Feb. 1979 by a South Yemeni invasion and warlike operations, S. succeeded in restoring a delicate balance between Sa'udi Arabia (on whose financial aid Yemen remained dependent) and South Yemen (with whom he achieved a reconciliation culminating in the 1990 merger). He also followed a pronouncedly neutralist policy and kept Yemen balanced between the USA, who supported and aided Yemen against South Yemen, and the USSR (who had in the past supplied most of Yemen's military equipment). He visited Moscow in Oct. 1981, and concluded a Treaty of Friendship and Cooperation with the USSR in Oct. 1984. In inter-Arab affairs he also followed, at first, a policy of low-profile neutrality. In 1989 he brought Yemen into a closer alliance with Egypt, Iraq and Jordan (the "Arab Cooperation Council"). However, in the crisis caused by Iraq's invasion of Kuwait, Aug 1990, he took, though joining the all-Arab and international demand that Iraq withdraw from Kuwait and rescind its annexation, a markedly pro-Iraqi and anti-U.S. position.

SALEM, MAMDUH (1920–88)   Egyptian administrator and politician. A graduate of the Police academy, S. served as a police officer, reaching the rank of General. From 1967 he was governor of various provinces, including Alexandria. A loyal aide of President *Sadat, S. prepared the ouster of the rival leftist faction of 'Ali *Sabri and supervised its implementation in May 1971. He was thereupon appointed Minister of the Interior the same month, and from Jan. 1972 also Deputy Premier. In Apr. 1975 he became Prime Minister. In that capacity he also headed the Arab Socialist

Union, the government party. When the party divided into institutionalized factions, from 1976, he headed its central, mainstream faction, later renamed "Misr Socialist Party" (which in effect dissolved itself in 1978 when Sadat founded his own National Democratic Party). S. headed the goverment until Oct. 1978. Upon his resignation, he was appointed Special Adviser to the President, in effect a nominal honorific, and no longer took an active part in political affairs.

AL-SALLAL, 'ABDULLAH (b. 1917? c. 1920?) Yemeni officer and politician. Leader of the revolution of 1962, President of the Yemen Republic 1962-67. Son of a lower-class Zeidi family, S. was sent in the 1930s to the Baghdad Military Academy, from which he graduated in 1938. Upon his return he was suspected of anti-regime activities and detained for some time, but was then allowed to resume his army career. He took part in the abortive al-Wazir coup of 1948 and was sentenced to death; the sentence was commuted to seven years' imprisonment and he was appointed Governor of Hodeida. S. was close to Prince al-Badr, who made him commander of his guard in the mid-1950s, and of the newly established Military Academy in 1959. When al-Badr became Imam-King in Sept. 1962, S., then a Major, became Commander of the Royal Guard and, according to some reports, Commander in Chief of the army. He was the main leader of the revolution of Sept. 1962 that toppled the monarchy, became President of the Republic and led the Republican camp in the civil war that erupted. He was concurrently also Prime Minister 1962-63 and 1966-67.

S. was strongly pro-Egyptian and depended on Egyptian support, not only in the conduct of the civil war, in which an Egyptian expeditionary army was the main force on the Republican side, but also in the frequent factional struggles within the Republican camp and army. He advocated a union of Yemen with Egypt and twice concluded agreements for Yemen to join Egypt-led unions or federations — in Mar. 1958 (the UAR) and in July 1964 (a planned, abortive Egypt-Iraq union) — agreements that were not implemented. S. was immersed in factional controversies and had little influence on the officers' corps, and even less on the tribes, and he was, of course, anathema to the Royalist camp. When the Egyptians felt compelled to seek a settlement of the Yemen conflict, they removed him in Apr. 1965 and took him to Egypt, into forced residence (while the Republic was run

by a Presidential Council that formally included S. but was in fact composed of his adversaries). In Sept. 1966 S. was allowed to return to Yemen and resume power; he took the Premiership in addition to the Presidency. However, when Egypt withdrew her expeditionary force in 1967, after the Six Day War, S. was overthrown in a bloodless coup in Nov. 1967. He went into exile to Baghdad and lost all influence on Yemeni affairs. 1973 reports of his return did not materialize. Late in 1981, apparently no longer considered a dangerous rival, he was allowed to return to Yemen and retire.

SANJABI, KARIM (b.1904)   Iranian politician. First Foreign Minister of Iran following the Islamic Revolution in 1979. Born in Kermanshah (now Bakhtaran), S. graduated in political science and law from the University of Tehran (1928), and received his doctorate in Paris. His father, Sardar Nasser Sanjalu, was the leader of the Sanjalu tribe (arrested by the British during World War I).

S. served in the Department of Education (1934) and the Treasury (1938), and was Director of the Department of Statistics of the Economic Affairs Ministry. He was also a professor of law and deputy dean of the law school.

During World War II, S. was arrested several times by the British. Together with other intellectuals, he founded the leftist *Mihan* Party in the 1940s, and later joined the Iran Party (allied with the Communist *Tudeh* Party), becoming a member of its Central Committee. In 1949 he was a founding member of the National Front coalition. In 1951 he served briefly as Minister of Education under Prime Minister *Mossaddeq, with whom he continued cooperating until his fall in 1953. He was active in the National Resistance Movement reforms in the 1950s and was a leader of the second National Front in the 1960s. After the unrest of 1961 he was arrested.

In 1977, together with other leaders of the National Front (e.g., Darius *Foruhar and Shahpur *Bakhtiar), S. publicly denounced the rule of the Shah. In 1978 he became Secretary-General of the National Front. In Dec. 1978, he was among the opposition leaders who negotiated with the Shah on ways to save his rule by a program of liberal reform. The talks failed (S. claimed the Shah had offered to make him Prime Minister, which he had declined). Shortly after, S. met with the exiled Ayatullah *Khomeini in Paris and agreed to join his camp. In Feb. 1979 he became Foreign Minister in *Bazargan's interim Islamic

Revolution government. But he was critical of the Revolutionary Council (and in particular of Deputy Prime Minister Ibrahim *Yazdi) for meddling in foreign affairs and resigned in April 1979. Disassociating himself from the Islamic regime, S. migrated to the United States, where he published his memoirs in 1989.

AL-SANUSSI, AL-SAYYID AHMAD AL-SHARIF (1873–1933)   A nephew of the founder of the Sanussi order in Libya-Cyrenaica, head of the order from 1902. From 1911–12 he was the leader of Sanussi resistance to the Italian conquerors in Cyrenaica. In 1916, after a Sanussi force under Turkish command was defeated by the British at Sollum and his leadership of the order was disputed by a rival faction under Idris *S., he was taken to Turkey, reportedly on a German submarine. He never returned, but lived as a high-ranking refugee in Turkey and Arab countries. In the first years after World War I his name was sometimes mentioned as a possible King of Iraq or Syria, but such ideas were abortive. He spent some years of his exile in Hijaz; King *Ibn Sa'ud was reported to think highly of him and sometimes used his services — e.g., as a mediator with the Idrissi Amirs of 'Assir and the Imam of Yemen. He died in Medina.

AL-SANUSSI, AL-SAYYID MUHAMMAD IDRIS (1890–1983)   Head of the S. order in Libya-Cyrenaica, King of Libya 1951–69. Born at Jaghbub, Cyrenaica, the grandson of the founder of the

Al-Sayyid Muhammad Idris al-Sanussi (Bar-David)

S. order, Idris established contacts with the British in Egypt in 1914, stayed in Egypt during World War I and recruited a S. force on the side of Britain and her allies — while the S. guerrillas in their war against the Italians joined the other side and became a part of Ottoman Turkey's forces. In 1916 Britain recognized him as the "Grand S.," the leader of the order — in place of his uncle al-Sayyid Ahmad Sharif *S. who fought on the other side. After the victory of the Allies, Italy recognized him, in the Rajma Agreement of 1920, as Amir of Cyrenaica heading a self-governing regime in the interior centered on the S. oases of Jaghbub and Kufra. In 1922 S. accepted the additional title of Amir of Tripolitania offered to him by the nationalists of that region — against Italy's wish. His agreement with the Italians was anyway half-hearted and short-lived. When the S.'s resumed their rebellion and guerrilla war, he left in 1922 for exile in Cairo, and remined there for 20 years. When Italy entered World War II, S. called upon all Libyans to cooperate with the Allies in a joint effort to drive out the Italians, and initiated the recruitment of a S. force which took part in the North African campaign. In return, the British recognized his claim to head an independent or autonomous Cyrenaica. After the Allied victory, and while discussions on the future of Libya were still going on, he proclaimed himself in 1949 Amir of Cyrenaica — with British support, and under a provisional British military government. In 1951 the crown of a united Libya was offered to him, and on Oct. 7, 1951, the National Assembly proclaimed him King of Libya. He ascended the throne on Dec. 24, 1951, when Libya became independent.

His reign was ultra-conservative, and while he continued relying on his S.'s in Cyrenaica, there was frequent friction between him and the nationalists in Tripolitania. His position was weakened in 1963 by the abolition of the federal structure of Libya and the imposition of a unitarian regime dominated by Tripoli. The stability of his reign seemed to depend on his person, since he had no children. King S. was deposed by a military coup on Sept. 1, 1969; he was abroad at the time and did not fight for his throne. He spent the rest of his days in exile in Greece and Egypt.

SAPIR(original name: Kozlovsky), **PINHAS**(1907–75) Israeli economist and politician. Born in Poland where he was active in the pioneering movement *Hehalutz*. In 1929 he immigrated to Palestine and settled in Kfar Sava, where he lived until his death. During the early 1930s he was active in the local Workers' Council and in 1937, when Levi Shkolnik (*Eshkol) was appointed director of the Water Company (later *Mekorot*), he became his assistant and right-hand man in running the company. He worked for this company until 1947, serving as its Director 1945–47.

During the War of Independence he was a member of the "Negev Commission" and later purchased arms in Europe and the United States. After the war he served as Director General of the Ministry of Defense. From 1953 to 1955 he was Director-General of the Ministry of Finance, under Levi Eshkol. In November 1955, after the elections to the Third Knesset, he joined the government as Minister of Trade and Industry. He held this position 1955–65 and 1970–72. In this capacity, he was responsible for the development of Israel's industry, particularly in development areas. In 1963, after Eshkol became Prime Minister, he was appointed Minister of Finance. He held this position 1963–68 and 1970–74. As Finance Minister, S. was responsible for Israel's economy and all events taking place within this economy were identified with him. During these years he accumulated political power and became a most important figure on the Israeli political scene. In 1968–69 he was Minister without Portfolio and Secretary-General of the Labor Party.

S. held very dovish political views. He greatly feared that the continued occupation of the West Bank and Gaza and their annexation would damage Israel. In spite of this, he did not come out against the hawkish policies of Golda *Meir, to whom he was extremely loyal. After the Yom Kippur War and Meir's fall from power, he would have been her natural successor as Prime Minister. However, in a rare recognition of his limitations, he refused to accept this position and chose, instead, to leave the government. In 1974–75 he was Chairman of the Jewish Agency Executive and Head of its *Aliyah* Department — a political decline.

S. was known, even among his political opponents, as the father of Israel's industry, during whose terms of office economic growth reached unknown heights. His personal lifestyle was modest and unassuming.

SAPIR, YOSEF (1902–72)   Israeli politician. Leader of the moderate right wing, the General Zionists Party. Born in Petah Tikvah, he was active in public matters from his youth. During the 1930s he was a leader of the Farmers Union. In 1940 he was elected Mayor of Petah Tikvah and served in this position until 1951. During the 1940s, he was the moderate right wing's representative in the *Haganah* Central Command.

Elected in 1949 to the First Knesset, S. was a Member of Knesset until his death. From 1952 to 1955 he was Minister of Transport, in the National Unity Government in 1967, Minister without Portfolio, and in 1969–70 Minister of Trade and Industry. In 1957 he was elected chairman of the General Zionists Party's Executive, and after Peretz Bernstein retired from political life, he was party leader. In 1961 he was one of the architects of the union between his party and the Progressives, which led to the creation of the Liberal Party. In 1965 he dissolved this party and helped to found *Gahal* — the *Herut*-Liberal bloc, and became one of its two leaders, along with Menahem Begin. This bloc laid the groundwork for the change of government in 1977.

SARACOĞLU, ŞÜKRÜ (1887–1953)   Turkish politician. Prime Minister 1942–46. Born in Odemis, he was educated at the civil service school and studied law at the University of Lausanne. In World War I he served as a reserve officer. He joined *Ataturk in new Turkey's War of Independence, 1919–22, and became a member of the Grand National Assembly, 1923. He served as Minister of Education, 1925, and Finance, 1927–30,

Sukru Saracoglu (AP Photo)

and was then sent to the USA to study business and economics and to develop commercial ties. Upon his return, he was appointed Minister of Justice, 1933–38. In 1938 he became Foreign Minister, a post he held until 1942: he signed the Mutual Assistance Pact with France and Great Britain (1939) and the Amity and Consultation Pact with Germany (1941).

S. became acting Prime Minister in Nov. 1941, and following the death of Refik Saydam in July 1942, Prime Minister. He co-determined Turkey's policy of neutrality in World War II, until Feb. 1945, when Turkey joined the Allies and delared war on Germany. S. held the Premiership until 1946.

SARKIS, ELIAS (1922? 1924?–85)   Lebanese jurist, economist and politician. Governor of the Central Bank 1967–76, President of Lebanon 1976–82. A Maronite Christian of a lower middle-class family, S. was educated at French-Catholic institutions in Beirut and graduated in law from the Jesuit St. Joseph University. From 1953 he worked as a judge at the Audit Office (*cour des comptes*). Involved in an investigation of irregularities in the Defense Ministry, he came to the attention of President Fu'ad *Shihab and was transferred to the President's Office. He played an important part in turning that office into a powerful institution, in collaboration with the secret services built up by President Shihab, and in 1962 became its Director-General. In 1967 he was named Governor of the Central Bank, which he headed for nine years, during a time of increasing economic difficulties. In 1970 he was a candidacy for the Presidency, supported by the "Shihabist" camp; he lost to Suleiman *Franjiyeh by one vote. In 1976, Syria, then in *de facto* occupation of most of Lebanon, strongly supported his renewed candidacy and applied pressure, and S. was duly elected President. During the years of his Presidency the civil war, that had officially ended in Oct. 1976, resumed and escalated. The rival armed militias and/or the Syrian army dominated most of the country, the regular army disintegrated and the government was unable to function properly and virtually lost control. The last months of his term saw the Israeli invasion of June 1982. Thus S., while personally respected, was not an effective President. While doing his best to reconcile the warring factions and work out a peace settlement, he refrained from expressing forceful opinions or taking clear-cut positions in the constant struggle of the factions, coalitions and militias. Out of frustration, he was on the verge of resigning several times (e.g., in July 1978). When his term expired in Sept. 1982, he retired and in the three remaining years of his life took no further part in public affairs.

SARRAJ, 'ABD-UL-HAMID   Syrian officer and politician. Born in Hama, S. graduated from the Military Academy and underwent advanced training in France. He served in al-*Qawuqji's "Army of Deliverance" in Palestine in 1948 and later rose in rank in the Syrian army. He was close to the *Ba'th* group, but did not formally join it. From 1955, as a colonel, he headed army intelligence and security and was considered the strong man of Syria. He played a major part in preparing the merger of Syria and Egypt as the UAR, 1958, and became Minister of the Interior in the Syrian "Region" of the UAR. As his power grew, he was virtually President *Nasser's deputy and representative in Syria. In Sept. 1960 he was named head of the Syrian Region's Executive Council (i.e., Prime Minister, though not so termed), keeping the Interior Ministry and the Security Services, and Secretary of the single-party National Union in Syria. When the separate governments of the two regions were abolished in Aug. 1961, he became Vice-President of the UAR, in charge of internal affairs, but following differences with President Nasser he resigned a month later and returned to Syria. During the Syrian officers' coup of Sept. 1961 that led to Syria's withdrawal from the UAR he was arrested. He escaped to Egypt in 1962 and took part in abortive attempts to bring Syria back into the UAR. He has remained in Egypt, from 1967 as the director of the National Insurance Institute, but no longer plays a part in public, political affairs.

SA'UD, HOUSE OF (Arabic: Aal)   The ruling dynasty in the largest country of the Arabian peninsula, Sa'udi Arabia, giving the country its name. The family, of the 'Anaiza tribe, first ruled the Dar'yya area of Najd. Muhammad Ibn Sa'ud, who ruled Dar'iyya 1726–65, adopted the Wahhabi doctrine and set up a Wahhabi state in 1745, and as he expanded his area of control he spread the new faith over large parts of the peninsula. His son 'Abd-ul-'Aziz (ruled 1766–1803) and his grandson Sa'ud (ruled 1803–14) extended their power as far as the Syrian and Iraqi borders and raided the border areas and also Mecca and Med-

King Khaled ibn 'Abd-ul-'Aziz

ina. Under 'Abdullah Ibn Sa'ud (ruled 1814–18), the Sa'udis were defeated by Muhammad 'Ali of Egypt, on behalf of the Ottoman Sultan, and 'Abdullah was executed in Constantinople (Istanbul). During the years 1819–37 the Sa'udis reconsolidated their rule. From 1837 to about 1843 Egyptian-Ottoman units again took control, and from 1843 the HoS reasserted itself. From about 1865, however, it declined and had only limited control over the Dar'iyya-Riyadh area, the Ottomans and the rival House of *Rashid of the Shammar tribe preventing an extension of its power.

In the 1880s the Rashid clan gained the upper hand and in 1890–91 it defeated 'Abd-ul-Rahman Aal S. and conquered the Dar'iyya-Riyadh area. Survivors of the HoS found refuge in Kuwait, among them young 'Abd-ul-'Aziz ibn 'Abd-ul-Rahman, (*"Ibn Sa'ud") (1880–1953, ruled 1902–53). The latter resumed the fight and regained control of Riyadh in 1902. He soon began expanding his realm. In 1913 he took the al-Hassa region on the Persian Gulf and thus came into contact with the sphere of British interests and domination and in 1915 he made a pact with Britain. In the course of his expansion, he beat the Rashidis, who surrendered in 1921, and clashed with *Hussein,

the *Hashemite Sharif of Mecca and King of Hijaz; in 1924 he conquered Hijaz and deposed the Hashemites. Henceforth the HoS ruled most of the Arabian peninsula (except the southern, southeastern and some of the eastern parts).

Ibn Sa'ud, who named his kingdom "Sa'udi Arabia" in 1932, died in 1953 and was succeeded by his eldest son *Sa'ud ibn 'Abd-ul-'Aziz (1902–69). In 1964 Sa'ud was deposed and succeeded by his halfbrother *Feisal ibn 'Abd-ul-'Aziz (1904–75). Feisal ruled until 1975, when he was assassinated. He was succeeded by his halfbrother *Khaled ibn 'Abd-ul-'Aziz (1912–82). Upon Khaled's death, in 1982, his halfbrother *Fahd ibn 'Abd-ul-'Aziz (b. 1921) became King, with another half-brother, *'Abdullah ibn 'Abd-ul-'Aziz (b. 1923), as Crown Prince and First Deputy Prime Minister. These four successions consolidated the principle laid down by Ibn Sa'ud: the Kingship was to pass on among his sons, by and large according to seniority.

Other key figures among Ibn Sa'ud's surviving sons (he had over 40) are Prince Sultan (b. 1924), Defense Minister since 1962 and Second Deputy Prime Minister since 1982, and Prince Na'if (b. 1934), Minister of Interior since 1975 — both full brothers of King Fahd, members of a powerful group of brothers called, after their mother, the Sudairis. Other surviving sons of Ibn Sa'ud serve as government ministers, provincial governors, etc., and some are active in business. Many members of the third generation, Ibn Sa'ud's grandsons, are also active, and some are prominent, in business and/or government and army positions. Of King Feisal's sons, for instance, 'Abdullah (b. 1921), was Minister of Interior 1953–60; Sa'ud (b. 1941), has been Foreign Minister since 1975; Turki (b. 1945) is Director of Foreign Intelligence. Of Prince Sultan's sons, Bandar is since 1983 Sa'udia's ambassador in the USA, and Khaled is commander of the armed forces (he formally commanded the forces of the U.S.-led international coalition against Iraq, 1990/91).

SA'UD IBN 'ABD-UL-'AZIZ (1902–69)   King of Sa'udi Arabia 1953–64. Eldest son of King 'Abdul-'Aziz ibn 'Abd-ul-Rahman (*Ibn Sa'ud) (after the death of his brother Turki in 1919). With the consolidation of the Sa'udi kingdom, his father named him Crown Prince in 1932 (with the understanding that his halfbrother *Feisal would be second in line) and Viceroy of Najd. When Ibn Sa'ud died in 1953, S. mounted the throne and also assumed the Premiership, despite reports of sharpening rivalry

King Sa'ud Ibn 'Abd-ul-'Aziz (Bar-David, Tel Aviv)

between him and Feisal. But differences escalated when the country underwent a severe financial crisis, despite its increasing oil revenues, as a result of extravagance and unbridled spending. At the same time, relations with Egypt deteriorated, and in Mar. 1958 President 'Abd-ul-*Nasser publicly accused S. of plotting his assassination. S.'s poor health also made him go abroad frequently. In 1958 he was compelled to hand over actual executive power to Feisal. However, he continued struggling. He made a partial comeback and took the Premiership in 1960, but in 1962 he had to restore it to Feisal. In 1964 he demanded that Feisal give up his powers. In the crisis that ensued, Feisal gained the upper hand. On Nov. 2, 1964, the Council of *'Ulama'* (Muslim Sages) deposed S. and crowned Feisal in his place. S. went into exile, at first in Europe; in 1966 he settled in Egypt and allowed Nasser to use him in his conflict with Feisal. When Nasser toned down his inter-Arab activities after 1967 and strove for a reconciliation with Feisal, S. was pushed into the background and ceased public and political activities. He died in exile in 1969.

AL-SAYYAB, BADR SHAKER (1926–64)   Iraqi poet, considered by some as one of the greatest modern Arab poets. Born in a village near Basra, S. graduated from the Teachers' College in Baghdad where he specialized in Arabic and English literature.

Having joined the clandestine Communist Party, he was soon dismissed from his teaching post. Under the influence of the Anglo-American poet T.S. Eliot, he developed, from about 1947 together with the Iraqi poetess Nazik al-Mala'ika, an Iraqi version of Arabic free verse, which soon became a main style of poetry in the whole Arab world, especially among leftist-modernist poets. His poems use the symbol of Tammuz (the Babylonian Adonis) and other Eastern deities, as well as Christ, to express his hopes for the spiritual, cultural and political revival of Iraq and the Arab world and for personal happiness. His poetry is frequently political: it decries massacres carried out in Mosul by the Communists, symbolized sometimes by the hell-dog Cerberus of Greek mythology; these massacres are the scythe cutting the veins of Tammuz.

Drought — symbolized by the thirsty dying Astarte wandering from village to village — is caused by the Tatars (the Communists); there is no spring, the rain (the revolution) which he hoped for has brought no salvation, and the prayers for Adonis have not borne fruit. S. celebrates the victory of the Algerian warriors against France — using the symbol of Sisyphus throwing away his rock.

Under the rule of 'Abd-ul-Karim *Qassem (1958–63), S. left the Communist Party. He was again dismissed from his government job and joined the *Shi'r* magazine group which published his anthology *The Song of the Rain* (Beirut, 1960). When he fell seriously ill, he expressed his despair and suffering, in several anthologies, seeing himself as a new Job.

AL-SHA'BI, QAHTAN MUHAMMAD (1920–81) South Yemeni politician, President of South Yemen 1967–69. Born in Lahej Sultanate in the 'Aden Protectorates, Sh. worked for several years in the Lahej Land Department and became its Director in 1955. He left the government service in 1958 to work for the nationalist insurgents and joined the South Arabian League. In 1960 he fled to Yemen. Around 1963, while still in exile in Yemen, he co-founded the National Liberation Front for the Liberation of South Yemen (NLF) and became one of its main leaders. He proclaimed an armed rebellion in Oct. 1963 and led a guerrilla war against the British and the South Arabia federal authorities, as well as against rival nationalist groups, chiefly FLOSY. In 1967 he overcame these rival factions, and the NLF emerged as the only organization with which the transfer of power was to be negotiated. Sh. headed the NLF delegation to the Nov.

1967 Geneva talks on independence. With independence achieved, the same month, he became South Yemen's first President, Prime Minister and Commander in Chief. He was, however, soon involved in factional struggles within the FLN and the government, and in June 1969 he was deposed. He was expelled from the ruling party, detained, and from Apr. 1970, imprisoned. He was also ailing, and did not return to active public and political life before his death in 1981.

AL-SHAFE'I, HUSSEIN(b. 1919) Egyptian officer and politician, Vice-President of Egypt, 1962–67 and 1970–75. A professional army officer, Sh. was among the "Free Officers" who planned and mounted the coup of July 1952, and after the coup he became a member of the 12-man Revolutionary Council. He joined the government in 1954, serving for a few months as Minister of War and then as Minister of Social Affairs. After the merger of Egypt and Syria as the UAR in 1958, he kept the Social Affairs portfolio — at first in the "regional" government of Egypt and then in that of the UAR. In Aug. 1961 he became one of the seven Vice-Presidents of the UAR — for one month, as the UAR broke up in Sept. In Oct. 1961 he again became Minister of Social Affairs in the government of Egypt, with the rank of Deputy Premier. From 1962 he was a member of the Presidential Council, quitting his Cabinet post, and from 1964 to 1967 he was a Vice-President. In 1967 he again became Deputy Premier and Minister of Social Affairs, taking also the portfolio of *Waqf* (Religious Endowments) until 1968. In 1967–68 he presided over the revolutionary court that tried 55 officers accused of plotting. After the death of President 'Abd-ul-*Nasser in Sept. 1970, the new President, Anwar *Sadat, appointed Sh. one of his two Vice-Presidents (from May 1971 to Jan. 1972 and from Sept. 1974 — the only Vice-President). Sh. was dismissed as Vice-President in Apr. 1975, and apart from occasional interviews or statements (e.g., one denouncing the Camp David Agreement in Oct. 1978, together with three other former Vice-Presidents) he played no further role in public-political affairs. Sh. loyally served President Nasser and until 1975 President Sadat, going along with the policies decided by the leader. He was not a decision-maker but was regarded as rather colorless with no independent views.

SHAMIR, MOSHE(b. 1921) Israeli writer, one of the prominent representatives of the Israel-born generation of writers. Born in Safed and raised in Tel Aviv, S. was a member and leader of the *Hashomer Hatza'ir* movement. From 1941 to 1947 he was a member of Kibbutz Mishmar Ha'emek, and in 1944 he joined the *Palmah*. During the 1948 War of Independence he was an education officer and the first editor of *Bamahaneh*, the IDF publication. In the war he lost his brother Elik, about whom he wrote his book *Bemo Yadav (With His Own Hands)*.

His first novel, *Hu Halakh Basadot (He Walked in the Fields)*, published in 1947, earned him a place as one of the most promising young writers. His books include historical novels, *Melech Basar Vadam (King of Flesh and Blood)* which tells the story of King Alexander Yanai, and *Kivsat Harash (The Poor Man's Lamb)*, the biblical tale of David and Bathsheva, both published in the mid-1950s. Sh. also published poems under the pen name Asaf Keller. For many years he wrote for the newspapers. He was a member of the editorial board of *Ma'ariv* and edited its literary supplement. He won the Israel Prize for Literature in 1988.

During the first years of the State Sh. was a member of the left-wing *Mapam* Party. After the Six Day War his political views underwent a change and he was one of the founders of the Movement for the Whole Eretz Yisrael (Greater Israel). In 1973, when the right-wing *Likud* Party was established, he joined that party, and was elected on its list to the Ninth Knesset in 1977. In 1979, after the signing of the peace agreement with Egypt, he left the party and was one of the founders of the right-wing radical *Tehiyah* Party. In 1981 he refused to be a candidate for the Knesset, and since then he has withdrawn from almost all public activity.

SHAMIR (original name: Yzernitzky), **YITZHAK** (b. 1915) Israeli political leader. Born in Poland and active in the *Betar* youth movement. In 1935 he immigrated to Palestine and joined the *Etzel (Irgun Z'vai Leumi)*. In 1940, when that organization split and Avraham *Stern (Yair) founded the "*Etzel* in Israel," (later the Fighters for the Freedom of Israel, *Lehi*), he joined the new body. After Yair's assassination in 1942, he was one of the three members of the *Lehi* Command and was responsible for its operational and organizational activity. In 1946 he was arrested and sent to a detention camp at Eritrea. After four months he escaped and lived in Paris until May 1948.

Upon his return to Israel Sh. was active in the

Yitzhak Shamir (GPO, Jerusalem)

"Fighters Party" founded by *Lehi*; according to reports never confirmed, he was involved in the assassination of Count Bernadotte. Later he joined the Intelligence Service (*Mossad*) where he served in various senior positions until 1965. After that he ran a mattress factory in Kfar Sava and in 1970 he joined the *Herut* movement. In 1973 he was elected chairman of the *Herut* Executive and in 1974 was elected to the Eighth Knesset.

In 1977, after the victory of the right, Sh. was elected Knesset Speaker. In 1978 he abstained from ratifying the Camp David Agreement. In 1980 he was appointed Foreign Minister. In 1983, after Menahem *Begin's retirement, he successfully contested David *Levy for the position of party leader (and Prime Minister). He began his term under difficult conditions: the army was embroiled in the Lebanese war, bank stocks had collapsed and inflation had skyrocketed. In addition to serving as Prime Minister he continued to act as Foreign Minister.

After the elections to the Eleventh Knesset in 1984, he signed a rotation agreement with the Labor Party's Shimon *Peres and until 1986 acted as his deputy and Foreign Minister. During this time he opposed the withdrawal of the army from Lebanon but acquiesced in it; he supported pro-

grams to stabilize the economy. In October 1986 he began his term as Prime Minister and after the elections of Nov. 1988 continued in that position with his own coalition, at first with the Labor Party and since June 1990 with right-wing parties only. The man chosen as Menahem Begin's temporary successor has shown a remarkable acumen for political survival.

SHAPIRA, MOSHE HAIM (1902–1970) Israeli politician. Leader of the national religious movement. Born in Grodno, Russia, in his youth he was active in the *Mizrahi* and in 1926 immigrated to Palestine. In 1935 he was elected deputy member of the Zionist Executive and during the Second World War acted as Deputy Head of the Aliyah (Immigration) Department of the Jewish Agency.

After the establishment of the State of Israel he was a member of the Provisional Government, as Minister of Aliyah and Health. Until his death he served as Minister of the Interior, Minister of Religion, Minister of Health and Minister of Welfare. He was one of the architects of the National Unity Government formed on the eve of the Six Day War. At the end of the war he signed the order which brought about the unification of Jerusalem. He was a Member of Knesset from its first day until his death.

During the 1950s and 1960s Sh. was the leader of the *Hapoel Hamizrahi* and afterwards the leader of *Mafdal* (the National Religious Party). He was known for his moderate political views and his support of the "historical pact" between his party and *Mapai*. During a confrontation between David *Ben Gurion and Moshe *Sharett, in 1955–56, he supported the more moderate Sharett. His death was a milestone in the political radicalization of his party.

In 1957 he was seriously injured by a hand grenade which was thrown into the Knesset. The wounds he incurred caused his death 13 years later.

SHAPIRA, YA'AKOV SHIMSHON (b. 1902) Israeli jurist and politician. Born in Russia. In 1924 he immigrated to Palestine and was one of the founders of Kibbutz Giv'at Hashlosha. After he left the *kibbutz* he studied law. His law office, very prominent in Mandatory Palestine, dealt with trials of the *Haganah* and "illegal" immigration. After the establishment of the State he was the first Attorney General, a position he held until 1950.

After his resignation, he was politically active within the framework of *Mapai*. He was a member of the Second and Third Knessets and was chairman of the coalition executive. In 1956 he was forced to resign from the Knesset due to public criticism over a high legal fee which he had collected, and returned to his law office.

In the late 1960s he returned to political life. In 1965 he acted as prosecutor in an internal trial which *Mapai* held against David *Ben Gurion and his associates. As a result, Ben Gurion was expelled from the party. In 1966 he was appointed Minister of Justice in Levi *Eshkol's government. He served in this position, first under Eshkol and later under Golda *Meir, until the end of 1973. After the Six Day War he served as chairman of the Ministerial Committee on Jerusalem.

Sh. was considered an influential Minister of Justice — in both the political and professional spheres. He was very close to the Prime Ministers under whom he served. A number of important laws were passed during his term, e.g., the Basic Law of Government (1966) and the law establishing National Commissions of Inquiry (1968).

In 1973, after the Yom Kippur War, he resigned from the government, sharply criticizing the leaders who did not resign despite their responsibility for the political and military failures of the war, and retired from the political and public stage.

SHARABI, HISHAM (b. 1927)   Palestinian-Arab American writer and scholar, Professor at Georgetown University. Born in Jaffa, Sh. settled in the USA completing his studies. He has been active as a supporter and spokesman of the Palestinian-Arab struggle, identified with the Palestine Liberation Organization (PLO) and a member of the Palestine National Council. Sh. authored several books: *A Handbook of the Contemporary Middle East* (1957); *Governments and Politics of the Middle East in the Twentieth Century* (1962); *Nationalism and Revolution in the Arab World* (1966); *The Lethal Dilemma: Palestine and Israel* (1969); *Arab Intellectuals and the West (1970); Palestine Guerrillas: Their Credibility and Effectiveness* (1970). Sh. also published several books in Arabic on the Palestinian problem as well as an *Introduction to the Study of Arab Society* (Beirut, 1975), criticizing Arab social behavior, mentality and customs.

SHARETT (original name: Shertok), **MOSHE** (1894–1965)   Israeli statesman. Foreign Minister 1948–56, Prime Minister 1954–55. He laid the foundation for the foreign policy of the *Yishuv* and the State of Israel. Born in Russia to *Bilu* member

Ya'akov Shertok, who immigrated to Palestine with his family in 1906. For a short while his family stayed at a farm near Arab villages in the Nablus area; afterwards it moved to Tel Aviv. Sh. was in the first graduating class of the Gymnasia Herzliah high school. In the First World War he volunteered for the Turkish army, and became an officer.

During the 1920s Sh. studied at the London School of Economics. Upon his return, in 1925 he joined the editorial board of the *Histadrut*'s just founded *Davar* daily. He was active in the *Ahdut Ha'avodah* Party, and from 1930 the Labor Party (*Mapai*). In 1931 he joined the staff of the Jewish Agency's Political Department and in 1933, after the assassination of Haim *Arlosoroff, he replaced him as head of the department. From then on he was "Foreign Minister" of the *Yishuv* and the Zionist movement and number two (after *Ben Gurion) in the *Yishuv*'s leadership. He was chiefly responsible for the volunteering of Palestinian Jews into the British army during the Second World War, the creation of the Jewish Brigade in 1944 and the political struggle which led to the partition solution of Nov. 29, 1947.

With the establishment of the State of Israel he was appointed Foreign Minister. He was a member of the Knesset from 1949 to 1965. His policies on most matters — such as the reparations from Germany and the American orientation which Israel adopted since the Korean War, 1950 — conformed to Ben-Gurion's. However, a split began to emerge as Sh.'s position was more diplomatic and moderate, while Ben Gurion's was more activist and military-oriented.

After Ben-Gurion's resignation in 1953, Sh. was chosen to replace him, and from Jan. 1954 until Nov. 1955 was both Prime Minister and Foreign Minister. This period was the apex of his political career, but he felt that his position at the head of the political pyramid was in reality a formal one. Ben-Gurion, retired at S'deh Boker, was a rival center of leadership. The defense forces, led by Defense Minister *Lavon and Chief of Staff *Dayan, did not carry out the orders of the Prime Minister and even submitted untruthful reports. For Sh. it was a tragedy that during his term of office incidents such as the "Lavon Affair" and the Gaza Operation of Feb. 1955 lessened the chances for the peace negotiations with the Arab countries, particularly Egypt, that were his chief aim and aspiration.

After the elections to the Third Knesset, 1955, Sh. returned to serve as Foreign Minister under Ben

Gurion. He led a group of moderate ministers who opposed Ben Gurion's military plans and even succeeded in thwarting some of them. In June 1956, Ben Gurion, planning the Sinai Campaign, forced Sh. to resign from the government. This forced resignation deeply wounded Sh. and he did not recover before his death. During the Sinai Campaign Sh. was on a trip to the Far East and had to defend that operation which he vehemently opposed.

After he resigned from the government he headed the *Histadrut*'s *Am Oved* publishing company and from 1960 to 1965 was Chairman of the Jewish Agency Executive. He refused to hold positions such as Knesset Speaker and President of the State of Israel, when these were offered to him.

Sh. was a man of many talents. He was fluent in many languages and at home in many cultures. He created Israeli diplomacy and dared to present an alternative to Ben Gurion's policies when the latter was at the zenith of his power.

SHARI'ATI, ALI (1933–77)   Iranian thinker, the outstanding ideologist of the Islamic Revolution outside the religious establishment. Born in Mazinan, a village near Mashhad, son of a well-known preacher and commentator of Islamic law who had a great deal of influence on him. In the early 1950s, as a student at Mashhad University, he was active in groups linked with Muhammad *Mossaddeq and was arrested. In 1960, he went to Paris to continue his studies and in 1964 received a Ph.D. in sociology and theology. In Paris, he met writers, philosophers, and Islamologists and was much influenced by the Algerian revolution which achieved success during his stay in Paris.

Upon his return to Iran, he taught at Mashhad University, but was soon dismissed and went to Tehran. There he became a popular lecturer and in 1967 co-founded *Husseiniya Arashad*, a progressive religious and social institution. The *Savak* (secret police) soon closed that institute and arrested Sh. He was jailed for a year and a half and endured house arrest for an additional two years. In June 1977 he was permitted to travel abroad and went to London. He died there and was buried in Damascus.

Sh. differed from *Khomeini in many ways, but there were some similarities between the two. They both opposed the Shah's regime and any influence from the West. They preached activism to the masses, sought to use the religious establishment to spread their views, guide the public and prevent opposing views and activities, and saw Islam as the ideology of the revolution. They opposed imperialism (especially cultural imperialism, alienating the people from its heritage), liberalism, capitalism, Marxism and socialism. But Sh. believed in Islamic humanism and rejected the determinist fatalism widespread in the Islamic establishment, because it deprived the individual of responsibility for his fate and that of society. According to Sh., Muslims should not wait for Shi'i Islam's secret Imam, but should act here and now, and an important precondition for action was preparing the soul and making an ideological change. He believed the ultimate goal was a society based on equality, a society that required leadership, but not necessarily a leader. Thus, Sh.'s tenets, though influential and respected, were not in accord with the official doctrine of Shi'i Islam and Khomeini's regime.

SHARIATMADARI, AYATULLAH MUHAMMAD KAZEM (1899? 1903?–86)   Iranian religious leader. Born in Tabriz, Sh. went to Qom to study Islamic law and doctrine; he was a classmate of the Ruhullah *Khomeini. In the mid-1930s he continued his religious studies in Najaf in Iraq, returning to Tabriz to teach. After 15 years there he returned to Qom.

After the death of Ayatullah Borujerdi in 1961, Sh. and Khomeini were rivals for the leadership of the Shi'ite establishment. In 1970, after the death of Borujerdi's successor, Muhsin Hakim, the Shah gave his support to Sh. During Khomeini's exile, Sh. remained the leader of the Shi'ite community in Iran, while Khomeini remained its leader in exile.

After the Islamic Revolution of 1979, Sh. opposed most of Khomeini's actions against the toppled Shah and the members of his regime. Sh. was an Iranian nationalist, moderate toward the West and conciliatory toward minorities. He was critical of the undemocratic character of the new Islamic Republic, opposed the trials and executions of the regime's enemies and condemned the capture of American hostages in 1979. He called for a modern Islamic state, which would, while Islamic in character, not ignore modern technology and the world developments that had occurred in the 1400 years since the beginning of Islam. He denounced Khomeini's use of the title Imam, a sacred messianic figure in Shi'i Islam. He believed that the Islamic Republic should be based on democracy, and called for freedom for all political movements, including the Communists. Sh. thus headed — with Ayatullah *Taleghani — the Islamic opposition to the new regime. Khomeini offered to make small concessions to him in exchange for his cooperation, but Sh. rejected that offer. From Feb. 1979 he tried to set up an "Islamic People's Party" in opposition, but had little success, and in early 1980 advised that group to suspend its activities and in fact disband itself. The regime did not allow him to operate freely; and his past moderate views, contacts with the Shah's regime, his allegedly "pro-U.S." position (he was even accused of cooperating with the CIA), were not in line with the mood of the public (though minorities and some intellectuals supported him).

Sh. was put under house arrest for some time, but due to his exalted religious position the regime did not treat him too harshly or eliminate him. Anyway, from 1980 he lapsed into silence. Sh.'s death removed Khomeini's chief opponent within the religious establishment.

SHARON (original name: Sheinerman), **ARIEL** (b. 1928)   Israeli military man and politician. Born in Kfar Malal, in his youth he joined the *Haganah* and during the War of Independence he was a platoon commander. After the war he continued in the regular army as Intelligence Officer of the Northern Command. In 1953 he formed a new unit, "Unit 101," for reprisal strikes across the borders. The unit, which played an important role in developing the army's fighting spirit, later was incorporated with the paratroopers. Thus, the young Sh. became a paratroop commander.

During the Sinai Campaign, the brigade he commanded was parachuted into the area near the Mitla Pass and Sh., loosely interpreting the commands he received, entered into a bloody battle which claimed many victims. His breach of discipline angered the army command, and his advancement in the army ranks was suspended for years. Only in 1965, after Yitzhak *Rabin became Chief of Staff, did Sh. become Head of the Training Department of the General Staff. In 1967 he was awarded the rank of Brigadier-General.

During the Six Day War Sh. commanded a division on the southern front which captured the Umm Katef range. In 1969 he was appointed Commander of the Southern Command. His appointment resulted from political pressure by Pinhas *Sapir, who feared that Sh. would resign from the army and enter politics for *Gahal*, the bloc composed of *Herut* and the Liberal Party. As Commander of the Southern Command, Sh. was responsible for fighting terrorism in the Gaza Strip. The means by which he carried this out

caused a sharp public debate. In the summer of 1973, shortly before the outbreak of the Yom Kippur War, Sh. resigned from the army, joined the Liberal Party and brought about the creation of the *Likud* — the bloc of right-wing parties.

During the Yom Kippur War Sh. commanded a division on the southern front. During the months of his command he tangled with the army high brass — including Chief of Staff Eleazar. In January 1974, after issuing a controversial order of the day on the occasion of his demobilization, his emergency appointment was cancelled.

In 1974 Sh. was elected to the Eighth Knesset; however, several months later he resigned from the Knesset to become an advisor to Prime Minister Yitzhak Rabin. In 1976 he formed a new party — *Shlomzion*. While forming this party, he negotiated with several leaders of the moderate camp, espousing moderate ideas. In the 1977 elections his party won two mandates. He joined the *Likud* — this time the *Herut* faction — and was appointed Minister of Agriculture. In this capacity he was responsible for creating "fake" settlements in the Rafiah area, which complicated the negotiations with Egypt. In 1981, after the elections to the Tenth Knesset, he was appointed Minister of Defense. He immediately began planning a war against the PLO in Lebanon — which broke out in June 1982. Within a short time the war became a matter of great public debate. This debate widened in Sept. 1982 following the Sabra and Shatila massacres. A huge demonstration, with 400,000 participants, forced the government to establish an official Commission of Inquiry.

The findings of this commission, published in Feb. 1983, caused Sh. to be dismissed from the Ministry of Defense. He became a Minister without Portfolio and was relegated to the political wilderness. In the summer of 1984, during negotiations over the formation of a National Unity government, Shimon *Peres returned him to center stage by appointing him Minister of Trade and Industry and a member of the inner political cabinet. He served in this capacity until Jan. 1990. From May 1990 onward he is Minister of Housing.

SHAWQI, AHMAD (1868–1932)   Egyptian-Arab poet. An outstanding neoclassical poet and playwright given the title "the Prince of Arab Poets." Born to a wealthy family of Turkish-Greek-Kurdish-Arab origin related to the Khedival family of Muhammad 'Ali, Sh. studied at the Cairo Law School (1885), but graduated from the Literature (Translation) faculty, and continued his studies at the Universities of Montpellier and Paris (1891–93). Back in Egypt, he was appointed to the Khedival palace; in 1905 he received the title of Bey.

When in 1914 the Khedive *'Abbas Hilmi was deposed by the British, Sh., who was his "poet laureate," accompanied him into exile in Istanbul. When Sh. returned to Egypt he was exiled to Spain and lived in Barcelona during the war. When in 1923 a Parliament was elected in Egypt, he became a member of the Senate.

In 1927 he was elected by all Arab poets, in a ceremony in Cairo, as "the Prince of Arab Poets," and in 1932 he was elected chairman of the *Apollo* poetic society. Soon afterwards he died in Cairo.

His collected poetry, *Diwan al-Shawqiyyat*, was published in 1899 and revised in 1926. He wrote 6 novels and 7 plays, most of them in verse.

SHAZAR (original name: Rubashov), **SHNEOR ZALMAN** (1889–1974)   Israeli intellectual and politician, President of Israel 1963–73. Born in Russia, Sh. was active from his youth in the Zionist-Socialist *Poalei Zion* movement. He studied in St. Petersburg, Germany, and Switzerland. During the first World War he engaged in Judaica research and studied in Berlin where he co-founded a branch of *Poalei Zion* and *Hehalutz*. In 1924 he immigrated to Palestine. There he was active in

Zalman Shazar (GPO, Jerusalem)

public affairs and the press, as a leader of *Ahdut Ha'avodah* and from 1930 *Mapai*, a member of the executive of the *Histadrut* and one of the editors of the *Histradrut*'s *Davar* daily. He was also active in the Zionist movement and a delegate to the Zionist Congresses. In 1944, after the death of Berl *Katznelson, he became the editor in chief of *Davar*.

After the establishment of the State of Israel, he was elected to the First Knesset and in 1949–1950 served as the first Minister of Education and Culture. After resigning from the government, he was elected to the Jewish Agency Executive and became head of the Department for Education and Culture in the Diaspora. From 1957 to 1961 he was acting Chairman of the Jewish Agency Executive. In 1963 he was elected the third President of the State of Israel and was reelected in 1968 to a second term of office.

Sh., a descendant of the leading rabbis of the *Habad Hassidim*, was an orator with great pathos and a leading intellectual. Throughout his life he was torn between his responsibilities as a public and political figure and his personal inclination towards activity in the intellectual field.

SHELAH (original name: Halperin), **URIEL (YONATAN RATOSH)** (1909–81)   Israeli poet and thinker. Founder of the "Canaanite" movement. Born in Warsaw (his father Yehiel Halperin was a prominent educator and poet). Immigrated to Palestine with his family and graduated from the Gymnasia Herzliah high school in Tel Aviv, 1926. In the 1930s he was part of a radical-maximalist Revisionist group and edited its newspaper *Hayarden*. In a series of articles in 1937 he called for the immediate establishment of a Hebrew state in all of Palestine. *Jabotinsky disagreed with his views, but they greatly influenced youth in the movement, particularly Avraham (Yair) *Stern.

In 1938–39 he studied linguistics in Paris. It was there that he formed his "Canaanite" concept: a new, "Hebrew" nation had been created in Palestine, which was no part of the Jewish people. Upon his return he established a Committee to Unify the Hebrew Youth and began to preach his ideas. While many young people were attracted by them, the political and cultural establishment vehemently fought him and his views. After the establishment of the State of Israel he founded a publication entitled *Alef*, which appeared until 1953. After the Six Day War he was a staunch supporter of establishing a Hebrew national entity in all of Palestine (Eretz Israel, the land of Israel).

From the mid-1920s Sh. published poems with a clear ideological message — first a radical Zionist one and afterwards a "Hebrew"-nationalist one — which caused him to be boycotted by the literary establishment. From the 1950s his poems were of a more lyrical and personal nature. During the last years of his life, and particularly after his death, he was recognized as a great Hebrew poet.

Though few accepted his views literally, he had a great deal of indirect influence.

SHIHAB, FU'AD (1902–73)   Lebanese officer and politician, President of Lebanon 1958–64. Maronite Christian of a renowned family whose heads had in the past borne the title Amir. During the French Mandate, Sh. served in the "Special Troops" recruited by the French, reaching the rank of Lieutenant-Colonel. In 1946, when Lebanon became independent, he was appointed Commander of the Army as a General, and did much to build it up into a modern, professional force. In Sept. 1952, when a "National Front" staged demonstrations against the corrupt administration of President Bishara al-*Khouri, Sh. refused to order the army to suppress the demonstrators, and Khouri was in consequence forced to resign. For an interim period of a few weeks, Sh. served as Prime Minister and Minister of the Interior and Defense. He adopted a similar attitude in the civil war in 1958, when fighting broke out between supporters of President Camille *Chamoun and a Nasserist "National Front." Sh. once again refused to order out the army against the insurgents, holding that the army ought to be above the rival camps and constitute a force for national unity, fearing it might break into rival factions if used in a civil war. Sh. thus acquired a reputation for impartiality, and on July 31, 1958, he was elected President — as a compromise, the first step towards a reconciliation of the parties in the civil war. Sh. continued that reconciliation, though somewhat favoring the Nasserist Muslims. In response to their demands, and to appease them, he moved closer to Egypt and her camp. He initiated a series of reforms in the administration aimed at strengthening the Muslim share in power, initiated public works in the backward north and south populated mainly by Muslims and enhanced the powers of the Presidency, striving for efficient, centralized government. His opponents claimed that he was employing bureaucratic and dictatorial methods, using the Secret Service for his own purpose and emptying the parliamentary system of content. Even after he retired

from the presidency in 1964 (declining urgent offers to arrange for an amendment of the constitution and his election for a second term), Sh. retained much influence through his supporters in Parliament, who formed a "Shihabist" bloc, through numerous army officers who remained loyal to him and through the Secret Services. In 1970, he was urged to stand again for the presidency (as permitted by the constitution after an interval of one term), but refused.

SHISHAKLI, ADIB (1901–64)   Syrian officer and politician. President of Syria, 1953–54. Born in Hama, Sh. served in the "Special Troops" set up by the French Mandate regime. In 1948 he was a senior officer in al-*Qawuqji's "Army of Deliverance" which fought the Jews in Palestine. He is said to have been a member of the Syrian Nationalist Party of Antoun *Sa'adeh. Sh. played a major part in Husni *Za'im's coup in 1949, but was suspected by Za'im of disloyalty and was dismissed from the army. He was reinstated by Sami *Hinnawi, after his coup, in Aug. 1949. On Dec. 19, 1949, he led a military coup which overthrew Hinnawi. At first, Sh. permitted the formal parliamentary regime established by Hinnawi to continue and he himself assumed only the title of Deputy Chief of Staff, though in fact he ruled behind the scenes. Sh. opposed the pro-Iraqi bent of the People's Party then in power, and on Nov. 29, 1951, carried out a second coup. His rule now became more openly dictatorial, although he appointed as a figurehead President and Prime Minister Marshal Fawzi Selo, one of his supporters. He assumed formal power in June 1953, when he became Premier and had himself elected President in a referendum. The same referendum approved a new constitution, which gave the President wide powers.

Sh. attempted to introduce several economic and social reforms, but did not persist in them. In 1952 he banned all political parties and established an Arab Liberation Movement as the single political organization. The ALM did not take root, and the parliament elected under its aegis in 1953 remained a nonrepresentative puppet-body. Since Sh. created order and stability in Syria, the West supported him, and he was considered pro-Western.

In Jan. 1954 resistance to his oppressive regime and antagonism he had aroused among the Druze community erupted in violent demonstrations. On Feb. 25, 1954, a coup forced Sh. to resign. He left Syria and lived in Lebanon, Sa'udia and France. In 1957 he was charged with plotting a coup with the support of Iraq and the West, and was tried *in absentia* several times. In 1960 he emigrated to Brazil. There he was assassinated in 1964 by a Druze in revenge for the bombing of the Druze Mountain during his rule.

SHPRINZAK, YOSEF (1885–1959)   Israeli political leader. Born in Russia he was one of the founders of the Socialist-Zionist movement *Ze'irei Zion* there. In 1910 he immigrated to Palestine and was elected Secretary-General of the *Hapoel Hatza'ir* party. He became the *de facto* leader of this party during all the years of its existence (until 1930). In the 1920s he was a member of the Zionist Executive.

When *Mapai* was founded in 1930 he became one of its main leaders and head of the moderate, pro-*Weizmann faction. He was also one of the leaders of the *Histadrut* and from 1945 to 1949 its Secretary-General.

With the establishment of the State of Israel S. was Chairman of the provisional Parliament and after the elections to the First Knesset, 1949, was elected Speaker. He served in this capacity until his death and had a formative influence on its patterns of functioning. In 1952, after the death of Chaim Weizmann, he was a candidate for President of Israel; but due to Ben Gurion's opposition, his party's Central Committee did not elect him.

AL-SHUQEIRI, AHMAD(1908–80)   Palestinian Arab politician, chairman of the PLO 1964–67. Born in Acre, the son of Sheikh As'as Sh., a prominent political and Muslim religious figure in Mandatory Palestine. A lawyer by profession, trained at the Jerusalem Law School and the American University of Beirut, Sh. in 1945 headed a Palestinian-Arab propaganda office in the USA, and later in Jerusalem. Briefly a member of the Palestinian Arab Higher Committee (Mar. to June 1946); member of the Syrian delegation to the UN 1949–50; Under Secretary for Political Affairs of the Arab League 1951–57 (according to his own account, he continued at the same time to represent Syria at the UN — from 1954 as Ambassador). Sh. was Sa'udi Arabian Minister of State for UN affairs and Ambassador to the UN 1957–62. During his tenure as Ambassador to the UN (Syrian or Sa'udi), he was the most active and vituperative spokesman for the Arab cause against Israel. In Apr. 1963 he was appointed as the representative of the Palestinian Arabs at the Arab League and was asked to prepare a plan and statutes for an

Ahmad al-Shuqeiri (AP Photo)

organization representing a Palestinian-Arab "entity." When the Palestinian Liberation Organization was established in 1964 under the auspices of the Arab League, Sh. became its Chairman. His leadership of the PLO was considered a failure — he was later also blamed for his violent and irresponsibly extremist speeches advocating the physical extermination of the Jews of Israel — and he was relieved of his post in Dec. 1967 (formalized July 1968) and retired from the political scene. Sh. published a book of memoirs (*Forty Years of Arab and International Life*, Arabic, Beirut 1969).

AL-SIBA'I, YUSUF(1917–78)   Egyptian officer, politician and writer. Born in Cairo to the Egyptian writer and scholar Muhammad al-Siba'i, S. graduated from the Military College in 1937 and served in the Army as an officer. In 1952 he was appointed Director of the Military Museum. Later the leaders of the Officers' Revolution of 1952 named him General Secretary of the Council for Literature and Art, as well as Chairman of the Writers' Association and the Cinema Critics' Association. He served as Secretary of the Asian and African Solidarity Conference, Cairo, Dec. 1957, and continued as Secretary-General of its permanent council.

S. became an active journalist. From 1966 he edited the weekly *Akher Sa'a*, and then was appointed Chairman of the Board of Directors of the *Dar al-Hilal* publishing house and later Chief Editor of the weekly *al-Musawwar*. From 1973 to 1976 he served as Minister of Culture and Information. In 1977 he was elected chairman of the Journalists' Association.

S. also wrote fiction committed to serving the Egyptian Revolution. He published more than 20 novels and short story collections; from some of them movies and TV films were made.

S. backed *Sadat's initiative for peace with Israel, 1977, and was seen by Palestinian-Arab activists as a foe. He was assassinated on 18 Feb. 1978, in the course of a Palestinian terrorist attack on an Afro-Asian Solidarity Congress held in Cyprus.

SIDQI, BAKR (1890–1937) Iraqi officer and politician, reportedly of Kurdish origin. A graduate of the Ottoman military academy, he served in command positions in the Ottoman army throughout World War I. In 1921 he joined the newly-formed Iraqi army. In 1933, as commanding officer of the army in northern Iraq, S. crushed what was described as an Assyrian rebellion (others saw it as a massacre of the Assyrians), and was promoted to the rank of General. In 1935 he put down several tribal rebellions in southern Iraq. He headed a group of army officers who looked with distaste at the disputes of civilian politicians and wished to emulate their colleagues in Iran and Turkey who had played so prominent a part in modernizing their country. S. collaborated clandestinely with the civilian politician Hikmat Suleiman and the leftist reformist *Ahali* Group. In Oct. 1936, when he was Acting Chief of the General Staff, S. moved military units to Baghdad and forced Prime Minister Yassin al-*Hashemi to resign. Hikmat Suleiman became Prime Minister and S. Chief of the General Staff and the strong man and real ruler of the country. His was the first straightforward military coup d'etat in the newly independent Arab countries. His reformist plans remained largely unimplemented. S. was assassinated in Aug. 1937 by a group of dissident officers.

SIDQI, ISMA'IL (1875–1950) Egyptian politician. Trained as a lawyer at Cairo Law School and abroad, S. was a minister in Egypt's semi-independent government from 1914 (Agriculture; *Waqf*). In 1918–19 he supported the nationalists under Sa'd *Zaghlul and accompanied him to exile in the Seychelles in 1919. He subsequently left Zaghlul's *Wafd* Party and participated in setting up the Liberal Constitutional Party in 1922. He was Minister of the Interior in 1924–25 on behalf of that party. S. became Prime Minister in June 1930 and substituted for the 1923 constitution — suspended since 1928 — a more conservative one and altered the election law. He founded a party to support him in Parliament — the People's Party (*Hizb al-Sha'b*) — and won the elections of May 1931 under the new election law. His rule, in collaboration with the King and under his orders, was conservative and considered by many as autocratic. His aim was also to strengthen the monarchy and weaken the *Wafd* Party. S.'s harsh rule aroused much opposition and growing popular resistance. When his government became involved in a corruption scandal, it fell in Sept. 1933. As a former Prime Minister, he was a member of the delegation which negotiated and signed the Anglo-Egyptian Treaty of 1936. In Feb. 1946, he again became Prime Minister. He reached an agreement with the British Foreign Secretary, Ernest Bevin, on the evacuation of British forces from Egypt within three years and the establishment of a joint defense council. The agreement was not ratified, as both sides published conflicting interpretations of the clause dealing with the future self-determination of Sudan, and S. was compelled to resign in Dec. 1946. He never again held government office. S. was also President of the Association of Industrialists and a protagonist of conservative capitalism. He did not believe in Arab unity and in 1946, while head of the government, had contacts with Zionist envoys towards a settlement of the Palestine problem. In 1948 S. had the courage to warn in the Senate, alone, against the Egyptian invasion of Palestine. He later published a series of articles in which he advocated an understanding with Israel. His memoirs were published, in Arabic, in 1950.

SMILANSKY, YIZHAR (S. YIZHAR) (b. 1916) Israeli writer. Born in Rehovot, son of Ze'ev Smilansky, a journalist and one of the founders of *Hapoel Hatzair*. A graduate of the Jerusalem Beit Hakerem Teachers' College, he taught in the Ben-Shemen Youth Village and in Rehovot. His first story was published in 1938 in Yitzhak Lamdan's literature magazine *Gilyonot*. During the 1940s S. published several collections of stories which established him as a leading representative of the young, Israel-born generation of writers.

In the War of Independence, 1948, he served as

an education officer. In 1949 he was elected to the First Knesset on the *Mapai* list, at the insistence of *Ben Gurion, though he was not a member of *Mapai*; he remained a member of the Knesset until 1967, first for *Mapai* and from 1965 for Ben Gurion's *Rafi*. Since leaving the Knesset he has been a professor of literature at Tel Aviv University.

In 1958 he published his *magnum opus*, the novel *The Days of Ziklag*, considered the most important novel about the War of Independence, making him the leading writer of the "Generation of 1948." He received the Brenner and Israel Prizes for this novel. Since *The Days of Ziklag* he has not written another major work.

Even after his resignation from the Knesset he continued to be active in public life. At first he was a member of Ben-Gurion's *Tenuah La'am*, and afterwards he expressed his views primarily through articles published in *Davar*. During the past few years he is a prominent spokesman of the dovish camp.

SNEH(original name: Kleinbaum), MOSHE(1909–72) Israeli political leader. Born in Radzin, Poland, at a young age he stood out as a leader of the Zionist movement in Poland. In 1930 he was chairman of the Zionist Students Union in Warsaw, in 1932 he

Moshe Sneh (GPO, Jerusalem)

was elected to the Central Committee of the Zionist Organization in Poland and in 1935 he became the political editor of the widely circulated daily *Haint*. S. was an associate of Yitzhak *Greunbaum, head of the Zionist movement in Poland, and a leader of his Radical Faction which opposed *Weizmann and his policies. In 1935, after Greunbaum immigrated to Palestine, S. inherited his position as chairman of the Zionist Organization in Poland.

With the outbreak of World War II he served as an officer in the Polish army and in 1940 succeeded in leaving occupied Poland and immigrating to Palestine. Despite his youth and the fact that he had just arrived, within a short time he became an outstanding leader of the *Yishuv*. In 1941 he was named Head of the *Haganah*'s Central Command, thus becoming the "Defense Minister" of the *Yishuv*. In 1945 he was elected to the Jewish Agency Executive. He was considered to be part of *Ben Gurion's inner circle.

In 1946, on the eve of the "Black Sabbath," the imprisonment of the *Yishuv*'s leadership, S. managed to leave for Paris. There he resigned from his post as Head of the *Haganah*'s Central Command. At the 22nd Zionist Congress of Dec. 1946 he was elected head of the "Illegal" Immigration Department of the Jewish Agency Executive.

In 1947 his views underwent a marked change and he began advocating an alliance with the Soviet Union. At the end of 1947 he resigned from the Jewish Agency Executive due to that disagreement over the international orientation of the Zionist Movement. In Jan. 1948 he joined *Mapam*, just founded, and became one of its prominent leaders. In 1949 he was elected to the First Knesset. S. became a leader of the leftist faction, in *Mapam*. In 1953, in connection with the Prague Trials, he resigned from the party and formed the Israeli Socialist Left Party. In 1954 that party joined the Israel Communist Party (*Maki*). S. became one of its leaders and served as the editor of its daily organ *Kol Ha'am* (The Voice of the People). Thus, within a few years he went all the way from being one of the leaders of the establishment to the fringe of the country's political and social life. Despite this isolation, even during those years his rhetorical and literary abilities awarded him a great deal of esteem. He was considered to be one of the outstanding speakers in the Knesset.

In 1965 he played a central role in a split within *Maki* and became a leader of the more national and less doctrinal faction thus beginning a comeback to the center of public life. After the Six Day War, he was a vocal spokesmen in favor of peace based upon compromise. His death in early 1972 was widely mourned and his funeral became a mass demonstration of empathy with him.

STERN, AVRAHAM ("YAIR") (1907–42) Founder and commander of the *Lohamei Herut Israel* military underground formation. Born in Poland, S. immigrated to Palestine in 1925, graduated from the Gymnasia Ivrit high school in Jerusalem and studied philosophy at the Hebrew University. He joined the *Haganah* and was active in defending Jerusalem during the 1929 Arab riots. In 1931 he was one of those who left the *Haganah* and founded the more activist *Irgun B*, becoming its command secretary.

In 1937, after most of the *Irgun B* rejoined the *Haganah*, he was one of the founders of the *Irgun Zva'i Leumi* (IZL) and became one of its top commanders. He strongly opposed the policy of restraint followed by the *Yishuv*'s political leadership and the *Haganah*. He also opposed the subordination of the IZL to the political leadership of the Revisionist Party, seeing it as an autonomous underground movement which decided its own goals and policies. *Jabotinsky also opposed his extreme anti-British orientation and his concept of "total war" against the "foreign ruler" (Britain).

In 1938 he left for Poland on an IZL mission to achieve cooperation with the Polish authorities and to plan bringing 40,000 fighters to Palestine for an uprising; he also worked on explanding IZL cells in Poland and establishing a daily newspaper *in Yiddish, Die Tat*, (Action). Upon his return to Palestine and with the outbreak of the Second World War the conflict between him and the Revisionist leadership and the IZL command escalated. He strongly opposed their decision to cease attacks on the British for the duration of the war and their cooperation with the *Haganah*.

In June 1940 he seceded from the IZL and in Sept. 1940 he formed a new organization called "the IZL in Israel," which later became known as *Lehi*. This organization maintained, even at the height of the war, that the British were the most dangerous enemy of the Jewish people and in order to fight them one might even negotiate with the Nazis. Indeed, contact was made with the German embassy in Ankara (but failed). This collaboration with the Nazis and terror attacks the *Lehi* carried out against the British isolated the organization from most of the *Yishuv*. "Yair" himself, in hiding,

was discovered in Feb. 1942 by British police and shot dead on the spot.

AL-SULH, RIYAD (1894–1951) Arab nationalist and Lebanese politician. Prime Minister, 1943–45 and 1946–51. Scion of a prominent Sunni Muslim family in Beirut (which provided also other Prime Ministers — Sami S.; Taqi-ul-Din S. [b. 1909, Premier 1973–74]; Rashid S. [b. 1926, Premier 1974–75]), S. studied law in Beirut and Istanbul. He was active from his youth in the Arab nationalist movement. He was sentenced to death by a Turkish military court during World War I, but was pardoned. In 1918, he joined the administration set up by Amir *Feisal in Damascus and was one of the co-founders of the *Istiqlal* Party. When Feisal's rule collapsed, S. escaped from Syria. He worked in Egypt and Geneva for Syrian independence, in the framework of the Syrian-Palestinian Congress. Despite his Pan-Arab views, he had contacts with the Zionist leadership in the 1920s, and in 1921 tried to persuade the Palestinian-Arab leaders to accept Britain's Zionist policy. He returned to Lebanon only in 1936, when relations between the nationalist movement and France improved, and soon became one of the most prominent Sunni leaders.

In 1943, S. helped lay the foundations for independent Lebanon by agreeing with the Maronite Christian leader Bishara al-*Khouri on an unwritten "National Pact" which determined the regime and character of the state, based on an intercommunal equilibrium. He became the first Prime Minister of independent Lebanon and held this office for more than five years, 1943–45 and 1946–51. He was highly regarded also in the other Arab countries and was a co-founder of the Arab League, 1945. It was largely his influence that led Lebanon to join that body, despite her doubts and hesitations.

In 1949, while S. was Prime Minister, the right-wing Pan-Syrian leader Antoun *Sa'adeh was sentenced to death by a military court, in a summary trial, and executed. Sa'adeh's supporters held S. responsible and in revenge assassinated him in July 1951, on a visit to Jordan.

SUNALP, TURGUT (b.1917) Turkish officer and politician. He studied in the Kuleli Military Lyceum and in the War Academy in Ankara and became a professional officer. In 1959/60 he represented the Turkish General Command in the London talks about the future of Cyprus. S. commanded the Cyprus Regiment. Upon his return from Cyprus, he was awarded the rank of General and commanded a division and later the Land War Academy in Istanbul. S. has also served as Turkey's representative to NATO, Deputy Chief of Staff, and Commander of the Aegean Army. From 1976 to 1982 he was Turkey's ambassador to Canada. In May 1983, S. founded a National Democratic Party (NDP). In the elections of 1983 it won c. 70 seats, defeated by Turgut *Ozal's Motherland Party. Consequently, the party was in disarray and S. was expelled from its General Committee. After the NDP dissolved itself in 1986, he continued to represent Izmir as an independent member of Parliament.

SUNAY, CEVDET (1900–82) Turkish officer and politician, President, 1966–73. Born in Trabzon, S. attended Kuleli Military Lyceum and the Military Academy and served in the armed forces from 1916 to 1966. During World War I, he was stationed in Palestine and later joined *Ataturk in the battles against Greece. He gradually advanced in rank and became a General Staff officer in 1933. From 1942 to 1947 he taught at the Military College and in 1959 was promoted to the rank of General. Following the military coup of May 1960, he served as the Commander of the Land Forces and as Chief of the General Staff until 1966. In that year he was elected, with the support of all the major political parties, as the Turkish Republic's fifth President.

AL-SUWEIDI, TAWFIQ (1890–1968) Iraqi politician. S. served as Legal Adviser to the Iraqi government 1921–27, Minister of Education 1927–28, Prime Minister and Foreign Minister 1929, Speaker of Parliament 1929–30, Minister to Iran 1931–33. He was again Foreign Minister 1937–38, 1941 (in the restored pro-British government, after the ouster of Rashid 'Ali *Kilani), 1950 and 1953, Prime Minister 1946 and 1950, and Deputy Prime Minister 1958. S. also served as Foreign Minister of the short-lived Iraqi-Jordanian "Arab Federation," May-July 1958. After the July 1958 coup he was sentenced to life imprisonment; his sentence was reduced to 10 years, but he was released in July 1961 and left for Lebanon. S. was one of the leaders of the conservative and pro-British faction loyal to the *Hashemite dynasty.

T

TABATABAI, ZIYA-UL-DIN (1890–1969) Iranian politician. Born in Yazd, the son of a religious leader. Considered a prominent writer and reformer, he cooperated with Colonel Reza Khan (later *Reza Shah Pahlavi) in the coup of Feb. 1921 that forced Ahmad Shah to hand over power to Reza Khan as Commander in Chief and Minister of War and T. as Prime Minister.

As his first act of state, T., who had opposed a draft Anglo-Iranian Treaty of 1919, which he saw as humiliating, signed a treaty with the Soviet Union (Feb. 1921) in which the Soviets, in order to break British influence and ascendancy, agreed to relinquish most of their privileges and concessions and to evacuate Iran.

T. fell out with Reza Khan after some time, was dismissed and went into exile. The British granted T. refuge in Palestine where he lived until 1943. He returned to Iran in 1943 and founded a political party, National Will (*Irade-i-Melli*), considered pro-British. In 1944, he was elected to the *Majlis* (Parliament). In 1946, he pressured Prime Minister *Qavam-as-Saltana to expel from the cabinet ministers from the Communist *Tudeh* Party who had joined the government the same year, and take other anti-Communist and anti-Soviet steps. However, he himself was arrested that same year by Qavam in an effort to appease the Soviets. His party faded away, and he failed in his efforts to carve out for himself a position as a right-wing reformist leader.

TABENKIN, YITZHAK (1887–1971) A leader of the Israel Labor movement. Born in Bobruysk, Russia, T. was one of the founders and main activists of the socialist-Zionist *Poalei Zion* movement. In 1912 he immigrated to Palestine and was a farm worker in several places, becoming one of the leaders of the union of agricultural workers. At first, though active in the Labor movement, he did not join any of its political factions. At the end of the First World War he was a co-founder of the *Ahdut Ha'avodah* Party, together with David *Ben Gurion and Berl *Katznelson. He was also one of the founders of the *Histadrut*. From the early 1920s he devoted most of his energy to forming the kibbutz movement. He was a founder of *Kibbutz* Ein Harod, and of the *Kibbutz Hameuhad*, during the 1930s and 1940s the largest association of *kibbutz* settlements. In 1925 he headed the *Histadrut* delegation to Poland and laid the foundations for the strong ties of *"Hehalutz"* in Poland with the *Kibbutz Hameuhad*.

In 1930 he was one of the founders of *Mapai*. He led a faction which opposed Ben Gurion's policy of shaping *Mapai* into a party which would dominate the Zionist movement, claiming that that would water down the party's socialist character. He thus became the leader of the opposition within the party. He opposed the agreement which Ben Gurion signed with *Jabotinsky in 1934. He also opposed the partition of Palestine proposed in 1937. During those years T. did not fill any executive position in the *Yishuv* and his power stemmed primarily from his position as leader of the *Kibbutz Hameuhad*.

In 1944 he led his faction ("Faction B," *Si'ah Beth*) to secede from *Mapai* and headed the new party which was formed, *"Ahdut Ha'avodah"*. During those years he was a staunch supporter of the *Palmah* and was its spiritual leader. In 1948 he led *Ahdut Ha'avodah* to unite with *Kibbutz Artzi (Hashomer Hatza'ir)* and from the *Mapam* Party and he headed its list to the First Knesset (1949). But in 1954 his faction seceded from *Mapam* and reestablished *Ahdut Ha'avodah*, which he led again. He headed its list to the Third Knesset, 1955, and served as a Member of Knesset until 1957. In 1965 he reunited his party with the Labor Party, in the Alignment. In 1967, after the Six Day War, he was one of the founders and leaders of the movement for a greater Israel (the Whole Land of Israel).

T. was one of the central leaders of the Israel Labor movement. For many years — before and after the establishment of the State of Israel — he refused to hold an executive position and only served in the Knesset for a short period. He always put great stress on ideological principles and opposed Ben Gurion's pragmatism. He also consistently advocated radical, "activist" policies. Within his movement — the *Kibbutz Hameuhad* — he was the admired mentor and nearly unchallenged leader. However, his influence on Israeli society as a whole was limited.

TALAL IBN 'ABDULLAH (1909–72)   King of Jordan 1951–52. The elder son of King *'Abdullah Ibn Hussein, born in Mecca, T. ascended the Jordanian throne in 1951, after the assassination of his father. His reign was short-lived and his personality or policy left no imprint, though he was popular as being supposedly "nationalist" and "democratic." T. was found to suffer from a mental illness and was dethroned in Aug. 1952, his son *Hussein succeeding. T. spent the remaining twenty years of his life in a mental institution in Istanbul.

TALAT PASHA MEHMED (1874–1921)   One of the leaders of the "Young Turks'" Revolution, 1908, and the regime they set up; Prime Minister 1917–18. Born into a poor family in Adrianople (Edirne), he studied at local schools and became a PTT official in Edirne Salonika. T. was active in the Young Turks' movement, and after their revolt (1908), became a member of Parliament for Edirne and soon Minister of the Interior. Together with *Enver Pasha and *Cemal Pasha he seized the government in a coup, 1913, and in practice that triumvirate governed Turkey during the First World War. In 1917, he became Prime Minister (Grand Vizier).

When the Ottoman Empire fell T. escaped to Europe. He was assassinated in 1921 in Berlin by an Armenian, as he was considered co-responsible for the massacre of Armenians during the war.

TALEGHANI, AYATULLAH MAHMUD(1910–79) Iranian religious leader. Born in Taleghan near Qazvin, T. studied Islamic law and theology in Qom. Considered a rather progressive and liberal cleric, he joined the struggle against the Shah and was first arrested in 1939. In the early 1950s he supported *Mossaddeq, and after the Shah's and *Zahedi's counter-coup in 1953 he was arrested again.

In 1961 he and Mehdi *Bazargan founded the left-of-center Iran Liberation Movement, which tried to revive Mossaddeq's National Front coalition in the 1960s. He was again arrested and in 1971 was exiled to southeast Iran. In 1977 he was arrested on the accusation of supporting the leftist-Islamic *Mujahidin Khalq* militants. Released in Nov. 1978, when Islamic resistance neared its peak, he used his contacts with the various resistance factions — Islamic-clerical, right, and left, including groups like the *Mujahidin* (one of his sons was a leader of the *Mujahidin* and another reportedly was with the Marxist *Fedayin Khalq*) — to forge a united revolutionary camp in anticipation of the Islamic takeover of 1979. T. was thus co-instrumental in the Islamic Revolution, accepting *Khomeini's supreme leadership. He was popular among intellectuals and students, who referred to him as the "intellectual Ayatullah"; when Iran's Kurds rebelled they would accept only his mediation; and because of his contacts with leftists, he was sometimes called the "Red Mullah." But he soon found himself in growing discord with the leaders of the new Islamic Republic. He believed that it was forbidden to force the government on the people — and said so. He upheld the rights of political and religious minorities, including the Communist *Tudeh* Party. While he agreed that the heads of the Shah's regime should be brought to trial, he warned against taking revenge against the innocent. He refused to sit on the Islamic court trying members of the former regime and to become a member of the Council of the Revolution. In his writings and lectures he laid down guidelines for a just Islamic order, rejecting both capitalism and Communism, because they valued material gains over the individual's freedom, and seeing freedom as the most important aspect of life. Taking a position between Khomeini and *Shari-atmadari, he accepted some intervention by the clergy in government affairs, but opposed the concentration of power in their hands.

In Apr. 1979, after two of his sons were arrested and tortured for their left-wing activities, T. left Tehran, threatening to leave Iran altogether in protest against the return of despotism and dictatorship. After a few days, he met with Khomeini and accepted a reconciliation, expressing his loyalty to him (thereby disappointing many radicals). One month before his death, he also accepted a seat in the Council of Experts, the body guiding the regime.

TALHOUNI, BAHJAT(b. 1913)   Jordanian jurist and politician. Born in Ma'an, southern Jordan, a

Bahjat Talhouni (Bar-David, Tel Aviv)

graduate in law from Damascus University, T. served as Attorney General and later as a judge. He was Minister of the Interior 1953–54, Chief of the Royal Court 1954–60 and 1963–64, Prime Minister 1960–61 (serving also as his own Foreign Minister), 1964–65, 1967–69, 1969–70. He was appointed President of the Senate in 1974 and held that position until Jan. 1983. In 1984 and 1989 he was reappointed to the Senate and served as its Vice-President. T. was mainly an administrator executing the King's will, and his political and decision-making influence was limited.

AL-TALL, 'ABDULLAH (1918–73)   Jordanian officer and politician. Born in Irbid, T. rose in the ranks of the Arab Legion, Transjordan's army. In the Palestine War of 1948 he served in the Jerusalem area, and when Jordan occupied East Jerusalem he became commander of the city, with the rank of Lieutenant-Colonel. In that capacity he was the chief liaison with the Israel army and negotiated agreements and arrangements for the Jerusalem area. He was, however, considered a radical nationalist, anti-British and anti-Israel, and

opposed to King *'Abdullah's efforts to reach a peace agreement with Israel. He was suspected of plotting, with Egyptian and Syrian support, to overthrow the regime. In 1949 he resigned from the army and went to Egypt, where he attempted to organize Jordanian opposition groups in preparation for a future takeover. He was tried *in absentia* and convicted of playing a part in the assassination of King 'Abdullah. In 1959 he published his memoirs, in which he bitterly attacked the Hashemite dynasty and the Jordanian regime. In 1965 T. was allowed to return to Jordan. He settled down in Irbid and was no longer active in public life, though King Hussein later appointed him a member of the Senate, to replace his relative, Prime Minister Wasfi al-*Tall, assassinated in Nov. 1971.

AL-TALL, WASFI (1920–71)   Jordanian politician. Born in Irbid, a graduate of the American University of Beirut, T. began his career as a teacher. From 1942 to 1945 he served in the British army, reaching the rank of captain. In 1945 he became a member of Mussa al-*'Alami's team and worked until 1947 in his information/propaganda offices in London and Jerusalem. During the Palestine War of 1948 he joined *Qawuqji's "Army of Deliverance." In 1949 he joined Jordan's

Wasfi al-Tall (Bar-David, Tel Aviv)

diplomatic and civil service. After rising in its ranks, he was Ambassador to Iraq in 1961–62. T. became Prime Minister and Minister of Defense in 1962, for one year, and was again Prime Minister in 1965–67 and 1970–71. An able administrator, he was considered loyal to the King and a hard-line anti-Nasserist. He assumed his last Premiership during the decisive crisis between the royal regime and the PLO and continued and completed the liquidation of the PLO establishment in Jordan that had begun in Sept. 1970. He was assassinated in Nov. 1971 by Palestinian-Arab terrorists, while on a visit to Cairo; his murder was the first appearance of the extremist "Black September" organization.

TAMIR (original name: Katznelson), **SHMUEL** (1923–87)   Israeli jurist and politician. Born in Jerusalem to a prominent family — his uncle was Zalman *Shazar, the third president of the State of Israel, and his mother was a member of the Knesset. A graduate of the Gymnasia Ivrit high school, he joined the IZL in his youth and held command positions; in 1944 and 1946 he was arrested and in 1947 sent to a detention camp in Kenya. There he was allowed to sit for the final law examinations of the Government School of Law.

In 1948, with the establishment of the State of Israel, he was released from detention, returned to Israel and opened a law practice. He was a founder of the *Herut* movement, but left it after a short time. In the 1950s he became widely known as he appeared in a number of political trials — such as the "*Kasztner Trial," which he turned from a defense of Malkiel Greenwald accused of libel into an attack on Kasztner and the *Mapai*-led establishment, and the libel suit in which he defended a right-wing "Group of Volunteers." During those years he co-founded a "New Regime" group aiming to reform the system of government.

In the mid-1960s he returned to the *Herut* movement and in 1965 was elected on its list to the Sixth Knesset. But soon his relations with the movement's leader, Menahem *Begin, worsened, and at the beginning of 1967 he was forced to leave *Herut*. He formed a new right-wing Free Center Party. After the Six Day War he coined the slogan "Liberated territory will not be returned." In the elections to the Seventh Knesset, 1969, his Free Center Party won only two seats.

In 1973, after the establishment of the *Likud*, T. returned to the party, but soon afterwards again left it. In 1977 he joined the Democratic Movement for Change (*Dash*) and was elected on its list to the Ninth Knesset. In Oct. 1977 he was the architect of *Dash*'s joining the government and was appointed Minister of Justice. He resigned in 1980 and tried to rejoin the *Likud*, but was not welcomed back. He was not elected to the Tenth Knesset, 1981, and returned to his legal practice. In his last public activity, he participated in negotiations for the release of Israeli prisoners of the Lebanon War.

T. was a prominent political figure of the Israel-born generation. He was highly controversial — a gifted jurist and politician with an unusual talent of expression, but seen by many as a demagogue, frequently changing his position on many matters. However, he never changed his basic views — nationalist and right-wing.

TIMISI, MUSTAFA (b. 1934)   Turkish politician, former Secretary-General of the Social Democratic Populist Party. Born in Divrigi, he graduated from the Academy of Economics and Commerce in Ankara. After his army service he entered politics, serving two terms as a member of Parliament for the Republican People's Party (1969–74). Later he defected and tried to set up a Turkish United Party of his own.

When party activity was banned after the military take-over of Sept. 1980, T. continued to be active underground. When political activity was renewed in 1983 he joined the Social Democratic Party (SODEP) and became a member of its Central Committee. When this party merged with the Populist Party, 1985, he was chosen as Secretary-General of the united party (SODEPOP). Though T. soon lost this position, he continued as an active member of the party's Central Committee.

TOUMA, EMIL (1918–85)   Palestinian-Arab writer and journalist in Israel, a leading member of the Israeli Communist Party. Born in Haifa to a Greek Orthodox family, T. went to high school in Haifa and Jerusalem. In 1939 T. joined the Palestinian Communist Party and was one of the founders of the Arab Trade Unions. In 1943 he joined in establishing the National Liberation Organization. In 1944 T. founded the Communist biweekly *al-Ittihad.* Conforming to the party line, he supported the partition of Palestine in 1947/48 and stayed in Israel, becoming one of the leaders of the Israeli Communist Party and continuing as editor of its chief organ *al-Ittihad.* Later he received his Ph.D. in history at the Soviet Oriental Institute. He represented the Israeli Communist Party at several international conferences and published several books on Arab affairs, mainly on the national movement of the Arabs in Palestine, such as *The Roots of the Palestinian Problem* (Nazareth, 1962) and *Sixty Years of the National Movement in Palestine* (Ramallah, 1978), both in Arabic.

TOUQAN (TAWQAN) Prominent Palestinian Arab family centered in Nablus, with a large branch in Jordan; the origin of the clan seems to have been in Jordan. For generations, the T. clan has been competing for supremacy in Nablus with the al-Nimr, *'Abd-ul-Hadi and other families. During the Ottoman period, members of the T. family served in many government positions; several of them were governors of the Nablus district. Under the Palestine Mandate the T. clan was a mainstay of the *Nashashibi-led camp of the "Opposition" (the camp opposing the dominance of the *Husseini-led camp), though not all its members always conformed to that rule. Several T.'s were prominent in the Jordan administration.

The outstanding member of the family in recent decades was Suleiman *T. Other prominent members: **Haidar T.** (1871–1952) was Mayor of Nablus in the Ottoman days and from 1912 represented the district in the Ottoman Parliament. **Hafez T.** (d. 1927) headed the Nablus Muslim-Christian Association in the 1920s and was from 1923 a member of the Arab Executive. His son **Qadri T.** (1908? 1910?-71) was a mathematician, the author of textbooks, and the principal of al-Najah College in Nablus. He also wrote books on national and political problems and was active in politics. He served as Jordan's Foreign Minister in 1964–64. A present-generation member, **Hafez T.**, a Nablus business, was in Mar. 1986 appointed acting Mayor of Nablus by the Israeli authorities, but resigned in 1988. **Baha'-ul-Din T.** (b. 1910) was prominent in Jordan's diplomatic service (Minister in Cairo 1948–51 and Ankara 1951–54, Ambassador in London 1956–58, at the UN 1958 and again 1971–72, in Rome 1973, and in Belgrade 1975–78, Minister of the Royal Court, 1973–75, and a member of the Senate). King *Hussein married T.'s daughter 'Aliya in 1972 (she died in 1977 in an accident), and he is the grandfather of two of the King's children. **Ahmad T.** (1903–81), Nablus-born, was Director of Education in the Jordan-occupied West Bank and from 1950 to 1954 Minister in the Jordanian Cabinet (Education, Public Works, Communications, Foreign Affairs). From 1954 to 1963 he was on the staff of UNESCO. After

returning to Jordan, he became Foreign Minister, 1967–69, with the rank of Deputy Prime Minister, in 1969 briefly also Defense Minister. In 1970 he was Prime Minister for one month, taking over from a short-lived military government during the bloody confrontation with the Palestinian-Arab guerrillas; his Premiership was a compromise between the pro-guerrilla pressure of all-Arab mediators and counter-pressure by the army and anti-PLO hard-liners. T. was Chief of the Royal Cabinet in 1970–71 and again in 1972–73. He became a Senator in 1973, and Chairman of the Board of Trustees of the University of Jordan in 1972. **Jamal T.** (b. 1906) was a senior official and district governor and served as Foreign Minister in 1954 and Minister of Education in 1957, each time briefly. **Salah-ul-Din T.** (b. 1914) also of the Jordanian branch, a Damascus-trained jurist, served in various judicial posts. In 1956 he joined the leftist opposition and became Finance Minister in its al-*Nabulsi government, until 1957. But he returned to the camp loyal to the establishment and was appointed a member of the Senate in 1961. He was elected to Parliament in 1962 and was its Speaker in 1962–63. He was again a Senator in 1973–74 and in 1979–83. **Taysir T.** held several ambassadorial posts (Libya, Italy). **Ibrahim T.** (1905–41) was a well-known Palestine-Arab poet; his younger sister **Fadwa T.** also writes poetry with a strongly nationalist message.

TOUQAN, SULEIMAN 'ABD-UL-RAZZAQ (1888? 1890?-1958)   Palestinian-Arab and Jordanian politician. Educated in Istanbul (Law School and Military Academy), T. ran his family's olive oil and soap factories and other business enterprises in Nablus. He was mayor of Nablus from 1925 to 1948 and the dominant leader of the towns. He was close to Amir *'Abdullah of Transjordan and to the *Nashashibi-led Palestinian-Arab camp opposing the dominance of the *Husseini faction; in 1934 he was among the founders of that camp's National Defense Party. He was considered pro-British and moderate in the Arab-Jewish conflict. When Arab guerrillas turned against the Arab opposition, in 1937–39, T. organized counterguerrillas (the "Peace Gangs"), in collaboration with some branches of the British military and to some extent with the Jews. After 1948, he helped consolidate Jordanian rule in the West Bank. From 1950 he was a member, and later Deputy-President, of the Jordanian Senate. T. was Minister of Defense in 1951–52, and Minister of the Royal Court

1953–55. During the crisis of Apr. 1957 — the restoration of the King's power after an attempted coup — he was again Minister of Defense, and Military Governor, until July. After serving again as Minister of the Royal Court, 1957–58, T. became Minister of Defense in the Federal Government of the short-lived Jordan-Iraq "Arab Federation," 1958. He was assassinated in July 1958 in Baghdad, during the coup that put an end to *Hashemite rule in Iraq.

TRUMPELDOR, YOSEF (1880–1920)   Zionist pioneer and soldier. Born in southern Russia, in 1902 he was inducted into the Czar's army, partici- pated in the Port Arthur battles of the Russo- Japanese War, 1904/05, was severely wounded and lost his left arm. When he recuperated, he returned to the battlefront and was taken prisoner. In the prison camp in Japan he organized the Jew- ish prisoners of war. In 1906 he was released, returned to Russia and, despite being a Jew, attained the rank of officer and received medals for his bravery and leadership in battle.

After his return, he studied law at the University of St. Petersburg. During this period he organized a Zionist group of young people who dreamed of founding agricultural communes in Palestine.

In 1912 he immigrated to Palestine and joined Degania, the first *kvutzah*. In 1914, with the out- break of the First World War, he tried to return to Russia and join the Russian army, but the Ottoman authorities deported him to Egypt. There he met Ze'ev *Jabotinsky and together they worked to establish Jewish Battalions. He was one of the founders of the Zion Mule Corps which fought on the Gallipoli front (1914–1915) as part of the Brit- ish army. After the Corps was dissolved, he went to London where he continued his efforts to form Jewish battalions within the British army.

In 1917 he returned to Russia where he organized Jewish youth in the *Hehalutz* organization, prepar- ing youth for immigration to Palestine, and chaired its founding conference in 1919. That same year he returned to Palestine and tried to prevent the disso- lution of the Jewish Battalions.

In Jan. 1920, as the security situation in the north of Palestine worsened, he went to Tel-Hai in Upper Galilee to assist its settlers. On Mar. 1, 1920, he was killed defending Tel-Hai. His death became a legend, a symbol of heroic self-defense. The *G'dud Ha'avodah* (Labor Battalion) founded half a year after his death was named for him, as was Kibbutz Tel-Yosef in the Jezreel Valley. T. is the hero of the two main, and rival, political trends in the *Yishuv* — the Labor movement and the Revisionists, whose youth movement — *Betar* (an acronym for *Brit Yosef Trumpeldor*) — is named for him. On the site where he fell, a statue of a roaring lion was erected and every year thousands of youngsters visit it on the anniversary of his death.

TÜRKEŞ, ALPARSLAN (b.1917)   Turkish officer and politician. Born in Nicosia, Cyprus, T. moved with his family to Istanbul in 1932, graduated from the Military Academy there in 1938 and became a professional officer. He had strong pro-German sympathies and claimed that Nazism and German principles of strong government were quite similar to Turkish Kemalism. He took part in an anti- Communist demonstration in 1944, and was arrested and put on trial, but was released. After the war T. served as a military attache and with NATO. He participated in the military coup of May 1960, and became a member of the "National Unity Committee," the junta that ruled Turkey in 1960–61, and a chief aide to General *Gursel, its head. He advocated the extension of military rule and speedy radical reforms that would implement *Ataturk's principles. Due to his radical views and his opposition to the return to civilian-political rule he was expelled from the National Unity Committee and was sent as a military attache to India.

In 1963, after returning from India, he was accused of conspiring against the government, but was found not guilty. He resigned from the army and joined the right-wing Republican Peasants' Nation Party. In 1965 he became leader of the party, eventually exercising dictatorial power and appointing his supporters to key posts (causing the old founder-leaders of the party to leave it and reestablish their own party). He also changed the name of the party — which was widely considered to be fascist — to the "Nationalist Action Move- ment Party." In the elections of 1969 his party lost heavily, and he remained its only representative in Parliament. He now increasingly fostered Pan- Turkish ideas stressing Turkey's ties to all peoples of Turkish origin or speaking Turkish languages, outside Turkey, e.g., in Soviet Central Asia, and her willingness to help them and reestablish a "Greater Turkish" nation and state.

In 1975–76 and again in 1977–78 T. was named Deputy Prime Minister in *Demirel's right-wing government. T. used his position to put his suppor- ters in key military, police, and government posts.

He was accused of using extreme means to achieve and maintain his power, including the murder of political opponents, and of stepping up his extreme-rightist propaganda, translating and distributing even Nazi propaganda.

After the military coup of 1980 he went into hiding, but gave himself up. He was put on trial in 1981, with several hundreds of his men, but after a heart attack he was hospitalized in 1983 and provisionally released in 1985. In Apr. 1987 he was sentenced to 11 years' imprisonment (the prosecution had asked for a death sentence), but remained free for health reasons. The days of his political activity and influence, however, ended in 1980.

U

ÜLÜSÜ, BÜLENT (b.1923) Turkish officer and politician. Prime Minister 1980–83. U. graduated from the Naval Academy in 1942 with advanced studies 1952 and served in the Turkish navy. In 1964 U. was appointed Navy Chief of Operations; he was promoted to Rear Admiral in 1967, Vice Admiral in 1970, and Admiral in 1974. He became Under Secretary in the Defense Ministry (1975) and Admiral of the Fleet (1977–80).

After the military coup of Sept. 1980, U. was appointed Prime Minister — a position he held until the military regime was replaced by the elections of Nov. 1983; his government was composed of technocrats and politicians acceptable to the army. He was considered an able administrator with moderate political views.

Bulent Ulusu (AP Photo)

ÜRGÜPLÜ, SUAT (1903–81) Turkish politician. Born in Damascus, U. was educated in the English High School and studied law at the University of Istanbul. He was a judge of commercial courts, 1929–32, and from 1932 to 1939 had a private law practice. He was elected to Parliament in 1939 for Kayseri and chaired the Istanbul section of the Republican People's Party (1942–43). He was Minister of Customs and Monopolies (1943–46) and again worked in private law practice from 1946 to 1950. In 1950, he was elected as a representative of Kayseri for the Democratic Party and headed the Turkish delegation to the Council of Europe in Strasbourg. He was ambassador to West Germany in 1952 and Spain in 1960. In the early 1960s he was elected to the Senate and was its President from 1963 to 1965. When the Inonu government was defeated in Feb. 1965 and opposition parties formed a coalition, U. was named Prime Minister. He headed the government until the elections of Oct. 1965.

USSISHKIN, MENAHEM (MENDEL) (1863–1941) Zionist leader, President of the Jewish National Fund. Born in Dubrovno, Russia, U. moved to Moscow with his family in 1871. From 1882 he studied at the Moscow Technological Institute, graduating in 1889 as an engineer. At the university he founded a Zionist group. In 1884 he was elected to the council of *B'nei Zion*, and in 1885 to that of *Hovevei Zion* — groups which nurtured many future Zionist leaders.

In 1891 he first visited Palestine and published his travel diary. He participated at all the Zionist Congresses, from the First (Basel, 1897). From 1898 until his death he was a member of the Zionist Action Committee. U. opposed Herzl's pure "Political Zionism," advocating "Practical Zionism" that would engage in settlement activity in Palestine. At the Sixth Zionist Congress, 1903, he vehemently opposed Herzl's suggestion to accept an offer of settling Jews in Uganda, and published a pamphlet entitled "Our Program" in which he formulated the main tenets of "Synthetic Zionism": a combination of political-diplomatic activity with practical activity of purchasing and settling land in Palestine.

From 1906 to 1919 U. headed the *Hovevei Zion* Council in Odessa which assisted in the establishment of settlements such as Ein Ganim near Petah Tikvah. In 1912 he visited Palestine and laid the groundwork for operations of the Zionist Organization in Palestine. At the Zionist Congress of 1913 he was one of the initiators of the idea of a university in Palestine. He was a member of the Zionist delegation to the Versailles Peace Conference, 1919.

In Nov. 1919 he immigrated to Palestine. For three years (1919–1923) he headed the *Va'ad Hatzirim*, the Zionist delegation provisionally in charge of Jewish affairs in Palestine. He was also active in attaining for Hebrew the status of an official language in Palestine. In 1921 he supported the extensive land purchases in the Jezreel Valley. From 1923 until his death he headed the Jewish National Fund. In this capacity he was a chief architect of land purchases and all settlement activities. He also continued promoting the establishment of a university in Jerusalem, 1925, and served on its board. In 1935 he was elected Chairman of the Zionist Action Committee. Politically he took a hard line and was considered right-wing. In 1937 he strongly opposed the partition plan proposed by the Peel Commission.

U. was one of the central leaders of the *Yishuv* and the Zionist movement. He wielded great influence and was highly respected. In 1939 a group of settlements in the Upper Galilee were named for him. K'far Menahem in the northern Negev is also named for him.

V

VILAYATI, 'ALI AKBAR (b.1945)   Iranian politician, Foreign Minister since Dec. 1981. Born in Tehran, V. in 1971 completed medical studies at the University of Tehran. After some postgraduate studies in the United States he taught at the Tehran Medical School.

After the Islamic Revolution (1979), V. served as Assistant Minister of Health and as a member of Parliament from Tehran. He was appointed Foreign Minister in Dec. 1981, when Iranian diplomacy was in disarray and succeeded in reforming the Foreign Service and reestablishing an orderly foreign policy.

V., considered a conservative, stood fast against pressure by radical groups demanding a revolutionary foreign policy and resisted extreme undiplomatic approaches accompanied by slogans and rhetoric as practiced during the first years of the revolution. He strengthened Iran's participation in international organizations, resumed relations with some Western nations, and advanced ties with Islamic countries and nations of the Third World. In Nov. 1989 Supreme Leader *Khamenei appointed him a member of the Council of the Islamic Revolution. As Foreign Minister he also is a member of the National Security Council.

W

AL-WAZIR, KHALIL ("ABU JIHAD")(1936–88) Palestinian-Arab guerrilla/terrorist organizer. Born in Ramla, W. left his home with the Palestinian refugees in 1948, when Israel became independent. In the 1960s he was among the founders of the guerrilla/terrorist organization *al-Fatah* (which in 1969 became dominant in the Palestine Liberation Organization, PLO) and its "military" arm, *al-'Asifa*. In the 1970s he emerged as *al-Fatah*'s chief "military" leader and was thus co-responsible for most of its guerrilla/terrorist operations. He was a loyal associate of PLO chairman *'Arafat and stood by him in his efforts to impose PLO discipline and a centralized military command on the various dissident factions. He was a member of the Executive Council of *al-Fatah*, but not of the PLO Executive (as a "military" man, not a political leader). W. was killed at his home in Tunis in Apr. 1988 — reportedly by an Israeli commando.

WEIZMANN, CHAIM(1874–1952)   Zionist statesman, the first President of the State of Israel. Born in the village of Motol, near Pinsk in Russia, W. studied chemistry at universities in Switzerland and Germany. In 1904 he was appointed Professor of Chemistry at Manchester University in Britain.

W. was active in the Zionist movement since its inception. In 1901 he established a "Democratic Faction," which criticized the movement's leadership and stressed "Practical Zionism" with settlement activity in Palestine as the central aim, as against "Political Zionism" with diplomatic activity and obtaining a charter as its central aim. After Herzl's death, 1904, he was one of the founders of "Synthetic Zionism" which sought to find a synthesis of these two trends.

During the First World War, W. began to play a central role in the Zionist movement. He was primarily responsible for obtaining the Balfour Declaration, 1917, which later served as the basis for the British Mandate for Palestine. In 1920 he was elected President of the World Zionist Organi-

Chaim Weizmann (GPO, Jerusalem)

zation. In 1918 he headed the "Delegates' Committee" (*Va'ad Hatzirim*) sent by the Zionist Executive to supervise activities in Palestine. In 1919 he represented the Zionist movement at the Versailles Peace Conference.

During the 1920s he was the chief leader of the Zionist movement. His power base was the network of relations which he developed with the heads of the British government, his alliance with the Labor movement of the Palestine Jewish *Yishuv*, and his influence on Jewish financiers throughout the world, whose contributions served as the financial base for developing Palestine. During this decade he was active in establishing an enlarged Jewish Agency, the association of non-Zionist groups which supported building Jewish Palestine with the Zionist Executive. The establishment of the Jewish Agency, in Aug. 1929, was considered his personal achievement.

As W.'s policy was one of moderation and cooperation with the British government, the latter's reaction to the Arab riots of 1929, mainly severe restrictions on immigration and settlement, weakened his position. Despite the "MacDonald Letter" of February 1931, which in practice cancelled these restrictions, he was not reelected at the 17th Zionist Congress in 1931 as President of the World Zionist Organization. After his resignation he was active in collecting funds to establish an institute of science in Rehovot. The Daniel Sieff Institute, established there in 1934, was the basis for the later Weizmann Institute. During these years he built his home in Rehovot.

In 1935 W. was again elected as President of the World Zionist Organization. In 1937 he supported the partition plan proposed by the Peel Commission. After World War II broke out, he supported cooperation with the British in the war and was active in the recruitment of Jewish-Palestinian volunteers and the creation of the Jewish Brigade in 1944. His son Michael, a pilot in the R.A.F., was killed in the war. W. supported David *Ben Gurion's Biltmore Program, calling for the creation of a Jewish "Commonwealth" in Palestine.

But his relations with Ben Gurion deteriorated despite their cooperation in several fields, e.g., at the Biltmore Conference. The tension between the two men also had a personal basis, but it was mainly political. W. was out of touch with the violent struggle against the British, from 1945, and remained identified with a pro-British line, while Ben Gurion tended then more and more towards an American orientation. The tension reached its zenith during the 22nd Zionist Congress in 1946, when W. resigned from the Presidency of the Zionist movement. Yet he retained much prestige as the leader of Zionism, and in 1947 he was a main spokesman for the Zionist movement in the United Nations deliberations which led to the establishment of the State of Israel.

After the establishement of the State of Israel, May 1948, W. was elected its provisional President,

but as he was abroad he could not sign the Declaration of Independence. In February 1949 the First Knesset elected him President of the State of Israel — a position which he held until his death. As President of the State his position was primarily representative and symbolic, with no real authority. His declining health did not permit him to struggle to strengthen his position as President. In November 1949, when he reached the age of 75, the Weizmann Institute of Science was established in Rehovot.

W.'s death in November 1952 was deeply mourned. He is remembered as one of the founding fathers of the Zionist movement and played a central role in the establishment of the State of Israel. His autobiography, *Trial and Error*, was published in 1949, and his letters were collected in many volumes.

WEIZMAN, EZER (b. 1924)   Israeli military and political leader. He was born in Palestine to a prominent family: his uncle was Chaim *Weizmann, the first President of the State of Israel. During the Second World War he served in the British army as a pilot. In the War of Independence he was one of the founders of the Israel Air Force and during the 1950s one of its senior Commanders. In 1958 he was appointed Commander of the Air Force and in 1959 received the rank of General.

Weizmann commanded the air force for eight years — longer than any other commander. He built up its strenght, while giving special attention to the human factor, preparing the Air Force for the role it would play during the Six Day War. In 1966, a year before the war, he left the air force and was appointed Chief of Operations of the IDF. He served in this position for three and a half years.

At the end of 1969, after he lost all hope of becoming Chief of Staff, W. left the army and became Minister of Transport, one of the six members of *Gahal* in the government. This was the only time in the history of the State that a senior officer in the army traded his army commission for an immediate transfer to the government. In Aug. 1970, when *Gahal* seceded from the government, he resigned. He went into private business and was elected chairman of the *Herut* Executive. He held this position until Dec. 1972, when he was forced to resign after a disagreement with Menahem *Begin.

At the beginning of 1977 he returned to political life, was appointed head of the *Likud* Election Headquarters, and led the *Likud* to victory. After the elections he served as Defense Minister in the

Begin government. During his term as Minister he changed from hawk to dove, playing a central role in the negotiations which led to peace with Egypt. In the summer of 1980 he resigned, as he disagreed with the government's position on autonomy for the Palestinians. He had hoped that his resignation would topple the government, but his hopes were not realized. He left political life and retreated to his home in Caesarea. He refused to voice his opinions even during the most difficult days of the Lebanese War.

In early 1984, before the elections to the Eleventh Knesset, W. returned to political life. He founded a new party — *Yahad* (Together) — which won three mandates. In spite of his disappointment, this gave W., holding the balance, the opportunity to determine who would become Prime Minister. Despite the entreaties of the *Likud*, he supported Shimon *Peres and thus paved the way for the National Unity Government headed by Peres. W. joined the Alignment and served as Minister without Portfolio and as a member of the inner political cabinet. From 1988 to 1990 he was Minister of Science and Development. During the elections to the Twelfth Knesset (1988) he was the Head of the Alignment Election Headquarters, but did not repeat his 1977 success. W. paid a heavy price for his ideological reversal — from extremist hawk to radical dove supporting negotiations with the PLO — and his political career is considered to have failed.

Y

YA'ARI (original name: Wald), **MEIR** (1897–1987) Israeli political leader, one of the founders of the Israel Labor movement. Born in Galicia, he was a founder of the *Hashomer Hatza'ir* Zionist-Socialist youth movement. In the First World War he served as an officer in the Austrian army. In 1920 he immigrated to Palestine and was the founder and leader of the first *kibbutz* of *Hashomer Hatza'ir* in Upper Bitania. He was one of the founders of the *Histadrut*.

After Bitania was disbanded, after bitter ideological debates, Y. struggled to turn *Hashomer Hatza'ir* from a youth movement with abstract socialist ideas into a radical socialist settlement movement with a Marxist ideology. In 1927 he established the *Kibbutz Artzi* — the association of all the *kibbutzim* of *Hashomer Hatza'ir*. In 1929 he was one of the founders of Kibbutz Merhavia, where he lived until his death. He represented his movement in the Secretariat of the *Histadrut* Executive and in the Zionist Executive Committee.

During the 1930s and 1940s Y. was the main leader of the process which turned *Hashomer Hatza'ir* into a political party. The climax of this process was the establishment of *Mapam* in 1948. In 1949 he was elected on its list to the First Knesset and remained a member until 1973. Y. headed *Mapam* during the early 1950s when the party was torn over the Prague Trials and its attitude to the Soviet Union. He and *Hazan ensured that *Mapam*, while radically socialist, remained an integral part of the Zionist movement. In 1955, after the elections to the Third Knesset, he brought his party into a coalition with *Mapai*, but refused to serve as a Minister. In 1969 he brought *Mapam* into an alignment with the Labor Party. Known for his analytical ability, and his talents as a writer, Y. was the chief ideologue of his party and drafted its political program.

During the 1970s he retired from official political activity. In 1972 he resigned as Secretary-General of *Mapam*, a position which he had held for many years and in 1973 he resigned from the Knesset. But even after his resignation he continued to be the leader of *Mapam* and of the *Kibbutz Ha'artzi* and their supreme ideological mentor.

YADIN (original name: Sukenik), **YIGAL** (1917–84) Israeli archaeologist and military and political leader. Born in Jerusalem (his father was the archaeologist Eliezer Lipa Sukenik), Y. graduated from the Gymnasia Ha'ivrit high school (1935) and the Hebrew University. At the end of the 1930s he joined the permanent staff of the *Haganah* and served as aide to Chief of Staff Ya'akov Dostrovsky (Dori). During the War of Independence, aged 31, he served as Chief of Operations; however, due to Chief of Staff Dori's illness, he acted in practice as Chief of Staff. In December 1949 Y. was appointed Chief of Staff of the IDF and served in this position for three years, until Dec. 1952. In this capacity he laid the foundations for the organization of the army in general and of the reserves in particular. He resigned in protest against *Ben Gurion's decision to cut the defense budget.

After leaving the army he completed his studies in archaeology and within a few years became a world-renowned archaeologist. He led excavations in Hazor and Massada. The latter dig had more than archaeological significance, and shed light upon an ancient national myth. In 1956 he was awarded the Israel Prize for his accomplishments in the field of archaeology.

For many years Y. was proposed as a potential candidate for high office, and some saw him as the "Israeli De Gaulle" who, at some future date, would save the nation. In 1973 he was appointed member of the Agranat Commission — an official commission investigating the functioning of the army during the early days of the Yom Kippur War. Y. appears to have had much influence over the Commission's report, which shook the nation and caused a great deal of public debate. In 1976 he founded a new political movement — The Democratic Movement. This body united with several other political groups to form The Democratic Movement for Change (*Dash*), with the reform of the election system as its main plank.

In the elections of May 1977, Y.'s movement won 15 seats — not a small success for a new party. However, Menahem *Begin was able to form a government without it. After several months of bitter argument the movement decided, by a small majority, to join the government. Y. was appointed Deputy Prime Minister and Chairman of the Cabinet Committee for Social Welfare. But after *Dash* joined the government, the debate within it grew sharper, and from 1978 onward the party began to split. Y. remained the leader of a three-member faction and soon he became, but a Deputy Prime Minister by the grace of Menahem Begin with little political power or influence and his stature was much diminished. In the summer of 1981 he resigned from public life, leaving behind him a trail of deep disappointment over the failure of his attempt to form a moderate liberal center party. In the summer of 1984 Yadin succumbed to a sudden heart attack.

AL-YAFI, 'ABDULLAH (b. 1901)   Lebanese politician, a leader of the Muslim-Sunni community in Beirut. A French-educated lawyer, Y. was elected to most Parliments from 1932. He first served as Prime Minister in 1938–39. He was Minister of Justice in 1946–47 and again Prime Minister in 1951–52. He allied himself with Camille *Chamoun in the opposition front that brought down President Bishara al-*Khouri in 1952 and was Chamoun's Prime Minister in 1953–54 and 1956. But when President Chamoun took an increasingly pro-Western line and refused to sever relations with Britain and France during the Suez crisis and war of 1956, Y. resigned and became a strong opponent of Chamoun. In 1957 he was defeated in the elections, with other opposition leaders. He adopted a Nasserist line, welcoming the Syrian-Egyptian merger of 1958 and advocating Lebanon's integration in an Egyptian-led Arab alignment. When a civil war broke out in 1958, Y. was one of the leaders of the rebellion. After the civil war a bitter rivalry ensued for the Premiership between him and Sa'eb *Salam, his colleague in Beirut's Muslim-Nasserist leadership. This rivalry led to Y.'s defeat in the elections of 1960 and 1964. He again became Prime Minister in 1966, 1968 and 1972. He seems to have reverted to the moderate-conservative position traditionally taken by the Beirut Sunni leadership. However, during the civil war since 1975 he lost much of his influence, along with that conservative Sunni group of leaders — the more so because that group had no armed militia of its own. In recent years Y. has not been active in public political life.

YAHYA HAMID-UL-DIN (1869–1948)   Imam-King of Yemen. Scion of a noble family of the Shi'i-Zeidi sect, Y. was elected Imam — religious head of the sect, and ruler of Yemen — in 1904. He continued a rebellion against the Ottoman sovereign that had been simmering for years, and in 1911 obtained an agreement granting him wide autonomy under nominal Ottoman sovereignty. During World War I he remained loyal to the Ottoman Empire, but with its dismemberment he gained complete independence for Yemen in 1918 without a struggle. In 1925 he expanded Yemen's territory by reconquering the port of Hodeida that had been occupied in 1921 by the rulers of neighboring 'Asir with British connivance. A dispute over 'Asir itself led to war between Yemen and Sa'udi Arabia in 1934, ending in defeat for the Imam and the loss of the disputed territory. Y.'s rule was ultraconservative and authoritarian. He prevented economic and social modernization and the creation of a modern administrative and representative regime other than the traditional Council of Notables. He even hesitated to maintain regular economic and diplomatic ties with other nations and tried to keep Yemen isolated and closed to foreign influence. His harsh administration drove many antagonists of the regime into exile and caused sporadic plots and rebellions inside Yemen. Y. was assassinated during a revolt in 1948; but the revolt failed to topple the regime, and his son Ahmad ibn Yahya succeeded him as Imam.

YALMAN, AHMET EMIN (1888–1972)   Leading Turkish journalist and editor. Born in Thessaloniki, Y. obtained his doctorate from Columbia University in New York. He worked for the *Saban* and *Tanin* newspapers, becoming Chief Editor of *Saban*. From 1923 to 1925 he edited the *Vatan* newspaper. After *Vatan* ceased publication, Y. revived it in 1940. Y. was considered one of Turkey's most influential journalists. He also taught statistics at the political science faculty of Istanbul University.

AL-YAMANI, AHMAD ZAKI (b. 1930)   Sa'udi Arabian oil economist. After studying law in Cairo

Ahmad Zaki al-Yamani (IPS, Tel Aviv)

and the USA (New York and Harvard), Y. became an outstanding representative of a new generation of young, Western-trained technocrats and rapidly advanced to senior positions. He was Legal Adviser to the Sa'udi government 1958–60 and a Minister of State from 1960. In 1962 he was appointed Minister of Oil and Natural Resources; he held that post — which involved also the chairmanship of the Sa'udi General Petroleum and Mineral Organization and the Fertilizer Company from the mid-1960s, and a directorship of Aramco — for 26 years, and powerfully determined Sa'udi Arabia's oil policies. He was also a chief architect of OPEC, the cartel of oil-producing countries, from 1960, serving in 1968–69 as its Seecretary-General. He was chiefly responsible for the upheaval in the world's oil economy in 1973 and 1979 caused by the enormous upsurge of prices enforced by OPEC. Yet he later advocated, in the course of shifting tactics and manipulations, increases in OPEC's, and particularly Sa'udia's, oil production, so as to keep up OPEC's share in world production, even if that would depress the oil price; and he was therefore considered in the West as a "moderate." Y. was unexpectedly dismissed in Oct. 1986 — appar-

ently because he was held responsible for the collapse of oil prices and the drop in Sa'udi Arabia's oil production and revenue.

YAZDI, AYATULLAH MUHAMMAD (b.1931) Iranian Islamic cleric and politician. Member of the Council of the Islamic Revolution, 1979, member of the *Majlis* (Parliament).

Born in Qom, Y. studied and taught theology. In his struggle against the regime of Shah *Muhammad Reza he was jailed several times. After the Islamic Revolution he became President of the Islamic Revolutionary Court in Qom and director of *Khomeini's office, as well as a member of the Assembly of Experts and of the Council of the Islamic Revolution. In 1980 Y. was appointed a representative of the Islamic Republic Party to the committee which dealt with the conflicts between President *Bani-Sadr and Prime Minister *Raja'i.

In 1980 he was elected a member of the *Majlis* from Qom, and in 1984 was reelected, this time from Tehran. In 1988, he failed to be reelected. In the *Majlis* he was head of the Committee for Judicial Affairs and the committee for reviewing the Decrees of the Council of the Islamic Revolution, as well as first Deputy Speaker under *Rafsanjani as Speaker. He headed the Iranian delegation to the Interparliamentary Union Convention in 1987.

Despite his defeat in the 1988 elections, he continued to fill public offices. Among others, he was appointed by Khomeini as a member of the Constitution Review Panel in 1989, and during recent years was also head of a theological seminary. Y. has published several religious books, including *The King and Knowledge of God, General Outlines of Islamic Government*, and *Jurisprudence in the Qur'an*. Y. was critical of government involvement in small details of the citizen's life, believing that government involvement should be limited to setting general frameworks. Aligned with the conservative-moderate faction, he has frequently been attacked by hard-line radicals.

YAZDI, MORTEZA (b. 1890)   Iranian Communist leader. He served as a physician in the Ministry of Health and professor at the University of Tehran. In 1936 he was arrested as a Communist. He was released in 1941 and was among the founders of the Communist *Tudeh* Party, 1942, and a member of its Central Committee. He became Health Minister in 1940–41, and 1946. He was also involved with the Social Insurance Organization and social welfare groups. He was arrested again in

1954 and sentenced to death, but was pardoned by the Shah and released in 1954.

YEHOSHUA, AVRAHAM (A.B.) (b. 1936)   Israeli writer. One of the most prominent writers of the younger Israel-born generation. Born in Jerusalem to a veteran Sefardi family, Y. studied at the Gymnasia Ivrit high school in Jerusalem and at the Hebrew University. Since 1972 he has taught in the Department of Literature at Haifa University.

Y.'s first stories, published in the *Lamerhav* newspaper and in the publication *Keshet*, were collected in 1963 in the book *Mot Hazaken* (*The Death of the Old Man*). *Mul Haya'arot* (*Across from the Forests*), also composed of short stories, was published in 1968. Later he exchanged the genre of short stories for novels (*The Lover*; *Late Divorce*; *Molkho* [*Five Seasons* in the English translation]; *Mr. Mani*) which quickly received much acclaim and were widely translated.

Y. has been active in public and political life, mainly in peace movements advocating territorial compromise and opposing Israel's continued occupation of the West Bank and Gaza as a danger to Israeli democracy and society. He frequently writes on these and other topics, such as the relationship between Israel and the Jews of the Diaspora, in newspaper articles, some of which were collected in a book.

YOSEF, DOV (original name: Bernard Joseph) (1899–1980)   Israeli jurist and politician. Born in Canada, during the First World War he served in the Jewish Battalion and after his demobilization he immigrated to Palestine and settled in Jerusalem. After finishing his legal studies, he opened a law office, one of the most prominent in Mandatory Palestine.

In 1933 he joined *Mapai* and from 1936 onward was the legal adviser of the Jewish Agency. During the Second World War he was in charge of enlistment in the British Army under the auspices of the Jewish Agency. In 1945 he was elected to the Jewish Agency Executive and on "Black Saturday" (June 1946) was arrested together with other Zionist leaders and spent over four months in the Latrun detention camp.

During the War of Independence he lost his daughter Leylah. At that time he was the Military Governor of Jerusalem. He governed the besieged city with an iron hand, but with great honesty. After the war he was elected to the Knesset and joined the government. Between 1949 and 1955 he served in various ministerial posts, the best known of which was Minister of Supply and Rationing (1949–1950). In this capacity he supervised the distribution of food and other necessities during the austerity period. From 1957 to 1961 he was treasurer of the Jewish Agency and in 1961–1966, Minister of Justice. In 1966 he was removed from his position by Prime Minister Levi *Eshkol in a manner which he bitterly resented. From then until his death he lived in Jerusalem, retired from political life.

Z

ZAGHLUL, (AHMAD) SA'D (1860–1927) Egyptian politician and main leader of Egyptian nationalism. Born in a prosperous landowning family of farmers in Ibiana in the Delta, Z. studied law, after a traditional Islamic education. At the beginning of the century he was one of the young modernists close to the *Umma* Party who opposed the conservative-Islamic trend and who were seen by some as collaborating with the British administrators, although he also remained close to the Islamic revivalist circles around Muhammad *'Abduh. In 1906 he was appointed Minister of Education and in 1910 Minister of Justice. He resigned in 1913 to head the opposition in the Legislative Assembly. At the end of World War I he emerged as a leader of the nationalists and headed a delegation (Arabic: *Wafd*) to the British which demanded full independence; from this delegation the *Wafd* evolved as a political party and the main proponent of the national struggle. In an effort to suppress nationalist ferment, the British exiled Z. twice — in Mar. 1919 to Malta (released in Apr.), and in 1922 to 'Aden, the Seychelles and Gibraltar. In 1923–24 Z. led the *Wafd* Party to victory in nominally independent Egypt's first elections and in Jan. 1924 he became Prime Minister. However, when the British High Commissioner, Lord Allenby, reacted to the murder of the Governor-General of Sudan and Commander of the Egyptian army, Sir Lee Stack, in Nov. 1924, by presenting to the government an ultimatum and conditions considered extreme and humiliating, Z. resigned. In new elections, Mar. 1925, the *Wafd* won a partial victory and Z. was elected Speaker of the House — whereupon the House was dissolved. In the elections of May 1926 Z. again led the *Wafd* to victory, but declined to form a government and was reelected Speaker. His death in Sept. 1927 was a great blow to the nationalist movement.

ZAHEDI, FAZLULLAH (1890–1963) Iranian officer and politician, Prime Minister 1953–55. Born in Hamadan, to a landowning family, Z. attended the Military Academy in Tehran and served as a professional officer from 1916, eventually attaining the rank of General. During World War II he was arrested by the British. In 1951, he served for several months as Minister of the Interior. When *Mossaddeq in Aug. 1953 forcibly resisted his dismissal from the premiership, Z. used military power to oust him, arrested him and restored the Shah to power. Z. himself became Prime Minister. During his term, he renewed diplomatic relations with Britain, severed under Mossaddeq, and signed a new oil treaty with a Western consortium. He resigned in 1955 due to poor health. His ties to the Shah were close, his son marrying one of the Shah's daughters.

ZA'IM, HUSNI (1889? 1896?–1949) Syrian officer and politician. President of Syria in 1949. Born in Aleppo, reportedly of Kurdish origin, Z. served as a professional officer in the Ottoman Army and after World I in the "Special Troops" formed by the French authorities. During World War II Z. remained loyal to the Vichy-French authorities, and after the conquest of Syria by the British and Free French in 1941 he was detained, but returned to the army after his release. During the Palestine War of 1948, he was Chief of Staff with the rank of Brigadier. On Mar. 30, 1949 Z. mounted Syria's first military coup, deposed President al-*Quwwatli and dissolved Parliament. In June he held a referendum which endorsed him as President with wide powers. He dissolved all political parties and ruled without a legislative or parliamentary body. Z. had ambitious plans for reforms inspired by those of *Ataturk. He was the first Arab leader to give women the franchise and tried to separate state and religion. He was pro-French and anti-*Hashemite and strengthened relations with Egypt, Sa'udi Arabia and Turkey. He also tried to establish contacts with the leaders of Israel, indicating that he was interested in peace and the constructive settlement of issues in dispute, such as the refugee problem.

Z. did not have the time to implement any of his far-reaching plans. He was overthrown on Aug. 14, 1949, by a pro-Hashemite coup staged by Col. Sami *Hinnawi. A military court summarily sentenced him to death, together with his Prime Minister Muhsin al-*Barazi, and he was immediately executed.

ZORLU, FATIN RÜŞTÜ (1910–61)   Turkish politician. Born in Istanbul, he studied law and political science at the Universities of Geneva and Paris.

A member of the Turkish National Assembly (1954–60) for the Democratic Party, Z. served as an ambassador to NATO and was Foreign Minister, 1955 and 1957–60. After the military coup of May 1960 he was tried — *inter alia*, for inciting riots against the Greeks in Istanbul (Sept. 1955), breaking foreign currency regulations, misusing the radio for political purposes, stirring up riots against former President Ismet *Inonu, and other political crimes. He was sentenced to death and executed on Sept. 15, 1961.

Fatin Rüştü, Zorlu

ZURAYQ, QUSTANTIN(b. 1909)   Syrian historian and writer. Born in Damascus, he studied at the American University of Beirut (AUB) and in Chicago and Princeton. After receiving a Ph.D. degree in history he lectured at the AUB, from 1938 as a full professor. In 1946 he was appointed Syrian Minister to the USA, and in 1947 he was a member of the Syrian delegation to the UN General Assembly that dealt with the Palestine problem. In 1949 he was appointed the Rector of Damascus University.

In his writings he called on the Arabs to seek three things: full independence, in all its aspects; unity among themselves; and modernization.

Among his books: *The Yazidiyya, Past and Present*, 1935; *al-Wa'i al-Qawmi* (National Consciousness), 1940, preaching the revival of Arab nationalism and Arab unity; *Ma'na al-Nakba (The Meaning of the Calamity)*, 1949, analyzing the Arab defeat by Israel in Palestine and urging the Arabs to start a total revolution in all aspects of their life which alone would enable them to solve their social, cultural and political problems.

ZU'AYYIN, YUSSUF (b. 1931)   Syrian politician. A Sunni Muslim born in Abu Kamal in the Euphrates region, Z. studied medicine at Damascus University and practiced as a physician. He was active in the *Ba'th* Party and became a member of its "national," i.e., all-Arab, and "regional," i.e., Syrian, leadership. He first joined the government in 1963, after the *Ba'th* coup, as Minister of Land Reform. In 1964 he was named Ambassador to Britain but did not take up that post. In 1964–65 he became Prime Minister. He was deposed late in Dec. 1965 when *Bitar and his "moderate" *Ba'th* faction tried to return to power. Z. supported the extremist "military" wing of Gen. Salah *Jadid who deposed the Bitar-al-*Hafez group in a coup in Feb. 1966, and became Prime Minister under the ruling junta of Generals Jadid and al-*Asad. He included Communists in his government and advocated closer relations with the USSR. When the ruling military *Ba'th* wing split into rival factions, Z. supported Jadid and his doctrinaire group against Asad, and lost the Premiership in Oct. 1968 when Asad gained the upper hand. When Asad completed his take-over in Nov. 1970, Z. was detained, along with other leaders of the Jadid faction. He was reportedly offered his release from detention late in 1980, but refused to pledge cooperation with the regime and stayed in prison. He was released in 1983, but was not allowed to resume any public-political activity.

THE HASHEMITE DYNASTY

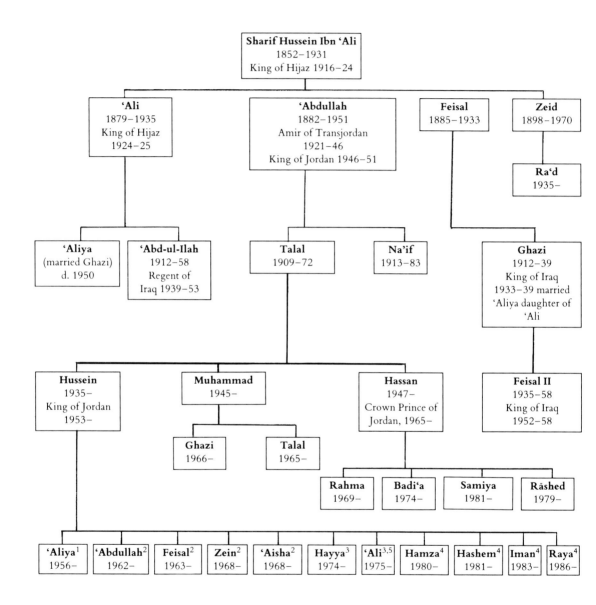

[1] Mother: Dina 'Abd-ul-Hamid al-'Awn, from another H. branch, whom Hussein married in 1955 and divorced in 1957.

[2] Mother: Tony Gardiner (after converted to Islam: Muna), whom Hussein married in 1961 and divorced in 1972.

[3] Mother: 'Aliya Touqan, whom Hussein married in 1972; died in 1977.

[4] Mother: Lisa Halabi (after converted to Islam: Nur-al-Hussein), whom Hussein married in 1978.

[5] Named in 1978 (second) Crown Prince after Hassan.

THE RULING DYNASTY OF EGYPT, 1805–1953

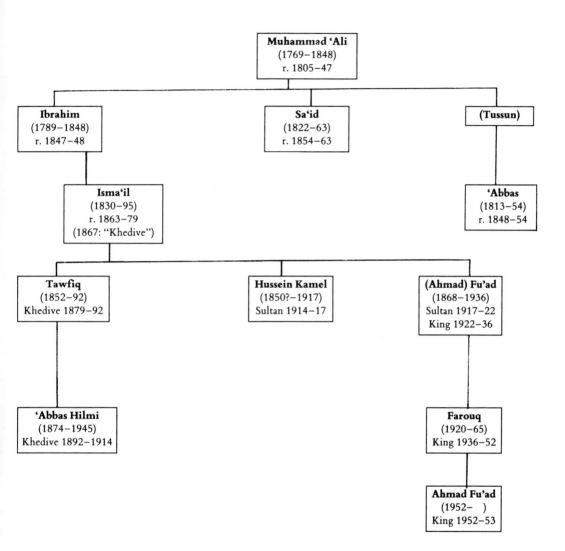

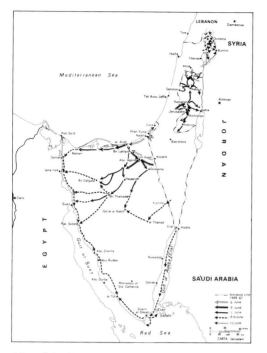

Map of the Six Day War

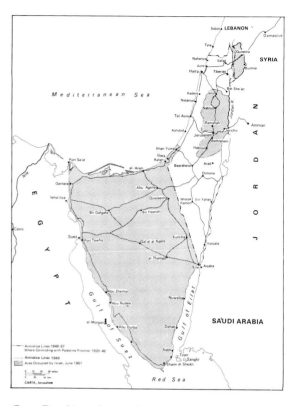

Cease-Fire Lines, June 1967

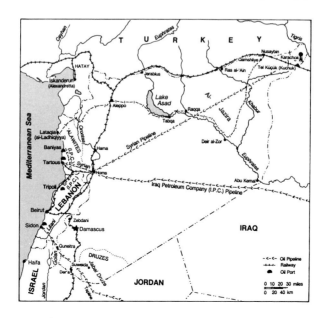

Map of Syria

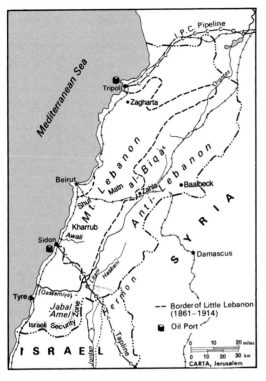

Map of Lebanon

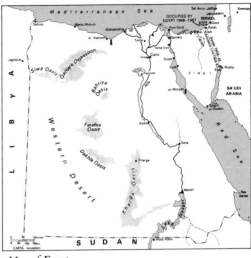

Map of Egypt

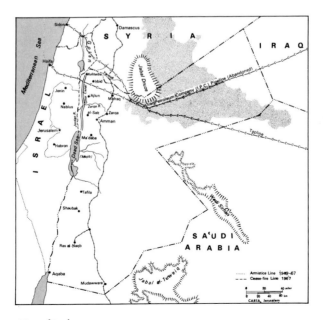

Map of Jordan

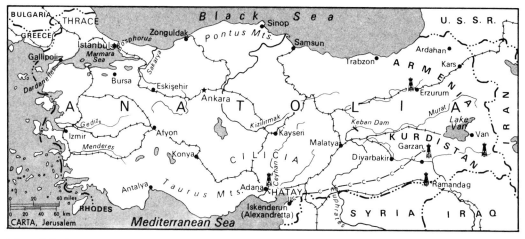

Map of Turkey

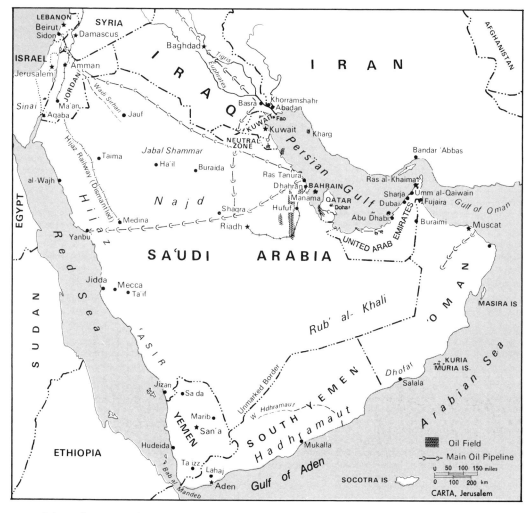

Map of the Arabian Peninsula

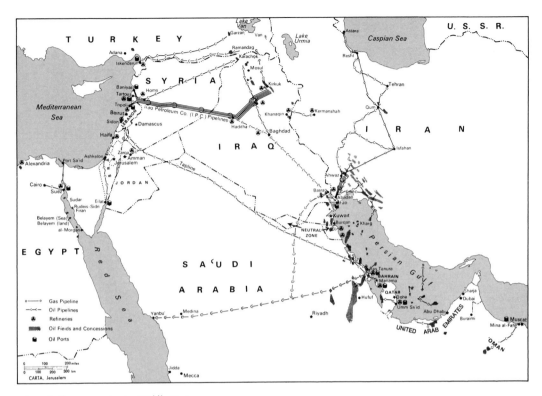

Map of oil resources in the Middle East

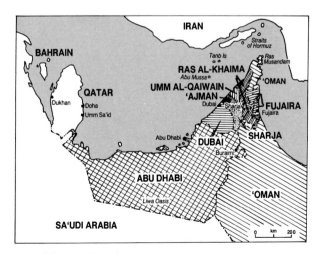

Map of the United Arab Emirates

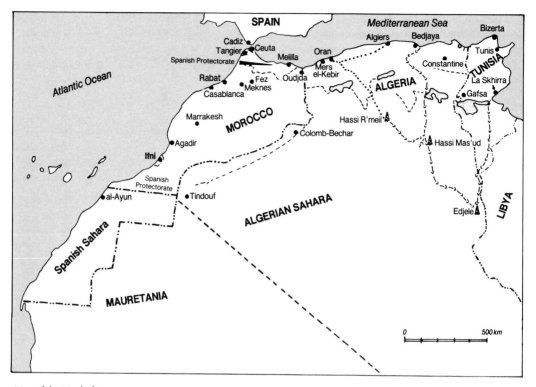

Map of the Maghrib

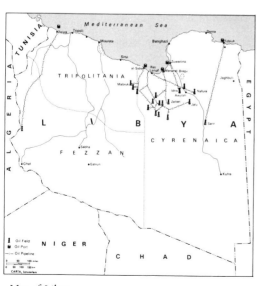

Map of Libya

Map of Sudan

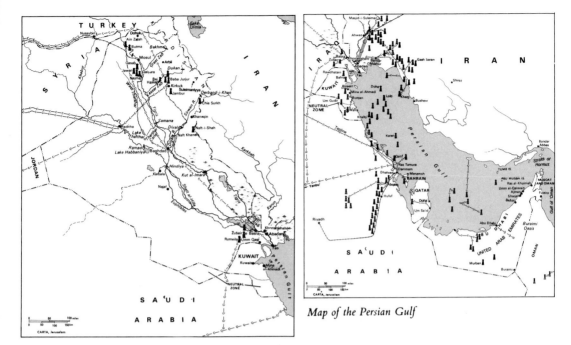

Map of the Persian Gulf

Map of Iraq

Map of Iran

ADDENDUM

MADRID PEACE CONFERENCE

Convened Oct. 30 — Nov. 1, 1991 under the auspices of Presidents Bush and Gorbachev of the USA and the USSR, as well as the EEC (European Economic Community) and chaired by Secretary of State James Baker and Foreign Minister of the USSR Boris Pankin.

ISRAELI DELEGATION

*SHAMIR, YITZHAK (b. 1915) Prime Minister. Head of the delegation.
AS'AD, AS'AD (b. 1944) Prime Minister *Shamir's adviser on Druze Affairs.
BEN-AHARON, YOSSI (b. 1932) Head of the Prime Minister's Office.
BEN-AMI, SHLOMO (b. 1943) Ambassador to Spain.
BEN-ELISSAR, ELIAHU (b. 1942) Member of the Knesset and head of its Foreign Affairs and Defense Committee.
BEN-TSUR, EITAN (b. 1948) Deputy Director General of the Foreign Ministry. He was also a delegate to the Geneva Conference in 1973.
DORON, SARAH (b. 1922) Member of the Knesset and head of the Likud Knesset faction.
HADAS, YOSEF (b. 1928) Acting Director General of the Foreign Ministry.
LANDAU, UZI (b. 1943) Likud member of Knesset.
MERIDOR, SALAI (b. 1955) Adviser to Defense Minister *Arens.
MOR, YEKUTIEL (b. 1946) Brigadier-General. Military Intelligence chief of analysis and adviser to Defense Minister *Arens.
NETHANYAHU, BENJAMIN (1950) Deputy Foreign Minister in charge of relations with the media at the Peace Conference.
RUBINSTEIN, ELYAKIM (b. 1947) Cabinet Secretary. Was also a delegate in the peace talks with Egypt, 1978/79.
SHOVAL, ZALMAN (b. 1930) Ambassador to the United States.

JORDANIAN-PALESTINIAN JOINT DELEGATION

ABU-JABBER, KAMAL (b. 1932) Head of the Joint-Delegation. Foreign Minister of Jordan.

JORDANIAN DELEGATION

MAJALI, 'ABD-UL-SALAM (b. 1925) Head of the Jordanian Delegation. General (ret.), former Minister of Health and Education.
'ADWAN, MUHAMMAD Ambasssador to Moscow.
AYYUB, FU'AD (b. 1944) Ambassador-designate to the U.K. Former Secretary to the King.
BAKHIT, 'ADNAN (b. 1941) Vice-President of the University of Jordan, Professor of History.
BANI-HANI, MUHAMMAD Head of Jordan Water Authority.
BREIZAT, MUSSA Palace official
HASSAN, TALAL Ambassador to Belgium.
JUNDI, GHASSAN Lecturer in international law.
KHALIDI, 'AWAD General. Ambassador to France.
KHALIDI, WALID Professor of international law at Harvard University.
KHASAWNA, 'AWN International law expert.

MAR'I, 'ABD-UL-HAFEZ General. Deputy Chief of Staff, Head of Military Intelligence.
(MU'ASHSHAR, MARWAN (b. 1954) of Jordan Information Office, Washington — Adviser.)

PALESTINIAN DELEGATION:

'ABD-UL-SHAFI, Dr. HAIDAR (b. 1919) Head of the delegation. Medical doctor, born in Gaza; a founding member of the Palestine National Council, 1964; head of the Palestinian Red Crescent Society in Gaza.
'ABDULLAH, SAMIR (b. 1950) Chairman of the Economics Department at al-Najah University in Nablus.
ABU MIDAIN, FREIH (b. 1944) Lawyer born in Gaza. Chairman of the Gaza Bar Association
AL-AGHA, Dr. ZAKARIA (b. 1942) Chairman of the Gaza Arab Medical Society; head of the Internal Medicine section at Ahli Hospital in Gaza. He took part in several meetings of Palestinian leaders with US Secretary of State James Baker.
AL-'AQER, Dr. MAHMOUD (b. 1943) Urologist at several hospitals in the West Bank and East Jerusalem.
EREKAT ('ARIQAT), SA'EB (b. 1955) Ph.D. in international relations. Associate professor of political science at al-Najah University in Nablus.
FREIJ, ELIAS (b. 1920) Mayor of Bethlehem since 1972; Chairman of the Bethlehem Chamber of Commerce.
HAMAD, 'ABD-UL-RAHMAN (b. 1946) Born in the Gaza Strip. Dean of the College of Engineering at Bir-Zeit University; head of the Palestinian Academic Society.
JA'BARI, Dr. NABIL Practicing dentist since 1973; Chairman of the Board of Trustees of Hebron University.
KAN'AN, SAMEH (b. 1954) Works for the Nablus Chamber of Commerce. Arrested in 1973 and sentenced to 20 years in prison, S. was released in 1985 in a prisoner exchange between Israel and the Damascus-based "Popular Front for the Liberation of Palestine — General Command" (the *Jibril Group).
AL-KHATIB, GHASSAN (b. 1954) Lecturer in cultural studies at Bir-Zeit University; head of the Jerusalem Media and Communication Center in East Jerusalem.
KILANI, SAMI (b. 1952) Writer and poet; physics instructor at al-Najah University in Nablus.
AL-NATSHEH, MUSTAFA (b. 1930) Acting Mayor of Hebron from 1980 to 1982 when he was deposed by the Israeli military authorities.
QASSIS, NABIL (b. 1947) Ph.D. in Physics. Vice president of Bir-Zeit University.

PALESTINIAN ADVISORY COMMITTEE (not all its members proceeded to Madrid, and the membership of some remained in doubt amid conflicting reports).
ABU-'AYASH, RADWAN (b. 1950) Journalist. In frequent contact with Israeli and US representatives.
ABU-ZAYYAD, ZAYYAD (b. 1940) Journalist and lawyer. In frequent contact with Israeli representatives.
'ASHRAWI, HANAN Lecturer in English literature at Bir-Zeit University. In frequent contact with Israeli and US representatives, including Secretary of State James Baker. She is considered to be close to the Leftist "Democratic Front for the Liberation of Palestine."
*HUSSEINI, FEISAL (b. 1940) See entry Husseini family.
JARA'I, RADI (b. 1941) Journalist. Sentenced in 1976 to 15 years imprisonment, released 1985 in exchange with *Jibril's "Popular Front for the Liberation of Palestine — General Command."
KAMAL, ZUHEIRA (b. 1945) Leader of Palestinian women's organizations, considered close to the "Democratic Front for the Liberation of Palestine."
KHALIDI, RASHID (b. 1948) Professor at the University of Chicago.
MANSUR, KAMEL
*NUSSEIBA, SARI (b. 1946) Lecturer on Islamic History, Bir-Zeit University. See entry Nusseiba family.

QASSEM, ANIS (b. 1925) Jurist. Adviser to the Libyan Ministry of Justice in the 1950s. In recent years in Lebanon.

TARIFI, JAMIL (b. 1947) Ramallah businessman.

EGYPTIAN DELEGATION

'AMR, MUSSA Head of the Delegation. Foreign Minister, a career diplomat and veteran of Islamic and Arab summits.

ABU AL-GHEIT, AHMAD Head of the Foreign Minister's office.

ABU-NASR, MAHMUD Former Deputy Foreign Minister and former Ambassador to Spain.

'AMER, Dr. SALAH Professor of international law at Cairo University.

BARAKAT, 'ALA Ambassador to Spain, former chief of the Air Force.

FAHMI, NABIL Diplomat; son of former Foreign Minister Isma'il *Fahmi.

FAKHR, AHMED Major-General (ret.). Former military adviser to the Prime Minister and head of an independent think-tank in Cairo.

HAMDI, WAGIH Diplomat, director of the Foreign Ministry East Arab department.

HIFNI, Dr. QADRI Professor of psychology at 'Ain Shams University.

HILLAL, Dr. 'ALA-UL-DIN Professor of political science at Cairo University, specializing in regional affairs.

AL-KHOLI, LOFTI Writer and veteran Leftist commentator at Egypt's most influential daily newspaper *Al-Ahram*.

RIZK, Dr. YUNAN LABIB Professor of modern history at 'Ain Shams University. Was a member of the team that negotiated with Israel the return of Taba.

AL-SHA'ER, Dr. RAMZI President of Zagazig University and specialist in international law.

SHIHATA, Dr. RIDA Diplomat, director of the international organizations department at the Foreign Ministry.

SYRIAN DELEGATION

SHAR', FARUK Foreign Minister. Head of delegation.

'ALAF, MUWAFFAQ Former ambassador to the U.N. Geneva Offices.

'ARNAWAS, AHMAD Diplomat

'AQQAD, ZUHEIR Ambassador to Spain.

FATTAL, DIA'ULLAH Ambassador to the U.N.

FALHUT, SABR Chairman of Journalists Association.

HAIDAR, NASRAT ULLAH (b. 1931) Legal adviser.

ISMA'IL, ZAKARIYA (b. 1924) Diplomat. Former Ambassador to Czechoslovakia.

JAZZAR, MAJDI (b.1936) Director, Department of International Organizations at the Foreign Ministry.

KHADR, MUHAMMAD Ambassador to the U.K.

AL-MASRI, AHMAD FATHI Diplomat, Foreign Ministry.

AL-MU'ALLEM, WALID Ambassador to the USA.

RIZQALLAH, ELIAS Professor of history at Damascus University.

TAYARA, 'ADNAN General.

LEBANESE DELEGATION

BUWEIZ, FARES Foreign Minister. Head of the delegation

ABU 'ASSI, NAJI Ambassador to Senegal.

ARSNIUS, YUSUF

EDDE, ISABELLE

HAMIYAH, 'ABBAS Ambassador to Spain

HAMUD, MAHMUD Ambassador to the U.K.
HASSAN, ZAFER Acting Secretary-General of the Foreign Ministry
KHEIR, ANTOINE Expert in international law.
MAHRAN, SHAFIQ
MU'AWIYA, JA'FAR Head of the Economic Department at the Foreign Ministry.
MUBARAK, SAMIR of the Foreign Ministry
MURTADA, JIHAD of the Foreign Ministry
SALAMA, GHASSAN Expert in international law
TUFAILI, MAHER

President George Bush addressing the delegates at the opening session of the Madrid Peace Conference. (Photo GPO)

ACKNOWLEDGEMENTS

The source of the illustrations has been indicated with the captions, and the Publishers have attempted to observe the legal requirements with respect to copyright. However, in view of the number of illustrations included in this volume, the Publishers wish to apologize in advance for any involuntary omission or error and invite persons or bodies concerned to write to the Publishers.